CANTI

CANTI

GIACOMO

Leopardi

TRANSLATED AND ANNOTATED BY

JONATHAN GALASSI

FARRAR STRAUS GIROUX

NEW YORK

FARRAR STRAUS GIROUX
18 West 18th Street, New York 10011

Distributed in Canada by D&M Publishers, Inc.
Printed in the United States of America
First edition, 2010

Some of these translations originally appeared, certain of them in very different form, in *The Antioch Review*, *The New Republic*, *The New York Review of Books*, *The New Yorker*, *Paragone*, *Ploughshares*, *Poesia*, and *Poetry*.

Library of Congress Cataloging-in-Publication Data
Leopardi, Giacomo, 1798–1837.
[Canti. English]
Canti / Giacomo Leopardi ; translated and annotated by Jonathan Galassi. — 1st ed.
p. cm.
Includes bibliographical references and index.
ISBN 978-0-374-23503-1 (hardcover : alk. paper)
1. Leopardi, Giacomo, 1798–1837. Canti.
I. Galassi, Jonathan. II. Title.

PQ4708.A2 2010
851'.7—dc22

2010005698

Designed and composed by Quemadura

www.fsgbooks.com

1 3 5 7 9 10 8 6 4 2

Frontispiece: *Monument to Clelia Severini* (1825), by Pietro Tenerani. San Lorenzo in Lucina, Rome. Photograph by Annie Schlechter

TO

Nicola Gardini

AND

Shirley Hazzard

CONTENTS

Other Texts

INTRODUCTION

POET OF PROBLEMS

Leopardi's *Canti*, one of the most influential works of the nineteenth century and one of the great achievements in Italian poetry, is not a conventional collection of poems. A mere forty-one compositions make up the Book of Life and Thought of Italy's first modern poet—a series of beginnings, of constantly evolving experiments in style and thematics, obsessively reworked and reorganized over a lifetime. They include both the most public and the most personal work of a writer who also spent his enormous if not inexhaustible energies on countless other literary endeavors: classical translations, philological studies, and the editing of texts and anthologies; philosophical dialogues and social criticism; and the enormous notebook of ideas and impressions, the *Zibaldone*,[1] which is the seedbed of all of Leopardi's work.

Among the canti are the first truly modern lyrics, the wellspring of everything that follows in the European poetic tradition. But they are not merely evocations of private suffering and grief, for the poet "not only had feelings to sing about but things to say," as one critic has put it.[2] The canti posit and explicate and, at their greatest, embody Leopardi's ideas and beliefs about human life. For all their beauty, for all their dedication to *vaghezza*, to the grace and mystery of indeterminacy, they are always crystallizations in poetic form of Leopardi's thought, unlike anything that preceded or followed them.[3] They are exemplars of *pensiero poetante*, thinking in poetry, as Martin Heidegger has called it, and they proved inspirational for some of the nineteenth century's deepest, most radical thinkers, among them Schopenhauer and Nietzsche.[4]

Leopardi's complex structuring of the *Canti* has been ably dissected and theorized,[5] but to us the book reads like a compendium of disparate undertakings. Beyond the poet's celebrated idylls, with which any reader new to his work should begin, there are public poems (the canzoni and epistles on history and politics); sentimental "novellas"; harsh philosophical satires; and translations and imitations; and the shifts in tone and material at times feel drastic. The book's title altered, too, from the aulic, Petrarchan *Canzoni* of 1824 to the more anthologistic *Versi* of 1826, to, finally, the more musical, open *Canti*, or "Songs" of the 1831 and 1835 editions, this original and magisterial new name indicative of Leopardi's expanded confidence in and willingness to assert the significance of his project.[6] His book was, as he himself pointed out, a "reliquary" in which he "deposited" what he had felt and thought; it was his version of Petrarch's *canzoniere*, or "songbook," in which he gave significant form to his deepest preoccupations and convictions, where his ideas devolved out of abstract thought back into concrete if not "unpremeditated" art.[7]

A classicist by education and mental inclination, Leopardi was severely critical of a world that had added to the comforts of religion—which he rejected as a young man—an equally credulous and self-deluding new faith in the ability of scientific knowledge to ameliorate the essentially tragic nature of life. He grew up in the small, backward town of Recanati in the papal Marche, in a household of ultramontane reactionary Catholic nobles. His father had amassed a great library stocked not only with the church fathers but with all of Greek and Latin literature, which he read and studied so intently and voraciously that by the time he was fifteen there was nothing more for his tutors to teach him and he had seriously compromised his health. Instead of leading him to holy orders, as his parents had hoped, his studies exposed him to illicit Greek sensuality and stoicism. He yearned for love, and for liberation from the clutches of his family, for the place in the great world that his great brilliance seemed to promise him; and indeed his philological and literary work earned him widespread fame at a young age. Yet he was always financially dependent on his parents—a benevolent but uncomprehending and rigidly conventional father and a withholding, judgmental mother (maternal imagery in Leopardi's poetry is usually negative)—and he never really won full emancipation from them. His sallies forth—to Rome, to Bologna, to Florence and Pisa—habitually ended in defeat, in a return to Recanati. He learned that he was unsuited for worldly life, just as he found that his amorous forays met with the indifference or disdain of the women with whom he became infatuated, his poor health and unprepossessing appearance no doubt contributing substantially to his sense of isolation and hopelessness. It was only in his last years, when he joined forces with a young Neapolitan, Antonio Ranieri, that he managed to establish an independent life in Naples.

Leopardi's first, adolescent writings were works of classical philology, scientific inquiry, and obligatory religiosity, but by the age of twenty, after apprenticing himself to his calling by way of translation and imitation, first of Horace and other canonical Latin writers and then, significantly, of the "prohibited" Greeks,[8] he began to embark on original work of several kinds. His social ideas found voice in exhortatory canzoni, public poems in which he called on the Italians to reclaim their culture's forgotten greatness and liberate themselves from the political oppression of the post-Napoleonic Restoration. (This made him a forefather of the Risorgimento and to other national liberation movements of the nineteenth century.) At the same time, he was inscribing into the *Zibaldone* copious profound and original reflections on his broad and deep studies in all branches of knowledge, which would remain unread until they were finally published at the very end of the century. And, more or less simultaneously, in the poems he called his idylls, he was writing about his own anguish in an entirely direct and new poetry that was to become the basis for his enduring international reputation.

Here is what is arguably the first of the idylls, written when the poet was barely twenty-one:

To the Moon

O graceful moon, I can remember, now
the year has turned, how, filled with anguish,
I came here to this hill to gaze at you,
and you were hanging then above those woods
the way you do now, lighting everything.
But your face was cloudy,
swimming in my eyes, thanks to the tears
that filled them, for my life
was torment, and it is, it doesn't change,
beloved moon of mine.
And yet it helps me, thinking back, reliving
the time of my unhappiness.
Oh in youth, when hope has a long road ahead

and the way of memory is short,
how sweet it is remembering what happened,
though it was sad, and though the pain endures!

Everything that will follow in two centuries of Western lyric poetry is here: a new self-consciousness of the writer's alienation from life, with the constant companionship of pain and the consolation of the power of memory—all evoked with unmediated directness and haunting expressive beauty. This is the Leopardi we think we know, the voice of suffering self-knowledge and lovely torment. But it is important to understand that the different modes of Leopardi's poetry, the lyric and the didactic, the pastoral and the historic, the metaphoric and the argumentative, derive from the same vision, express the same spirit in diverse ways. Even Leopardi's most articulated political exhortations are studded with classically inspired similes and lyric interludes that illustrate his ideas poetically; while the poems we read as pure lyrics likewise need to be seen as embodiments of his ideas, with the didacticism largely though not entirely suppressed.

The rhetoric of the early canzoni derives from a received, elevated style that had dominated Italian verse since the Renaissance; the verse epistle to Carlo Pepoli and the "Palinodia," too, exhibit what the idealist philosopher Benedetto Croce called the argumentative "non-poetry" that also finds its way into Leopardi's testament, "La ginestra," which many have seen as the great poem of Italian national identity. But the mind that was analyzing and deriding the headlong liberal belief in unending self-improvement and societal betterment—

. . . having failed to make a single
person on earth happy, they abandoned man

and tried to find a universal bliss;
and having found it easily,
out of many wretched and unhappy persons
made a joyful, happy race:

is the same mind that is preoccupied in his intimate lyrics with his—and our—inability to achieve serenity. "Each creature born will be / simply unhappy, in whatever era . . . by universal law": our natural mere unhappiness, about which nothing can be done, is the subject and stuff of his most personal lyrics, a distillation of a vision of life conditioned by Greek philosophy and confirmed by personal experience of the omnipresence of pain, offset only by the power of illusions to conceal it from us for a time. Leopardi's ultimate cast of mind, then, is disabused and, at its darkest, utterly hopeless. The trajectory from his best-known idyll, "L'infinito," to its mirror-poem, "A se stesso," is the trajectory from a stunned contemplation of the mysterious "sea of being"—which arouses an amorous desire to lose oneself in existence—to disgusted resignation and withdrawal from life. It runs the gamut, one might say, from an overpowering urge to fuse with overbrimming "immensity," to a bitter leave-taking of the emptiness of "all"—one, as in a Möbius strip, the obverse of the other. And it makes him, in spite of himself, one of the major figures of European romanticism.

The poems of the *Canti* fall into several periods, which are presented in roughly chronological order in the book. In the early, "extravagant," radical canzoni (1817–23),[9] Leopardi explores political, historical, and philosophical subjects, using the received rhetoric of public poetry with great virtuosity, suppleness, and concision. He also makes his first experiments in creating a poetic "character" for himself: in the song of the poet Simonides that brings alive the last part of the first canzone, "All'Italia," the young Leopardi impersonates the great bard of ancient Greece in a bid to speak as the public voice of emergent Italy—a declaration of ambition and intentions that amounts to an *ars poetica*. Likewise, in the "Ultimo canto di Saffo," he portrays the "unloved lover," the unbeautiful, undesired singer of human pain that will become his other principal persona. These dramatic monologues are cousins of "Alla luna" and "L'infinito," lyric "poems" in our modern, delimited sense of the word. And these two kinds of composition, public canzone and intimate idyll, set him on the course of alternating voices that will be fundamental to his ever-evolving approach to poetic creation.

From the very start Leopardi is formally revolutionary, gradually revising and relaxing the rules of his genre. In the early elegies and especially in the idylls (1819–21), many of them written contemporaneously with the canzoni and inspired by Hellenistic pastoral, we find the first instances of the private, ur-modern Leopardi, evoking a solitary character at odds with his native setting, in a kind of alienated antipastoral, in fact. The great odes of the Pisa-Recanati period (1828–30), composed after a long hiatus during which he was preoccupied with the satirical dialogues that became the *Operette morali*, represent a complex, mature return to the lyric impulse of the first idylls, but in a darker, more despairing, more memory-obsessed key; indeed, in later masterworks such as "A Silvia" and the "Canto notturno," the poet makes the canzone form an instrument entirely his own, in which rhyme is used originally and sparingly to overwhelmingly powerful effect.

In the poems written in Florence and Bologna (1831–35) during the poet's thirties, in the throes of his one intense attempted love affair, Leopardi oscillates between an austerely beautiful, almost abstract idiosyncratic Platonism and a novelistic sentimentality (in "Consalvo," in particular) that, while popular in Leopardi's time, is vexing to us today. (It is notable that most of Leopardi's poetic activity in his last years, when he had more or less withdrawn from society and given up on love, was largely devoted to the political satire of the *Paralipomeni della Batracomiomachia*, a long and caustic poem about Bourbon Naples that is not part of the *Canti*, and the social criticism of the "Palinodia.") Finally, in the last great Neapolitan poems of 1836, "La ginestra" and "Il tramonto della luna," written as his health was failing, he offers a resigned vision of human life devoid of illusions, considered from above and afar, by moonlight.

So many of the greatest moments in Leopardi's poetry take place under the aegis of the moon. Unabashed, obsessive repetition of theme, imagery, and trope are characteristic of his work, as if he is saying, over and over, "*This* is what matters; this is what I'm talking—and talking—about." Except for the poet's own persona, the figures in his poems are not individuals, by and large, but represent existential categories; as his sympathetic English biographer, Iris Origo, wrote, the women of Leopardi's poetry are really only vehicles for his emotions.[10] Indeed, the moon is the poet's most constant interlocutor, the only feminine presence in his lyrics, apart from safely dead figures like Virginia and Silvia and Nerina, with whom he can calmly converse, though he, or his stand-in the wandering shepherd, does all the talking. (Harold Bloom calls the moon "a trope of male self-negation" for Leopardi, as for Keats and Lawrence.) In "Bruto minore," "Alla luna," "La vita solitaria," and the "Canto notturno," the speaker addresses the moon directly (as he talks to the Big Dipper in "Le ricordanze"); in fourteen of the forty-one canti, in fact, the poem transpires under moonlight. Moonlight, then, *is* the medium of Leopardi's preferred mode of thought, a representation of the cool, removed contemplation that his most serene poetry achieves, and in which the poet is perhaps most wholly himself. In the countervailing mode, embodied by the heat of midday, life is at a standstill, and, as in "L'infinito" and "Le ricordanze," the self is shipwrecked, virtually overwhelmed by conflicting forces. Under the moon, by contrast, the "potent fire" of day has passed, the unendurable pressures of being are relaxed, and half-light allows for a certain indeterminacy and openness to illusion. The poet can observe celestial and earthly activity at a remove, almost as on Keats's urn (in Leopardi's late "sepulchral" odes "Sopra un basso rilievo antico sepolcrale" and "Sopra il ritratto di una bella donna," moonlight is reified as stone, carrying this motif into the tomblike realm of art). Moonlight is half-life, the realm of memory, of aftermath, a silent, death-haunted eternity.

For Leopardi, poetry was an intermittent mode of expression, albeit the highest one, the ultimate distillation, the *summum* of his work, one might say.[11] It was not, however, a constant practice the way it was for many of the major poets of his time, such as, say, Wordsworth, possibly his nearest contemporary in our language, though Eamon Grennan, himself an intrepid Leopardi translator, makes a good case for Coleridge's "mixture of the lyrical and meditative manner" as most congruent with the Italian's in certain respects. Grennan goes on to imagine a "translation committee" for Leopardi that would include "Coleridge, Wordsworth, Keats, Arnold, James Thomson—who translated some of Leopardi's prose and whose own poems show Leopardi's influence—Sam Johnson, Sam Beckett, and Wallace Stevens."[12] D. S. Carne-Ross, more plausibly, has suggested the Milton of *Lycidas* or *Samson Agonistes* as an appropriately daunting model for anyone foolhardy enough to attempt versions of this maddeningly various, inventive, sinuously decisive poetry. In fact, there have been many tries at translating Leopardi into English, and few successes. Nicolas Perella quotes the critic G. Singh to the effect that the best translations seem to be paraphrases in prose that aspire to be poetry, adding, "We can only wince in recalling that Leopardi spoke harshly of paraphrases."[13] In approaching Leopardi, the hapless translator is often confronted with impenetrably perfect, sonorous expressiveness; in the end, the best he can manage is likely a close approximation of the poem's literal thrust, which, if he or she is faithful and lucky, attains a modest aptness in the translator's own language.

In tone and style, Leopardi is a precursor of our modernists, who a hundred years later brought chaste, nude elision to an overstuffed, overly familiar Edwardian language. At its most successful, his grave, meditative voice attains an air of spare finality, of "unstrained dignity," as Perella puts it, in which each word feels entirely inevitable, the most surprising and efficient possible use of his instrument. Leopardi's diction may appear "contorted" to us, as Patrick Creagh has said; the willful remoteness of his style is no doubt related to his reaction against the "progressive" fashion of his moment.[14] In any case, Perella notes, his "recourse to words of an archaic or quasi-archaic nature and to unusual syntactical forms" has the effect of raising "the 'reality' of his subject matter into a sphere where myth and memory reign." Like John Heath-Stubbs, who associates his classicism with "the passionate paganism of Hölderlin,"[15] Carne-Ross asserts that Leopardi's work at its height is closest in spirit and form to ancient Greek poetry, claiming that "Leopardi, a great Latinist in Latinate Italy, achieved in his best work a Greek ease and fluidity,"[16] and reminding us that the *Zibaldone* shows his deep familiarity with the Greek language and his "sensitivity to its slightest nuances." In his hands, Italian verse gradually attained a radical new freedom as he melded the rigidly formal canzone with the unrhymed hendecasyllable to produce a poetic instrument that attained the impersonal authority of the choruses of Greek tragedy,[17] moving "from I to we," as Michel Orcel puts it, "from *coeur* to *choeur*."[18]

Leopardi thought of himself as a writer who never finished anything.[19] His papers are full of sketches and outlines, often highly articulated, for discourses, operas, odes. This, too, is something truly modern about him. He is a poet of the industrial revolution who writes about railroads, printing presses, and California, all the while deploring his times and their comfortable, ill-conceived faith in progress and social "usefulness." Like most poets, he felt that we are here "too late, / and in the evening of human life" and he yearned for an idealized, "naïve" pre-lapsarian world, before the arrival of degenerate, "sentimental" self-consciousness, the awareness of illusions that carried with it the loss of a primal integrity and happiness. In the *Zibaldone* he describes what he called the "philosophical conversion . . . the passage from poetry to philosophy, from the 'ancient' to the modern condition," in which the individual recapitulates the journey of the human spirit from a mythic wholeness and "ignorance" to alienated awareness.[20] For him, poetry represents, and seeks to re-create and hence to recuperate, man's ancient oneness with the world, when

> Nature, Queen and Goddess once, ordained
> a life that wasn't suffering
> and guilt, but free and pure in the forests.

In some ways Leopardi resembles today's antiglobalist; he was a fierce opponent of triumphalist adventurism in politics and of the utilitarian notion that knowledge entails improvement. As the great Italian critic Francesco De Sanctis wrote, his "skepticism heralds the end of that world of theology and metaphysics, and the inauguration of the aridly true, of the real. Leopardi's canti are the deepest, most occult voices of that laborious transition that was called 'the nineteenth century' . . . And what matters in this 'century of progress' . . . is the exploration of one's own soul . . . This tenacious life of his inner world, in spite of the death of every philosophical and metaphysical world, is the original quality in Leopardi."[21]

Leopardi was not a willing participant in life. He remained an "implacable innocent,"[22] a kind of emotional child, and his constant lament for his unspent youth and his pleasure in desperation can sometimes seem more like unresolved adolescent angst than true Baudelairean spleen.[23] Yet he bitterly rejected the criticism of some of his contemporaries that his negativity was in any way a subjective effect of his own situation. Cyril Connolly wrote in *The Unquiet Grave* (1945) that Pascal and Leopardi "are the Grand Inquisitors who break down our alibis of health and happiness. Are they pessimistic because they are ill? Or does their illness act as a short cut to reality—which is intrinsically tragic?"[24] Leopardi insisted that love is an illusion. Yet, not unlike the Stevens who posits the necessity of "supreme fictions," he also knew that such illusions are what make life worth living. This, perhaps, is why the *Canti*, this book of pain and grief, ends with the light and touching command to pursue one's illusions, to live and love life as it occurs:

> Ai presenti diletti
> La breve età commetti.
> [commit to present pleasure
> your brief life.]

Nicola Gardini posits Leopardi's approach to poetry as alternating between historical and pastoral modes—or, as others have put it, between thought and memory (one might even say between Latin and Greek inspirations)—in a book "centered around an ultimately insoluble conflict between decline and utopia." Pastoral—the mode of the idylls, what we today think of as his "truest" poetry—represents "escape from history and oblivion of one's own historicity: the only possible form of human happiness."[25] "The *Canti*," Gardini adds, "are run through by constant, irresistible impulses to return to origins (something Leopardi shares with Vico) and to resolve or repair the negative—in a virtually infinite chain of attempts. Leopardi is not a poet of solutions . . . [but] of problems . . . [He] puts forward questions and provokes provisional answers that will eventually be superseded by new questions."

All this is available to us as we ponder the staggering output of his rich and paradoxical mind, even when the intense musicality of his poetry cannot fully be brought over. It is hard to think of a poet in our tradition with such riches at his command. Let the translation committee form and reform, trying "in vain"—one of Leopardi's favorite phrases—to catch his inimitable sound. However we fail, we are the better for it.

Canti

I

ALL'ITALIA

O patria mia, vedo le mura e gli archi
E le colonne e i simulacri e l'erme
Torri degli avi nostri,
Ma la gloria non vedo,
Non vedo il lauro e il ferro ond'eran carchi
I nostri padri antichi. Or fatta inerme,
Nuda la fronte e nudo il petto mostri.
Oimè quante ferite,
Che lividor, che sangue! oh qual ti veggio,
Formosissima donna! Io chiedo al cielo
E al mondo: dite dite;
Chi la ridusse a tale? E questo è peggio,
Che di catene ha carche ambe le braccia;
Sì che sparte le chiome e senza velo
Siede in terra negletta e sconsolata,
Nascondendo la faccia
Tra le ginocchia, e piange.
Piangi, che ben hai donde, Italia mia,
Le genti a vincer nata
E nella fausta sorte e nella ria.

Se fosser gli occhi tuoi due fonti vive,
Mai non potrebbe il pianto

I

TO ITALY

O my country, I can see the walls
and arches and the columns and the statues
and lonely towers of our ancestors,
but I don't see the glory;
I don't see the laurel and the sword
our ancient fathers wore.
Your forehead and your breast are naked,
undefended. Ah, so many wounds,
contusions, blood: beautiful lady,
this is how you look! I ask heaven and earth
to tell me, Who did this to her?
And, worse, her arms
are bound with chains;
hair undone, without her veil,
she sits alone and hopeless on the ground,
her face between her knees,
and weeps.
Weep; for you have reason to, my Italy,
born to outdo others
in both happiness and misery.

Even if your eyes were fountains,
your tears could never equal

Adeguarsi al tuo danno ed allo scorno;
Che fosti donna, or sei povera ancella.
Chi di te parla o scrive,
Che, rimembrando il tuo passato vanto,
Non dica: già fu grande, or non è quella?
Perchè, perchè? dov'è la forza antica,
Dove l'armi e il valore e la constanza?
Chi ti discinse il brando?
Chi ti tradì? qual arte o qual fatica
O qual tanta possanza
Valse a spogliarti il manto e l'auree bende?
Come cadesti o quando
Da tanta altezza in così basso loco?
Nessun pugna per te? non ti difende
Nessun de' tuoi? L'armi, qua l'armi: io solo
Combatterò, procomberò sol io.
Dammi, o ciel, che sia foco
Agl'italici petti il sangue mio.

Dove sono i tuoi figli? Odo suon d'armi
E di carri e di voci e di timballi:
In estranie contrade
Pugnano i tuoi figliuoli.
Attendi, Italia, attendi. Io veggio, o parmi,
Un fluttuar di fanti e di cavalli,
E fumo e polve, e luccicar di spade
Come tra nebbia lampi.
Nè ti conforti? e i tremebondi lumi
Piegar non soffri al dubitoso evento?
A che pugna in quei campi

your suffering and humiliation;
you were a lady, and now you are a slave.
Whoever speaks or writes about you,
who, remembering you in your pride,
wouldn't say: She was great once; but no longer?
Why? What happened to our ancient strength,
the arms, the courage, the resolve?
Who stripped you of your sword?
Who betrayed you?
What treachery, what sabotage, what power
could take away your cloak and golden crown?
When did you fall, and how,
so low from such great heights?
No one fights for you? None of your own defend you?
To arms! Bring me my sword:
I'll fight alone, I'll fall alone.
Let my blood, O heaven,
be inspiring to Italian hearts.

Where are your sons? I hear the sound
of arms and chariots, voices, drums:
Your sons are making war
in foreign lands.
Hear me, Italy. I see
a wave of infantry and cavalry,
smoke and dust, and flashing swords
like lightning in the fog.
Does it comfort you? Or don't you dare
to witness the uncertain outcome?
Why are young Italians

L'itala gioventude? O numi, o numi:
Pugnan per altra terra itali acciari.
Oh misero colui che in guerra è spento,
Non per li patrii lidi e per la pia
Consorte e i figli cari,
Ma da nemici altrui
Per altra gente, e non può dir morendo:
Alma terra natia,
La vita che mi desti ecco ti rendo.

Oh venturose e care e benedette
L'antiche età, che a morte
Per la patria correan le genti a squadre;
E voi sempre onorate e gloriose,
O tessaliche strette,
Dove la Persia e il fato assai men forte
Fu di poch'alme franche e generose!
Io credo che le piante e i sassi e l'onda
E le montagne vostre al passeggere
Con indistinta voce
Narrin siccome tutta quella sponda
Coprìr le invitte schiere
De' corpi ch'alla Grecia eran devoti.
Allor, vile e feroce,
Serse per l'Ellesponto si fuggia,
Fatto ludibrio agli ultimi nepoti;
E sul colle d'Antela, ove morendo
Si sottrasse da morte il santo stuolo,
Simonide salia,
Guardando l'etra e la marina e il suolo.

fighting in those fields? Gods, O gods:
Italian steel fights for another land.
Oh miserable is he who dies in battle,
not for his country's soil, his faithful
wife and precious children,
but who dies serving someone else,
dies at the hands of that man's enemies,
and can't say at the end: Beloved native land,
the life you gave me I give back to you.

Oh happy and beloved and blessed
were those ancient days, when whole battalions
raced to die for their country;
and you were ever honored and renowned,
Thessalian passes,
where Persia and destiny failed to overpower
a few bold and noble souls!
It seems to me your trees and rocks,
your sea and mountains
murmur to the passing traveler
how the undefeated ranks
covered the entire shore
with undefeated bodies sworn to Greece.
Then cowardly and vicious
Xerxes fled by Hellespont, and became
an emblem of contempt to his descendants.
And climbing the Antela hill, where
the sacred band who died became immortal,
Simonides surveyed
the sky and shore and land.

E di lacrime sparso ambe le guance,
E il petto ansante, e vacillante il piede,
Toglieasi in man la lira:
Beatissimi voi,
Ch'offriste il petto alle nemiche lance
Per amor di costei ch'al Sol vi diede;
Voi che la Grecia cole, e il mondo ammira.
Nell'armi e ne' perigli
Qual tanto amor le giovanette menti,
Qual nell'acerbo fato amor vi trasse?
Come sì lieta, o figli,
L'ora estrema vi parve, onde ridenti
Correste al passo lacrimoso e duro?
Parea ch'a danza e non a morte andasse
Ciascun de' vostri, o a splendido convito:
Ma v'attendea lo scuro
Tartaro, e l'onda morta;
Nè le spose vi foro o i figli accanto
Quando su l'aspro lito
Senza baci moriste e senza pianto.

Ma non senza de' Persi orrida pena
Ed immortale angoscia.
Come lion di tori entro una mandra
Or salta a quello in tergo e sì gli scava
Con le zanne la schiena,
Or questo fianco addenta or quella coscia;
Tal fra le Perse torme infuriava
L'ira de' greci petti e la virtute.
Ve' cavalli supini e cavalieri;
Vedi intralciare ai vinti

And, cheeks wet with tears,
out of breath, unsteady,
he lifted up his lyre:
Most blessed, you
whose chests took the foe's spears
for love of her who gave you to the Sun;
you whom Greece adores and the world admires.
What love was strong enough to send the young
into the peril of battle,
what kind of love sent you to bitter death?
How happy, sons of ours,
the last hour seemed,
when you ran smiling toward the tearful end?
It appeared that each of you was going
to a dance or splendid banquet, not to death:
yet dark Tartarus was waiting,
and the somber river;
nor were your wives or children with you
when you died on that wild shore
not kissed goodbye, unmourned.

But not before inflicting horrible
suffering and destruction on the Persians.
The way a lion in a field of bulls
pounces now on that one's back
and tears into him with his teeth,
and now shreds this one's flank and that one's thigh;
so the anger and the valor of Greek hearts
tore the Persian hordes apart.
Look! horses and their riders on the ground;
Look! chariots and fallen tents

La fuga i carri e le tende cadute,
E correr fra' primieri
Pallido e scapigliato esso tiranno;
Ve' come infusi e tinti
Del barbarico sangue i greci eroi,
Cagione ai Persi d'infinito affanno,
A poco a poco vinti dalle piaghe,
L'un sopra l'altro cade. Oh viva, oh viva:
Beatissimi voi
Mentre nel mondo si favelli o scriva.

Prima divelte, in mar precipitando,
Spente nell'imo strideran le stelle,
Che la memoria e il vostro
Amor trascorra o scemi.
La vostra tomba è un'ara; e qua mostrando
Verran le madri ai parvoli le belle
Orme del vostro sangue. Ecco io mi prostro,
O benedetti, al suolo,
E bacio questi sassi e queste zolle,
Che fien lodate e chiare eternamente
Dall'uno all'altro polo.
Deh foss'io pur con voi qui sotto, e molle
Fosse del sangue mio quest'alma terra.
Che se il fato è diverso, e non consente
Ch'io per la Grecia i moribondi lumi
Chiuda prostrato in guerra,
Così la vereconda
Fama del vostro vate appo i futuri
Possa, volendo i numi,
Tanto durar quanto la vostra duri.

blocking the defeated from escaping,
and the coward tyrant,
pale and disheveled, with the first to flee.
See how, drenched
in barbarian blood, the hero Greeks,
cause of endless torment to the Persians,
one by one, defeated by their wounds,
fall on one another.
Oh live, oh live, forever. You are blessed
as long as men will live to tell your story.

The stars will fall from the sky and into the sea
and scream as they're put out
before we forget you
and our love for you will die.
Your tomb is an altar
where mothers will bring their children
to see your glorious bloodstains.
I'll lie down, blessed ones,
and kiss these stones, this earth,
which shall be praised and glorious forever
from pole to pole.
If only I were down below with you,
and this sweet earth were wet with my blood, too.
But if my fate is unlike yours,
and will not let me shut my eyes
dying fallen on the field for Greece,
still may the modest glory of your bard,
if the gods will it,
endure as long as yours
in times to come.

II

SOPRA IL MONUMENTO DI DANTE CHE SI PREPARAVA IN FIRENZE

Perchè le nostre genti
Pace sotto le bianche ali raccolga,
Non fien da' lacci sciolte
Dell'antico sopor l'itale menti
S'ai patrii esempi della prisca etade
Questa terra fatal non si rivolga.
O Italia, a cor ti stia
Far ai passati onor; che d'altrettali
Oggi vedove son le tue contrade,
Nè v'è chi d'onorar ti si convegna.
Volgiti indietro, e guarda, o patria mia,
Quella schiera infinita d'immortali,
E piangi e di te stessa ti disdegna;
Che senza sdegno omai la doglia è stolta:
Volgiti e ti vergogna e ti riscuoti,
E ti punga una volta
Pensier degli avi nostri e de' nepoti.

D'aria e d'ingegno e di parlar diverso
Per lo toscano suol cercando gia

II

ON THE MONUMENT TO DANTE BEING ERECTED IN FLORENCE

Although Peace is gathering
our people under her white wings,
Italian minds will not be freed
from their age-old drowsiness
if this great land will not return
to the example our forefathers set.
O Italy, let it be in your heart
to honor the ancients; for this land
has no such men today,
and no one to honor.
Turn back, my country,
look back on that infinity of immortals,
and weep with shame;
for grieving without shame is senseless:
turn back and be ashamed and shake yourself awake
and let the memory of those ancestors
and what feebly followed stab you.

A stranger, singular in attitude
and cast of mind and speech,

L'ospite desioso
Dove giaccia colui per lo cui verso
Il meonio cantor non è più solo.
Ed, oh vergogna! udia
Che non che il cener freddo e l'ossa nude
Giaccian esuli ancora
Dopo il funereo dì sott'altro suolo,
Ma non sorgea dentro a tue mura un sasso,
Firenze, a quello per la cui virtude
Tutto il mondo t'onora.
Oh voi pietosi, onde sì tristo e basso
Obbrobrio laverà nostro paese!
Bell'opra hai tolta e di ch'amor ti rende,
Schiera prode e cortese,
Qualunque petto amor d'Italia accende.

Amor d'Italia, o cari,
Amor di questa misera vi sproni,
Ver cui pietade è morta
In ogni petto omai, perciò che amari
Giorni dopo il seren dato n'ha il cielo.
Spirti v'aggiunga e vostra opra coroni
Misericordia, o figli,
E duolo e sdegno di cotanto affanno
Onde bagna costei le guance e il velo.
Ma voi di quale ornar parola o canto
Si debbe, a cui non pur cure o consigli,
Ma dell'ingegno e della man daranno
I sensi e le virtudi eterno vanto
Oprate e mostre nella dolce impresa?

traveled through Tuscany
seeking the tomb of the poet thanks to whom
Homer doesn't stand alone.
And to our shame he learned
that since that poet's death
his ashes and his bones
still lie in exile, and, incredibly,
not a single monument was raised
within your walls to him whose greatness, Florence,
means the whole world honors you.
Oh patriots, who will set
our country free from this disgrace!
You undertake a noble task,
generous and noble band, and anyone
who loves Italy will love you for it.

Love of Italy, my friends—let love
for this unhappy country triumph in you
since loyalty to her otherwise has gone,
for after her bright day
came bitter ones.
Let mercy give you energy
and bless your work, you patriots,
who know so well how Italy's misery
floods her cheeks and veil with tears.
But how to praise you, citizens,
for the noble work you do,
the care and wisdom that you showed,
and the genius and gifts
that will always bring you honor?

Quali a voi note invio, sì che nel core,
Sì che nell'alma accesa
Nova favilla indurre abbian valore?

Voi spirerà l'altissimo subbietto,
Ed acri punte premeravvi al seno.
Chi dirà l'onda e il turbo
Del furor vostro e dell'immenso affetto?
Chi pingerà l'attonito sembiante?
Chi degli occhi il baleno?
Qual può voce mortal celeste cosa
Agguagliar figurando?
Lunge sia, lunge alma profana. Oh quante
Lacrime al nobil sasso Italia serba!
Come cadrà? come dal tempo rosa
Fia vostra gloria o quando?
Voi, di ch'il nostro mal si disacerba,
Sempre vivete, o care arti divine,
Conforto a nostra sventurata gente,
Fra l'itale ruine
Gl'itali pregi a celebrare intente.

Ecco voglioso anch'io
Ad onorar nostra dolente madre
Porto quel che mi lice,
E mesco all'opra vostra il canto mio,
Sedendo u' vostro ferro i marmi avviva.
O dell'etrusco metro inclito padre,
Se di cosa terrena,
Se di costei che tanto alto locasti

What else can I say
to strike a new spark in your heart
that will inspire you?

This greatest of all themes will spur you on
and pierce your heart;
who can tell the wave and whirlwind
of your fury and enormous love?
Who imagines your impassioned look,
the lightning in your eyes?
What human voice does justice
describing something superhuman?
Away, profane spirit. How many tears
will Italy shed for this great monument!
How or when
will time erase your glory?
You still live, O divine arts
to console us in our misery,
comfort for our luckless people,
bent on celebrating
Italian greatness in the ruins of Italy.

Look: I want
to honor our grieving mother, too;
I bring what I have,
and sing my song beside you as you work,
sitting where your chisel brings the stone alive.
O noble father of Tuscan poetry,
if you hear some news of things on earth,
or about the woman you so loved,

Qualche novella ai vostri lidi arriva,
Io so ben che per te gioia non senti,
Che saldi men che cera e men ch'arena,
Verso la fama che di te lasciasti,
Son bronzi e marmi; e dalle nostre menti
Se mai cadesti ancor, s'unqua cadrai,
Cresca, se crescer può, nostra sciaura,
E in sempiterni guai
Pianga tua stirpe a tutto il mondo oscura.

Ma non per te; per questa ti rallegri
Povera patria tua, s'unqua l'esempio
Degli avi e de' parenti
Ponga ne' figli sonnacchiosi ed egri
Tanto valor che un tratto alzino il viso.
Ahi, da che lungo scempio
Vedi afflitta costei, che sì meschina
Te salutava allora
Che di novo salisti al paradiso!
Oggi ridotta sì che a quel che vedi,
Fu fortunata allor donna e reina.
Tal miseria l'accora
Qual tu forse mirando a te non credi.
Taccio gli altri nemici e l'altre doglie;
Ma non la più recente e la più fera,
Per cui presso alle soglie
Vide la patria tua l'ultima sera.

Beato te che il fato
A viver non dannò fra tanto orrore;

I know that for yourself you feel no joy,
that bronze and marble are less permanent
than wax or sand next to the fame
you left behind; and if you ever
vanish from our minds again,
may our unhappiness,
if possible, increase
and your descendants weep,
unknown to the whole world, in endless misery.

But not you; you'll rejoice
for your poor country,
if the example of their ancestors
ever gives its drowsy, sickly sons
the courage to lift their eyes for once.
You can tell
what endless trouble worried her,
she who so unhappily said farewell
when you rose to paradise again!
She is so reduced today
that next to what you see she was a queen.
Such misery assails her
you won't believe it, seeing her.
I'll ignore her other enemies and hardships;
but not the newest and most cruel,
because of which your country feared
her final evening was here.

You were lucky fate did not condemn you
to live among these horrors;

Che non vedesti in braccio
L'itala moglie a barbaro soldato;
Non predar, non guastar cittadi e colti
L'asta inimica e il peregrin furore;
Non degl'itali ingegni
Tratte l'opre divine a miseranda
Schiavitude oltre l'alpe, e non de' folti
Carri impedita la dolente via;
Non gli aspri cenni ed i superbi regni;
Non udisti gli oltraggi e la nefanda
Voce di libertà che ne schernia
Tra il suon delle catene e de' flagelli.
Chi non si duol? che non soffrimmo? intatto
Che lasciaron quei felli?
Qual tempio, quale altare o qual misfatto?

Perchè venimmo a sì perversi tempi?
Perchè il nascer ne desti o perchè prima
Non ne desti il morire,
Acerbo fato? onde a stranieri ed empi
Nostra patria vedendo ancella e schiava,
E da mordace lima
Roder la sua virtù, di null'aita
E di nullo conforto
Lo spietato dolor che la stracciava
Ammollir ne fu dato in parte alcuna.
Ahi non il sangue nostro e non la vita
Avesti, o cara; e morto
Io non son per la tua cruda fortuna.
Qui l'ira al cor, qui la pietade abbonda:

you didn't see Italian wives
in barbarian soldiers' arms;
you didn't see the angry enemy
lay waste to our cities and our fields,
or divine works of Italian genius
carted across the Alps to abject slavery,
or the highway blocked by groaning wagons,
the sharp looks and the insolent commands;
you didn't hear the insults
and the abused word "freedom"
they mocked us with
amidst chains and whipping.
Who doesn't grieve? What have we not suffered?
What did those felons leave untouched—
what temple, altar, crime?

How did we come to these corrupted times?
Bitter fate, why give us life,
or else why not an earlier death,
when you see our country
enslaved by profane foreigners,
her virtue cut to ribbons
by their biting steel?
No help or comfort: we weren't given
any way of lessening
the relentless pain that tore at her.
Alas, you didn't take our blood or life,
beloved country,
and I haven't died for your cruel fate.
So rage and pity overwhelm the heart,

Pugnò, cadde gran parte anche di noi:
Ma per la moribonda
Italia no; per li tiranni suoi.

Padre, se non ti sdegni,
Mutato sei da quel che fosti in terra.
Morian per le rutene
Squallide piagge, ahi d'altra morte degni,
Gl'itali prodi; e lor fea l'aere e il cielo
E gli uomini e le belve immensa guerra.
Cadeano a squadre a squadre
Semivestiti, maceri e cruenti,
Ed era letto agli egri corpi il gelo.
Allor, quando traean l'ultime pene,
Membrando questa desiata madre,
Diceano: oh non le nubi e non i venti,
Ma ne spegnesse il ferro, e per tuo bene,
O patria nostra. Ecco da te rimoti,
Quando più bella a noi l'età sorride,
A tutto il mondo ignoti,
Moriam per quella gente che t'uccide.

Di lor querela il boreal deserto
E conscie fur le sibilanti selve.
Così vennero al passo,
E i negletti cadaveri all'aperto
Su per quello di neve orrido mare
Dilaceràr le belve;
E sarà il nome degli egregi e forti
Pari mai sempre ed uno

for many of us also fought and fell,
but not for dying Italy:
for her tyrants.

Father (that is, if you don't disdain us),
you're no longer what you were on earth.
Brave Italians who deserved another death
fell on the lonely Russian steppe,
and the freezing weather
pitilessly attacked both men and beasts.
Squad after squad they fell,
half naked, mangled, bloodied,
and the ice became a bed for their poor bodies.
And as they breathed their painful last
they recalled the mother they had longed for,
saying: Not clouds and wind, but iron
should have killed us, and for you, our country.
Here, so far away from you,
while time smiles most benevolently on us,
unknown to all the world, we die
for those who are murdering you.

The northern wasteland heard them cry,
and the whispering woods were witness, too.
So their moment came,
and wild beasts
tore up their deserted corpses
on that enormous horrid sea of snow.
And the stragglers and malingerers
will always be remembered

Con quel de' tardi e vili. Anime care,
Bench'infinita sia vostra sciagura,
Datevi pace; e questo vi conforti
Che conforto nessuno
Avrete in questa o nell'età futura.
In seno al vostro smisurato affanno
Posate, o di costei veraci figli,
Al cui supremo danno
Il vostro solo è tal che s'assomigli.

Di voi già non si lagna
La patria vostra, ma di chi vi spinse
A pugnar contra lei,
Sì ch'ella sempre amaramente piagna
E il suo col vostro lacrimar confonda.
Oh di costei ch'ogni altra gloria vinse
Pietà nascesse in core
A tal de' suoi ch'affaticata e lenta
Di sì buia vorago e sì profonda
La ritraesse! O glorioso spirto,
Dimmi: d'Italia tua morto è l'amore?
Dì: quella fiamma che t'accese, è spenta?
Dì: nè più mai rinverdirà quel mirto
Ch'alleggiò per gran tempo il nostro male?
Nostre corone al suol fien tutte sparte?
Nè sorgerà mai tale
Che ti rassembri in qualsivoglia parte?

In eterno perimmo? e il nostro scorno
Non ha verun confine?

with the noble and the strong. Beloved spirits,
though your agony will never end,
be at peace, and let it comfort you
that you will have no comfort
now or in any future time.
Rest on the breast
of your unmeasured pain,
O true sons of her whose final ruin
only yours resembles.

Your country doesn't grieve for you
but for him
who made you fight against her;
so she weeps as bitterly as ever
and her tears are mixed with yours.
If only pity for her whose glory
excelled all others' came alive
in those who love her and can save her,
exhausted and lethargic as she is,
from such abyssal darkness! Glorious spirit,
tell me: Has your love for your Italy died?
Has the fire that gave you life gone cold?
Will the myrtle that assuaged our sadness for so long
never turn green again?
Have all our crowns been scattered on the ground?
Will she never rise again
to resemble you in any way?

Did we die for all eternity?
Will our shame never end?

Io mentre viva andrò sclamando intorno,
Volgiti agli avi tuoi, guasto legnaggio;
Mira queste ruine
E le carte e le tele e i marmi e i templi;
Pensa qual terra premi; e se destarti
Non può la luce di cotanti esempli,
Che stai? levati e parti.
Non si conviene a sì corrotta usanza
Questa d'animi eccelsi altrice e scola:
Se di codardi è stanza,
Meglio l'è rimaner vedova e sola.

I, while I'm alive, shall keep exhorting,
Turn back to your ancestors, corrupted sons.
Look at these ruins,
these pages, canvases, these stones and temples.
Think what earth you walk on. And if the light
of these examples fails to inspire you,
what are you waiting for? Arise and go.
Such low behavior is unworthy
of this nurse and teacher of great spirits.
If she is the home of cowards,
better she be a widow and alone.

III

AD ANGELO MAI

Quand'ebbe trovato i libri di
Cicerone Della Repubblica

Italo ardito, a che giammai non posi
Di svegliar dalle tombe
I nostri padri? ed a parlar gli meni
A questo secol morto, al quale incombe
Tanta nebbia di tedio? E come or vieni
Sì forte a' nostri orecchi e sì frequente,
Voce antica de' nostri,
Muta sì lunga etade? e perchè tanti
Risorgimenti? In un balen feconde
Venner le carte; alla stagion presente
I polverosi chiostri
Serbaro occulti i generosi e santi
Detti degli avi. E che valor t'infonde,
Italo egregio, il fato? O con l'umano
Valor forse contrasta il fato invano?

Certo senza de' numi alto consiglio
Non è ch'ove più lento
E grave è il nostro disperato obblio,

III

TO ANGELO MAI

On His Finding the Manuscript
of Cicero's De re publica

Ardent Italian, how do you constantly
bring our ancestors to life again;
and let them speak to this dead century
in its haze of tedium?
And, language of our fathers
silent so long, how is it
we hear you loud and clear and often now?
Why all these resurrections?
Suddenly the pages
wake and speak;
dusty cloisters hid the precious writings
of our ancestors till now.
Great Italian, is it destiny
that has inspired you? Or does fate
contend to no avail with human courage?

Clearly it is the high will of the gods
that just when we
have wholly lost

A percoter ne rieda ogni momento
Novo grido de' padri. Ancora è pio
Dunque all'Italia il cielo; anco si cura
Di noi qualche immortale:
Ch'essendo questa o nessun'altra poi
L'ora da ripor mano alla virtude
Rugginosa dell'itala natura,
Veggiam che tanto e tale
È il clamor de' sepolti, e che gli eroi
Dimenticati il suol quasi dischiude,
A ricercar s'a questa età sì tarda
Anco ti giovi, o patria, esser codarda.

Di noi serbate, o gloriosi, ancora
Qualche speranza? in tutto
Non siam periti? A voi forse il futuro
Conoscer non si toglie. Io son distrutto
Nè schermo alcuno ho dal dolor, che scuro
M'è l'avvenire, e tutto quanto io scerno
È tal che sogno e fola
Fa parer la speranza. Anime prodi,
Ai tetti vostri inonorata, immonda
Plebe successe; al vostro sangue è scherno
E d'opra e di parola
Ogni valor; di vostre eterne lodi
Nè rossor più nè invidia; ozio circonda
I monumenti vostri; e di viltade
Siam fatti esempio alla futura etade.

Bennato ingegno, or quando altrui non cale
De' nostri alti parenti,

the memory of our heritage,
our fathers rouse themselves to lead us on.
Heaven does have charity for Italy;
some god still cares for us:
now is the moment—this is the hour—
to regain the strength
and valor of Italianness;
the clamor from the tombs is loud,
and the earth is setting
our forgotten heroes free,
asking, my countrymen, if you
still want to be cowards.

Glorious ancestors, is there
still hope for us? Are we not completely dead?
Can you see the future? I'm exhausted,
nothing shields me from suffering,
the way ahead is dark, and all I see
makes hope phantasmagorical.
Noble spirits, rabble
inherited your houses;
your descendants
disdain excellence;
they resent your glory
and neglect
your monuments;
and they have made us all
exemplars of baseness for the future.

Noble mind, now when no one else
takes an interest in our noble forebears,

A te ne caglia, a te cui fato aspira
Benigno sì che per tua man presenti
Paion que' giorni allor che dalla dira
Obblivione antica ergean la chioma,
Con gli studi sepolti,
I vetusti divini, a cui natura
Parlò senza svelarsi, onde i riposi
Magnanimi allegràr d'Atene e Roma.
Oh tempi, oh tempi avvolti
In sonno eterno! Allora anco immatura
La ruina d'Italia, anco sdegnosi
Eravam d'ozio turpe, e l'aura a volo
Più faville rapia da questo suolo.

Eran calde le tue ceneri sante,
Non domito nemico
Della fortuna, al cui sdegno e dolore
Fu più l'averno che la terra amico.
L'averno: e qual non è parte migliore
Di questa nostra? E le tue dolci corde
Susurravano ancora
Dal tocco di tua destra, o sfortunato
Amante. Ahi dal dolor comincia e nasce
L'italo canto. E pur men grava e morde
Il mal che n'addolora
Del tedio che n'affoga. Oh te beato,
A cui fu vita il pianto! A noi le fasce
Cinse il fastidio; a noi presso la culla
Immoto siede, e su la tomba, il nulla.

be interested, for your inspired work
brings back those days
when the godlike ancients
roused themselves from the oblivion
that had buried them and their achievements—
our fathers to whom nature used to speak,
although she never gave herself away,
and pleased the great of Athens and of Rome.
Oh times, snowbound in eternal sleep!
Italy's ruin then was still to come,
we still looked down on idleness as shameful,
and the wind still lifted countless sparks
of inspiration from this soil.

Your holy ashes still were warm,
undefeated enemy of fortune, [*Dante*]
to whose disdain and pain
hell was friendlier than earth.
Yes, even hell: for what place isn't preferable
to ours? And your sweet strings
still murmured at your hand's touch,
suffering lover. [*Petrarch*]
Ah, Italian song
begins, is born, in pain. And yet the pain
we're suffering weighs us down and stings
less than the tedium we're sinking into.
Oh happy one for whom lament was life!
Boredom wrapped us in our swaddling clothes;
and nothingness guards our cradle and our tomb.

Ma tua vita era allor con gli astri e il mare,
Ligure ardita prole,
Quand'oltre alle colonne, ed oltre ai liti
Cui strider l'onde all'attuffar del sole
Parve udir su la sera, agl'infiniti
Flutti commesso, ritrovasti il raggio
Del Sol caduto, e il giorno
Che nasce allor ch'ai nostri è giunto al fondo;
E rotto di natura ogni contrasto,
Ignota immensa terra al tuo viaggio
Fu gloria, e del ritorno
Ai rischi. Ahi ahi, ma conosciuto il mondo
Non cresce, anzi si scema, e assai più vasto
L'etra sonante e l'alma terra e il mare
Al fanciullin, che non al saggio, appare.

Nostri sogni leggiadri ove son giti
Dell'ignoto ricetto
D'ignoti abitatori, o del diurno
Degli astri albergo, e del rimoto letto
Della giovane Aurora, e del notturno
Occulto sonno del maggior pianeta?
Ecco svaniro a un punto,
E figurato è il mondo in breve carta;
Ecco tutto è simile, e discoprendo,
Solo il nulla s'accresce. A noi ti vieta
Il vero appena è giunto,
O caro immaginar; da te s'apparta
Nostra mente in eterno; allo stupendo
Poter tuo primo ne sottraggon gli anni;
E il conforto perì de' nostri affanni.

But your life then was with the stars and sea,
bold son of Liguria, [*Columbus*]
when beyond the columns and the shores
where it seemed one heard the waves
screaming as the sun set,
you ventured out onto the boundless ocean
and happened on the light of the gone Sun,
and the day that starts when He's reached the end of ours;
and having broken nature's every bond,
a boundless, unfamiliar earth was the glorious
reward for your voyage and your perilous return.
Alas, the world when once known doesn't expand:
it shrinks; and the echoing heaven
and the gentle earth and sea
seem far vaster to the infant than to the sage.

Where have they gone, our happy dreams
of the exotic homelands
of exotic peoples, or the stars' diurnal
resting place, or young Aurora's distant bed,
or the hidden sleep of the great planet?
Look, they vanished in a moment,
and the world's described on one brief page;
look, now everything's the same,
and discovery only adds to nothingness.
Truth is taken from us
in the moment it arrives,
O sweet imaginination; our mind's cut off
from you forever; the years removed us
from your stupendous primal power;
and the comfort for our troubles died.

Nascevi ai dolci sogni intanto, e il primo
Sole splendeati in vista,
Cantor vago dell'arme e degli amori,
Che in età della nostra assai men trista
Empièr la vita di felici errori:
Nova speme d'Italia. O torri, o celle,
O donne, o cavalieri,
O giardini, o palagi! a voi pensando,
In mille vane amenità si perde
La mente mia. Di vanità, di belle
Fole e strani pensieri
Si componea l'umana vita: in bando
Li cacciammo: or che resta? or poi che il verde
È spogliato alle cose? Il certo e solo
Veder che tutto è vano altro che il duolo.

O Torquato, o Torquato, a noi l'eccelsa
Tua mente allora, il pianto
A te, non altro, preparava il cielo.
Oh misero Torquato! il dolce canto
Non valse a consolarti o a sciorre il gelo
Onde l'alma t'avean, ch'era sì calda,
Cinta l'odio e l'immondo
Livor privato e de' tiranni. Amore,
Amor, di nostra vita ultimo inganno,
T'abbandonava. Ombra reale e salda
Ti parve il nulla, e il mondo
Inabitata piaggia. Al tardo onore
Non sorser gli occhi tuoi; mercè, non danno,
L'ora estrema ti fu. Morte domanda
Chi nostro mal conobbe, e non ghirlanda.

But you were born to gentle dreams,
and the early sun shone in your face,
graceful bard of arms and loves [*Ariosto*]
which, in an age less malcontent than ours,
filled life with glad illusions:
new hope of Italy. O towers, chambers,
damsels, knights, O gardens, palaces!
When I think of you, my mind
traces a thousand empty vagaries.
Human life was made of vanities,
glad fantasies, and strange ideas:
we chased them together; what survives,
now that the green has leached out of things?
The certain, lonely knowledge
that everything is vain but grief.

O Torquato, Torquato, heaven made [*Tasso*]
your sublime mind for us,
but only sorrow, nothing else, for you.
Miserable Torquato! Your sweet song
couldn't console you, couldn't melt the ice
that the hatred and foul jealousy
of men and tyrants locked your spirit in,
that was so warm. Love,
the last illusion of our life,
deserted you. Nothingness to you
seemed an actual, substantial shadow
and the world a desert. You didn't notice
your late honors; your last moment
was relief, not pain for you. He who has known
our pain wants death and not a wreath.

Torna torna fra noi, sorgi dal muto
E sconsolato avello,
Se d'angoscia sei vago, o miserando
Esemplo di sciagura. Assai da quello
Che ti parve sì mesto e sì nefando,
È peggiorato il viver nostro. O caro,
Chi ti compiangeria,
Se, fuor che di se stesso, altri non cura?
Chi stolto non direbbe il tuo mortale
Affanno anche oggidì, se il grande e il raro
Ha nome di follia;
Nè livor più, ma ben di lui più dura
La noncuranza avviene ai sommi? o quale,
Se più de' carmi, il computar s'ascolta,
Ti appresterebbe il lauro un'altra volta?

Da te fino a quest'ora uom non è sorto,
O sventurato ingegno,
Pari all'italo nome, altro ch'un solo,
Solo di sua codarda etate indegno
Allobrogo feroce, a cui dal polo
Maschia virtù, non già da questa mia
Stanca ed arida terra,
Venne nel petto; onde privato, inerme,
(Memorando ardimento) in su la scena
Mosse guerra a' tiranni: almen si dia
Questa misera guerra
E questo vano campo all'ire inferme
Del mondo. Ei primo e sol dentro all'arena
Scese, e nullo il seguì, che l'ozio e il brutto
Silenzio or preme ai nostri innanzi a tutto.

Come back, come back among us,
rise out of the silent, lonely tomb,
if you long for anguish, O unhappy
exemplar of calamity. The life
that seemed so dark and wrong to you
has become far worse for us.
Loved one, who would mourn you,
if everyone cares only for himself?
Who wouldn't call your mortal struggle
foolish too now, when the great and rare
are called insane? Is it not mere jealousy
but something far more cruel: indifference,
that assaults the greatest?
Who, when mathematics is preferred to song,
would offer you the laurel wreath again?

No man has appeared since you till now,
O unfortunate intelligence,
worthy to be called Italian, except one,
one man unworthy of his cowardly age, [*Alfieri*]
fierce Allobrogian,
endowed with manly courage from on high,
not by this worn-out, arid land of mine;
with it, as a simple citizen,
and (memorable audacity) unarmed,
he battled tyrants from the stage:
so that this hopeless fight and empty field,
at least, should be devoted to the powerless
angers of the world. He was the first to go
down alone into the arena, and no one followed,
for idleness and brutal silence now own us most of all.

Disdegnando e fremendo, immacolata
Trasse la vita intera,
E morte lo scampò dal veder peggio.
Vittorio mio, questa per te non era
Età nè suolo. Altri anni ed altro seggio
Conviene agli alti ingegni. Or di riposo
Paghi viviamo, e scorti
Da mediocrità; sceso il sapiente
E salita è la turba a un sol confine,
Che il mondo agguaglia. O scopritor famoso,
Segui; risveglia i morti,
Poi che dormono i vivi; arma le spente
Lingue de' prischi eroi; tanto che in fine
Questo secol di fango o vita agogni
E sorga ad atti illustri, o si vergogni.

Disdainful and enraged, he lived
pure his whole life,
and death prevented him from seeing worse.
My Vittorio, this age and land
were not for you. Other times, another place
are fit for genius. Now we live
ready for rest, with mediocrities
as company: the wise man has come down
and the crowd has risen to his level,
with the world. O famed discoverer, [*Mai*]
continue. Raise the fallen,
since the living sleep. Rearm the dead tongues
of our pristine heroes, so at last
this age of mud will either want to live
and rise to noble action, or be shamed.

IV

NELLE NOZZE DELLA SORELLA PAOLINA

Poi che del patrio nido
I silenzi lasciando, e le beate
Larve e l'antico error, celeste dono,
Ch'abbella agli occhi tuoi quest'ermo lido,
Te nella polve della vita e il suono
Tragge il destin; l'obbrobriosa etate
Che il duro cielo a noi prescrisse impara,
Sorella mia, che in gravi
E luttuosi tempi
L'infelice famiglia all'infelice
Italia accrescerai. Di forti esempi
Al tuo sangue provvedi. Aure soavi
L'empio fato interdice
All'umana virtude,
Nè pura in gracil petto alma si chiude.

O miseri o codardi
Figliuoli avrai. Miseri eleggi. Immenso
Tra fortuna e valor dissidio pose
Il corrotto costume. Ahi troppo tardi,

IV

ON THE MARRIAGE OF HIS SISTER PAOLINA

Now you're abandoning the peace and quiet
of your parental nest, with its beloved
ghosts and the old illusion, heaven's gift,
that makes this lonely place seem lovely to you,
destiny leads you to the dust and noise
of life. Learn the shame
that cruel heaven
ordained for us, sister:
that in terrible times
you'll bear luckless children
for unlucky Italy.
Set them a strong example. Fate is heartless
and denies fair weather
to human courage,
and a pure heart won't survive in a weak breast.

The children that you'll have will either be
cowards or unhappy. Let them be unhappy.
Corruption opened up a yawning chasm
between character and circumstance.

E nella sera dell'umane cose,
Acquista oggi chi nasce il moto e il senso.
Al ciel ne caglia: a te nel petto sieda
Questa sovr'ogni cura,
Che di fortuna amici
Non crescano i tuoi figli, e non di vile
Timor gioco o di speme: onde felici
Sarete detti nell'età futura:
Poichè (nefando stile,
Di schiatta ignava e finta)
Virtù viva sprezziam, lodiamo estinta.

Donne, da voi non poco
La patria aspetta; e non in danno e scorno
Dell'umana progenie al dolce raggio
Delle pupille vostre il ferro e il foco
Domar fu dato. A senno vostro il saggio
E il forte adopra e pensa; e quanto il giorno
Col divo carro accerchia, a voi s'inchina.
Ragion di nostra etate
Io chieggo a voi. La santa
Fiamma di gioventù dunque si spegne
Per vostra mano? attenuata e franta
Da voi nostra natura? e le assonnate
Menti, e le voglie indegne,
E di nervi e di polpe
Scemo il valor natio, son vostre colpe?

Ad atti egregi è sprone
Amor, chi ben l'estima, e d'alto affetto

Alas, a man who's born today
learns to act and feel too late,
and in the evening of human life.
That is heaven's doing; but let this concern
surpass all others: that your children not be raised
as fortune's friends or playthings
of base fear or hope.
For this you'll be called happy in the future;
for a lazy and false people
tend to disdain virtue while it lives
and praise it once it's gone.

Women, the fatherland expects
much from you. And it wasn't to harm and scorn
the human race that the loving light of your eyes
was given the power to tame both iron and fire.
The wise and strong man acts and thinks
according to your will; and everything
that the sun circles in his heavenly chariot
inclines to you.
I ask you to explain our age:
Did you put out youth's holy fire?
Have you weakened and debased our character?
And our sleepy minds and low desires,
our native strength
that lack for nerve and fiber—
is all this because of you as well?

Love, for him who sees it clearly,
is a spur to noble actions,

Maestra è la beltà. D'amor digiuna
Siede l'alma di quello a cui nel petto
Non si rallegra il cor quando a tenzone
Scendono i venti, e quando nembi aduna
L'olimpo, e fiede le montagne il rombo
Della procella. O spose,
O verginette, a voi
Chi de' perigli è schivo, e quei che indegno
È della patria e che sue brame e suoi
Volgari affetti in basso loco pose,
Odio mova e disdegno;
Se nel femmineo core
D'uomini ardea, non di fanciulle, amore.

Madri d'imbelle prole
V'incresca esser nomate. I danni e il pianto
Della virtude a tollerar s'avvezzi
La stirpe vostra, e quel che pregia e cole
La vergognosa età, condanni e sprezzi;
Cresca alla patria, e gli alti gesti, e quanto
Agli avi suoi deggia la terra impari.
Qual de' vetusti eroi
Tra le memorie e il grido
Crescean di Sparta i figli al greco nome;
Finchè la sposa giovanetta il fido
Brando cingeva al caro lato, e poi
Spandea le negre chiome
Sul corpo esangue e nudo
Quando e' reddia nel conservato scudo.

and beauty is the mistress of deep feeling.
The man whose soul cannot take pleasure
when the winds rage and the sky
fills with clouds and thunder strikes
the hills, is lacking in love.
Brides! Young virgins!
may you despise the man
who fears danger,
who's unworthy of the fatherland
and squandered his desires and vulgar loves
on worthless trifles.
If you are women, let your hearts
be warm with love for men and not for boys.

Don't be known as mothers of timid children.
Let your offspring learn to bear the pains
and sorrows of goodness,
and condemn and hate
what this shameful age admires.
May they be raised for their country and great deeds,
and learn what their homeland owes their ancestors.
So the sons of Sparta
grew up hearing legends
in praise of ancient heroes with Greek names,
and the young bride belted
her husband's trusty sword to his loved side,
and later spread her jet-black hair
across his bloodless, naked corpse
when he came home on the shield he'd saved.

Virginia, a te la molle
Gota molcea con le celesti dita
Beltade onnipossente, e degli alteri
Disdegni tuoi si sconsolava il folle
Signor di Roma. Eri pur vaga, ed eri
Nella stagion ch'ai dolci sogni invita,
Quando il rozzo paterno acciar ti ruppe
Il bianchissimo petto,
E all'Erebo scendesti
Volonterosa. A me disfiori e scioglia
Vecchiezza i membri, o padre; a me s'appresti,
Dicea, la tomba, anzi che l'empio letto
Del tiranno m'accoglia.
E se pur vita e lena
Roma avrà dal mio sangue, e tu mi svena.

O generosa, ancora
Che più bello a' tuoi dì splendesse il sole
Ch'oggi non fa, pur consolata e paga
È quella tomba cui di pianto onora
L'alma terra nativa. Ecco alla vaga
Tua spoglia intorno la romulea prole
Di nova ira sfavilla. Ecco di polve
Lorda il tiranno i crini;
E libertade avvampa
Gli obbliviosi petti; e nella doma
Terra il marte latino arduo s'accampa
Dal buio polo ai torridi confini.
Così l'eterna Roma
In duri ozi sepolta
Femmineo fato avviva un'altra volta.

Virginia, all-powerful
beauty touched your tender cheek
with her celestial fingers, and your proud refusal
incensed the insane
master of Rome. You were still lovely,
and in the season that inspires sweet dreams,
when your father's cruel blade
pierced your snowy breast,
and you went willingly to Erebus.
Father, let age deflower me and loose my limbs;
prepare the tomb for me, she said,
rather than that the impious
tyrant should have me.
And if Rome may still draw life and breath
from my blood, unvein me.

Generous one, although the sun
shone lovelier in your days than it does now,
still your tomb, which the beloved homeland
honors with her tears,
is mourned and atoned for. See
around your lovely corpse the sons of Romulus
ignited by fresh anger. See
the tyrant's mane dragged in the dirt,
as freedom inspires forgetful hearts,
and in the conquered land
the cruel Latin god of war
rules from the dark North to the torrid South.
So eternal Rome
entombed in heavy sleep
finds life again thanks to a woman's death.

V

A UN VINCITORE NEL PALLONE

Di gloria il viso e la gioconda voce,
Garzon bennato, apprendi,
E quanto al femminile ozio sovrasti
La sudata virtude. Attendi attendi,
Magnanimo campion (s'alla veloce
Piena degli anni il tuo valor contrasti
La spoglia di tuo nome), attendi e il core
Movi ad alto desio. Te l'echeggiante
Arena e il circo, e te fremendo appella
Ai fatti illustri il popolar favore;
Te rigoglioso dell'età novella
Oggi la patria cara
Gli antichi esempi a rinnovar prepara.

Del barbarico sangue in Maratona
Non colorò la destra
Quei che gli atleti ignudi e il campo eleo,
Che stupido mirò l'ardua palestra,
Nè la palma beata e la corona
D'emula brama il punse. E nell'Alfeo
Forse le chiome polverose e i fianchi
Delle cavalle vincitrici asterse

V

TO A CHAMPION AT FOOTBALL

Learn the look and happy sound of glory,
noble youth, and how much hard-won virtue
has over girlish laziness.
Hear, great-hearted champion
(if your courage can protect your name
from the threatening headlong flood of time),
hear, and dedicate your heart to high ambition.
The echoing arena and the stadium
and the people's thundering adulation
urge you on to brilliant feats.
Your beloved fatherland
calls you in the prime of youth today
to reenact the great deeds of the past.

The man who wasn't moved to see
the nude athletes on the field at Elis
or in its intimidating ring,
was not the man
who stained his hand
with barbarian blood at Marathon,
or coveted the sacred palm or crown.
But he who wetted down the dusty manes and flanks

Tal che le greche insegne e il greco acciaro
Guidò de' Medi fuggitivi e stanchi
Nelle pallide torme; onde sonaro
Di sconsolato grido
L'alto sen dell'Eufrate e il servo lido.
Vano dirai quel che disserra e scote
Della virtù nativa
Le riposte faville? e che del fioco
Spirto vital negli egri petti avviva
Il caduco fervor? Le meste rote
Da poi che Febo instiga, altro che gioco
Son l'opre de' mortali? ed è men vano
Della menzogna il vero? A noi di lieti
Inganni e di felici ombre soccorse
Natura stessa: e là dove l'insano
Costume ai forti errori esca non porse,
Negli ozi oscuri e nudi
Mutò la gente i gloriosi studi.

Tempo forse verrà ch'alle ruine
Delle italiche moli
Insultino gli armenti, e che l'aratro
Sentano i sette colli; e pochi Soli
Forse fien volti, e le città latine
Abiterà la cauta volpe, e l'atro
Bosco mormorerà fra le alte mura;
Se la funesta delle patrie cose
Obblivion dalle perverse menti
Non isgombrano i fati, e la matura

of his victorious mares in the Alpheus
may have raised Greek banners and Greek swords
against the pale swarms of exhausted, fleeing Medes,
whose desperate cries were heard across
the deep Euphrates and its conquered shore.
Will you say what reignites
the scattered embers of our innate power,
what rouses the flickering fervor
in our faint hearts, is useless? From the moment
Phoebus started spinning his sad wheels,
have the works of men been anything but a game?
And is the truth less meaningless than lies?
Nature herself
fed us on sweet illusions and happy phantoms:
and, where unhealthy habits
didn't foment grandiose illusions,
the people favored squalid laziness
over glorious accomplishments.

Maybe the time will come when herds
will browse the ruins of Italian palaces
and the seven hills will feel the plow.
In a few years the wily vixen
may live in Latin cities and dark forests
will murmur inside their high walls,
if the fates do not erase
fatal forgetting of what's patriotic
from corrupt minds,
and heaven, turned benevolent again,

Clade non torce dalle abbiette genti
Il ciel fatto cortese
Dal rimembrar delle passate imprese.

Alla patria infelice, o buon garzone,
Sopravviver ti doglia.
Chiaro per lei stato saresti allora
Che del serto fulgea, di ch'ella è spoglia,
Nostra colpa e fatal. Passò stagione;
Che nullo di tal madre oggi s'onora:
Ma per te stesso al polo ergi la mente.
Nostra vita a che val? solo a spregiarla:
Beata allor che ne' perigli avvolta,
Se stessa obblia, nè delle putri e lente
Ore il danno misura e il flutto ascolta;
Beata allor che il piede
Spinto al varco leteo, più grata riede.

recalling the achievements of the past,
won't rescue an abject people
from imminent destruction.

Noble youth, may it be painful to you
to live on after your unhappy country.
You would have been great for her then,
when the crown shone that she's missing now,
to our shame, and fate's. The times have changed;
for no son of this mother is honored now.
Yet think of heaven, for your own sake.
What is our life worth? Nothing but disdain.
Blessed then, when, danger all around,
it forgets itself and doesn't count the loss
of the slow, stagnant hours, or hear them ebb;
blessed when, having grazed the shores of Lethe,
it returns more cherished.

VI

BRUTO MINORE

Poi che divelta, nella tracia polve
Giacque ruina immensa
L'italica virtute, onde alle valli
D'Esperia verde, e al tiberino lido,
Il calpestio de' barbari cavalli
Prepara il fato, e dalle selve ignude
Cui l'Orsa algida preme,
A spezzar le romane inclite mura
Chiama i gotici brandi;
Sudato, e molle di fraterno sangue,
Bruto per l'atra notte in erma sede,
Fermo già di morir, gl'inesorandi
Numi e l'averno accusa,
E di feroci note
Invan la sonnolenta aura percote.

Stolta virtù, le cave nebbie, i campi
Dell'inquiete larve
Son le tue scole, e ti si volge a tergo
Il pentimento. A voi, marmorei numi,
(Se numi avete in Flegetonte albergo
O su le nubi) a voi ludibrio e scherno

VI

BRUTUS

Now that Italian valor lies uprooted,
one huge ruin in the dust of Thrace,
where fate is readying barbarian horses
to trample the green valleys of Hesperia
and Tiber's shore,
exhorting Gothic swordsmen
from the wild forests
lorded over by the freezing Bear
to breach the venerable walls of Rome,
Brutus, sweating, soaked in brothers' blood,
sitting the dark night out alone
prepared to die,
curses the implacable gods and hell itself,
and assails the sleeping air in vain
with savage cries:

Foolish valor, empty mists
and the fields of restless ghosts
are where you live,
and remorse dogs your footsteps. Gods of stone,
(whether you live by Phlegethon
or in the clouds), you mock and scorn

È la prole infelice
A cui templi chiedeste, e frodolenta
Legge al mortale insulta.
Dunque tanto i celesti odii commove
La terrena pietà? dunque degli empi
Siedi, Giove, a tutela? e quando esulta
Per l'aere il nembo, e quando
Il tuon rapido spingi,
Ne' giusti e pii la sacra fiamma stringi?

Preme il destino invitto e la ferrata
Necessità gl'infermi
Schiavi di morte: e se a cessar non vale
Gli oltraggi lor, de' necessarii danni
Si consola il plebeo. Men duro è il male
Che riparo non ha? dolor non sente
Chi di speranza è nudo?
Guerra mortale, eterna, o fato indegno,
Teco il prode guerreggia,
Di cedere inesperto; e la tiranna
Tua destra, allor che vincitrice il grava,
Indomito scrollando si pompeggia,
Quando nell'alto lato
L'amaro ferro intride,
E maligno alle nere ombre sorride.

Spiace agli Dei chi violento irrompe
Nel Tartaro. Non fora
Tanto valor ne' molli eterni petti.
Forse i travagli nostri, e forse il cielo

the unhappy race from whom
you exacted temples and a fraudulent
law harmful to mortals.
So, is this how piety on earth
arouses heaven's rage? Do you sit there, Jupiter,
and shield the blasphemous? And when the storm cloud
rages in the air and you let loose
swift thunder, do you brandish sacred fire
against the just and faithful?

Omnipotent fate and iron necessity
oppress the sickly slaves of death:
and, without a means
to end their suffering, the people
look for comfort for the pain they can't avoid.
Is an incurable disease any less cruel?
Does a man stripped of hope not suffer torment?
The brave man, who's incapable of surrender,
fights you without quarter to the death,
unworthy fate.
And when your tyrant right hand pins him down,
undefeated he exults
as the harsh blade
slices deep into his side,
and bitterly he smiles at the black shades.

Breaking violently into Tartarus
displeases the Gods. No such power should be,
according to these tender deathless hearts.
Did heaven make a happy spectacle

I casi acerbi e gl'infelici affetti
Giocondo agli ozi suoi spettacol pose?
Non fra sciagure e colpe,
Ma libera ne' boschi e pura etade
Natura a noi prescrisse,
Reina un tempo e Diva. Or poi ch'a terra
Sparse i regni beati empio costume,
E il viver macro ad altre leggi addisse;
Quando gl'infausti giorni
Virile alma ricusa,
Riede natura, e il non suo dardo accusa?

Di colpa ignare e de' lor proprii danni
Le fortunate belve
Serena adduce al non previsto passo
La tarda età. Ma se spezzar la fronte
Ne' rudi tronchi, o da montano sasso
Dare al vento precipiti le membra,
Lor suadesse affanno;
Al misero desio nulla contesa
Legge arcana farebbe
O tenebroso ingegno. A voi, fra quante
Stirpi il cielo avvivò, soli fra tutte,
Figli di Prometeo, la vita increbbe;
A voi le morte ripe,
Se il fato ignavo pende,
Soli, o miseri, a voi Giove contende.

E tu dal mar cui nostro sangue irriga,
Candida luna, sorgi,

of our unhappiness, our cruel fates
and miserable loves, for their amusement?
Nature, Queen and Goddess once, ordained
a life for us that wasn't suffering
and guilt, but free and pure in the forests.
Now, since sacrilegious ways
have destroyed the blessed realms on earth
and subjected meager life to other laws,
when a manly soul rejects his luckless life,
does nature rear up and denounce
the weapon that's not hers?

Serene old age delivers
the lucky animals, unaware of sin
and their own suffering, to an end
they can't imagine. But if misery
made them beat their foreheads on rough trees
or toss their bodies headlong to the winds
from a mountain cliff,
no arcane law or shadowy idea
would make objection
to their miserable wish.
Only for you, of all the progeny
that heaven gave breath to, children of Prometheus,
was life made unendurable.
Only you, unhappy ones, if death comes late,
does Jove bar from the fatal shore.

And you, bright moon, you rise
out of the sea our blood turns red,

E l'inquieta notte e la funesta
All'ausonio valor campagna esplori.
Cognati petti il vincitor calpesta,
Fremono i poggi, dalle somme vette
Roma antica ruina;
Tu sì placida sei? Tu la nascente
Lavinia prole, e gli anni
Lieti vedesti, e i memorandi allori;
E tu su l'alpe l'immutato raggio
Tacita verserai quando ne' danni
Del servo italo nome,
Sotto barbaro piede
Rintronerà quella solinga sede.

Ecco tra nudi sassi o in verde ramo
E la fera e l'augello,
Del consueto obblio gravido il petto,
L'alta ruina ignora e le mutate
Sorti del mondo: e come prima il tetto
Rosseggerà del villanello industre,
Al mattutino canto
Quel desterà le valli, e per le balze
Quella l'inferma plebe
Agiterà delle minori belve.
Oh casi! oh gener vano! abbietta parte
Siam delle cose; e non le tinte glebe,
Non gli ululati spechi
Turbò nostra sciagura,
Nè scolorò le stelle umana cura.

and scan the unquiet night and the field
that proved fatal to Italian courage.
The victor tramples on his brothers' bodies,
the hillsides echo, ancient Rome
crumbles from her heights—
are you so calm?
You saw Lavinia's children born,
their happy years and memorable victories,
and still you'll pour your changeless light
silent on the mountain peaks
when this lonely place will echo
under the barbarian's heel,
staining the name of enslaved Italy.

Here, among bare rocks or on green branches,
beast and bird, breasts heavy
with their usual oblivion,
know nothing of the great decay
and changed fate of the world:
and once the toiling farmer's roof turns red,
the one will wake
the valleys with its morning song
while on the heights the other will go chasing
the helpless multitude of little creatures.
Oh fates! Oh worthless race! We are a miserable
part of things, and neither bloodstained earth
nor the caves resounding with our cries
were troubled by our torment;
nor did human pain discolor the stars.

Non io d'Olimpo o di Cocito i sordi
Regi, o la terra indegna,
E non la notte moribondo appello;
Non te, dell'atra morte ultimo raggio,
Conscia futura età. Sdegnoso avello
Placàr singulti, ornàr parole e doni
Di vil caterva? In peggio
Precipitano i tempi; e mal s'affida
A putridi nepoti
L'onor d'egregie menti e la suprema
De' miseri vendetta. A me dintorno
Le penne il bruno augello avido roti;
Prema la fera, e il nembo
Tratti l'ignota spoglia;
E l'aura il nome e la memoria accoglia.

I call not on the heedless kings
of Olympus or Cocytus,
nor on unworthy earth, nor night before I die;
and not on you, conscious future generation,
last hope of lightless death. Will tears appease
a scornful man's tomb? Will the vile crowd's
praise and offerings turn it beautiful?
The times are swiftly worsening,
and honoring great minds
and the last vindication of the suffering
are wrongly left to our corrupt descendants.
Let the voracious bird flap his black wings
above me, let the beast have at me,
and the shades carry off my nameless corpse,
and the wind take my name and memory.

VII

ALLA PRIMAVERA,

O

DELLE FAVOLE

ANTICHE

Perchè i celesti danni
Ristori il sole, e perchè l'aure inferme
Zefiro avvivi, onde fugata e sparta
Delle nubi la grave ombra s'avvalla;
Credano il petto inerme
Gli augelli al vento, e la diurna luce
Novo d'amor desio, nova speranza
Ne' penetrati boschi e fra le sciolte
Pruine induca alle commosse belve;
Forse alle stanche e nel dolor sepolte
Umane menti riede
La bella età, cui la sciagura e l'atra
Face del ver consunse
Innanzi tempo? Ottenebrati e spenti
Di febo i raggi al misero non sono
In sempiterno? ed anco,

VII

TO SPRING, OR ON THE ANCIENT MYTHS

Although the sun is working to repair
the damage in the sky,
a breeze is freshening the sickly air,
and the clouds' dark shadow, chased away, dispersed,
fades in the valley; now the birds
are trusting their defenseless breasts
to the wind, and daylight brings
new desire for love, new hope
to the dappled woods and cattle
restless in the melting frosts;
can that sweet time return perhaps
for weary human minds shut up in sadness,
the time calamity and the dark fire
of knowledge ended too soon?
Is Apollo's light not hidden and gone forever
for the unhappy? And, scented Spring,

Primavera odorata, inspiri e tenti
Questo gelido cor, questo ch'amara
Nel fior degli anni suoi vecchiezza impara?

Vivi tu, vivi, o santa
Natura? vivi e il dissueto orecchio
Della materna voce il suono accoglie?
Già di candide ninfe i rivi albergo,
Placido albergo e specchio
Furo i liquidi fonti. Arcane danze
D'immortal piede i ruinosi gioghi
Scossero e l'ardue selve (oggi romito
Nido de' venti): e il pastorel ch'all'ombre
Meridiane incerte ed al fiorito
Margo adducea de' fiumi
Le sitibonde agnelle, arguto carme
Sonar d'agresti Pani
Udì lungo le ripe; e tremar l'onda
Vide, e stupì, che non palese al guardo
La faretrata Diva
Scendea ne' caldi flutti, e dall'immonda
Polve tergea della sanguigna caccia
Il niveo lato e le verginee braccia.

Vissero i fiori e l'erbe,
Vissero i boschi un dì. Conscie le molli
Aure, le nubi e la titania lampa
Fur dell'umana gente, allor che ignuda
Te per le piagge e i colli,
Ciprigna luce, alla deserta notte

do you still inspire and tempt this frozen heart,
this heart that learns of bitter age
in the very prime of life?

Are you living, holy Nature?
Are you alive; is it your mother's voice
our unaccustomed ear is welcoming?
Bright nymphs walked on your shores once,
your clear springs were their tranquil home and mirror.
Hidden dancing of immortal feet
beat on the ruined heights
and in the impenetrable forests
(distant nest for winds today). And the shepherd boy
who led his thirsty lambs among the fleeting
noontime shadows and the flowering banks
could hear the shrill of woodland Pans
piping on the shores
and saw the water's surface
shimmer and, in amazement,
watched the arrow-bearing Goddess [*Diana*]
enter the warm waves unrecognized
to wash the foul dust of the bloody hunt
from her snow-white sides and virgin arms.

Flowers and herbs bloomed once,
and the woods were green. The gentle breeze,
the clouds, and the Titanic sun
knew man, when the traveler
followed you intently as he walked,
pure Cyprian moonlight, in the desert night [*Venus*]

Con gli occhi intenti il viator seguendo,
Te compagna alla via, te de' mortali
Pensosa immaginò. Che se gl'impuri
Cittadini consorzi e le fatali
Ire fuggendo e l'onte,
Gl'ispidi tronchi al petto altri nell'ime
Selve remoto accolse,
Viva fiamma agitar l'esangui vene,
Spirar le foglie, e palpitar segreta
Nel doloroso amplesso
Dafne o la mesta Filli, o di Climene
Pianger credè la sconsolata prole
Quel che sommerse in Eridano il sole.

Nè dell'umano affanno,
Rigide balze, i luttuosi accenti
Voi negletti ferìr mentre le vostre
Paurose latebre Eco solinga,
Non vano error de' venti,
Ma di ninfa abitò misero spirto,
Cui grave amor, cui duro fato escluse
Delle tenere membra. Ella per grotte,
Per nudi scogli e desolati alberghi,
Le non ignote ambasce e l'alte e rotte
Nostre querele al curvo
Etra insegnava. E te d'umani eventi
Disse la fama esperto,
Musico augel che tra chiomato bosco
Or vieni il rinascente anno cantando,
E lamentar nell'alto

by shore and over hill, and thought of you
as his companion, watching over mortals.
Or if someone, fleeing corrupt crowds
and the city's murderous shame and rage,
clung to shaggy trees in the dark forest,
he could feel a living flame
burn in their exhausted veins,
the leaves themselves breathed
as Daphne or sad Phyllis quivered
hidden in his sorrowing embrace,
while Clymene's offspring
mourned unconsoled
for him who sank the sun in Eridanos. [*Phaeton*]

Nor did the mournful sound of human suffering
strike you unheard, harsh cliffs,
while lonely Echo
was living in your fearful caves
not as an empty, wandering wind
but as the sad spirit of a nymph,
whom unrequited love and cruel fate
had separated from her tender body.
In grottoes, on bare rocks, in lonely places,
she repeated her familiar woes
and our strident, broken-voiced laments
to the overarching sky.
And fame said you were versed in human doings,
musical bird who in the leafy grove [*the nightingale*]
now comes to sing of the reviving year,
and mourn in the deep languor of the fields

Ozio de' campi, all'aer muto e fosco,
Antichi danni e scellerato scorno,
E d'ira e di pietà pallido il giorno.

Ma non cognato al nostro
Il gener tuo; quelle tue varie note
Dolor non forma, e te di colpa ignudo,
Men caro assai la bruna valle asconde.
Ahi ahi, poscia che vote
Son le stanze d'Olimpo, e cieco il tuono
Per l'atre nubi e le montagne errando,
Gl'iniqui petti e gl'innocenti a paro
In freddo orror dissolve; e poi ch'estrano
Il suol nativo, e di sua prole ignaro
Le meste anime educa;
Tu le cure infelici e i fati indegni
Tu de' mortali ascolta,
Vaga natura, e la favilla antica
Rendi allo spirto mio; se tu pur vivi,
E se de' nostri affanni
Cosa veruna in ciel, se nell'aprica
Terra s'alberga o nell'equoreo seno,
Pietosa no, ma spettatrice almeno.

and in the heavy, silent, still-dark air,
ancient wrong and criminal disgrace,
and the daylight, dimmed by rage and pity.

But your race is not the same as ours.
Suffering doesn't shape your changing notes,
and hidden in the dark valley, you sound guiltless
and therefore that much less adored by us.
Alas, for the halls of Olympus
are abandoned, and blind thunder
echoes in the black clouds and the mountains,
shattering evil and pure hearts alike
with icy terror, while our native land,
alien and ignorant of its offspring,
nurtures sad souls. Hear the troubles
and unworthy fates of mortals,
lovely Nature, and imbue my spirit
with the old spark—
if indeed you live,
if there is anything
in heaven, on sunlit earth,
or on the ocean's breast that, if not pitying,
can testify at least to what we suffer.

VIII

INNO AI PATRIARCHI,

O

DE' PRINCIPII DEL GENERE UMANO

E voi de' figli dolorosi il canto,
Voi dell'umana prole incliti padri,
Lodando ridirà; molto all'eterno
Degli astri agitator più cari, e molto
Di noi men lacrimabili nell'alma
Luce prodotti. Immedicati affanni
Al misero mortal, nascere al pianto,
E dell'etereo lume assai più dolci
Sortir l'opaca tomba e il fato estremo,
Non la pietà, non la diritta impose
Legge del cielo. E se di vostro antico
Error che l'uman seme alla tiranna
Possa de' morbi e di sciagura offerse,
Grido antico ragiona, altre più dire
Colpe de' figli, e irrequieto ingegno
E demenza maggior l'offeso Olimpo

VIII

HYMN TO THE PATRIARCHS, OR ON THE ORIGINS OF THE HUMAN RACE

Your grieving sons will sing in praise of you
again, illustrious fathers of the race;
will sing in praise of you, so much more loved
than we are by the stars' eternal mover,
and born into the nurturing daylight
with far less cause for mourning. It wasn't piety
or the just law of heaven that ordained
incurable pain for miserable mortals:
to be born to weep, and have
the dark tomb and death seem so much gentler
than daylight. And if long tradition
tells of your old transgression that betrayed
humans to the tyrannizing power
of illness and disaster, your children's other,
far worse failings, restlessness of mind
and greater madness, armed offended Olympus

N'armaro incontra, e la negletta mano
Dell'altrice natura; onde la viva
Fiamma n'increbbe, e detestato il parto
Fu del grembo materno, e violento
Emerse il disperato Erebo in terra.

Tu primo il giorno, e le purpuree faci
Delle rotanti sfere, e la novella
Prole de' campi, o duce antico e padre
Dell'umana famiglia, e tu l'errante
Per li giovani prati aura contempli:
Quando le rupi e le deserte valli
Precipite l'alpina onda feria
D'inudito fragor; quando gli ameni
Futuri seggi di lodate genti
E di cittadi romorose, ignota
Pace regnava; e gl'inarati colli
Solo e muto ascendea l'aprico raggio
Di febo e l'aurea luna. Oh fortunata,
Di colpe ignara e di lugubri eventi,
Erma terrena sede! Oh quanto affanno
Al gener tuo, padre infelice, e quale
D'amarissimi casi ordine immenso
Preparano i destini! Ecco di sangue
Gli avari colti e di fraterno scempio
Furor novello incesta, e le nefande
Ali di morte il divo etere impara.
Trepido, errante il fratricida, e l'ombre
Solitarie fuggendo e la secreta
Nelle profonde selve ira de' venti,

and the neglected hand of Mother Nature
against us; till the flame of life itself
became inimical, and being born
from a mother's womb was hateful,
and violent, hopeless Erebus appeared on earth.

You, ancient guide and father [*Adam*]
of the human family, were the first to see the day,
the purple fires of the revolving stars,
the newborn flowering fields,
the wind that blows across the freshened meadows,
when the cascading alpine waters
struck the cliffs and uninhabited
valleys with unheard sound; when unheard-of peace
reigned in the pleasing future habitats
of happy peoples and their busy cities,
when, silent and alone,
Phoebus's brilliant light and the gold moon
climbed the unplowed hills.
Oh blessed, gentle home on earth,
unaware of sin and tragedy! Oh, how much pain
does destiny imagine for your offspring,
unhappy father, what a vast array
of bitterness! See, new madness stains
the parched fields with the blood
of a brother's murder, and the holy air [*Cain, murderer of Abel*]
knows the abominable wings of death.
Wandering in fear, the fratricide,
fleeing lonely shadows and the hidden winds
that rage deep in the forest,

Primo i civili tetti, albergo e regno
Alle macere cure, innalza; e primo
Il disperato pentimento i ciechi
Mortali egro, anelante, aduna e stringe
Ne' consorti ricetti: onde negata
L'improba mano al curvo aratro, e vili
Fur gli agresti sudori; ozio le soglie
Scellerate occupò, ne' corpi inerti
Domo il vigor natio, languide, ignave
Giacquer le menti; e servitù le imbelli
Umane vite, ultimo danno, accolse.

E tu dall'etra infesto e dal mugghiante
Su i nubiferi gioghi equoreo flutto
Scampi l'iniquo germe, o tu cui prima
Dall'aer cieco e da' natanti poggi
Segno arrecò d'instaurata spene
La candida colomba, e delle antiche
Nubi l'occiduo Sol naufrago uscendo,
L'atro polo di vaga iri dipinse.
Riede alla terra, e il crudo affetto e gli empi
Studi rinnova e le seguaci ambasce
La riparata gente. Agl'inaccessi
Regni del mar vendicatore illude
Profana destra, e la sciagura e il pianto
A novi liti e nove stelle insegna.

Or te, padre de' pii, te giusto e forte,
E di tuo seme i generosi alunni
Medita il petto mio. Dirò siccome

builds the first houses in the city, home and realm
of gnawing worry; and for the first time
desperate repentance, gasping, miserable,
gathers and pens blind mortals up
in hiding together:
so evil hands shunned the curved plow
and farmwork was seen as inferior;
laziness invaded corrupt families; minds decayed,
sluggish in torpid bodies, their native strength
gone slack; and slavery, the worst of evils,
became the rule for cowardly human life.

But you protect your wicked offspring [*Noah*]
from the angry sky and roaring ocean flood
that drowned the cloud-supporting peaks, you to whom
the white dove brought a first sign of new hope
out of the blind air and the swimming hills,
and the sunken setting Sun,
emerging from the old clouds,
paints the black sky bright with rainbows.
The rescued race returns to earth,
their sad desires and impious ways,
and their attendant misery.
A profane hand menaces unconquered lands
beyond the jealous sea and teaches
crimes and tears to new shores and new stars.

My heart is meditating on you now,
father of the faithful, just and strong, [*Abraham*]
and on your brave descendants. I shall tell

Sedente, oscuro, in sul meriggio all'ombre
Del riposato albergo, appo le molli
Rive del gregge tuo nutrici e sedi,
Te de' celesti peregrini occulte
Beàr l'eteree menti; e quale, o figlio
Della saggia Rebecca, in su la sera,
Presso al rustico pozzo e nella dolce
Di pastori e di lieti ozi frequente
Aranitica valle, amor ti punse
Della vezzosa Labanide: invitto
Amor, ch'a lunghi esigli e lunghi affanni
E di servaggio all'odiata soma
Volenteroso il prode animo addisse.

Fu certo, fu (nè d'error vano e d'ombra
L'aonio canto e della fama il grido
Pasce l'avida plebe) amica un tempo
Al sangue nostro e dilettosa e cara
Questa misera piaggia, ed aurea corse
Nostra caduca età. Non che di latte
Onda rigasse intemerata il fianco
Delle balze materne, o con le greggi
Mista la tigre ai consueti ovili
Nè guidasse per gioco i lupi al fonte
Il pastorel; ma di suo fato ignara
E degli affanni suoi, vota d'affanno
Visse l'umana stirpe; alle secrete
Leggi del cielo e di natura indutto
Valse l'ameno error, le fraudi, il molle
Pristino velo; e di sperar contenta
Nostra placida nave in porto ascese.

how, as you sat alone at sunset in the shade
of your peaceful house, along the gentle banks
that fed and rested your flock,
heaven's holy pilgrims dressed as men
blessed you; also how,
O son of wise Rebecca, in the evening, [*Jacob, son of Isaac*]
beside the well in the sweet Haran valley,
home to shepherds and delightful ease,
love for Laban's fetching daughter pierced you: [*Rachel*]
unvanquished love, which bound your noble soul
to exile and long labor
and voluntary servitude
under the hated yoke.

Surely once this miserable place
was friendly to our race (heroic song and story
can't satisfy a hungry people
with empty falsehood and obscurity);
this place was loved and lovely,
and our short life was golden.
Not that an unsullied stream of milk
carved the flanks of the maternal hills
it flowed from, or that the shepherd led
the tiger with his flock to their usual fold,
or had wolves cavorting in the fountain;
but the human race lived ignorant
of its fate and troubles then,
free of sadness; sweet illusions,
fantasies, the gentle, pristine veil possessed the power
to cloak the hidden laws of heaven and nature;
and happy in hope our calm ship came to port.

Tal fra le vaste californie selve
Nasce beata prole, a cui non sugge
Pallida cura il petto, a cui le membra
Fera tabe non doma; e vitto il bosco,
Nidi l'intima rupe, onde ministra
L'irrigua valle, inopinato il giorno
Dell'atra morte incombe. Oh contra il nostro
Scellerato ardimento inermi regni
Della saggia natura! I lidi e gli antri
E le quiete selve apre l'invitto
Nostro furor; le violate genti
Al peregrino affanno, agl'ignorati
Desiri educa; e la fugace, ignuda
Felicità per l'imo sole incalza.

So in the boundless California forests
a blessed race is born, whose breast
is never nursed by pallid care, whose body
implacable disease does not destroy;
and with the woods for food, the hidden crags for nests,
and the irrigated valley giving water,
the day of dark death hangs over them unseen.
Oh kingdoms of wise nature, undefended
from our evil greed! Our boundless rage
storms her shores and caves and peaceful forests,
drives her assaulted natives to strange labor
and desires they never knew,
and hunts down fleeting, fragile happiness
till the sun sets.

IX

ULTIMO CANTO DI SAFFO

Placida notte, e verecondo raggio
Della cadente luna; e tu che spunti
Fra la tacita selva in su la rupe,
Nunzio del giorno; oh dilettose e care
Mentre ignote mi fur l'erinni e il fato,
Sembianze agli occhi miei; già non arride
Spettacol molle ai disperati affetti.
Noi l'insueto allor gaudio ravviva
Quando per l'etra liquido si volve
E per li campi trepidanti il flutto
Polveroso de' Noti, e quando il carro,
Grave carro di Giove a noi sul capo,
Tonando, il tenebroso aere divide.
Noi per le balze e le profonde valli
Natar giova tra' nembi, e noi la vasta
Fuga de' greggi sbigottiti, o d'alto
Fiume alla dubbia sponda
Il suono e la vittrice ira dell'onda.

Bello il tuo manto, o divo cielo, e bella
Sei tu, rorida terra. Ahi di cotesta
Infinita beltà parte nessuna

IX

SAPPHO'S LAST SONG

Tranquil night, and bashful light
of the fading moon, and you, emerging
from the quiet woods above the cliff,
herald of day; oh you were joyous, much-loved
sights when I was ignorant of torment
and of fate, but now no gentle scene
comforts my hopelessness.
Unfamiliar joy excites us
when the dust-filled tide of winds
swirls in the bright sky and across
the waving fields, and overhead
Jove's chariot, Jove's heavy chariot,
rumbles, shattering the darkened air.
We love it swimming in the clouds,
along the high cliffs and deep in the valleys,
we love the scattering of the nervous flocks,
and the roaring anger of the rising
river water from the threatened bank.

Your cloak is lovely, divine heaven,
and you are lovely also, dewy earth.
Alas, the gods and pitiless fate

Alla misera Saffo i numi e l'empia
Sorte non fenno. A' tuoi superbi regni
Vile, o natura, e grave ospite addetta,
E dispregiata amante, alle vezzose
Tue forme il core e le pupille invano
Supplichevole intendo. A me non ride
L'aprico margo, e dall'eterea porta
Il mattutino albor; me non il canto
De' colorati augelli, e non de' faggi
Il murmure saluta: e dove all'ombra
Degl'inchinati salici dispiega
Candido rivo il puro seno, al mio
Lubrico piè le flessuose linfe
Disdegnando sottragge,
E preme in fuga l'odorate spiagge.

Qual fallo mai, qual sì nefando eccesso
Macchiommi anzi il natale, onde sì torvo
Il ciel mi fosse e di fortuna il volto?
In che peccai bambina, allor che ignara
Di misfatto è la vita, onde poi scemo
Di giovanezza, e disfiorato, al fuso
Dell'indomita Parca si volvesse
Il ferrigno mio stame? Incaute voci
Spande il tuo labbro: i destinati eventi
Move arcano consiglio. Arcano è tutto,
Fuor che il nostro dolor. Negletta prole
Nascemmo al pianto, e la ragione in grembo
De' celesti si posa. Oh cure, oh speme
De' più verd'anni! Alle sembianze il Padre,

saved none of this endless beauty for poor Sappho.
In your proud kingdoms I am worthless, Nature,
an uninvited guest, an unloved lover.
My heart and eyes address your gracious form
in hopeless supplication. The sunlit shore
or the bright dawn out of heaven's gate
doesn't smile on me. No brilliant birdsong
or beeches' murmur
greets me:
and where a bright brook
shows its pure white curve
in the shadow of the bending willows,
its lilting water
shrinks from my unsteady foot,
running ahead to lap the fragrant bank.

What failing was it, what heinous excess
marked me before my birth, so heaven
and the face of fortune were so stern with me?
How did I sin as a child, when we can't know
what evil is, so later, my youth gone
and out of flower, my iron-colored thread
got wound on the spindle of unyielding Fate?
Your lips spill foolish words: mysterious wisdom
determines destined things.
All is mystery except our pain.
Neglected children, we were born to weep,
and the reason lies in the lap of the gods.
Oh cares, oh hope of our greenest years.
The Father granted

Alle amene sembianze eterno regno
Diè nelle genti; e per virili imprese,
Per dotta lira o canto,
Virtù non luce in disadorno ammanto.

Morremo. Il velo indegno a terra sparto,
Rifuggirà l'ignudo animo a Dite,
E il crudo fallo emenderà del cieco
Dispensator de' casi. E tu cui lungo
Amore indarno, e lunga fede, e vano
D'implacato desio furor mi strinse,
Vivi felice, se felice in terra
Visse nato mortal. Me non asperse
Del soave licor del doglio avaro
Giove, poi che perìr gl'inganni e il sogno
Della mia fanciullezza. Ogni più lieto
Giorno di nostra età primo s'invola.
Sottentra il morbo, e la vecchiezza, e l'ombra
Della gelida morte. Ecco di tante
Sperate palme e dilettosi errori,
Il Tartaro m'avanza; e il prode ingegno
Han la tenaria Diva,
E l'atra notte, e la silente riva.

eternal power over men to appearances
to beauty; and, for doing manly deeds,
for learned poetry or song,
genius won't shine in an unlovely form.

We're going to die. Once the unworthy veil
falls to the ground, the naked soul will fly
to Dis again, and right the cruel wrong
of the blind dispenser of fates. And you,
for whom long hopeless love, and faithfulness,
and hopeless, raging, unfulfilled desire
held me hostage, be happy on earth,
if any who are born to die live happy.
Zeus anointed me with none of that sweet liquor
from his miser's jar, once the illusions
and the dream of childhood died. The happiest day
of life is first to fly. Then sickness follows,
and old age, and the shadow
of cold death. So, after endless
hoped-for honors and enjoyed illusions,
only Tartarus remains,
and the Tenarian goddess and black night
and the still shore own the valiant mind.

X

IL PRIMO AMORE

Tornami a mente il dì che la battaglia
D'amor sentii la prima volta, e dissi:
Oimè, se quest'è amor, com'ei travaglia!

Che gli occhi al suol tuttora intenti e fissi
Io mirava colei ch'a questo core
Primiera il varco ed innocente aprissi.

Ahi come mal mi governasti, amore!
Perchè seco dovea sì dolce affetto
Recar tanto desio, tanto dolore?

E non sereno, e non intero e schietto,
Anzi pien di travaglio e di lamento
Al cor mi discendea tanto diletto?

Dimmi, tenero core, or che spavento,
Che angoscia era la tua fra quel pensiero
Presso al qual t'era noia ogni contento?

Quel pensier che nel dì, che lusinghiero
Ti si offeriva nella notte, quando
Tutto queto parea nell'emisfero:

X

FIRST LOVE

That day comes back to mind when I first knew
the strife of love, and said: Ah me,
if this is love, it is such misery!

When, with eyes still staring at the ground,
I saw the one who, in all innocence,
first opened up a way into this heart.

Oh how badly did you treat me, love!
Why did such sweet feeling have to bring
so much desire and pain along with it?

And why not tranquil, why not whole and pure,
but full of suffering and lament instead,
did so much joy descend into my heart?

Tell me now, tender heart, about the fear,
the anguish you felt, consumed by this idea
compared to which all happiness was pain?

This idea that enticingly
revealed itself to you both day and night,
when all seemed quiet in the hemisphere:

Tu inquieto, e felice e miserando,
M'affaticavi in su le piume il fianco,
Ad ogni or fortemente palpitando.

E dove io tristo ed affannato e stanco
Gli occhi al sonno chiudea, come per febre
Rotto e deliro il sonno venia manco.

Oh come viva in mezzo alle tenebre
Sorgea la dolce imago, e gli occhi chiusi
La contemplavan sotto alle palpebre!

Oh come soavissimi diffusi
Moti per l'ossa mi serpeano, oh come
Mille nell'alma instabili, confusi

Pensieri si volgean! qual tra le chiome
D'antica selva zefiro scorrendo,
Un lungo, incerto mormorar ne prome.

E mentre io taccio, e mentre io non contendo,
Che dicevi, o mio cor, che si partia
Quella per che penando ivi e battendo?

Il cuocer non più tosto io mi sentia
Della vampa d'amor, che il venticello
Che l'aleggiava, volossene via.

Senza sonno io giacea sul dì novello,
E i destrier che dovean farmi deserto,
Battean la zampa sotto al patrio ostello.

you exhausted me, so full of anguish,
lying glad and suffering in bed,
heart beating wildly hour after hour.

And when sad, tormented, and exhausted,
I closed my eyes to sleep, as in a fever,
sleep, broken and delirious, wouldn't come.

Oh how the sweet image rose alive
amidst the shadows, and how my closed eyes
contemplated it beneath their lids!

Oh how those soft, elusive movements
snaked around my bones, oh how
a thousand confused, uncertain thoughts

roiled in my soul! The way a wind
riffling in the hair of an old wood
excites a long, uncertain murmuring.

And though I was silent and uncomplaining,
what did I say, my heart, when she for whom
you were suffering and beating left?

No sooner did I feel the burning heat
of the flame of love than the little breeze
that could relieve it up and flew away.

I lay sleepless till the new day dawned,
and the horses that soon would leave me lonely
pawed the ground outside my father's house.

Ed io timido e cheto ed inesperto,
Ver lo balcone al buio protendea
L'orecchio avido e l'occhio indarno aperto,

La voce ad ascoltar, se ne dovea
Di quelle labbra uscir, ch'ultima fosse;
La voce, ch'altro il cielo, ahi, mi togliea.

Quante volte plebea voce percosse
Il dubitoso orecchio, e un gel mi prese,
E il core in forse a palpitar si mosse!

E poi che finalmente mi discese
La cara voce al core, e de' cavai
E delle rote il romorio s'intese;

Orbo rimaso allor, mi rannicchiai
Palpitando nel letto e, chiusi gli occhi,
Strinsi il cor con la mano, e sospirai.

Poscia traendo i tremuli ginocchi
Stupidamente per la muta stanza,
Ch'altro sarà, dicea, che il cor mi tocchi?

Amarissima allor la ricordanza
Locommisi nel petto, e mi serrava
Ad ogni voce il core, a ogni sembianza.

E lunga doglia il sen mi ricercava,
Com'è quando a distesa Olimpo piove
Malinconicamente e i campi lava.

And I, afraid and still and maladroit,
leaned out my window in the dark
watching in vain, cocking my eager ear

to hear her voice, if it would only issue
from those lips one final time; her voice,
for heaven, alas, was taking the rest of her.

How many times a peasant's sounds assailed
my uncertain ear, a chill took hold of me,
and my doubting heart began to throb!

But finally, when the beloved voice
entered my heart and the commotion
of the horses and carriage wheels was heard,

I was orphaned then, and hid myself
trembling in my bed, and shut my eyes.
I held my hand to my heart, and sighed.

Then, stupefied, knees shaking, dragged
myself across the silent room, and asked,
What else will ever touch my heart again?

Then the very bitter memory
settled in my breast, and locked my heart
against every other voice and face.

And long suffering entered in my breast,
as when Olympus rains down desolation
everywhere around and floods the fields.

Ned io ti conoscea, garzon di nove
E nove Soli, in questo a pianger nato
Quando facevi, amor, le prime prove.

Quando in ispregio ogni piacer, nè grato
M'era degli astri il riso, o dell'aurora
Queta il silenzio, o il verdeggiar del prato.

Anche di gloria amor taceami allora
Nel petto, cui scaldar tanto solea,
Che di beltade amor vi fea dimora.

Nè gli occhi ai noti studi io rivolgea,
E quelli m'apparian vani per cui
Vano ogni altro desir creduto avea.

Deh come mai da me sì vario fui,
E tanto amor mi tolse un altro amore?
Deh quanto, in verità, vani siam nui!

Solo il mio cor piaceami, e col mio core
In un perenne ragionar sepolto,
Alla guardia seder del mio dolore.

E l'occhio a terra chino o in se raccolto,
Di riscontrarsi fuggitivo e vago
Nè in leggiadro soffria nè in turpe volto:

Che la illibata, la candida imago
Turbare egli temea pinta nel seno,
Come all'aure si turba onda di lago.

Nor did I, a boy of eighteen, know you
when you made your first experiments,
Love, on him who was born to lament.

When I disdained all pleasures, and the stars'
smile was inimical, or the stillness
of the calm dawn, or the meadow's greening.

Even the love of glory, which before
had moved me so, was silenced in my breast then,
for love had made it beauty's dwelling place.

Nor did I turn back to my normal work;
for it seemed empty now, though it had made me
think all other desires were empty once.

Ah, how was I so alien to myself,
And how did so much love replace another?
Ah, in truth, how changeable we are!

Only my heart pleased me; and being entombed
in constant conversation with it,
so as to safeguard my unhappiness.

And my eyes, downcast or focused inward,
fleeting and vague, would not allow themselves
to meet a lovable or evil face:

for they feared the blameless, candid image
painted in my heart would be disturbed
the way a lake is troubled by the wind.

E quel di non aver goduto appieno
Pentimento, che l'anima ci grava,
E il piacer che passò cangia in veleno,

Per li fuggiti dì mi stimolava
Tuttora il sen: che la vergogna il duro
Suo morso in questo cor già non oprava.

Al cielo, a voi, gentili anime, io giuro
Che voglia non m'entrò bassa nel petto,
Ch'arsi di foco intaminato e puro.

Vive quel foco ancor, vive l'affetto,
Spira nel pensier mio la bella imago,
Da cui, se non celeste, altro diletto

Giammai non ebbi, e sol di lei m'appago.

And that regret at not having fully
enjoyed a thing, which weighs our spirits down
and turns the pleasure that is past to poison,

regret for bygone days still pierced
my breast: for as of yet this heart
had not experienced the pain of shame.

Noble souls, to heaven and you I swear
that no base desire entered my heart:
I burned with pure, untainted fire.

That fire is still alive, my love lives on,
the lovely image breathes inside my mind
from which I never had another joy

than the divine, and only it fulfills me.

XI

IL PASSERO SOLITARIO

D'in su la vetta della torre antica,
Passero solitario, alla campagna
Cantando vai finchè non more il giorno;
Ed erra l'armonia per questa valle.
Primavera dintorno
Brilla nell'aria, e per li campi esulta,
Sì ch'a mirarla intenerisce il core.
Odi greggi belar, muggire armenti;
Gli altri augelli contenti, a gara insieme
Per lo libero ciel fan mille giri,
Pur festeggiando il lor tempo migliore:
Tu pensoso in disparte il tutto miri;
Non compagni, non voli,
Non ti cal d'allegria, schivi gli spassi;
Canti, e così trapassi
Dell'anno e di tua vita il più bel fiore.

Oimè, quanto somiglia
Al tuo costume il mio! Sollazzo e riso,
Della novella età dolce famiglia,
E te german di giovinezza, amore,
Sospiro acerbo de' provetti giorni,

XI

THE SOLITARY THRUSH

High on the rooftop of the ancient tower,
solitary thrush, you keep on singing
to the countryside till the day dies,
and your music wanders in the valley.
All around, spring glistens in the air
and glories in the fields,
till the heart turns tender at the sight.
You can hear flocks bleating and herds lowing;
the other birds compete in happiness,
taking a thousand turns in the wide sky,
exulting in their best of times.
Pensive and apart, you watch it all.
No comrades and no flights,
no happiness for you. You shun their games;
you sing, and so you spend
the high time of the year and of your life.

Alas, how much your ways resemble mine!
Delight and laughter,
sweet companions of our early years,
and you, youth's sibling, love,
bitter regret of later on,

Non curo, io non so come; anzi da loro
Quasi fuggo lontano;
Quasi romito, e strano
Al mio loco natio,
Passo del viver mio la primavera.
Questo giorno ch'omai cede alla sera,
Festeggiar si costuma al nostro borgo.
Odi per lo sereno un suon di squilla,
Odi spesso un tonar di ferree canne,
Che rimbomba lontan di villa in villa.
Tutta vestita a festa
La gioventù del loco
Lascia le case, e per le vie si spande;
E mira ed è mirata, e in cor s'allegra.
Io solitario in questa
Rimota parte alla campagna uscendo,
Ogni diletto e gioco
Indugio in altro tempo: e intanto il guardo
Steso nell'aria aprica
Mi fere il Sol che tra lontani monti,
Dopo il giorno sereno,
Cadendo si dilegua, e par che dica
Che la beata gioventù vien meno.

Tu, solingo augellin, venuto a sera
Del viver che daranno a te le stelle,
Certo del tuo costume
Non ti dorrai; che di natura è frutto
Ogni vostra vaghezza.
A me, se di vecchiezza

I take no notice of, I can't say why.
In fact, I seem to run away from them.
Hermitlike,
a stranger in my native place,
I'm living out the springtime of my life.
This day, which is now becoming evening,
is a feast day in our town.
You hear the sound of bells in the bright sky
and often rifle-fire reports far off
from farm to farm.
Dressed up to celebrate,
the young people of the place
leave their homes and gather in the streets,
and, seeing and being seen, are glad.
Only I, who make for this
remote spot in the countryside,
put off every pleasure and enjoyment
to another time. And as I stare
into the cloudless air
the sun's rays strike me,
fading as it sets in the far hills
after the clear day, as if to say
that blessed youth is failing, too.

Lonely bird, when you come to the evening
of the life the stars will set for you,
surely you won't regret the way you lived,
for every wish of yours
is nature's doing.
But I, if I cannot avoid

La detestata soglia
Evitar non impetro,
Quando muti questi occhi all'altrui core,
E lor fia vóto il mondo, e il dì futuro
Del dì presente più noioso e tetro,
Che parrà di tal voglia?
Che di quest'anni miei? che di me stesso?
Ahi pentirommi, e spesso,
Ma sconsolato, volgerommi indietro.

crossing the hateful
threshold of old age,
when these eyes say nothing to another's heart,
and the world is blank to them, and the day to come
duller and darker than the one at hand,
what will I think then of this wish of mine?
And of my life? And my own self?
Ah, I'll repent, and often
look back, unconsoled.

XII

L'INFINITO

Sempre caro mi fu quest'ermo colle,
E questa siepe, che da tanta parte
Dell'ultimo orizzonte il guardo esclude.
Ma sedendo e mirando, interminati
Spazi di là da quella, e sovrumani
Silenzi, e profondissima quiete
Io nel pensier mi fingo; ove per poco
Il cor non si spaura. E come il vento
Odo stormir tra queste piante, io quello
Infinito silenzio a questa voce
Vo comparando: e mi sovvien l'eterno,
E le morte stagioni, e la presente
E viva, e il suon di lei. Così tra questa
Immensità s'annega il pensier mio:
E il naufragar m'è dolce in questo mare.

XII

INFINITY

This lonely hill was always dear to me,
and this hedgerow, which cuts off the view
of so much of the last horizon.
But sitting here and gazing, I can see
beyond, in my mind's eye, unending spaces,
and superhuman silences, and depthless calm,
till what I feel
is almost fear. And when I hear
the wind stir in these branches, I begin
comparing that endless stillness with this noise:
and the eternal comes to mind,
and the dead seasons, and the present
living one, and how it sounds.
So my mind sinks in this immensity:
and foundering is sweet in such a sea.

XIII

LA SERA DEL DÌ DI FESTA

Dolce e chiara è la notte e senza vento,
E queta sovra i tetti e in mezzo agli orti
Posa la luna, e di lontan rivela
Serena ogni montagna. O donna mia,
Già tace ogni sentiero, e pei balconi
Rara traluce la notturna lampa:
Tu dormi, che t'accolse agevol sonno
Nelle tue chete stanze; e non ti morde
Cura nessuna; e già non sai nè pensi
Quanta piaga m'apristi in mezzo al petto.
Tu dormi: io questo ciel, che sì benigno
Appare in vista, a salutar m'affaccio,
E l'antica natura onnipossente,
Che mi fece all'affanno. A te la speme
Nego, mi disse, anche la speme; e d'altro
Non brillin gli occhi tuoi se non di pianto.
Questo dì fu solenne: or da' trastulli
Prendi riposo; e forse ti rimembra
In sogno a quanti oggi piacesti, e quanti
Piacquero a te: non io, non già ch'io speri,
Al pensier ti ricorro. Intanto io chieggo
Quanto a viver mi resti, e qui per terra

XIII

THE EVENING OF THE HOLIDAY

The night is soft and bright and without wind,
and the moon hangs still above the roofs
and kitchen gardens, showing every mountain
clear in the distance. O my lady,
every lane is quiet now, and night lights
glow in the windows only here and there.
You sleep, for sleep came easily to you
in your still room. No worry troubles you,
nor can you imagine
what a wound you opened in my heart.
Yes, you sleep, while I come to my window
to salute this sky that seems so kind,
and eternal, all-commanding nature
who created me for suffering.
I deny you hope, she told me, even hope;
let your eyes never shine except with tears.
This was a holiday. Tonight you rest
from play, and maybe in your sleep
you dream of all the men you charmed today,
and those who charmed you, too; but I don't come to mind,
not that I hoped to. So I ask myself
what's left in life for me,

Mi getto, e grido, e fremo. Oh giorni orrendi
In così verde etate! Ahi, per la via
Odo non lunge il solitario canto
Dell'artigian, che riede a tarda notte,
Dopo i sollazzi, al suo povero ostello;
E fieramente mi si stringe il core,
A pensar come tutto al mondo passa,
E quasi orma non lascia. Ecco è fuggito
Il dì festivo, ed al festivo il giorno
Volgar succede, e se ne porta il tempo
Ogni umano accidente. Or dov'è il suono
Di que' popoli antichi? or dov'è il grido
De' nostri avi famosi, e il grande impero
Di quella Roma, e l'armi, e il fragorio
Che n'andò per la terra e l'oceano?
Tutto è pace e silenzio, e tutto posa
Il mondo, e più di lor non si ragiona.
Nella mia prima età, quando s'aspetta
Bramosamente il dì festivo, or poscia
Ch'egli era spento, io doloroso, in veglia,
Premea le piume; ed alla tarda notte
Un canto che s'udia per li sentieri
Lontanando morire a poco a poco,
Già similmente mi stringeva il core.

and fall down on the ground and rage, and shake.
Horrific days at such a tender age!
On the road not far from me I hear
the lonely song of the workman, coming late
from his evening out to his poor home,
and my heart is stricken
to think how everything in this world passes
and barely leaves a trace. Look,
the holiday is gone, the workday follows,
and time makes off with every human thing.
Where is the clamor of those ancient peoples?
Where is the renown
of our famed ancestors, and the great empire
of their Rome, her armies,
and the din she made on land and sea?
Everything is peace and quiet now,
the world is calm, and speaks no more of them.
In my young years, in the time of life
when we wait impatiently for Sunday,
afterward I'd lie awake unhappy,
and late at night a song heard on the road
dying note by note as it passed by
would pierce my heart
the same way even then.

XIV

ALLA LUNA

O graziosa luna, io mi rammento
Che, or volge l'anno, sovra questo colle
Io venia pien d'angoscia a rimirarti:
E tu pendevi allor su quella selva
Siccome or fai, che tutta la rischiari.
Ma nebuloso e tremulo dal pianto
Che mi sorgea sul ciglio, alle mie luci
Il tuo volto apparia, che travagliosa
Era mia vita: ed è, nè cangia stile,
O mia diletta luna. E pur mi giova
La ricordanza, e il noverar l'etate
Del mio dolore. Oh come grato occorre
Nel tempo giovanil, quando ancor lungo
La speme e breve ha la memoria il corso,
Il rimembrar delle passate cose,
Ancor che triste, e che l'affanno duri!

XIV

TO THE MOON

O graceful moon, I can remember, now
the year has turned, how, filled with anguish,
I came here to this hill to gaze at you,
and you were hanging then above those woods
the way you do now, lighting everything.
But your face was cloudy,
swimming in my eyes, due to the tears
that filled them, for my life
was torment, and it is, it doesn't change,
beloved moon of mine.
And yet it helps me, thinking back, reliving
the time of my unhappiness.
Oh in youth, when hope has a long road ahead
and the way of memory is short,
how sweet it is remembering what happened,
though it was sad, and though the pain endures!

XV

IL SOGNO

Era il mattino, e tra le chiuse imposte
Per lo balcone insinuava il sole
Nella mia cieca stanza il primo albore;
Quando in sul tempo che più leve il sonno
E più soave le pupille adombra,
Stettemi allato e riguardommi in viso
Il simulacro di colei che amore
Prima insegnommi, e poi lasciommi in pianto.
Morta non mi parea, ma trista, e quale
Degl'infelici è la sembianza. Al capo
Appressommi la destra, e sospirando,
Vivi, mi disse, e ricordanza alcuna
Serbi di noi? Donde, risposi, e come
Vieni, o cara beltà? Quanto, deh quanto
Di te mi dolse e duol: nè mi credea
Che risaper tu lo dovessi; e questo
Facea più sconsolato il dolor mio.
Ma sei tu per lasciarmi un'altra volta?
Io n'ho gran tema. Or dimmi, e che t'avvenne?
Sei tu quella di prima? E che ti strugge
Internamente? Obblivione ingombra
I tuoi pensieri, e gli avviluppa il sonno,

XV

THE DREAM

It was morning, and the sun's first light
was filtering into my dark room
through the closed shutters;
at the time when sleep
most lightly, gently veils the eyes,
the image of the woman who first showed me love,
then left me in tears, stood next to me,
staring into my eyes. She wasn't dead, it seemed,
but downcast, the way unhappy people are.
She laid her right hand on my head and sighed,
and said, Are you alive? Do you remember anything
about us? I answered, Where have you come from,
and how, O lovely thing? Oh, how I've grieved
and grieve for you. But I never thought
you'd know it, and this made my grief
all the more inconsolable. Are you leaving
me again? I'm so afraid you will.
Tell me, what became of you?
Are you who you once were?
And what's devouring you inside?
Forgetfulness disturbs your way of thinking,
and sleep has overwhelmed it,

Disse colei. Son morta, e mi vedesti
L'ultima volta, or son più lune. Immensa
Doglia m'oppresse a queste voci il petto.
Ella seguì: nel fior degli anni estinta,
Quand'è il viver più dolce, e pria che il core
Certo si renda com'è tutta indarno
L'umana speme. A desiar colei
Che d'ogni affanno il tragge, ha poco andare
L'egro mortal; ma sconsolata arriva
La morte ai giovanetti, e duro è il fato
Di quella speme che sotterra è spenta.
Vano è saper quel che natura asconde
Agl'inesperti della vita, e molto
All'immatura sapienza il cieco
Dolor prevale. Oh sfortunata, oh cara,
Taci, taci, diss'io, che tu mi schianti
Con questi detti il cor. Dunque sei morta,
O mia diletta, ed io son vivo, ed era
Pur fisso in ciel che quei sudori estremi
Cotesta cara e tenerella salma
Provar dovesse, a me restasse intera
Questa misera spoglia? Oh quante volte
In ripensar che più non vivi, e mai
Non avverrà ch'io ti ritrovi al mondo,
Creder nol posso. Ahi ahi, che cosa è questa
Che morte s'addimanda? Oggi per prova
Intenderlo potessi, e il capo inerme
Agli atroci del fato odii sottrarre.
Giovane son, ma si consuma e perde
La giovanezza mia come vecchiezza;

she answered, I'm dead; you saw me
for the last time many months ago.
At her words huge grief weighed on my heart.
She continued: I died in my prime,
when life is sweetest, long before the heart
knows for sure all human hope is vain.
It's not long till the miserable mortal
wants what will cure him of all suffering;
but there's no consolation for a child's death,
and it's a cruel fate indeed
when our hope is buried underground.
Those without experience of life
can't know what nature hides from them,
and blind pain overpowers untried wisdom.
Enough, unhappy one, I said, be still.
You're breaking my heart
with these words. So you are dead,
my love, and I'm alive,
and was it already decreed in heaven
that your beloved, tender body
had to undergo that extreme suffering,
while my miserable flesh remained untouched?
Oh how often, remembering
you're not alive and I won't see you
in the world again, I can't believe it.
What is this thing called death? If only I
could know it now myself, and save
my unprotected head from savage fate.
I'm young, and yet my youth is being spent
and lost like old age,

La qual pavento, e pur m'è lunge assai.
Ma poco da vecchiezza si discorda
Il fior dell'età mia. Nascemmo al pianto,
Disse, ambedue; felicità non rise
Al viver nostro; e dilettossi il cielo
De' nostri affanni. Or se di pianto il ciglio,
Soggiunsi, e di pallor velato il viso
Per la tua dipartita, e se d'angoscia
Porto gravido il cor; dimmi: d'amore
Favilla alcuna, o di pietà, giammai
Verso il misero amante il cor t'assalse
Mentre vivesti? Io disperando allora
E sperando traea le notti e i giorni;
Oggi nel vano dubitar si stanca
La mente mia. Che se una volta sola
Dolor ti strinse di mia negra vita,
Non mel celar, ti prego, e mi soccorra
La rimembranza or che il futuro è tolto
Ai nostri giorni. E quella: ti conforta,
O sventurato. Io di pietade avara
Non ti fui mentre vissi, ed or non sono,
Che fui misera anch'io. Non far querela
Di questa infelicissima fanciulla.
Per le sventure nostre, e per l'amore
Che mi strugge, esclamai; per lo diletto
Nome di giovanezza e la perduta
Speme dei nostri dì, concedi, o cara,
Che la tua destra io tocchi. Ed ella, in atto
Soave e tristo, la porgeva. Or mentre
Di baci la ricopro, e d'affannosa

which I'm afraid of, though it's far away.
But sweet youth isn't very different
from age for me. The two of us
were born for suffering, she said.
There was nothing happy in our lives,
and heaven took pleasure in our pain.
Now since my eyes are blind with tears, I answered,
and since my face is pale because you're leaving
and my heart is heavy with anxiety:
tell me: Did the slightest spark
of love or pity for your miserable lover
ever strike your heart while you were living?
In both despair and hope then, I dragged out
the nights and days, and my heart is riven still
with pointless doubt. So if even once
you felt pity for my lightless life, I beg you
not to hide it from me, let the memory
help me, now the future has been stolen
from us. And she said: Take comfort,
my unhappy friend. I wasn't without pity
for you while I was alive, nor am I now;
I was unhappy, too. Don't grieve
for this child who was so miserable.
By our unhappiness, and by the love
that's tearing me apart, I cried,
in the beloved name of youth
and the lost hope of our days,
let me touch your hand, my dear. And gently,
sadly she extended it to me. Now, as I covered it
with kisses, and pressed it to my heaving heart,

Dolcezza palpitando all'anelante
Seno la stringo, di sudore il volto
Ferveva e il petto, nelle fauci stava
La voce, al guardo traballava il giorno.
Quando colei teneramente affissi
Gli occhi negli occhi miei, già scordi, o caro,
Disse, che di beltà son fatta ignuda?
E tu d'amore, o sfortunato, indarno
Ti scaldi e fremi. Or finalmente addio.
Nostre misere menti e nostre salme
Son disgiunte in eterno. A me non vivi
E mai più non vivrai: già ruppe il fato
La fe che mi giurasti. Allor d'angoscia
Gridar volendo, e spasimando, e pregne
Di sconsolato pianto le pupille,
Dal sonno mi disciolsi. Ella negli occhi
Pur mi restava, e nell'incerto raggio
Del Sol vederla io mi credeva ancora.

throbbing with pain and sweetness, my hot face
and chest were bathed in sweat, my voice
was in my throat, and the day swayed before me.
Then tenderly she looked me in the eye
and said, My dear, have you already forgotten
that I've been stripped of beauty and you're inflamed,
trembling with hopeless love,
unlucky man. Now finally, farewell.
Our unhappy minds and bodies
are separated for eternity. You're not alive for me,
nor will you ever come to life again.
Fate has already broken the vow you swore me.
Wanting to rage with anguish then,
and shaking, my eyes brimming
with unconsoled tears,
I roused myself from sleep. But she was there
in front of me, and in the sun's veiled light
I kept on believing I could see her.

XVI

LA VITA SOLITARIA

La mattutina pioggia, allor che l'ale
Battendo esulta nella chiusa stanza
La gallinella, ed al balcon s'affaccia
L'abitator de' campi, e il Sol che nasce
I suoi tremuli rai fra le cadenti
Stille saetta, alla capanna mia
Dolcemente picchiando, mi risveglia;
E sorgo, e i lievi nugoletti, e il primo
Degli augelli susurro, e l'aura fresca,
E le ridenti piagge benedico:
Poichè voi, cittadine infauste mura,
Vidi e conobbi assai, là dove segue
Odio al dolor compagno; e doloroso
Io vivo, e tal morrò, deh tosto! Alcuna
Benchè scarsa pietà pur mi dimostra
Natura in questi lochi, un giorno oh quanto
Verso me più cortese! E tu pur volgi
Dai miseri lo sguardo; e tu, sdegnando
Le sciagure e gli affanni, alla reina
Felicità servi, o natura. In cielo,
In terra amico agl'infelici alcuno
E rifugio non resta altro che il ferro.

XVI

THE SOLITARY LIFE

The morning rain—now that the hen
shut in her pen exults and beats her wings,
and the field hand gazes out his window,
and, coming alive, the Sun shoots glistening rays
among the falling droplets gently
beating on my roof—the morning rain
wakes me; and as I rise, I bless
the puffy little clouds,
the birds' first cooing,
and the cool air and the sunstruck hills:
for I have seen enough of you,
unhappy city walls, where hate
treads on the heel of his companion, pain;
where I live painfully and will die too,
let it be soon! Yet nature now and then
still shows a little kindness here,
though she was once far gentler.
For you too turn away from those in pain,
ignoring their troubles and calamities,
you too serve Queen Felicity, O Nature.
In heaven and on earth, the luckless have
no other friend and refuge but the sword.

Talor m'assido in solitaria parte,
Sovra un rialto, al margine d'un lago
Di taciturne piante incoronato.
Ivi, quando il meriggio in ciel si volve,
La sua tranquilla imago il Sol dipinge,
Ed erba o foglia non si crolla al vento,
E non onda incresparsi, e non cicala
Strider, nè batter penna augello in ramo,
Nè farfalla ronzar, nè voce o moto
Da presso nè da lunge odi nè vedi.
Tien quelle rive altissima quiete;
Ond'io quasi me stesso e il mondo obblio
Sedendo immoto; e già mi par che sciolte
Giaccian le membra mie, nè spirto o senso
Più le commova, e lor quiete antica
Co' silenzi del loco si confonda.

Amore, amore, assai lungi volasti
Dal petto mio, che fu sì caldo un giorno,
Anzi rovente. Con sua fredda mano
Lo strinse la sciaura, e in ghiaccio è volto
Nel fior degli anni. Mi sovvien del tempo
Che mi scendesti in seno. Era quel dolce
E irrevocabil tempo, allor che s'apre
Al guardo giovanil questa infelice
Scena del mondo, e gli sorride in vista
Di paradiso. Al garzoncello il core
Di vergine speranza e di desio
Balza nel petto; e già s'accinge all'opra
Di questa vita come a danza o gioco

Sometimes I sit alone, apart,
on a hillside, by a lake
ringed by silent reeds and bushes.
There, when high noon fills the sky,
the Sun paints his undisturbed reflection,
and no blade of grass or leaf
stirs in the wind, you neither see nor hear
wave break nor cicada shriek; no bird
moves a feather on a branch, no butterfly
flitters—there's no sound or movement, far or near.
Deepest quiet fills those shores,
and, sitting still, I seem to forget
myself and the world; my limbs relax,
no longer ruled by mind or spirit,
their immemorial calm
dissolving in the silence of the place.

Love, love, long ago you flew
out of my heart, which once had been so warm,
burning even. Sorrow held it
in her cold hand, and it turned to ice
in the prime of life. I can remember
when you came into my heart. It was that sweet
moment we can't bring back again when a young man
is first shown the world's unhappy scene,
which smiles on him and looks like paradise.
A heart of virgin hope and desire
leaps in his young breast,
and the miserable mortal girds himself
for the hard labor of this life

Il misero mortal. Ma non sì tosto,
Amor, di te m'accorsi, e il viver mio
Fortuna avea già rotto, ed a questi occhi
Non altro convenia che il pianger sempre.
Pur se talvolta per le piagge apriche,
Su la tacita aurora o quando al sole
Brillano i tetti e i poggi e le campagne,
Scontro di vaga donzelletta il viso;
O qualor nella placida quiete
D'estiva notte, il vagabondo passo
Di rincontro alle ville soffermando,
L'erma terra contemplo, e di fanciulla
Che all'opre di sua man la notte aggiunge
Odo sonar nelle romite stanze
L'arguto canto; a palpitar si move
Questo mio cor di sasso: ahi, ma ritorna
Tosto al ferreo sopor; ch'è fatto estrano
Ogni moto soave al petto mio.

O cara luna, al cui tranquillo raggio
Danzan le lepri nelle selve; e duolsi
Alla mattina il cacciator, che trova
L'orme intricate e false, e dai covili
Error vario lo svia; salve, o benigna
Delle notti reina. Infesto scende
Il raggio tuo fra macchie e balze o dentro
A deserti edifici, in su l'acciaro
Del pallido ladron ch'a teso orecchio
Il fragor delle rote e de' cavalli
Da lungi osserva o il calpestio de' piedi

as for a dance or game. But, love,
no sooner had I learned of you
than fate destroyed my life,
and all that my eyes knew were endless tears.
Still, if sometimes on an open hill,
in the silent dawn, or when the roofs
and hills and fields are gleaming in the sun,
I see a beautiful young woman's face,
or, in the languid calm of a summer night,
slowing in my wandering
as I come to houses once again,
I contemplate the lonely countryside,
or hear the soft song of a girl
continuing her handiwork
in her lonely room at night, this heart of stone
starts racing. But then soon enough
it falls back to its leaden sleep, for every tender
feeling has become alien to my heart.

Dear moon, underneath whose tranquil light
hares dance in the woods; and in the morning
the hunter curses their confusing,
scrambled tracks, their many trails
that hide their warrens from him: hail to you,
O benevolent queen of nights. Your light
falls unwelcome onto cliffs and thickets
or, in abandoned buildings, on the knife
of the pale thief who cocks his ear to hear
the sound of wheels and horses in the distance
or footsteps on the silent road; who suddenly,

Su la tacita via; poscia improvviso
Col suon dell'armi e con la rauca voce
E col funereo ceffo il core agghiaccia
Al passegger, cui semivivo e nudo
Lascia in breve tra' sassi. Infesto occorre
Per le contrade cittadine il bianco
Tuo lume al drudo vil, che degli alberghi
Va radendo le mura e la secreta
Ombra seguendo, e resta, e si spaura
Delle ardenti lucerne e degli aperti
Balconi. Infesto alle malvage menti,
A me sempre benigno il tuo cospetto
Sarà per queste piagge, ove non altro
Che lieti colli e spaziosi campi
M'apri alla vista. Ed ancor io soleva,
Bench'innocente io fossi, il tuo vezzoso
Raggio accusar negli abitati lochi,
Quand'ei m'offriva al guardo umano, e quando
Scopriva umani aspetti al guardo mio.
Or sempre loderollo, o ch'io ti miri
Veleggiar tra le nubi, o che serena
Dominatrice dell'etereo campo,
Questa flebil riguardi umana sede.
Me spesso rivedrai solingo e muto
Errar pe' boschi e per le verdi rive,
O seder sovra l'erbe, assai contento
Se core e lena a sospirar m'avanza.

with weapons drawn, rough words,
and murderous stare, will chill the heart
of the traveler, whom he soon abandons
half alive and naked on the rocks.
Your white light shines unwelcome, too,
on the vile adulterer in the city,
who hugs the walls of houses
and lurks in shadows, hanging back afraid
of lit lanterns and unshuttered windows.
The sight of you will always be unwelcome
to evil minds, but ever sweet to me
here on these slopes,
where all you let me see
are glad hills and open fields.
Yet, though I was innocent,
I used to resent your lovely light
in crowded places,
when I could be seen by other men,
and saw them, too.
Now I'll always praise it, when I watch you
sail among the clouds, or you look down,
serene mistress of the heavenly plains,
on this miserable human home.
Often you'll see me silent and alone
wandering in the woods, on the green banks,
or sitting on the grass, happy enough
that I have heart and breath to heave a sigh.

XVII

CONSALVO

Presso alla fin di sua dimora in terra,
Giacea Consalvo; disdegnoso un tempo
Del suo destino; or già non più, che a mezzo
Il quinto lustro, gli pendea sul capo
Il sospirato obblio. Qual da gran tempo,
Così giacea nel funeral suo giorno
Dai più diletti amici abbandonato:
Ch'amico in terra al lungo andar nessuno
Resta a colui che della terra è schivo.
Pur gli era al fianco, da pietà condotta
A consolare il suo deserto stato,
Quella che sola e sempre eragli a mente,
Per divina beltà famosa Elvira;
Conscia del suo poter, conscia che un guardo
Suo lieto, un detto d'alcun dolce asperso,
Ben mille volte ripetuto e mille
Nel costante pensier, sostegno e cibo
Esser solea dell'infelice amante:
Benchè nulla d'amor parola udita
Avess'ella da lui. Sempre in quell'alma
Era del gran desio stato più forte
Un sovrano timor. Così l'avea
Fatto schiavo e fanciullo il troppo amore.

XVII

CONSALVO

Consalvo was coming to the end
of his stay on earth. Once he'd disdained
his fate, but not now, for at twenty-two
the oblivion he'd sighed for was at hand.
He lay there on his dying day,
as he long had,
deserted by his most beloved friends:
for in the end he who disdains this earth
finds no one on earth is still his friend.
Yet by his side, come there out of pity
to console him in his solitude,
was the woman who was always on his mind,
Elvira, famous for her godly beauty,
conscious of her power, aware a happy
look of hers, or some sweet phrase
repeated over and over a thousand times
in his obsessive mind, had once been comfort
and sustenance for her unhappy lover—
although she'd never heard him say
a single word of love. A great timidity
had always had more power over his soul
than his great desire. And so excessive love
had made him into a slave and a child.

Ma ruppe alfin la morte il nodo antico
Alla sua lingua. Poichè certi i segni
Sentendo di quel dì che l'uom discioglie,
Lei, già mossa a partir, presa per mano,
E quella man bianchissima stringendo,
Disse: tu parti, e l'ora omai ti sforza:
Elvira, addio. Non ti vedrò, ch'io creda,
Un'altra volta. Or dunque addio. Ti rendo
Qual maggior grazia mai delle tue cure
Dar possa il labbro mio. Premio daratti
Chi può , se premio ai pii dal ciel si rende.
Impallidia la bella, e il petto anelo
Udendo le si fea: che sempre stringe
All'uomo il cor dogliosamente, ancora
Ch'estranio sia, chi si diparte e dice,
Addio per sempre. E contraddir voleva,
Dissimulando l'appressar del fato,
Al moribondo. Ma il suo dir prevenne
Quegli, e soggiunse: desiata, e molto,
Come sai, ripregata a me discende,
Non temuta, la morte; e lieto apparmi
Questo feral mio dì. Pesami, è vero,
Che te perdo per sempre. Oimè per sempre
Parto da te. Mi si divide il core
In questo dir. Più non vedrò quegli occhi,
Nè la tua voce udrò! Dimmi: ma pria
Di lasciarmi in eterno, Elvira, un bacio
Non vorrai tu donarmi? un bacio solo
In tutto il viver mio? Grazia ch'ei chiegga
Non si nega a chi muor. Nè già vantarmi

But in the end, death loosened the age-old
knot in his tongue. For, seeing clear indications
of the day that sets man free, he took
her snow-white hand as she was rising to go,
and held it, saying: Now you're leaving,
it's late and time to go. Farewell, Elvira.
I don't think I'll ever see you again.
Farewell. I want to offer you the greatest
thanks I can express for your concern.
He who can, will reward you, if heaven
rewards the faithful. The lovely woman
went pale hearing him, and her breast
started heaving: for the heart is always
struck with sadness when someone,
even a stranger, says as he is leaving,
Goodbye forever. She wanted
to contradict him and conceal his coming end
from the dying man. But he cut her off,
saying: The death that comes to me is wished for,
and, you know, much prayed for and not feared;
and my dying day seems happy to me.
True, it weighs on me I'm losing you
forever. Yes, alas, I'm leaving you forever.
My heart breaks saying this. I'll never see
these eyes, or hear your voice again. But first,
before you leave me for eternity,
Elvira, don't you want to give me a kiss?
One kiss in an entire life? You can't deny
a dying man's last favor.
Nor can I boast about your gift,

Potrò del dono, io semispento, a cui
Straniera man le labbra oggi fra poco
Eternamente chiuderà. Ciò detto
Con un sospiro, all'adorata destra
Le fredde labbra supplicando affisse.

Stette sospesa e pensierosa in atto
La bellissima donna; e fiso il guardo,
Di mille vezzi sfavillante, in quello
Tenea dell'infelice, ove l'estrema
Lacrima rilucea. Nè dielle il core
Di sprezzar la dimanda, e il mesto addio
Rinacerbir col niego; anzi la vinse
Misericordia dei ben noti ardori.
E quel volto celeste, e quella bocca,
Già tanto desiata, e per molt'anni
Argomento di sogno e di sospiro,
Dolcemente appressando al volto afflitto
E scolorato dal mortale affanno,
Più baci e più, tutta benigna e in vista
D'alta pietà, su le convulse labbra
Del trepido, rapito amante impresse.

Che divenisti allor? quali appariro
Vita, morte, sventura agli occhi tuoi,
Fuggitivo Consalvo? Egli la mano,
Ch'ancor tenea, della diletta Elvira
Postasi al cor, che gli ultimi battea
Palpiti della morte e dell'amore,
Oh, disse, Elvira, Elvira mia! ben sono

since I'm half gone already, and a strange hand
will close my lips forever before long.
This said, he sighed
and kissed her adored right hand
in supplication with his frigid lips.

The lovely one sat hesitant
and lost in thought; and her eyes,
shining with a thousand beauties,
met the dying man's,
in which a last tear glistened.
She didn't have the heart to tell him no
and embitter their sad parting with refusal;
rather, pity for his patent ardor
won her over.
And gently bringing that celestial face,
that mouth so long desired,
the stuff of dreams and sighs for years,
to his afflicted face, pale with the pain of dying,
she printed many kisses, all benign
signs of deep pity, on the fevered lips
of her trembling and enraptured lover.

What did you become then? How did life,
death, and unhappiness seem to you, Consalvo,
as you left? Placing the hand
of his beloved Elvira on his heart
beating with the final pulse
of death and love, he said: Oh, Elvira,
my Elvira! I know I'm still on earth,

In su la terra ancor; ben quelle labbra
Fur le tue labbra, e la tua mano io stringo!
Ahi vision d'estinto, o sogno, o cosa
Incredibil mi par. Deh quanto, Elvira,
Quanto debbo alla morte! Ascoso innanzi
Non ti fu l'amor mio per alcun tempo;
Non a te, non altrui; che non si cela
Vero amore alla terra. Assai palese
Agli atti, al volto sbigottito, agli occhi,
Ti fu: ma non ai detti. Ancora e sempre
Muto sarebbe l'infinito affetto
Che governa il cor mio, se non l'avesse
Fatto ardito il morir. Morrò contento
Del mio destino omai, nè più mi dolgo
Ch'aprii le luci al dì. Non vissi indarno,
Poscia che quella bocca alla mia bocca
Premer fu dato. Anzi felice estimo
La sorte mia. Due cose belle ha il mondo:
Amore e morte. All'una il ciel mi guida
In sul fior dell'età; nell'altro, assai
Fortunato mi tengo. Ah, se una volta,
Solo una volta il lungo amor quieto
E pago avessi tu, fora la terra
Fatta quindi per sempre un paradiso
Ai cangiati occhi miei. Fin la vecchiezza,
L'abborrita vecchiezza, avrei sofferto
Con riposato cor: che a sostentarla
Bastato sempre il rimembrar sarebbe
D'un solo istante, e il dir: felice io fui
Sovra tutti i felici. Ahi, ma cotanto

for those clearly were your lips, and this
is your hand I'm holding. It is like
a dead man's vision, or a dream, or something
unbelievable. Ah how much, Elvira,
how much I owe to death! My love was never
concealed from you before at any time,
not from you and not from anyone,
for true love can't be concealed on earth.
It was clear to you from what I did,
from my unhappy face and eyes—though not from what
I said. The endless love that rules my heart
would always have kept silent
if my dying hadn't lent it courage.
Now I'll die happy with my destiny,
and won't complain again my eyes saw daylight.
I didn't live in vain: I was allowed
to put my mouth on yours. Indeed,
I think my fate is happy. There are two fair
things in this world: love and death.
Heaven brought me one in the prime of my youth;
as for the other, I count myself
lucky indeed. Ah, if once, just once,
you'd have solaced and appeased
my long love, the world would have been
a heaven forever in my transformed eyes.
I'd even have endured old age,
abhorred old age, serenely:
for it would have been enough to bear it
always remembering a single moment
and saying, I was happy above all happy men.

Esser beato non consente il cielo
A natura terrena. Amar tant'oltre
Non è dato con gioia. E ben per patto
In poter del carnefice ai flagelli,
Alle ruote, alle faci ito volando
Sarei dalle tue braccia; e ben disceso
Nel paventato sempiterno scempio.

O Elvira, Elvira, oh lui felice, oh sovra
Gl'immortali beato, a cui tu schiuda
Il sorriso d'amor! felice appresso
Chi per te sparga con la vita il sangue!
Lice, lice al mortal, non è già sogno
Come stimai gran tempo, ahi lice in terra
Provar felicità. Ciò seppi il giorno
Che fiso io ti mirai. Ben per mia morte
Questo m'accadde. E non però quel giorno
Con certo cor giammai, fra tante ambasce,
Quel fiero giorno biasimar sostenni.

Or tu vivi beata, e il mondo abbella,
Elvira mia, col tuo sembiante. Alcuno
Non l'amerà quant'io l'amai. Non nasce
Un altrettale amor. Quanto, deh quanto
Dal misero Consalvo in sì gran tempo
Chiamata fosti, e lamentata, e pianta!
Come al nome d'Elvira, in cor gelando,
Impallidir; come tremar son uso
All'amaro calcar della tua soglia,
A quella voce angelica, all'aspetto

Ah, but heaven does not permit
any being on earth to be blessed this way.
We can't love this deeply and with joy.
Yet in exchange I would have delivered myself
out of your arms to the executioner,
the whip, the rack, the bonfire, and even gone
into terrifying eternal torment.

O Elvira, Elvira, happy is the man,
more blessed than the immortals,
on whom you smile in love! And he who sheds
his blood and gives his life for you
is almost as blessed! It's allowed, it's given to men,
not just a dream, as I believed so long:
we mortals can know happiness on earth.
I knew this the day that I set eyes on you.
And, for me, it happened as I died.
And yet, in spite of so much anguish, never,
never could I blame that cruel day.

Now live blessed, my Elvira,
and let your beauty beautify the world.
No one will love it as I have.
Another love like this will never be.
How often, yes, how often
and how long were you called to and lamented
and wept over by miserable Consalvo!
How pale I turned hearing the name Elvira,
how my heart froze, how I used to tremble
as I crossed your threshold bitterly,

Di quella fronte, io ch'al morir non tremo!
Ma la lena e la vita or vengon meno
Agli accenti d'amor. Passato è il tempo,
Nè questo dì rimemorar m'è dato.
Elvira, addio. Con la vital favilla
La tua diletta immagine si parte
Dal mio cor finalmente. Addio. Se grave
Non ti fu quest'affetto, al mio feretro
Dimani all'annottar manda un sospiro.

Tacque: nè molto andò, che a lui col suono
Mancò lo spirto; e innanzi sera il primo
Suo dì felice gli fuggia dal guardo.

hearing that angelic voice, seeing that forehead,
I who don't quake in the face of death!
But breath and life both fail me for words of love now.
That time is over, nor will I be able
to recall this day. Farewell, Elvira.
With the breath of life, your adored image
leaves my heart at last. Farewell.
If this love of mine was not a burden,
send a sigh to my bier tomorrow as night falls.

He was silent: and not much time passed
before his spirit, like his voice, departed,
and by night his first glad day had left his eyes.

XVIII

ALLA SUA DONNA

Cara beltà che amore
Lunge m'inspiri o nascondendo il viso,
Fuor se nel sonno il core
Ombra diva mi scuoti,
O ne' campi ove splenda
Più vago il giorno e di natura il riso;
Forse tu l'innocente
Secol beasti che dall'oro ha nome,
Or leve intra la gente
Anima voli? o te la sorte avara
Ch'a noi t'asconde, agli avvenir prepara?

Viva mirarti omai
Nulla spene m'avanza;
S'allor non fosse, allor che ignudo e solo
Per novo calle a peregrina stanza
Verrà lo spirto mio. Già sul novello
Aprir di mia giornata incerta e bruna,
Te viatrice in questo arido suolo
Io mi pensai. Ma non è cosa in terra
Che ti somigli; e s'anco pari alcuna
Ti fosse al volto, agli atti, alla favella,
Saria, così conforme, assai men bella.

XVIII

TO HIS LADY

Beloved beauty who inspires
love from afar, your face concealed
except when your celestial image
stirs my heart in sleep, or in the fields
where light and nature's laughter
shine more lovely;
was it maybe you who blessed the innocent
age they call golden,
and do you now, blithe spirit,
soar among men? Or does the miser, fate,
who hides you from us keep you for the future?

No hope of seeing you alive
remains for me now,
except when, naked and alone,
my soul will go down a new street
to an unfamiliar home. Already, at the dawn
of my dark, uncertain day,
I imagined you a fellow traveler
on this parched ground. But no thing on earth
is equal to you; and if there were someone
who had a face like yours, though she resembled
you in word and deed, she'd be less lovely.

Fra cotanto dolore
Quanto all'umana età propose il fato,
Se vera e quale il mio pensier ti pinge,
Alcun t'amasse in terra, a lui pur fora
Questo viver beato:
E ben chiaro vegg'io siccome ancora
Seguir loda e virtù qual ne' prim'anni
L'amor tuo mi farebbe. Or non aggiunse
Il ciel nullo conforto ai nostri affanni;
E teco la mortal vita saria
Simile a quella che nel cielo india.

Per le valli, ove suona
Del faticoso agricoltore il canto,
Ed io seggo e mi lagno
Del giovanile error che m'abbandona;
E per li poggi, ov'io rimembro e piagno
I perduti desiri, e la perduta
Speme de' giorni miei; di te pensando,
A palpitar mi sveglio. E potess'io,
Nel secol tetro e in questo aer nefando,
L'alta specie serbar; che dell'imago,
Poi che del ver m'è tolto, assai m'appago.

Se dell'eterne idee
L'una sei tu, cui di sensibil forma
Sdegni l'eterno senno esser vestita,
E fra caduche spoglie
Provar gli affanni di funerea vita;
O s'altra terra ne' superni giri

In spite of all the suffering
fate assigned to human life,
if there was anyone on earth
who truly loved you as my thought portrays you,
this life for him would be a joy.
And I see clearly how your love
would still inspire me to seek praise and virtue,
the way I used to in my early years.
Though heaven gave no comfort for our suffering,
still mortal life with you would be
like what in heaven becomes divinity.

In the valleys, where you hear
the weary farmer singing
and I sit and mourn
my youth's illusions fleeing;
and on the hills where I turn back
and lament my lost desires,
my life's lost hope, I think of you
and start to shake. In this sad age
and unhealthy atmosphere, I try
to keep your noble look in mind;
without the real thing, I enjoy the image.

Whether you are the one and only
eternal idea that eternal wisdom
disdains to see arrayed in sensible form,
to know the pains of mortal life
in transitory dress;
or if in the supernal spheres another earth

Fra' mondi innumerabili t'accoglie,
E più vaga del Sol prossima stella
T'irraggia, e più benigno etere spiri;
Di qua dove son gli anni infausti e brevi,
Questo d'ignoto amante inno ricevi.

from among unnumbered worlds receives you,
and a near star lovelier than the Sun
warms you and you breathe benigner ether,
from here, where years are both ill-starred and brief,
accept this hymn from your unnoticed lover.

XIX

AL CONTE CARLO PEPOLI

Questo affannoso e travagliato sonno
Che noi vita nomiam, come sopporti,
Pepoli mio? di che speranze il core
Vai sostentando? in che pensieri, in quanto
O gioconde o moleste opre dispensi
L'ozio che ti lasciàr gli avi remoti,
Grave retaggio e faticoso? È tutta,
In ogni umano stato, ozio la vita,
Se quell'oprar, quel procurar che a degno
Obbietto non intende, o che all'intento
Giunger mai non potria, ben si conviene
Ozioso nomar. La schiera industre
Cui franger glebe o curar piante e greggi
Vede l'alba tranquilla e vede il vespro,
Se oziosa dirai, da che sua vita
È per campar la vita, e per se sola
La vita all'uom non ha pregio nessuno,
Dritto e vero dirai. Le notti e i giorni
Tragge in ozio il nocchiero; ozio il perenne
Sudar nelle officine, ozio le vegghie
Son de' guerrieri e il perigliar nell'armi;
E il mercatante avaro in ozio vive:

XIX

TO COUNT CARLO PEPOLI

How do you bear this tortured and tormented
sleep that we call life, my Pepoli?
What hopes do you keep feeding to your heart?
What are the ideas, the many happy
or unhappy plans on which you spend
the idleness that your forefathers left you,
solemn, burdensome inheritance?
All life is idleness, at every human level,
if doing or getting with no worthy aim,
or that could never reach the goal
that it aspires to, can be seen as idle.
If you say the hardworking crowd is idle
who see the tranquil sunrise and the sunset
while they break clods or tend to crops or herds
you'll say the truth, because they spend their lives
living, and life in and of itself
has no value whatsoever for man.
The helmsman drags his nights and days
out in idleness, the endless sweat
in factories is idle, the soldiers' watch
and danger in battle is idle,
and the greedy merchant lives in idleness:

Che non a se, non ad altrui, la bella
Felicità, cui solo agogna e cerca
La natura mortal, veruno acquista
Per cura o per sudor, vegghia o periglio.
Pure all'aspro desire onde i mortali
Già sempre infin dal dì che il mondo nacque
D'esser beati sospiraro indarno,
Di medicina in loco apparecchiate
Nella vita infelice avea natura
Necessità diverse, a cui non senza
Opra e pensier si provvedesse, e pieno,
Poi che lieto non può, corresse il giorno
All'umana famiglia; onde agitato
E confuso il desio, men loco avesse
Al travagliarne il cor. Così de' bruti
La progenie infinita, a cui pur solo,
Nè men vano che a noi, vive nel petto
Desio d'esser beati; a quello intenta
Che a lor vita è mestier, di noi men tristo
Condur si scopre e men gravoso il tempo,
Nè la lentezza accagionar dell'ore.
Ma noi, che il viver nostro all'altrui mano
Provveder commettiamo, una più grave
Necessità, cui provveder non puote
Altri che noi, già senza tedio e pena
Non adempiam: necessitate, io dico,
Di consumar la vita: improba, invitta
Necessità, cui non tesoro accolto,
Non di greggi dovizia, o pingui campi,
Non aula puote e non purpureo manto

since, by care or effort, watchfulness or daring,
no one wins himself or anyone sweet happiness,
which is all mortal beings want and seek.
Yet, in answer to the sharp desire
that they have pined in vain for since the day
the world was created: to be happy,
nature, instead of remedies for misery,
invented various necessities
that only can be had by work and thought,
making the day chock-full instead of glad
for the human family, so if a man's desire
was aroused but left unsatisfied,
it would have less time to trouble him.
So with the countless species of the animals,
who also only wish for happiness
(and do so no less hopelessly than we);
for them, concentrated on this aim
that is their whole life's work, time seems to pass
less sadly than for us, and weighs less heavily,
and they don't complain about its sluggishness.
But we, who delegate the task
of managing our lives to others,
can't satisfy a deeper need,
which only we can answer,
without pain and boredom—
the need, I say, to use life up:
cruel, invincible necessity,
which not accumulated wealth,
the husbanding of herds or fertile fields,
or palaces or purple robes

Sottrar l'umana prole. Or s'altri, a sdegno
I vóti anni prendendo, e la superna
Luce odiando, l'omicida mano,
I tardi fati a prevenir condotto,
In se stesso non torce; al duro morso
Della brama insanabile che invano
Felicità richiede, esso da tutti
Lati cercando, mille inefficaci
Medicine procaccia, onde quell'una
Cui natura apprestò, mal si compensa.

Lui delle vesti e delle chiome il culto
E degli atti e dei passi, e i vani studi
Di cocchi e di cavalli, e le frequenti
Sale, e le piazze romorose, e gli orti,
Lui giochi e cene e invidiate danze
Tengon la notte e il giorno; a lui dal labbro
Mai non si parte il riso; ahi, ma nel petto,
Nell'imo petto, grave, salda, immota
Come colonna adamantina, siede
Noia immortale, incontro a cui non puote
Vigor di giovanezza, e non la crolla
Dolce parola di rosato labbro,
E non lo sguardo tenero, tremante,
Di due nere pupille, il caro sguardo,
La più degna del ciel cosa mortale.

Altri, quasi a fuggir volto la trista
Umana sorte, in cangiar terre e climi
L'età spendendo, e mari e poggi errando,

can free man of. So, if someone detests
his empty life and hates the light of heaven
and wants to hurry his slow fate along
not turning a murderous hand upon himself,
stung by the incurable desire
that searches hopelessly for happiness,
he is forced to go look everywhere,
chasing a thousand useless cures
for which the only one that nature offers
is small recompense.

For one, the cult of clothing and hairdressing,
of doing, coming, and going, the empty interest
in carriages and horses,
busy salons and noisy squares and gardens,
games and dinners and exclusive dances,
takes up his attention night and day.
Laughter never falls from his lips: but in his heart, alas,
deep down, heavy, massive, motionless,
immortal boredom sits like adamant,
against which all the energy of youth
is useless. Not even a sweet word
from a rosy lip will send it packing,
or the tender, trembling glance
of two dark eyes, the loving look,
the human thing that is most worthy of heaven.

Another, as if determined to escape
unhappy human fate by spending his days
in other lands and climates, wandering the seas and hills,

Tutto l'orbe trascorre, ogni confine
Degli spazi che all'uom negl'infiniti
Campi del tutto la natura aperse,
Peregrinando aggiunge. Ahi ahi, s'asside
Su l'alte prue la negra cura, e sotto
Ogni clima, ogni ciel, si chiama indarno
Felicità, vive tristezza e regna.

Havvi chi le crudeli opre di marte
Si elegge a passar l'ore, e nel fraterno
Sangue la man tinge per ozio; ed havvi
Chi d'altrui danni si conforta, e pensa
Con far misero altrui far se men tristo,
Sì che nocendo usar procaccia il tempo.
E chi virtute o sapienza ed arti
Perseguitando; e chi la propria gente
Conculcando e l'estrane, o di remoti
Lidi turbando la quiete antica
Col mercatar, con l'armi, e con le frodi,
La destinata sua vita consuma.

Te più mite desio, cura più dolce
Regge nel fior di gioventù, nel bello
April degli anni, altrui giocondo e primo
Dono del ciel, ma grave, amaro, infesto
A chi patria non ha. Te punge e move
Studio de' carmi e di ritrar parlando
Il bel che raro e scarso e fuggitivo
Appar nel mondo, e quel che più benigna
Di natura e del ciel, fecondamente

travels the whole globe, and, as he journeys, comes
to every end of the earth nature opened to man
in the boundless spaces of the universe.
Alas, black care sits on his ship's high prow,
and in every climate, under every sky,
where we seek hopelessly for happiness,
sadness lives and reigns.

Others choose to spend their days
doing the cruel work of Mars, and idly
stain their hands with their brothers' blood;
some take comfort in the woes of others,
and think that making others miserable
makes them less sad, and so they spend their time
doing evil. And there are those who use
their fated life up chasing after virtues,
wisdom, or the arts. Others oppress
their own, or someone else,
or trouble the age-old peace of distant shores
with commerce, armies, and dishonesty.

A gentler wish, a kindlier concern
drives you in the noontime of your youth,
the gentle April of your years,
heaven's glad first gift to some,
but heavy, bitter, hostile
to the man who has no country.
The study of song moves you and inspires you
to portray in words
the rare and scarce and fleeting beauty

A noi la vaga fantasia produce
E il nostro proprio error. Ben mille volte
Fortunato colui che la caduca
Virtù del caro immaginar non perde
Per volger d'anni; a cui serbare eterna
La gioventù del cor diedero i fati;
Che nella ferma e nella stanca etade,
Così come solea nell'età verde,
In suo chiuso pensier natura abbella,
Morte, deserto avviva. A te conceda
Tanta ventura il ciel; ti faccia un tempo
La favilla che il petto oggi ti scalda,
Di poesia canuto amante. Io tutti
Della prima stagione i dolci inganni
Mancar già sento, e dileguar dagli occhi
Le dilettose immagini, che tanto
Amai, che sempre infino all'ora estrema
Mi fieno, a ricordar, bramate e piante.
Or quando al tutto irrigidito e freddo
Questo petto sarà, nè degli aprichi
Campi il sereno e solitario riso,
Nè degli augelli mattutini il canto
Di primavera, nè per colli e piagge
Sotto limpido ciel tacita luna
Commoverammi il cor; quando mi fia
Ogni beltate o di natura o d'arte,
Fatta inanime e muta; ogni alto senso,
Ogni tenero affetto, ignoto e strano;
Del mio solo conforto allor mendico,
Altri studi men dolci, in ch'io riponga

that we find in this world, which most benignly,
fruitfully creates our lovely fantasies
of nature and heaven for us, and our illusions.
He is fortunate a thousand times
who doesn't lose the fleeting power
of sweet imagination with the passing years,
whom fate let keep his heart's eternal freshness,
who in adulthood and in tired old age
makes nature lovely in his inner thought
just as he did in youth,
and brings the desert, death, to life.
May heaven grant you such good luck;
may the spark that warms your heart now make you
a white-haired lover of poetry one day.
I feel the sweet illusions of my youth
all failing already, and the pleasing images
I loved so much are fading from my eyes;
recalling them I'll yearn and mourn forever,
till my last hour. When this heart
goes wholly hard and cold, not the serene,
lonely laughter of the sun-drenched fields
nor the morning song of birds in spring,
nor the still moon over hill and shore
under an open sky will move my heart;
when every beauty
of nature or of art
will be dead and meaningless for me,
and every deep emotion, every tender
feeling will be foreign and unfamiliar,
without my only consolation then,

L'ingrato avanzo della ferrea vita,
Eleggerò. L'acerbo vero, i ciechi
Destini investigar delle mortali
E dell'eterne cose; a che prodotta,
A che d'affanni e di miserie carca
L'umana stirpe; a quale ultimo intento
Lei spinga il fato e la natura; a cui
Tanto nostro dolor diletti o giovi;
Con quali ordini e leggi a che si volva
Questo arcano universo; il qual di lode
Colmano i saggi, io d'ammirar son pago.

In questo specolar gli ozi traendo
Verrò: che conosciuto, ancor che tristo,
Ha suoi diletti il vero. E se del vero
Ragionando talor, fieno alle genti
O mal grati i miei detti o non intesi,
Non mi dorrò, che già del tutto il vago
Desio di gloria antico in me fia spento:
Vana Diva non pur, ma di fortuna
E del fato e d'amor, Diva più cieca.

I shall choose less pleasant occupations
to turn to during the unwelcome onset
of inexorable old age. To learn
the bitter truth, the unseen fates of mortal
and eternal things—why the human race was made,
why it suffers pain and misery,
where ultimately fate and nature drive us,
whom our enormous pain brings pleasure
or profit to, according to what rules and laws
this mysterious universe revolves:
what the wise praise I'm happy to admire.

I shall spend my idleness
in speculating thus; because the truth, once known,
though it is sad, has pleasures of its own.
And if, speaking the truth, my words at times
will be unwelcome or misunderstood,
I shall not grieve, for all my fine desire
for the old glory will have run its course—
glory, not only a vain Goddess, but a Goddess
blinder still than fortune, fate, and love.

XX

IL RISORGIMENTO

Credei ch'al tutto fossero
In me, sul fior degli anni,
Mancati i dolci affanni
Della mia prima età:
I dolci affanni, i teneri
Moti del cor profondo,
Qualunque cosa al mondo
Grato il sentir ci fa.

Quante querele e lacrime
Sparsi nel novo stato,
Quando al mio cor gelato
Prima il dolor mancò!
Mancàr gli usati palpiti,
L'amor mi venne meno,
E irrigidito il seno
Di sospirar cessò!

Piansi spogliata, esanime
Fatta per me la vita;
La terra inaridita,
Chiusa in eterno gel;

XX

THE REAWAKENING

I felt, on the verge
of the springtime of life,
that I had lost all
the sweet torments of youth:
the sweet torments, the inner
heart's tender emotions,
what in the world
makes us happy to feel.

How hard I cried,
in this new state of mine,
when pain was first gone
from my frozen heart.
There was no throbbing,
love left me alone,
and my newly hard heart
didn't sigh anymore.

I was crying because
for me life was barren and dead,
the earth was arid,
permanent ice.

Deserto il dì; la tacita
Notte più sola e bruna;
Spenta per me la luna,
Spente le stelle in ciel.

Pur di quel pianto origine
Era l'antico affetto:
Nell'intimo del petto
Ancor viveva il cor.
Chiedea l'usate immagini
La stanca fantasia;
E la tristezza mia
Era dolore ancor.

Fra poco in me quell'ultimo
Dolore anco fu spento,
E di più far lamento
Valor non mi restò.
Giacqui: insensato, attonito,
Non dimandai conforto:
Quasi perduto e morto,
Il cor s'abbandonò.

Qual fui! quanto dissimile
Da quel che tanto ardore,
Che sì beato errore
Nutrii nell'alma un dì!
La rondinella vigile,
Alle finestre intorno
Cantando al novo giorno,
Il cor non mi ferì:

Day was a desert,
the silent night lonely.
The moon had died out
with the stars in the sky.

But my old feelings
gave birth to those tears:
deep in my breast
my heart was alive.
My worn-out fantasies
longed for old images,
and my unhappiness
still felt like pain.

Soon that last pain
had died in me, too;
I had no power
to keep on complaining.
I lay without feeling,
not wanting relief.
My heart had surrendered,
forgotten and gone.

How different I was
from the man who had fed
such ardor, so much
blessed pain in his soul!
The sentinel swallow
that sang at my window
at daybreak, he couldn't
break into my heart,

Non all'autunno pallido
In solitaria villa,
La vespertina squilla,
Il fuggitivo Sol.
Invan brillare il vespero
Vidi per muto calle,
Invan sonò la valle
Del flebile usignol.

E voi, pupille tenere,
Sguardi furtivi, erranti,
Voi de' gentili amanti
Primo, immortale amor,
Ed alla mano offertami
Candida ignuda mano,
Foste voi pure invano
Al duro mio sopor.

D'ogni dolcezza vedovo,
Tristo; ma non turbato,
Ma placido il mio stato,
Il volto era seren.
Desiderato il termine
Avrei del viver mio;
Ma spento era il desio
Nello spossato sen.

Qual dell'età decrepita
L'avanzo ignudo e vile,
Io conducea l'aprile
Degli anni miei così:

nor, in pale autumn
alone on the farm,
could the church bell at dusk,
or the fleeting Sun, as it fled.
I watched the sun glowing
in the still street,
and heard the lament
of the bird in the valley.

And you, gentle eyes,
with your wandering glances,
you first, undying
sweet lovers' love,
and the white, naked hand
that my own hand was given—
you were no help
in my cruel sleep.

Deprived of all sweetness,
sad but untroubled,
my state was calm
and my look was serene.
I could have wanted
my life to end then,
except desire had died
in my powerless heart.

Like the bare, hateful
remains of old age,
I lived out the April
of my young life.

Così quegl'ineffabili
Giorni, o mio cor, traevi,
Che sì fugaci e brevi
Il cielo a noi sortì.

Chi dalla grave, immemore
Quiete or mi ridesta?
Che virtù nova è questa,
Questa che sento in me?
Moti soavi, immagini,
Palpiti, error beato,
Per sempre a voi negato
Questo mio cor non è?

Siete pur voi quell'unica
Luce de' giorni miei?
Gli affetti ch'io perdei
Nella novella età?
Se al ciel, s'ai verdi margini,
Ovunque il guardo mira,
Tutto un dolor mi spira,
Tutto un piacer mi dà.

Meco ritorna a vivere
La piaggia, il bosco, il monte;
Parla al mio core il fonte,
Meco favella il mar.
Chi mi ridona il piangere
Dopo cotanto obblio?
E come al guardo mio
Cangiato il mondo appar?

So, heart, you lived
the incredible days
that heaven allotted us,
fleeting and brief.

Who is it wakes me
from this leaden old calm?
What is this new power
I'm sensing inside?
Sweet feelings, visions,
throbbings, illusions—
are you always forbidden
to this heart of mine?

Are you the singular
light of my days,
the love I lost
in this new age?
Wherever I look,
at the green banks, the sky—
all of it's pain,
all of it's joy.

The shore, grove, and mountain
have come back to life.
The fountain is talking,
the sea speaks to me.
Who gives me back tears
after so much forgetting?
How can the world
look so different to me?

Forse la speme, o povero
Mio cor, ti volse un riso?
Ahi della speme il viso
Io non vedrò mai più.
Proprii mi diede i palpiti,
Natura, e i dolci inganni.
Sopiro in me gli affanni
L'ingenita virtù;

Non l'annullàr: non vinsela
Il fato e la sventura;
Non con la vista impura
L'infausta verità.
Dalle mie vaghe immagini
So ben ch'ella discorda:
So che natura è sorda,
Che miserar non sa.

Che non del ben sollecita
Fu, ma dell'esser solo:
Purchè ci serbi al duolo,
Or d'altro a lei non cal.
So che pietà fra gli uomini
Il misero non trova;
Che lui, fuggendo, a prova
Schernisce ogni mortal.

Che ignora il tristo secolo
Gl'ingegni e le virtudi;
Che manca ai degni studi
L'ignuda gloria ancor.

Is hope maybe smiling
on you, my poor heart?
I'll never ever
see hope again.
Nature gave me my heart
and my own sweet illusions.
My pain had extinguished
my own native power;

but fate and bad luck
didn't ruin or defeat it,
nor did the blind sight
of unlucky truth.
I know it conflicts
with my own glad illusions.
I know nature's deaf,
and can't share in our pain,

she doesn't care about good,
what matters is being.
All that she wants
is to save us for pain.
I know the unhappy man
has no real fellows,
that everyone turns against
him as he flees;

that this sad century
knows nothing of genius,
that great work's still missing
the praise it deserves.

E voi, pupille tremule,
Voi, raggio sovrumano,
So che splendete invano,
Che in voi non brilla amor.

Nessuno ignoto ed intimo
Affetto in voi non brilla:
Non chiude una favilla
Quel bianco petto in se.
Anzi d'altrui le tenere
Cure suol porre in gioco;
E d'un celeste foco
Disprezzo è la mercè.

Pur sento in me rivivere
Gl'inganni aperti e noti;
E de' suoi proprii moti
Si maraviglia il sen.
Da te, mio cor, quest'ultimo
Spirto, e l'ardor natio,
Ogni conforto mio
Solo da te mi vien.

Mancano, il sento, all'anima
Alta, gentile e pura,
La sorte, la natura,
Il mondo e la beltà.
Ma se tu vivi, o misero,
Se non concedi al fato,
Non chiamerò spietato
Chi lo spirar mi dà.

And you, trembling eyes,
you, heaven's light,
I know what's shining
in you isn't love.

No hidden emotion
glimmers in you,
that white breast is hiding
no spark of its own.
In fact, it laughs
at the troubles of others,
disdains the reward
for celestial fire.

Yet I feel the familiar
illusions reviving,
my breast is amazed
at all that it feels.
From you, this new spirit,
heart, and my own fire:
all of my comfort
is coming from you.

I know that the high and pure
soul is deprived
of destiny, nature,
the world and its beauty.
But if you live, sad one,
and don't bow to fate,
I won't call heartless
who gives me breath.

XXI

A SILVIA

Silvia, rimembri ancora
Quel tempo della tua vita mortale,
Quando beltà splendea
Negli occhi tuoi ridenti e fuggitivi,
E tu, lieta e pensosa, il limitare
Di gioventù salivi?

Sonavan le quiete
Stanze, e le vie dintorno,
Al tuo perpetuo canto,
Allor che all'opre femminili intenta
Sedevi, assai contenta
Di quel vago avvenir che in mente avevi.
Era il maggio odoroso: e tu solevi
Così menare il giorno.

Io gli studi leggiadri
Talor lasciando e le sudate carte,
Ove il tempo mio primo
E di me si spendea la miglior parte,
D'in su i veroni del paterno ostello
Porgea gli orecchi al suon della tua voce,

XXI

TO SILVIA

Silvia, do you remember still
that moment in your mortal life
when beauty shimmered
in your smiling, startled eyes
as, bright and pensive, you arrived
at the threshold of youth?

The quiet rooms
and streets outside
echoed with your endless song
as you sat, bending to your woman's work,
happy enough with the hazy
future in your head.
It was fragrant May:
and so you spent your day.

Sometimes I left the cherished
books and labored pages
on which my young years
and the best of me were spent,
to listen from my father's balcony
for the sound of your singing

Ed alla man veloce
Che percorrea la faticosa tela.
Mirava il ciel sereno,
Le vie dorate e gli orti,
E quinci il mar da lungi, e quindi il monte.
Lingua mortal non dice
Quel ch'io sentiva in seno.

Che pensieri soavi,
Che speranze, che cori, o Silvia mia!
Quale allor ci apparia
La vita umana e il fato!
Quando sovviemmi di cotanta speme,
Un affetto mi preme
Acerbo e sconsolato,
E tornami a doler di mia sventura.
O natura, o natura,
Perchè non rendi poi
Quel che prometti allor? perchè di tanto
Inganni i figli tuoi?

Tu pria che l'erbe inaridisse il verno,
Da chiuso morbo combattuta e vinta,
Perivi, o tenerella. E non vedevi
Il fior degli anni tuoi;
Non ti molceva il core
La dolce lode or delle negre chiome,
Or degli sguardi innamorati e schivi;
Nè teco le compagne ai dì festivi
Ragionavan d'amore.

and your swift hand's back-and-forth
on the heavy loom.
I looked out on the cloudless sky,
the golden streets and gardens,
and, far off, the sea here and mountains there.
No mortal tongue can tell
all that I felt.

What light thoughts,
what hopes, what hearts, my Silvia!
What human life and fate
were to us then!
When I remember so much hope
I'm overcome,
bitter, inconsolable,
and rage against my own ill luck.
O Nature, Nature,
why don't you deliver later
what you promised then? Why do you lead on
your children so?

You, before winter had withered the grass,
stricken then overcome by hidden sickness,
died, gentle girl. You didn't see
your years come into flower.
Sweet talk about your raven hair
or your beguiling, guarded glance
never melted your heart,
and on holidays you never talked
about love with your friends.

Anche peria fra poco
La speranza mia dolce: agli anni miei
Anche negaro i fati
La giovanezza. Ahi come,
Come passata sei,
Cara compagna dell'età mia nova,
Mia lacrimata speme!
Questo è quel mondo? questi
I diletti, l'amor, l'opre, gli eventi
Onde cotanto ragionammo insieme?
Questa la sorte dell'umane genti?
All'apparir del vero
Tu, misera, cadesti: e con la mano
La fredda morte ed una tomba ignuda
Mostravi di lontano.

Before long, my sweet hope
died, too; the fates
denied me youth also.
Ah, how truly
past you are,
dear companion of my innocence,
my much-lamented hope!
Is this that world? Are these
the joys, love, deeds, experience
we spoke so often of?
Is this man's fate?
When the truth dawned
you fell away, poor thing, and from afar
pointed out cold death
and a naked grave.

Translated with Tim Parks

XXII

LE RICORDANZE

Vaghe stelle dell'Orsa, io non credea
Tornare ancor per uso a contemplarvi
Sul paterno giardino scintillanti,
E ragionar con voi dalle finestre
Di questo albergo ove abitai fanciullo,
E delle gioie mie vidi la fine.
Quante immagini un tempo, e quante fole
Creommi nel pensier l'aspetto vostro
E delle luci a voi compagne! allora
Che, tacito, seduto in verde zolla,
Delle sere io solea passar gran parte
Mirando il cielo, ed ascoltando il canto
Della rana rimota alla campagna!
E la lucciola errava appo le siepi
E in su l'aiuole, susurrando al vento
I viali odorati, ed i cipressi
Là nella selva; e sotto al patrio tetto
Sonavan voci alterne, e le tranquille
Opre de' servi. E che pensieri immensi,
Che dolci sogni mi spirò la vista
Di quel lontano mar, quei monti azzurri,

XXII

THE RECOLLECTIONS

Shimmering stars of the Bear, I never thought
that I'd be back again to see you shine
over my father's garden,
and talk with you from the windows
of this house I lived in as a child,
where I saw my happiness come to an end.
How many images, how many fantasies
seeing you and your companion-lights
created in my mind
when, sitting on the grass,
I used to spend a good part of the evening
watching the sky, and listening to the song
of the frog out in the countryside.
And the firefly floated over the hedges
and flower beds, while the perfumed avenues
and the cypresses there in the grove
whispered in the wind, and I heard voices
under my father's roof, and the servants
peaceably at work. And what immense ideas,
what tender dreams the sight of that far sea
inspired in me, those blue hills I can see

Che di qua scopro, e che varcare un giorno
Io mi pensava, arcani mondi, arcana
Felicità fingendo al viver mio!
Ignaro del mio fato, e quante volte
Questa mia vita dolorosa e nuda
Volentier con la morte avrei cangiato.

Nè mi diceva il cor che l'età verde
Sarei dannato a consumare in questo
Natio borgo selvaggio, intra una gente
Zotica, vil; cui nomi strani, e spesso
Argomento di riso e di trastullo,
Son dottrina e saper; che m'odia e fugge,
Per invidia non già, che non mi tiene
Maggior di se, ma perchè tale estima
Ch'io mi tenga in cor mio, sebben di fuori
A persona giammai non ne fo segno.
Qui passo gli anni, abbandonato, occulto,
Senz'amor, senza vita; ed aspro a forza
Tra lo stuol de' malevoli divengo:
Qui di pietà mi spoglio e di virtudi,
E sprezzator degli uomini mi rendo,
Per la greggia ch'ho appresso: e intanto vola
Il caro tempo giovanil; più caro
Che la fama e l'allor, più che la pura
Luce del giorno, e lo spirar: ti perdo
Senza un diletto, inutilmente, in questo
Soggiorno disumano, intra gli affanni,
O dell'arida vita unico fiore.

from here and planned to cross one day
as I invented secret worlds,
hidden gladness in my life!
ignorant of my fate and of how often
I would gladly have exchanged
this sad and barren life of mine with death.

Nor did my heart tell me I would be condemned
to waste my green age here in this barbaric
native place of mine, among a rude, low people
for whom learning and wisdom are strange notions,
and often the occasion
of ridicule and sport, who hate and shun me,
not really out of envy, for they don't feel
I'm better than they are, but because they sense
I think so in my heart, though outwardly
I make no sign of this to anyone.
I spend my years secluded here, shut in,
with no love and no life, and against my will
turn hard toward the crowd of my ill-wishers:
I strip myself of gentleness and kindness,
becoming someone who despises men,
thanks to the herd around me. And all the while
youth's beloved moment flies, more dear
than fame and laurel, dearer than the simple
light of day and breath: O single flower
of my arid life, I'm losing you
joylessly, for no good reason,
in this inhuman place beset by suffering.

Viene il vento recando il suon dell'ora
Dalla torre del borgo. Era conforto
Questo suon, mi rimembra, alle mie notti,
Quando fanciullo, nella buia stanza,
Per assidui terrori io vigilava,
Sospirando il mattin. Qui non è cosa
Ch'io vegga o senta, onde un'immagin dentro
Non torni, e un dolce rimembrar non sorga.
Dolce per se; ma con dolor sottentra
Il pensier del presente, un van desio
Del passato, ancor tristo, e il dire: io fui.
Quella loggia colà, volta agli estremi
Raggi del dì; queste dipinte mura,
Quei figurati armenti, e il Sol che nasce
Su romita campagna, agli ozi miei
Porser mille diletti allor che al fianco
M'era, parlando, il mio possente errore
Sempre, ov'io fossi. In queste sale antiche,
Al chiaror delle nevi, intorno a queste
Ampie finestre sibilando il vento,
Rimbombaro i sollazzi e le festose
Mie voci al tempo che l'acerbo, indegno
Mistero delle cose a noi si mostra
Pien di dolcezza; indelibata, intera
Il garzoncel, come inesperto amante,
La sua vita ingannevole vagheggia,
E celeste beltà fingendo ammira.

O speranze, speranze; ameni inganni
Della mia prima età! sempre, parlando,

The wind comes, with the hour that tolls
from the town tower. This sound, I can remember,
was a comfort to my nights,
when as a child I lay in my dark room
prey to unrelenting terrors, sighing for morning.
There's nothing here I see or feel
but that some image doesn't live in me again,
some sweet memory come to light.
Sweet in itself; but knowledge of the present
replaces it with pain, and a vain desire
for the past, however sad, and the wish
to say: I was. That loggia there, which faces
the day's last rays, these painted walls,
those pictured herds, and the Sun that rises
over lonely country, offered a thousand
pleasures as I lay with my omnipotent
imagination, ever eloquent
and always with me. In these ancient rooms
reflecting the snow's brightness, with the wind
whistling in these wide windows,
the sound of games and my glad shouting
echoed in the moment when the cruel,
unworthy mystery of things appears to us
as full of sweetness. The young boy,
like an untried lover, fantasizes
his illusionary life intact, untasted,
and wonders, dreaming of celestial beauty.

Hopes, hopes: O bright illusions
of my early years! Whenever I talk

Ritorno a voi; che per andar di tempo,
Per variar d'affetti e di pensieri,
Obbliarvi non so. Fantasmi, intendo,
Son la gloria e l'onor; diletti e beni
Mero desio; non ha la vita un frutto,
Inutile miseria. E sebben vóti
Son gli anni miei, sebben deserto, oscuro
Il mio stato mortal, poco mi toglie
La fortuna, ben veggo. Ahi, ma qualvolta
A voi ripenso, o mie speranze antiche,
Ed a quel caro immaginar mio primo;
Indi riguardo il viver mio sì vile
E sì dolente, e che la morte è quello
Che di cotanta speme oggi m'avanza;
Sento serrarmi il cor, sento ch'al tutto
Consolarmi non so del mio destino.
E quando pur questa invocata morte
Sarammi allato, e sarà giunto il fine
Della sventura mia; quando la terra
Mi fia straniera valle, e dal mio sguardo
Fuggirà l'avvenir; di voi per certo
Risovverrammi; e quell'imago ancora
Sospirar mi farà, farammi acerbo
L'esser vissuto indarno, e la dolcezza
Del dì fatal tempererà d'affanno.

E già nel primo giovanil tumulto
Di contenti, d'angosce e di desio,
Morte chiamai più volte, e lungamente
Mi sedetti colà su la fontana

I come around to you, for though time passes
and affections and ideas change,
I can't forget you. Yes, I understand
glory and honor are phantoms;
joys and things mere wishes; life produces nothing,
only senseless suffering. Yet though my years
are empty, though my mortal life
is barren and lightless, I can see
that fate is taking little from me.
Yet sometimes I think back on you, old hopes of mine,
and my sweet first imagining, and then
look at my life, so purposeless, so painful,
and see that death
is what remains for me of so much hope.
I feel my heart break, and I'm totally
inconsolable about my fate.
And when at last this death I've prayed for
is upon me and the end
of my misadventure will have come,
when earth will be an unfamiliar valley
and the future flies from view, I'm sure
I'll think of you again, and my imagining
will make me sigh again, will make me bitter
that I lived in vain, and the sweet release
of my last day will be alloyed with suffering.

But already, in the early youthful tumult
of happiness and anguish and desire,
there were many times I prayed for death,
and sat long by that fountain there,

Pensoso di cessar dentro quell'acque
La speme e il dolor mio. Poscia, per cieco
Malor, condotto della vita in forse,
Piansi la bella giovanezza, e il fiore
De' miei poveri dì, che sì per tempo
Cadeva: e spesso all'ore tarde, assiso
Sul conscio letto, dolorosamente
Alla fioca lucerna poetando,
Lamentai co' silenzi e con la notte
Il fuggitivo spirto, ed a me stesso
In sul languir cantai funereo canto.

Chi rimembrar vi può senza sospiri,
O primo entrar di giovinezza, o giorni
Vezzosi, inenarrabili, allor quando
Al rapito mortal primieramente
Sorridon le donzelle; a gara intorno
Ogni cosa sorride; invidia tace,
Non desta ancora ovver benigna; e quasi
(Inusitata maraviglia!) il mondo
La destra soccorrevole gli porge,
Scusa gli errori suoi, festeggia il novo
Suo venir nella vita, ed inchinando
Mostra che per signor l'accolga e chiami?
Fugaci giorni! a somigliar d'un lampo
Son dileguati. E qual mortale ignaro
Di sventura esser può, se a lui già scorsa
Quella vaga stagion, se il suo buon tempo,
Se giovanezza, ahi giovanezza, è spenta?

thinking I'd end my hope and suffering
in its waters. Later, when cruel illness
put my life in danger,
I wept for lovely youth, and for the best
of my unhappy days that died so soon.
And often, sitting late at night
on the bed that was my witness, miserably
writing poetry by my faint lantern,
I mourned my fleeting life
to the quiet night and sang myself
a song of lamentation, languishing.

Who can remember you without a sigh,
first entry into youth, delusive,
unsayable days, when girls first smile
on an enraptured mortal? Every thing
competes in smiling, envy holds its tongue,
either not yet excited or benign,
and it seems (rare miracle!)
that the world offers us a helping hand,
forgives our failings,
celebrates our fresh
arrival into life, and, with a bow
seems to acknowledge us and call us master.
Fleeting days! Like lightning they were gone.
And what mortal can stay unacquainted
with ill luck once that lovely season's over,
once his good time, youth,
ah youth, is spent?

O Nerina! e di te forse non odo
Questi luoghi parlar? caduta forse
Dal mio pensier sei tu? Dove sei gita,
Che qui sola di te la ricordanza
Trovo, dolcezza mia? Più non ti vede
Questa Terra natal: quella finestra,
Ond'eri usata favellarmi, ed onde
Mesto riluce delle stelle il raggio,
È deserta. Ove sei, che più non odo
La tua voce sonar, siccome un giorno,
Quando soleva ogni lontano accento
Del labbro tuo, ch'a me giungesse, il volto
Scolorarmi? Altro tempo. I giorni tuoi
Furo, mio dolce amor. Passasti. Ad altri
Il passar per la terra oggi è sortito,
E l'abitar questi odorati colli.
Ma rapida passasti; e come un sogno
Fu la tua vita. Ivi danzando; in fronte
La gioia ti splendea, splendea negli occhi
Quel confidente immaginar, quel lume
Di gioventù, quando spegneali il fato,
E giacevi. Ahi Nerina! In cor mi regna
L'antico amor. Se a feste anco talvolta,
Se a radunanze io movo, infra me stesso
Dico: o Nerina, a radunanze, a feste
Tu non ti acconci più, tu più non movi.
Se torna maggio, e ramoscelli e suoni
Van gli amanti recando alle fanciulle,
Dico: Nerina mia, per te non torna
Primavera giammai, non torna amore.

O Nerina! Isn't it of you
I hear these places speaking?
Could I have possibly forgotten you?
Where have you gone, that all that I find here
are memories of you, my sweetness?
This Earth where you were born sees you no more:
that window where you used to talk to me,
and which reflects the sad light of the stars,
is empty. Where are you, that I no longer
hear your voice the way I did,
when the slightest murmur from your lips
would turn me pale? Another time.
Your days are over, my sweet love.
You left.
Others walk the earth today
and live in these fragrant hills.
But you went quickly; and your life
was like a dream. You danced; joy glistened
on your forehead, and that confident
imagining, the light of youth,
shone in your eyes,
till fate extinguished them
and you fell. Ah, Nerina! The old love
rules in my heart. If now and then I go
to gatherings or parties, I say to myself:
O Nerina, you no longer dress your hair
or go to gatherings. When May returns
and boys give flowering branches to their girls
and sing to them, I say: My Nerina, neither spring
nor love will ever come for you again.

Ogni giorno sereno, ogni fiorita
Piaggia ch'io miro, ogni goder ch'io sento,
Dico: Nerina or più non gode; i campi,
L'aria non mira. Ahi tu passasti, eterno
Sospiro mio: passasti: e fia compagna
D'ogni mio vago immaginar, di tutti
I miei teneri sensi, i tristi e cari
Moti del cor, la rimembranza acerba.

Each brilliant day, each blooming hill I see,
whatever pleases me, I say:
Nothing can please Nerina now. She doesn't see
the fields, the air. You're gone,
lifelong regret of mine, you're gone;
and the bitter memory will last
with all my fond imagining, each tender feeling,
and every sad, sweet motion of my heart.

XXIII

CANTO NOTTURNO DI UN PASTORE ERRANTE DELL'ASIA

Che fai tu, luna, in ciel? dimmi, che fai,
Silenziosa luna?
Sorgi la sera, e vai,
Contemplando i deserti; indi ti posi.
Ancor non sei tu paga
Di riandare i sempiterni calli?
Ancor non prendi a schivo, ancor sei vaga
Di mirar queste valli?
Somiglia alla tua vita
La vita del pastore.
Sorge in sul primo albore;
Move la greggia oltre pel campo, e vede
Greggi, fontane ed erbe;
Poi stanco si riposa in su la sera:
Altro mai non ispera.
Dimmi, o luna: a che vale
Al pastor la sua vita,
La vostra vita a voi? dimmi: ove tende
Questo vagar mio breve,
Il tuo corso immortale?

XXIII

NIGHT SONG OF A WANDERING SHEPHERD IN ASIA

What are you doing, moon, up in the sky;
what are you doing, tell me, silent moon?
You rise at night and go,
observing the deserts. Then you set.
Aren't you tired
of plying the eternal byways?
Aren't you bored? Do you still want
to look down on these valleys?
The shepherd's life
is like your life.
He rises at first light,
moves his flock across the fields, and sees
sheep, springs, and grass,
then, weary, rests at evening,
and hopes for nothing more.
Tell me, moon, what good
is the shepherd's life to him
or yours to you? Tell me: where is it tending,
my brief wandering,
your immortal journey?

Vecchierel bianco, infermo,
Mezzo vestito e scalzo,
Con gravissimo fascio in su le spalle,
Per montagna e per valle,
Per sassi acuti, ed alta rena, e fratte,
Al vento, alla tempesta, e quando avvampa
L'ora, e quando poi gela,
Corre via, corre, anela,
Varca torrenti e stagni,
Cade, risorge, e più e più s'affretta,
Senza posa o ristoro,
Lacero, sanguinoso; infin ch'arriva
Colà dove la via
E dove il tanto affaticar fu volto:
Abisso orrido, immenso,
Ov'ei precipitando, il tutto obblia.
Vergine luna, tale
È la vita mortale.

Nasce l'uomo a fatica,
Ed è rischio di morte il nascimento.
Prova pena e tormento
Per prima cosa; e in sul principio stesso
La madre e il genitore
Il prende a consolar dell'esser nato.
Poi che crescendo viene,
L'uno e l'altro il sostiene, e via pur sempre
Con atti e con parole
Studiasi fargli core,
E consolarlo dell'umano stato:

Little old white-haired man,
weak, half naked, barefoot,
with an enormous burden on his back,
up mountain and down valley,
over sharp rocks, across deep sands and bracken,
through wind and storm,
in hot and freezing weather,
runs on, running till he's out of breath,
crosses rivers, wades through swamps,
falls and climbs and rushes on
ever faster, no rest or relief,
battered, bloodied; till at last he comes
to where his way
and all his effort led him:
terrible, immense abyss
into which he falls, forgetting everything.
This, O virgin moon,
is human life.

Man is born by labor,
and birth itself means risking death.
The first thing he feels
is pain and torment, and from the start
mother and father
seek to comfort him for being born.
As he grows,
they nurture him,
and constantly by word and deed
they seek to instill courage,
consoling him for being human.

Altro ufficio più grato
Non si fa da parenti alla lor prole.
Ma perchè dare al sole,
Perchè reggere in vita
Chi poi di quella consolar convenga?
Se la vita è sventura,
Perchè da noi si dura?
Intatta luna, tale
È lo stato mortale.
Ma tu mortal non sei,
E forse del mio dir poco ti cale.

Pur tu, solinga, eterna peregrina,
Che sì pensosa sei, tu forse intendi,
Questo viver terreno,
Il patir nostro, il sospirar, che sia;
Che sia questo morir, questo supremo
Scolorar del sembiante,
E perir dalla terra, e venir meno
Ad ogni usata, amante compagnia.
E tu certo comprendi
Il perchè delle cose, e vedi il frutto
Del mattin, della sera,
Del tacito, infinito andar del tempo.
Tu sai, tu certo, a qual suo dolce amore
Rida la primavera,
A chi giovi l'ardore, e che procacci
Il verno co' suoi ghiacci.
Mille cose sai tu, mille discopri,
Che son celate al semplice pastore.

Parents can do no more loving thing
for their children.
But why bring to light,
why educate
someone we'll console for living later?
If life is misery,
why do we bear it?
This, unblemished moon,
is mortal nature.
But you're not mortal,
and what I say may matter little to you.

Yet you, eternal solitary wanderer,
you who are so pensive,
understand this life on earth, perhaps,
what our suffering and sighing is,
what this death is, this last
paling of the face,
and leaving earth behind, deserting
all familiar, loving company.
And certainly you comprehend
the why of things, and see the usefulness
of morning, evening,
and the silent, endless pace of time.
Certainly you know for whose sweet love
spring smiles,
who enjoys the heat,
and what winter and its ice are for.
You know and understand a thousand things
that are hidden to a simple shepherd.

Spesso quand'io ti miro
Star così muta in sul deserto piano,
Che, in suo giro lontano, al ciel confina;
Ovver con la mia greggia
Seguirmi viaggiando a mano a mano;
E quando miro in cielo arder le stelle;
Dico fra me pensando:
A che tante facelle?
Che fa l'aria infinita, e quel profondo
Infinito seren? che vuol dir questa
Solitudine immensa? ed io che sono?
Così meco ragiono: e della stanza
Smisurata e superba,
E dell'innumerabile famiglia;
Poi di tanto adoprar, di tanti moti
D'ogni celeste, ogni terrena cosa,
Girando senza posa,
Per tornar sempre là donde son mosse;
Uso alcuno, alcun frutto
Indovinar non so. Ma tu per certo,
Giovinetta immortal, conosci il tutto.
Questo io conosco e sento,
Che degli eterni giri,
Che dell'esser mio frale,
Qualche bene o contento
Avrà fors'altri; a me la vita è male.

O greggia mia che posi, oh te beata,
Che la miseria tua, credo, non sai!
Quanta invidia ti porto!

Often, when I watch you
standing still above the empty plain
whose last horizon closes with the sky,
or moving with me step by step
as I wander with my flock,
or when I see the stars burn up in heaven,
I ask myself:
Why all these lights?
What does the endless air do, and that deep
eternal blue? What is the meaning of
this huge solitude? And what am I?
I ask myself: about this boundless,
wondrous space
and its numberless inhabitants,
and all these works and all this movement
of all heavenly and earthly things,
revolving without rest,
only to return to where they started;
any purpose, any usefulness
I cannot see. But you, immortal maiden,
surely understand it all.
This I know and feel:
that from the eternal motions,
from my fragile being,
others may derive
some good or gladness; life for me is wrong.

O resting flock of mine, you blessed beings,
who don't, I think, know your own misery!
How I envy you!

Non sol perchè d'affanno
Quasi libera vai;
Ch'ogni stento, ogni danno,
Ogni estremo timor subito scordi;
Ma più perchè giammai tedio non provi.
Quando tu siedi all'ombra, sovra l'erbe,
Tu se' queta e contenta;
E gran parte dell'anno
Senza noia consumi in quello stato.
Ed io pur seggo sovra l'erbe, all'ombra,
E un fastidio m'ingombra
La mente, ed uno spron quasi mi punge
Sì che, sedendo, più che mai son lunge
Da trovar pace o loco.
E pur nulla non bramo,
E non ho fino a qui cagion di pianto.
Quel che tu goda o quanto,
Non so già dir; ma fortunata sei.
Ed io godo ancor poco,
O greggia mia, nè di ciò sol mi lagno.
Se tu parlar sapessi, io chiederei:
Dimmi: perchè giacendo
A bell'agio, ozioso,
S'appaga ogni animale;
Me, s'io giaccio in riposo, il tedio assale?

Forse s'avess'io l'ale
Da volar su le nubi,
E noverar le stelle ad una ad una,
O come il tuono errar di giogo in giogo,

Not just because you move
as if nearly trouble-free
and soon forget each need, each pain,
each deathly fear,
but more because you're never bored.
When you lie down in the shade,
on the grass, you're calm, content,
and so you spend the great part of the year
and feel no boredom.
I sit on the grass, too, in the shade,
but an anxiousness invades my mind
as if a thorn were pricking me,
so that sitting there I'm even further
from finding peace or resting place.
Yet I want nothing, and thus far
I have no reason for complaint.
What you enjoy or how,
I can't say, but you're fortunate.
I enjoy much less, O flock of mine,
but it's not only this I mourn.
If you could speak, I'd ask you:
Tell me why it is
all animals are happy
resting, at ease, while I, if I lie down,
am plagued with tedium?

Maybe if I had wings
to fly above the clouds
and count the stars out one by one,
or, like thunder, graze from peak to peak,

Più felice sarei, dolce mia greggia,
Più felice sarei, candida luna.
O forse erra dal vero,
Mirando all'altrui sorte, il mio pensiero:
Forse in qual forma, in quale
Stato che sia, dentro covile o cuna,
È funesto a chi nasce il dì natale.

I'd be happier, my gentle flock,
happier, bright moon.
Or maybe my mind's straying from the truth,
imagining the destinies of others.
Maybe in whatever form or state,
be it in stall or cradle,
the day we're born is cause for mourning.

XXIV

LA QUIETE DOPO LA TEMPESTA

Passata è la tempesta:
Odo augelli far festa, e la gallina,
Tornata in su la via,
Che ripete il suo verso. Ecco il sereno
Rompe là da ponente, alla montagna;
Sgombrasi la campagna,
E chiaro nella valle il fiume appare.
Ogni cor si rallegra, in ogni lato
Risorge il romorio
Torna il lavoro usato.
L'artigiano a mirar l'umido cielo,
Con l'opra in man, cantando,
Fassi in su l'uscio; a prova
Vien fuor la femminetta a còr dell'acqua
Della novella piova;
E l'erbaiuol rinnova
Di sentiero in sentiero
Il grido giornaliero.
Ecco il Sol che ritorna, ecco sorride
Per li poggi e le ville. Apre i balconi,
Apre terrazzi e logge la famiglia:
E, dalla via corrente, odi lontano
Tintinnio di sonagli; il carro stride
Del passegger che il suo cammin ripiglia.

XXIV

THE CALM AFTER THE STORM

The storm is over:
I hear birds rejoicing, and the hen
is back in the road,
repeating her song. See, brightness
breaks through in the west, above the hills.
The countryside unveils,
and the river shimmers in the valley.
Every heart is happy,
and everywhere the hum revives,
the day's work starts anew.
The artisan comes to his door
singing, with his work in hand,
and stares up at the glistening sky. The young girl
rushes out to gather
fresh rainwater,
and the vegetable seller shouts
his daily shout again
from lane to lane.
Here's the Sun returning, see him smile
on hills and farms. The servants
open windows, terraces, and loggias.
And from the highway I can hear
bells chiming in the distance; the carriage screams
as the traveler sets off again.

Si rallegra ogni core.
Sì dolce, sì gradita
Quand'è, com'or, la vita?
Quando con tanto amore
L'uomo a' suoi studi intende?
O torna all'opre? o cosa nova imprende?
Quando de' mali suoi men si ricorda?
Piacer figlio d'affanno;
Gioia vana, ch'è frutto
Del passato timore, onde si scosse
E paventò la morte
Chi la vita abborria;
Onde in lungo tormento,
Fredde, tacite, smorte,
Sudàr le genti e palpitàr, vedendo
Mossi alle nostre offese
Folgori, nembi e vento.

O natura cortese,
Son questi i doni tuoi,
Questi i diletti sono
Che tu porgi ai mortali. Uscir di pena
È diletto fra noi.
Pene tu spargi a larga mano; il duolo
Spontaneo sorge: e di piacer, quel tanto
Che per mostro e miracolo talvolta
Nasce d'affanno, è gran guadagno. Umana
Prole cara agli eterni! assai felice
Se respirar ti lice
D'alcun dolor: beata
Se te d'ogni dolor morte risana.

Every heart is happy.
When is life as sweet,
as much enjoyed as now?
When does a man attend to what he does
with such devotion?
Return to work, or take up something new?
When is he less conscious of his troubles?
Pleasure, child of suffering,
empty joy, effect
of dread that's past
which made the man who hated life
tremble with fear of death,
which turned the people
cold and mute and pale
and made them sweat and shiver in long torment
seeing lightning, clouds, and wind
arrayed against us.

O gentle Nature,
these are what you give us,
these are the delights
you offer mortals. Surcease from suffering
is happiness for us.
You dole pain with a liberal hand: grieving
rises spontaneous, and the brief enjoyment
that now and then by miracle and marvel
is born of anguish, is great gain.
Race of men beloved of the immortals!
Happy indeed if you're allowed
relief from sorrow, blessed when
death cures you of all sorrow.

XXV

IL SABATO DEL VILLAGGIO

La donzelletta vien dalla campagna,
In sul calar del sole,
Col suo fascio dell'erba; e reca in mano
Un mazzolin di rose e di viole,
Onde, siccome suole,
Ornare ella si appresta
Dimani, al dì di festa, il petto e il crine.
Siede con le vicine
Su la scala a filar la vecchierella,
Incontro là dove si perde il giorno;
E novellando vien del suo buon tempo,
Quando ai dì della festa ella si ornava,
Ed ancor sana e snella
Solea danzar la sera intra di quei
Ch'ebbe compagni dell'età più bella.
Già tutta l'aria imbruna,
Torna azzurro il sereno, e tornan l'ombre
Giù da' colli e da' tetti,
Al biancheggiar della recente luna.
Or la squilla dà segno
Della festa che viene;
Ed a quel suon diresti
Che il cor si riconforta.

XXV

SATURDAY IN THE VILLAGE

The girl comes in from the country
as the sun is setting, carrying
her sheaf of grass, and in her hand
she holds a bunch of violets and roses
that, as always, she intends to use
to decorate her breast and hair
tomorrow, on the holiday.
The little old crone sits on the stairs
and spins with her neighbors,
facing where day is dying,
and goes on telling stories of her good times,
when she adorned herself on Sundays, too,
and danced the night away,
still light and lithe,
in her salad days, with all her beaux.
Now the air is darkening everywhere,
the sky turns blue again, and shadows
fall again from hills and roofs,
while the new moon goes white.
Now the bell announces
the coming holiday,
and you could say
the heart takes comfort at the sound.

I fanciulli gridando
Su la piazzuola in frotta,
E qua e là saltando,
Fanno un lieto romore:
E intanto riede alla sua parca mensa,
Fischiando, il zappatore,
E seco pensa al dì del suo riposo.

Poi quando intorno è spenta ogni altra face,
E tutto l'altro tace,
Odi il martel picchiare, odi la sega
Del legnaiuol, che veglia
Nella chiusa bottega alla lucerna,
E s'affretta, e s'adopra
Di fornir l'opra anzi il chiarir dell'alba.

Questo di sette è il più gradito giorno,
Pien di speme e di gioia:
Diman tristezza e noia
Recheran l'ore, ed al travaglio usato
Ciascuno in suo pensier farà ritorno.

Garzoncello scherzoso,
Cotesta età fiorita
È come un giorno d'allegrezza pieno,
Giorno chiaro, sereno,
Che precorre alla festa di tua vita.
Godi, fanciullo mio; stato soave,
Stagion lieta è cotesta.
Altro dirti non vo'; ma la tua festa
Ch'anco tardi a venir non ti sia grave.

The crowd of children
shouting in the little square
and running everywhere
make happy noises,
while the cobbler
goes home, whistling, to his frugal meal,
looking forward to his day of rest.

Later, when every other light around is out,
and everything besides is still,
you hear the beating hammer and the saw
of the carpenter,
up late in his shuttered shop,
hurrying as he works by lantern light
to have his job done before dawn.

This day is the most welcome of the seven,
alive with hope and joy.
Tomorrow time again will bring
sadness and boredom, and everyone
will turn back to his old preoccupations.

Playful boy,
this time in bloom
is like a day alive with happiness:
bright day, bright blue prelude
to the feast day of your life.
Enjoy it, son of mine: it is a gentle
hour, a radiant moment.
I won't say more, but may your Sunday
that is so slow to come not disappoint you.

XXVI

IL PENSIERO DOMINANTE

Dolcissimo, possente
Dominator di mia profonda mente;
Terribile, ma caro
Dono del ciel; consorte
Ai lúgubri miei giorni,
Pensier che innanzi a me sì spesso torni.

Di tua natura arcana
Chi non favella? il suo poter fra noi
Chi non sentì? Pur sempre
Che in dir gli effetti suoi
Le umane lingue il sentir propio sprona,
Par novo ad ascoltar ciò ch'ei ragiona.

Come solinga è fatta
La mente mia d'allora
Che tu quivi prendesti a far dimora!
Ratto d'intorno intorno al par del lampo
Gli altri pensieri miei
Tutti si dileguàr. Siccome torre
In solitario campo,
Tu stai solo, gigante, in mezzo a lei.

XXVI

THE DOMINANT IDEA

Sweetest, potent
lord of my profoundest mind,
terrible but precious
gift of heaven, companion of
my grieving days,
idea that recurs to me so often.

Who doesn't speak
of your mysterious nature?
Who hasn't felt its power among us?
Yet, whenever their emotion
moves men to explain your influence,
what they have to say seems new to hear.

How single-minded
has my mind become
ever since you took up residence.
As swift as lightning
any other idea of mine
vanished everywhere around.
Like a tower in an empty field,
you stand alone, gigantic, in my thinking.

Che divenute son, fuor di te solo,
Tutte l'opre terrene,
Tutta intera la vita al guardo mio!
Che intollerabil noia
Gli ozi, i commerci usati,
E di vano piacer la vana spene,
Allato a quella gioia,
Gioia celeste che da te mi viene!

Come da' nudi sassi
Dello scabro Apennino
A un campo verde che lontan sorrida
Volge gli occhi bramoso il pellegrino;
Tal io dal secco ed aspro
Mondano conversar vogliosamente,
Quasi in lieto giardino, a te ritorno,
E ristora i miei sensi il tuo soggiorno.

Quasi incredibil parmi
Che la vita infelice e il mondo sciocco
Già per gran tempo assai
Senza te sopportai;
Quasi intender non posso
Come d'altri desiri,
Fuor ch'a te somiglianti, altri sospiri.

Giammai d'allor che in pria
Questa vita che sia per prova intesi,
Timor di morte non mi strinse il petto.
Oggi mi pare un gioco

What are they in my eyes now
next to you,
all earthly works, the whole of life!
What intolerable boredom
are idleness and small talk
and the empty hope for empty pleasure,
next to the joy, the heavenly joy
that comes to me from you!

As from the barren boulders
of the craggy Apennine
the pilgrim turns his eager eyes
toward a green field smiling in the distance,
so I from arid, acrid,
worldly chatter willingly
return to you as to a joyous garden,
and my stay with you restores my senses.

It seems almost incredible to me
that I endured unhappy life
and the idiotic world
so long without you.
I can barely understand
how another man can sigh
desiring something else that isn't like you.

Before this I had no experience
that told me what this world is like,
fear of dying didn't grip my heart.
Today extreme necessity,

Quella che il mondo inetto,
Talor lodando, ognora abborre e trema,
Necessitade estrema;
E se periglio appar, con un sorriso
Le sue minacce a contemplar m'affiso.

Sempre i codardi, e l'alme
Ingenerose, abbiette
Ebbi in dispregio. Or punge ogni atto indegno
Subito i sensi miei;
Move l'alma ogni esempio
Dell'umana viltà subito a sdegno.
Di questa età superba,
Che di vote speranze si nutrica,
Vaga di ciance, e di virtù nemica;
Stolta, che l'util chiede,
E inutile la vita
Quindi più sempre divenir non vede;
Maggior mi sento. A scherno
Ho gli umani giudizi; e il vario volgo
A' bei pensieri infesto,
E degno tuo disprezzator, calpesto.

A quello onde tu movi,
Quale affetto non cede?
Anzi qual altro affetto
Se non quell'uno intra i mortali ha sede?
Avarizia, superbia, odio, disdegno,
Studio d'onor, di regno,
Che sono altro che voglie

which the inept world abhors and dreads,
though they sometimes praise it,
seems ridiculous.
And if danger comes, I steel myself
to contemplate its menace with a smile.

I've always had contempt
for cowards and ungenerous, mean spirits.
Now each unworthy act offends me instantly;
every type of human baseness
swiftly moves my spirit to disdain.
I disdain this prideful age,
which feeds itself on empty hopes,
in love with slogans, enemy of virtue,
this foolish age, which wants what's useful
and so doesn't see that life
is becoming constantly more useless.
I feel superior, and have contempt
for human judgment; and the motley crowd,
the enemies of beautiful ideas
who by nature denigrate you,
I trample on.

What love doesn't give up pride of place
to the one from which you move?
Indeed, what other love holds sway
among mortal men but this?
Greed, pride, hatred, and disdain,
desire for honor and the crown—
what are these but vulgar hankerings

Al paragon di lui? Solo un affetto
Vive tra noi: quest'uno,
Prepotente signore,
Dieder l'eterne leggi all'uman core.

Pregio non ha, non ha ragion la vita
Se non per lui, per lui ch'all'uomo è tutto;
Sola discolpa al fato,
Che noi mortali in terra
Pose a tanto patir senz'altro frutto;
Solo per cui talvolta,
Non alla gente stolta, al cor non vile
La vita della morte è più gentile.

Per còr le gioie tue, dolce pensiero,
Provar gli umani affanni,
E sostener molt'anni
Questa vita mortal, fu non indegno;
Ed ancor tornerei,
Così qual son de' nostri mali esperto,
Verso un tal segno a incominciare il corso:
Che tra le sabbie e tra il vipereo morso,
Giammai finor sì stanco
Per lo mortal deserto
Non venni a te, che queste nostre pene
Vincer non mi paresse un tanto bene.

Che mondo mai, che nova
Immensità, che paradiso è quello
Là dove spesso il tuo stupendo incanto

compared to it? One love alone
lives among us: the eternal laws
gave it to the human heart,
as its all-commanding lord.

Life has no worth, no reason
but this, which is everything to man.
In itself, it exculpates
fate, which put us mortals here on earth
to suffer so much for no other reason.
Only because of this sometimes,
not for the foolish but the valiant heart,
can life be more beautiful than death.

To harvest your joys, sweet idea,
it was worth knowing human suffering,
worth enduring
this mortal life for all these years.
And I'd come back again,
I who am so expert in our pain,
to take the road again to such a goal.
For never till now did I journey to you
across the mortal desert,
among its sands and stinging vipers,
so worn out that vanquishing
these pains of ours did not seem a great good.

What a world, what new immensity,
what a paradise it is
your overwhelming magic

Parmi innalzar! dov'io,
Sott'altra luce che l'usata errando,
Il mio terreno stato
E tutto quanto il ver pongo in obblio!
Tali son, credo, i sogni
Degl'immortali. Ahi finalmente un sogno
In molta parte onde s'abbella il vero
Sei tu, dolce pensiero;
Sogno e palese error. Ma di natura,
Infra i leggiadri errori,
Divina sei; perchè sì viva e forte,
Che incontro al ver tenacemente dura,
E spesso al ver s'adegua,
Nè si dilegua pria, che in grembo a morte.

E tu per certo, o mio pensier, tu solo
Vitale ai giorni miei,
Cagion diletta d'infiniti affanni,
Meco sarai per morte a un tempo spento:
Ch'a vivi segni dentro l'alma io sento
Che in perpetuo signor dato mi sei.
Altri gentili inganni
Soleami il vero aspetto
Più sempre infievolir. Quanto più torno
A riveder colei
Della qual teco ragionando io vivo,
Cresce quel gran diletto,
Cresce quel gran delirio, ond'io respiro.
Angelica beltade!
Parmi ogni più bel volto, ovunque io miro,

often seems to raise me to! Where, wandering
in another light than the usual,
I forget my earthly nature
and everything that's real!
Such are the immortals' dreams, I think.
In the end, in many ways,
you are a dream through which reality
becomes lovelier, sweet idea,
dream and patent error. But by nature,
among the pleasing errors you're divine;
because you're so alive and strong
that you hold up against the truth;
often you seem to be the truth,
and won't fade till we're in the lap of death.

But surely, O idea of mine,
you alone essential to my days,
beloved cause of endless suffering,
you'll be undone by death along with me:
for from strong signals in my soul I feel
you're given to me as my lord forever.
Other sweet illusions
would always weaken
the way that truth appeared to me.
But the more that I return
to see her whom I spend my life
telling about, the more the great joy grows,
the more that great delirium grows
by which I breathe. Angelic beauty!
Every lovely face, wherever I look,

Quasi una finta imago
Il tuo volto imitar. Tu sola fonte
D'ogni altra leggiadria,
Sola vera beltà parmi che sia.

Da che ti vidi pria,
Di qual mia seria cura ultimo obbietto
Non fosti tu? quanto del giorno è scorso,
Ch'io di te non pensassi? ai sogni miei
La tua sovrana imago
Quante volte mancò? Bella qual sogno,
Angelica sembianza,
Nella terrena stanza,
Nell'alte vie dell'universo intero,
Che chiedo io mai, che spero
Altro che gli occhi tuoi veder più vago?
Altro più dolce aver che il tuo pensiero?

seems like an image made
in imitation of your face.
You, only source of every other grace,
you seem to me to be the one true beauty.

   Since I first saw you,
what has the last object of my interest
been, if not you? How much of the day
passed without a thought of you?
How often was your sovereign image
gone from my dreams?
Lovely as a dream, angelic semblance,
in our earthly home or on the pathways
of the entire universe,
what more can I ask, what can I hope for,
than to see your eyes more radiant,
what sweeter thing to have than the thought of you?

XXVII

AMORE E MORTE

Ὃν οἱ θεοὶ φιλοῦσιν, ἀποθνήσκει νέος.

Muor giovane colui ch'al cielo è caro.

MENANDRO

Fratelli, a un tempo stesso, Amore e Morte
Ingenerò la sorte.
Cose quaggiù sì belle
Altre il mondo non ha, non han le stelle.
Nasce dall'uno il bene,
Nasce il piacer maggiore
Che per lo mar dell'essere si trova;
L'altra ogni gran dolore,
Ogni gran male annulla.
Bellissima fanciulla,
Dolce a veder, non quale
La si dipinge la codarda gente,
Gode il fanciullo Amore
Accompagnar sovente;
E sorvolano insiem la via mortale,
Primi conforti d'ogni saggio core.
Nè cor fu mai più saggio
Che percosso d'amor, nè mai più forte

XXVII

LOVE AND DEATH

Ὃν οἱ θεοὶ φιλοῦσιν, ἀποθνήσκει νέος.
He whom the gods love dies young.

MENANDER

Fate gave birth at one and the same time
to two siblings, Love and Death.
No other thing as beautiful
exists down here, or in the stars above.
Good is born of one,
the greatest pleasure
to be found upon the sea of being.
The other ends all major sorrow,
each worst wrong.
Often Love, the little boy, is pleased
to be the playmate of the lovely girl
who is delightful to behold,
not the way the craven crowd portrays her.
And they fly together
above life's highway,
the great comforts of all knowing hearts.
Nor was heart ever wiser
than when struck with love;

Sprezzò l'infausta vita,
Nè per altro signore
Come per questo a perigliar fu pronto:
Ch'ove tu porgi aita,
Amor, nasce il coraggio,
O si ridesta; e sapiente in opre,
Non in pensiero invan, siccome suole,
Divien l'umana prole.

Quando novellamente
Nasce nel cor profondo
Un amoroso affetto,
Languido e stanco insiem con esso in petto
Un desiderio di morir si sente:
Come, non so: ma tale
D'amor vero e possente è il primo effetto.
Forse gli occhi spaura
Allor questo deserto: a se la terra
Forse il mortale inabitabil fatta
Vede omai senza quella
Nova, sola, infinita
Felicità che il suo pensier figura:
Ma per cagion di lei grave procella
Presentendo in suo cor, brama quiete,
Brama raccorsi in porto
Dinanzi al fier disio,
Che già, rugghiando, intorno intorno oscura.

Poi, quando tutto avvolge
La formidabil possa,

never did it disdain unlucky life
more powerfully, nor was prepared to suffer
danger for any other lord:
for when you lend your hand, Love,
courage comes alive
or lives again, and human beings
turn wise in action,
not in empty thought, as is their wont.

When a loving feeling
is newborn deep within the heart,
at the same time
a languid and exhausted
wish to die arrives,
I don't know why; but this
is the first effect of true and potent love.
Maybe this desert terrifies the eyes then,
or the mortal
finds earth unlivable
without this new, unique, unending
happiness his mind conceives.
But sensing an ungovernable storm
brewing in his heart because of it,
he yearns for calm,
he yearns to come to port
ahead of fierce desire,
already roaring, turning the world dark.

Then when the terrifying power
envelops everything,

E fulmina nel cor l'invitta cura,
Quante volte implorata
Con desiderio intenso,
Morte, sei tu dall'affannoso amante!
Quante la sera, e quante
Abbandonando all'alba il corpo stanco,
Se beato chiamò s'indi giammai
Non rilevasse il fianco,
Nè tornasse a veder l'amara luce!
E spesso al suon della funebre squilla,
Al canto che conduce
La gente morta al sempiterno obblio,
Con più sospiri ardenti
Dall'imo petto invidiò colui
Che tra gli spenti ad abitar sen giva.
Fin la negletta plebe,
L'uom della villa, ignaro
D'ogni virtù che da saper deriva,
Fin la donzella timidetta e schiva,
Che già di morte al nome
Sentì rizzar le chiome,
Osa alla tomba, alle funeree bende
Fermar lo sguardo di costanza pieno,
Osa ferro e veleno
Meditar lungamente,
E nell'indotta mente
La gentilezza del morir comprende.
Tanto alla morte inclina
D'amor la disciplina. Anco sovente,
A tal venuto il gran travaglio interno

and undefeated fear
strikes lightning in the heart,
Death, how often are you called upon
with keen desire by the suffering lover!
How often in the evening,
how often nodding off at dawn exhausted,
would he say he was blessed
if he never had to move his bones again
or return to see the bitter light!
And at the sound of funeral bells,
the singing that accompanies the dead
to perpetual oblivion,
with many ardent sighs,
deep in his heart he envied him
who was going to stay with the dead.
Even simple people,
peasants, ignorant
of all the virtues that derive from knowledge,
even the timid, bashful girl
who feels her hair stand on end
at the very name of death,
dares to stare unflinchingly
at the tomb and widow's weeds,
dares to meditate at length
on iron and poison,
and in her uneducated mind
she understands death's gentleness.
So the law of love
inclines toward death.
And often the war within them is so great

Che sostener nol può forza mortale,
O cede il corpo frale
Ai terribili moti, e in questa forma
Pel fraterno poter Morte prevale;
O così sprona Amor là nel profondo,
Che da se stessi il villanello ignaro,
La tenera donzella
Con la man violenta
Pongon le membra giovanili in terra.
Ride ai lor casi il mondo,
A cui pace e vecchiezza il ciel consenta.

Ai fervidi, ai felici,
Agli animosi ingegni
L'uno o l'altro di voi conceda il fato,
Dolci signori, amici
All'umana famiglia,
Al cui poter nessun poter somiglia
Nell'immenso universo, e non l'avanza,
Se non quella del fato, altra possanza.
E tu, cui già dal cominciar degli anni
Sempre onorata invoco,
Bella Morte, pietosa
Tu sola al mondo dei terreni affanni,
Se celebrata mai
Fosti da me, s'al tuo divino stato
L'onte del volgo ingrato
Ricompensar tentai,
Non tardar più, t'inchina
A disusati preghi,

that humans lack the power to resist it.
Either the frail body
surrenders to its awful turbulence,
and Death prevails through her sibling's power,
or else Love wounds so deeply
that on their own the ignorant
peasant or the tender girl
bring their own young bodies
down by force.
The world, which heaven guarantees
peace and old age, derides their fate.

May destiny grant
to fervent, glad, courageous minds
one or the other of you,
gentle lords,
the human family's friends,
whose power no power
in the enormous universe can match,
and whom no might surpasses, except fate.
And you, whom from my earliest years
I've always honored,
lovely Death, who only in the world
pities earthly suffering,
if ever you were praised by me,
if ever I attempted
to answer the disdain
of the ungrateful crowd,
delay no longer,
answer these uncommon prayers,

Chiudi alla luce omai
Questi occhi tristi, o dell'età reina.
Me certo troverai, qual si sia l'ora
Che tu le penne al mio pregar dispieghi,
Erta la fronte, armato,
E renitente al fato,
La man che flagellando si colora
Nel mio sangue innocente
Non ricolmar di lode,
Non benedir, com'usa
Per antica viltà l'umana gente;
Ogni vana speranza onde consola
Se coi fanciulli il mondo,
Ogni conforto stolto
Gittar da me; null'altro in alcun tempo
Sperar, se non te sola;
Solo aspettar sereno
Quel dì ch'io pieghi addormentato il volto
Nel tuo virgineo seno.

shut these sad eyes now on the light,
O queen of time.
Surely you'll find me, at whatever hour
you spread your wings in answer to my prayers,
head held high,
armed, and resisting fate.
Don't weigh with praise
the hand that, whipping me,
is colored with my blameless blood;
don't glorify it as man does,
out of age-old cowardice.
Toss away from me
every vain desire with which the world
childishly consoles itself,
all foolish comfort. Let me never hope for anything
but you alone;
may I only wait serenely for
the day I'll lay my sleeping face
on your virgin breast.

XXVIII

A SE STESSO

Or poserai per sempre,
Stanco mio cor. Perì l'inganno estremo,
Ch'eterno io mi credei. Perì. Ben sento,
In noi di cari inganni,
Non che la speme, il desiderio è spento.
Posa per sempre. Assai
Palpitasti. Non val cosa nessuna
I moti tuoi, nè di sospiri è degna
La terra. Amaro e noia
La vita, altro mai nulla; e fango è il mondo.
T'acqueta omai. Dispera
L'ultima volta. Al gener nostro il fato
Non donò che il morire. Omai disprezza
Te, la natura, il brutto
Poter che, ascoso, a comun danno impera,
E l'infinita vanità del tutto.

XXVIII

TO HIMSELF

Now you'll rest forever,
worn-out heart. The ultimate illusion
that I thought was eternal died. It died.
I know not just the hope but the desire
for loved illusions is done for us.
Be still forever.
You have beaten enough.
Nothing deserves your throbbing, nor is earth
worth sighing over. Life is only
bitterness and boredom, and the world is filth.
Now be calm. Despair for the last time.
Death is the one thing
fate gave our kind.
Disdain yourself now, nature, the brute
hidden power that rules to common harm,
and the boundless vanity of all.

XXIX

ASPASIA

Torna dinanzi al mio pensier talora
Il tuo sembiante, Aspasia. O fuggitivo
Per abitati lochi a me lampeggia
In altri volti; o per deserti campi,
Al dì sereno, alle tacenti stelle,
Da soave armonia quasi ridesta,
Nell'alma a sgomentarsi ancor vicina
Quella superba vision risorge.
Quanto adorata, o numi, e quale un giorno
Mia delizia ed erinni! E mai non sento
Mover profumo di fiorita piaggia,
Nè di fiori olezzar vie cittadine,
Ch'io non ti vegga ancor qual eri il giorno
Che ne' vezzosi appartamenti accolta,
Tutti odorati de' novelli fiori
Di primavera, del color vestita
Della bruna viola, a me si offerse
L'angelica tua forma, inchino il fianco
Sovra nitide pelli, e circonfusa
D'arcana voluttà; quando tu, dotta
Allettatrice, fervidi sonanti
Baci scoccavi nelle curve labbra
De' tuoi bambini, il niveo collo intanto

XXIX

ASPASIA

Sometimes your image comes to mind again,
Aspasia. Either it shines fleetingly
in lived-in places, in other faces;
or in the empty fields, on a clear day,
under the silent stars,
as if evoked by gentle harmony,
that exalted vision reappears
in a soul still verging on dismay.
How adored, O gods! and what delight
and torment once! And I never smell
the fragrant breeze along a blooming shore,
or city streets perfumed with flowers,
that I don't see you as you were
that day when, in those lovely rooms
all scented with the spring's first blossoms,
I was first shown your angelic form
dressed in dark violet, and I bent
to greet you in the flesh,
veiled in secret sensuality,
while you, expert enticer,
showered fervent, noisy kisses
on the pursed lips of your children,
inclining your snowy neck just so,

Porgendo, e lor di tue cagioni ignari
Con la man leggiadrissima stringevi
Al seno ascoso e desiato. Apparve
Novo ciel, nova terra, e quasi un raggio
Divino al pensier mio. Così nel fianco
Non punto inerme a viva forza impresse
Il tuo braccio lo stral, che poscia fitto
Ululando portai finch'a quel giorno
Si fu due volte ricondotto il sole.

Raggio divino al mio pensiero apparve,
Donna, la tua beltà. Simile effetto
Fan la bellezza e i musicali accordi,
Ch'alto mistero d'ignorati Elisi
Paion sovente rivelar. Vagheggia
Il piagato mortal quindi la figlia
Della sua mente, l'amorosa idea,
Che gran parte d'Olimpo in se racchiude,
Tutta al volto ai costumi alla favella
Pari alla donna che il rapito amante
Vagheggiare ed amar confuso estima.
Or questa egli non già, ma quella, ancora
Nei corporali amplessi, inchina ed ama.
Alfin l'errore e gli scambiati oggetti
Conoscendo, s'adira; e spesso incolpa
La donna a torto. A quella eccelsa imago
Sorge di rado il femminile ingegno;
E ciò che inspira ai generosi amanti
La sua stessa beltà, donna non pensa,
Nè comprender potria. Non cape in quelle
Anguste fronti ugual concetto. E male

and held them, unaware of your intentions,
with your very graceful hand
to your open, much-desired breast.
To me it seemed new heaven, new earth,
almost a ray of heavenly light. And so,
into my not-at-all-protected side,
your arm let fly its arrow with great force,
which I carried lodged in me, lamenting,
till the sun had twice come to that day.

Lady, your beauty was a ray of heavenly
light to my thinking. Beauty and musical
harmony have similar effects,
for it often seems that they reveal
the mysteries of hidden Paradises.
So the wounded mortal dreams
the daughter of his mind, the amorous idea,
this high thing he keeps largely to himself,
in face, in habits, and expression equal
to the one the enraptured lover wants
to dream about and love in his confusion;
yet it's not she whom he reveres and loves,
even as he holds her, but the other.
At last he sees the error of his misplaced
feelings and becomes enraged, and often
wrongly blames the woman. Rarely
does feminine nature rise to this high ideal.
And what inspires her noble lovers,
her very beauty, woman doesn't see
and isn't capable of understanding;
their narrow minds can't take in such ideas.

Al vivo sfolgorar di quegli sguardi
Spera l'uomo ingannato, e mal richiede
Sensi profondi, sconosciuti, e molto
Più che virili, in chi dell'uomo al tutto
Da natura è minor. Che se più molli
E più tenui le membra, essa la mente
Men capace e men forte anco riceve.

Nè tu finor giammai quel che tu stessa
Inspirasti alcun tempo al mio pensiero,
Potesti, Aspasia, immaginar. Non sai
Che smisurato amor, che affanni intensi,
Che indicibili moti e che deliri
Movesti in me; nè verrà tempo alcuno
Che tu l'intenda. In simil guisa ignora
Esecutor di musici concenti
Quel ch'ei con mano o con la voce adopra
In chi l'ascolta. Or quell'Aspasia è morta
Che tanto amai. Giace per sempre, oggetto
Della mia vita un dì: se non se quanto,
Pur come cara larva, ad ora ad ora
Tornar costuma e disparir. Tu vivi,
Bella non solo ancor, ma bella tanto,
Al parer mio, che tutte l'altre avanzi.
Pur quell'ardor che da te nacque è spento:
Perch'io te non amai, ma quella Diva
Che già vita, or sepolcro, ha nel mio core.
Quella adorai gran tempo; e sì mi piacque
Sua celeste beltà, ch'io, per insino
Già dal principio conoscente e chiaro
Dell'esser tuo, dell'arti e delle frodi,

In the bright flash of her looks
the bewitched man wrongly hopes for, wrongly seeks,
deep, mysterious, and much more than manly
understanding, in one who naturally
is less than man in everything. For if her limbs
are softer and more tender, she's also given
a mind that's less capacious and less strong.

Nor could you, Aspasia,
ever imagine what you once inspired
in my mind. You don't know
what boundless love, what powerful suffering,
what indescribable emotions and delirium
you aroused in me, nor will there be a time
when you will understand. In a like way,
he who creates harmonies in music
is ignorant of the effect his hand or voice
has on his listener. The Aspasia I loved
so deeply is dead now. She who was once
the object of my life now rests forever.
If not as this, still as a cherished shade,
she now and then returns, and disappears.
You live, not simply lovely now, but still
so lovely in my eyes that you surpass all others.
But the ardor that was born of you has died,
because it wasn't you I loved, but the Goddess
who lived once but now is buried in my heart.
I worshipped her a long time, and her celestial
beauty so enthralled me that although
I was aware and clear from the beginning
as to your nature, your artifice and falseness,

Pur ne' tuoi contemplando i suoi begli occhi,
Cupido ti seguii finch'ella visse,
Ingannato non già, ma dal piacere
Di quella dolce somiglianza un lungo
Servaggio ed aspro a tollerar condotto.
Or ti vanta, che il puoi. Narra che sola
Sei del tuo sesso a cui piegar sostenni
L'altero capo, a cui spontaneo porsi
L'indomito mio cor. Narra che prima,
E spero ultima certo, il ciglio mio
Supplichevol vedesti, a te dinanzi
Me timido, tremante (ardo in ridirlo
Di sdegno e di rossor), me di me privo,
Ogni tua voglia, ogni parola, ogni atto
Spiar sommessamente, a' tuoi superbi
Fastidi impallidir, brillare in volto
Ad un segno cortese, ad ogni sguardo
Mutar forma e color. Cadde l'incanto,
E spezzato con esso, a terra sparso
Il giogo: onde m'allegro. E sebben pieni
Di tedio, alfin dopo il servire e dopo
Un lungo vaneggiar, contento abbraccio
Senno con libertà. Che se d'affetti
Orba la vita, e di gentili errori,
È notte senza stelle a mezzo il verno,
Già del fato mortale a me bastante
E conforto e vendetta è che su l'erba
Qui neghittoso immobile giacendo,
Il mar la terra e il ciel miro e sorrido.

still gazing on her lovely eyes in yours,
I eagerly obeyed you while she lived,
not really fooled, but led on by the pleasure
of that sweet resemblance to endure
a long and bitter servitude.
Now boast, because you can. Announce that you're
the one of all your sex who made me bend
my proud head, the one to whom I freely
gave my unvanquished heart.
Say you were the first, and certainly
the last, I hope, to see me bow to you,
to see me timid, trembling (telling it,
I'm burning with embarrassment and shame),
undone, attending humbly to your slightest
wish, or word, or deed, becoming pale
when you showed your proud displeasure, brightening
at a friendly nod, changing look and color
with every look of yours. The spell was broken,
and the yoke shattered on the ground: I'm glad.
And, though they may be
full of boredom, I embrace
wisdom and freedom happily at last,
having served out my long infatuation.
For if life, once empty of attachments
and sweet illusions, is a starless winter night,
still it's enough for me of mortal fate
and comfort and revenge that I can lie here
lazy, lifeless on the grass,
watching the sea and earth and sky, and smile.

XXX

SOPRA UN BASSO RILIEVO ANTICO SEPOLCRALE

Dove una giovane morta è rappresentata in atto di partire, accommiatandosi dai suoi

Dove vai? chi ti chiama
Lunge dai cari tuoi,
Bellissima donzella?
Sola, peregrinando, il patrio tetto
Sì per tempo abbandoni? a queste soglie
Tornerai tu? farai tu lieti un giorno
Questi ch'oggi ti son piangendo intorno?

Asciutto il ciglio ed animosa in atto,
Ma pur mesta sei tu. Grata la via
O dispiacevol sia, tristo il ricetto
A cui movi o giocondo,
Da quel tuo grave aspetto
Mal s'indovina. Ahi ahi, nè già potria
Fermare io stesso in me, nè forse al mondo

XXX

ON AN ANCIENT FUNERAL RELIEF

In Which a Dead Young Woman Is Represented in the Act of Leaving, Bidding Farewell to Her Own

Where are you going? Who is calling you
away from your loved ones,
beautiful young woman? Are you leaving
your father's house so soon to wander lonely?
Will you cross this threshold
ever again, will you bring joy someday
to those who stand beside you weeping now?

Your eyes are dry, your movements spirited,
and yet you're downcast. If your way
is glad or hard, the destination
that you travel to is dire or happy,
your grave expression doesn't indicate.
Alas, myself I couldn't say,
nor does the world yet know, perhaps,

S'intese ancor, se in disfavore al cielo
Se cara esser nomata,
Se misera tu debbi o fortunata.

Morte ti chiama; al cominciar del giorno
L'ultimo istante. Al nido onde ti parti,
Non tornerai. L'aspetto
De' tuoi dolci parenti
Lasci per sempre. Il loco
A cui movi, è sotterra:
Ivi fia d'ogni tempo il tuo soggiorno.
Forse beata sei; ma pur chi mira,
Seco pensando, al tuo destin, sospira.

Mai non veder la luce
Era, credo, il miglior. Ma nata, al tempo
Che reina bellezza si dispiega
Nelle membra e nel volto,
Ed incomincia il mondo
Verso lei di lontano ad atterrarsi;
In sul fiorir d'ogni speranza, e molto
Prima che incontro alla festosa fronte
I lúgubri suoi lampi il ver baleni;
Come vapore in nuvoletta accolto
Sotto forme fugaci all'orizzonte,
Dileguarsi così quasi non sorta,
E cangiar con gli oscuri
Silenzi della tomba i dì futuri,
Questo se all'intelletto
Appar felice, invade
D'alta pietade ai più costanti il petto.

if you should be seen
as cursed or blessed by heaven,
miserable or fortunate.

Death calls you:
daybreak is your final hour. You won't come back
to the nest you're leaving. You're letting go
of the sight of your dear
parents forever. The place you're going to
is underground:
it will be your lodging for all time.
It may be you're blessed, and yet whoever
contemplates your fate sighs all the same.

Never to see the light
was best, I think. But, given life,
and at the time when sovereign beauty
is resplendent in your face and body
and the world
starts to pay you homage from afar,
when every hope is flowering,
long before truth's dismal lightning
strikes the happy brow,
to fade as though you hadn't lived,
like mist condensed into a cloud
in shapes that disappear on the horizon
and to relinquish future days
for the dark silence of the tomb—
this, even if the mind
sees it as happy,
assails the stoutest hearts with deepest pity.

Madre temuta e pianta
Dal nascer già dell'animal famiglia,
Natura, illaudabil maraviglia,
Che per uccider partorisci e nutri,
Se danno è del mortale
Immaturo perir, come il consenti
In quei capi innocenti?
Se ben, perchè funesta,
Perchè sovra ogni male,
A chi si parte, a chi rimane in vita,
Inconsolabil fai tal dipartita?

Misera ovunque miri,
Misera onde si volga, ove ricorra,
Questa sensibil prole!
Piacqueti che delusa
Fosse ancor dalla vita
La speme giovanil; piena d'affanni
L'onda degli anni; ai mali unico schermo
La morte; e questa inevitabil segno,
Questa, immutata legge
Ponesti all'uman corso. Ahi perchè dopo
Le travagliose strade, almen la meta
Non ci prescriver lieta? anzi colei
Che per certo futura
Portiam sempre, vivendo, innanzi all'alma,
Colei che i nostri danni
Ebber solo conforto,
Velar di neri panni,
Cinger d'ombra sì trista,

Nature, mother feared and wept for
since the human family was born,
marvel that cannot be praised,
that bears and nurtures only to destroy,
if dying young brings mortals pain,
why have it come down
on these blameless heads?
And if good, then why is it unhappy,
why make this leaving inconsolable,
worse than any other woe,
for those who live, as well as those who go?

Unhappy everywhere they look,
wretched everywhere they turn or run,
is this feeling race.
You chose that life should disappoint
the hope of youth,
that the wave of years be full of pain,
with death our only
shield from suffering;
and this inevitable end, this changeless law,
you established for the human journey.
But why, after these streets of suffering,
did you not at least prescribe a happy end?
Indeed, why show us
what we hold up to the soul
as the certain future while we live,
the one comfort for our pains,
why show the port
arrayed in black

E spaventoso in vista
Più d'ogni flutto dimostrarci il porto?

Già se sventura è questo
Morir che tu destini
A tutti noi che senza colpa, ignari,
Nè volontari al vivere abbandoni,
Certo ha chi more invidiabil sorte
A colui che la morte
Sente de' cari suoi. Che se nel vero,
Com'io per fermo estimo,
Il vivere è sventura,
Grazia il morir, chi però mai potrebbe,
Quel che pur si dovrebbe,
Desiar de' suoi cari il giorno estremo,
Per dover egli scemo
Rimaner di se stesso,
Veder d'in su la soglia levar via
La diletta persona
Con chi passato avrà molt'anni insieme,
E dire a quella addio senz'altra speme
Di riscontrarla ancora
Per la mondana via;
Poi solitario abbandonato in terra,
Guardando attorno, all'ore ai lochi usati
Rimemorar la scorsa compagnia?
Come, ahi come, o natura, il cor ti soffre
Di strappar dalle braccia
All'amico l'amico,
Al fratello il fratello,

and closed in by such unhappy shadows,
more frightening to behold than any storm?

If it's already evil luck,
this dying you assign
to all whom sinless, unaware,
unwilling, you give up to life,
surely the fate of him who dies is enviable
compared to one who has to live
his loved one's death.
For if it's true, as I believe,
that life is bad luck and death grace,
who could ever, even so,
do what he should do:
hope for the last day of those he loves
and have to go on
shorn of himself,
to see the adored person
with whom he has lived for many years,
stolen from his doorstep,
and bid farewell to her
with no more hope
of meeting her again on the world's ways;
and later, left alone on earth,
to look around and think of his companions
at the old times and places?
How, O Nature, does your heart
allow you to sever
friend from friend,
brother from brother,

La prole al genitore,
All'amante l'amore: e l'uno estinto,
L'altro in vita serbar? Come potesti
Far necessario in noi
Tanto dolor, che sopravviva amando
Al mortale il mortal? Ma da natura
Altro negli atti suoi
Che nostro male o nostro ben si cura.

child from parent,
loved one from lover, and, when one has died,
expect the other to continue living?
How could you let so much pain
be needful for us, so that mortal
has to keep on loving mortal?
But Nature in her actions is concerned
with something else besides our pain or joy.

XXXI

SOPRA IL RITRATTO DI UNA BELLA DONNA

Scolpito nel monumento sepolcrale della medesima

Tal fosti: or qui sotterra
Polve e scheletro sei. Su l'ossa e il fango
Immobilmente collocato invano,
Muto, mirando dell'etadi il volo,
Sta, di memoria solo
E di dolor custode, il simulacro
Della scorsa beltà. Quel dolce sguardo,
Che tremar fe, se, come or sembra, immoto
In altrui s'affisò; quel labbro, ond'alto
Par, come d'urna piena,
Traboccare il piacer; quel collo, cinto
Già di desio; quell'amorosa mano,
Che spesso, ove fu porta,
Sentì gelida far la man che strinse;
E il seno, onde la gente
Visibilmente di pallor si tinse,
Furo alcun tempo: or fango
Ed ossa sei: la vista
Vituperosa e trista un sasso asconde.

XXXI

ON THE PORTRAIT OF A BEAUTIFUL WOMAN

Carved on Her Burial Monument

You were this: but here, now, underground
you're dust and skeleton. Raised and set
above your mud and bones to no avail,
the image of your former beauty stands
in silent witness while time flies,
sole guardian of memory and grief.
The gentle look that made men tremble
when you turned to them, as you do now,
the lip from which deep pleasure seemed to overflow
as from a brimming urn, the neck
once circled by desire, the loving hand,
which when it was given often felt
the hand it took go cold;
and the breast,
which meant that men
went visibly pale—
all of these were once upon a time.
Now you are mud and bones. A stone
hides the indecent, miserable sight.

Così riduce il fato
Qual sembianza fra noi parve più viva
Immagine del ciel. Misterio eterno
Dell'esser nostro. Oggi d'eccelsi, immensi
Pensieri e sensi inenarrabil fonte,
Beltà grandeggia, e pare,
Quale splendor vibrato
Da natura immortal su queste arene,
Di sovrumani fati,
Di fortunati regni e d'aurei mondi
Segno e sicura spene
Dare al mortale stato:
Diman, per lieve forza,
Sozzo a vedere, abominoso, abbietto
Divien quel che fu dianzi
Quasi angelico aspetto,
E dalle menti insieme
Quel che da lui moveva
Ammirabil concetto, si dilegua.

Desiderii infiniti
E visioni altere
Crea nel vago pensiere,
Per natural virtù, dotto concento;
Onde per mar delizioso, arcano
Erra lo spirto umano,
Quasi come a diporto
Ardito notator per l'Oceano:
Ma se un discorde accento
Fere l'orecchio, in nulla
Torna quel paradiso in un momento.

So destiny reduces
the look that seemed the brightest
image of heaven among us. Eternal
mystery of our being. Ineffable
source of noble and immense ideas
and feelings, beauty reigns today
and seems, like splendor
lavished on these sands by a divine being,
a sign of reassuring hope
for superhuman destinies,
for blessed realms
and golden worlds for mortals.
Tomorrow, without warning,
what was almost angelic to behold
becomes repulsive to the sight,
detestable, unworthy,
while the admirable idea
that emanated from it
fades from our minds.

Music's learned harmony
naturally engenders
infinite aspirations and exalted
visions in the dreaming mind;
thanks to which the human spirit
moves in a delicious, unknown sea,
almost the way a daring swimmer
dives into the ocean, for enjoyment.
But if a discordant
note assails the ear,
that heaven turns to nothing in an instant.

Natura umana, or come,
Se frale in tutto e vile,
Se polve ed ombra sei, tant'alto senti?
Se in parte anco gentile,
Come i più degni tuoi moti e pensieri
Son così di leggeri
Da sì basse cagioni e desti e spenti?

Human nature,
if you're merely weak and worthless,
dust and shadow, why aspire so high?
But if you're partly noble,
why are your best actions and intentions
so easily, by such unworthy causes,
both inspired and undone?

XXXII

PALINODIA AL
MARCHESE GINO CAPPONI

Il sempre sospirar nulla rileva.

PETRARCA

Errai, candido Gino; assai gran tempo,
E di gran lunga errai. Misera e vana
Stimai la vita, e sovra l'altre insulsa
La stagion ch'or si volge. Intolleranda
Parve, e fu, la mia lingua alla beata
Prole mortal, se dir si dee mortale
L'uomo, o si può. Fra maraviglia e sdegno,
Dall'Eden odorato in cui soggiorna,
Rise l'alta progenie, e me negletto
Disse, o mal venturoso, e di piaceri
O incapace o inesperto, il proprio fato
Creder comune, e del mio mal consorte
L'umana specie. Alfin per entro il fumo
De' sígari onorato, al romorio
De' crepitanti pasticcini, al grido
Militar, di gelati e di bevande
Ordinator, fra le percosse tazze

XXXII

RECANTATION FOR

MARCHESE GINO CAPPONI

Always sighing is no help.

PETRARCH

I was wrong, great Gino, far too long
and foolishly was wrong. I thought that life
was miserable and empty, and the age unfolding now
was duller than the rest. My words both seemed
and were intolerable to the blessed race
of mortals—if one must, or can, call mankind
mortal. With amazement and disdain,
from the fragrant Eden where it lives,
the noble progeny guffawed, and said
I felt ignored or otherwise unhappy,
incapable or ignorant of joy,
believing my own fate was universal
and mankind shared in my unhappiness.
At last, amidst the glory of cigar smoke,
the crunch of pastries, and a military
order that conscripted drinks and ice cream
to the clang of cups and brandished spoons,

E i branditi cucchiai, viva rifulse
Agli occhi miei la giornaliera luce
Delle gazzette. Riconobbi e vidi
La pubblica letizia, e le dolcezze
Del destino mortal. Vidi l'eccelso
Stato e il valor delle terrene cose,
E tutto fiori il corso umano, e vidi
Come nulla quaggiù dispiace e dura.
Nè men conobbi ancor gli studi e l'opre
Stupende, e il senno, e le virtudi, e l'alto
Saver del secol mio. Nè vidi meno
Da Marrocco al Catai, dall'Orse al Nilo,
E da Boston a Goa, correr dell'alma
Felicità su l'orme a gara ansando
Regni, imperi e ducati; e già tenerla
O per le chiome fluttuanti, o certo
Per l'estremo del boa. Così vedendo,
E meditando sovra i larghi fogli
Profondamente, del mio grave, antico
Errore, e di me stesso, ebbi vergogna.

Aureo secolo omai volgono, o Gino,
I fusi delle Parche. Ogni giornale,
Gener vario di lingue e di colonne,
Da tutti i lidi lo promette al mondo
Concordemente. Universale amore,
Ferrate vie, moltiplici commerci,
Vapor, tipi e *choléra* i più divisi
Popoli e climi stringeranno insieme:
Nè maraviglia fia se pino o quercia

the living daylight of the papers
shone in my eyes.
I saw and recognized the public joy
and the delights of mortal destiny.
I saw the exalted nature and the value
of earthly things, the whole blooming
human cavalcade, and understood how nothing
that isn't pleasing can survive down here.
Nor did I ignore the stupefying aims and plans,
the wisdom, virtues, and deep learning
of my own century; nor fail to see,
from Morocco to Cathay, the North Pole to the Nile,
Boston to Goa, kingdoms, empires,
dukedoms racing, gasping at the heels
of life-enhancing happiness,
trying to grasp her by her flowing locks,
or at the least by the end of her boa.
Seeing all this, and meditating deeply on
the broadsheets, I was ashamed of both
my dull, inveterate error and myself.

It's a golden age the Fates'
spools are unwinding, Gino. Every paper,
though languages and pagination differ,
promises it to the world in unison
in every country. Universal love,
railroads, expanded commerce, steam,
typography and cholera the most far-flung
peoples and climates will embrace together:
and it will be no marvel if pine or oak

Suderà latte e mele, o s'anco al suono
D'un *walser* danzerà. Tanto la possa
Infin qui de' lambicchi e delle storte,
E le macchine al cielo emulatrici
Crebbero, e tanto cresceranno al tempo
Che seguirà; poichè di meglio in meglio
Senza fin vola e volerà mai sempre
Di Sem, di Cam e di Giapeto il seme.

Ghiande non ciberà certo la terra
Però, se fame non la sforza: il duro
Ferro non deporrà. Ben molte volte
Argento ed or disprezzerà, contenta
A polizze di cambio. E già dal caro
Sangue de' suoi non asterrà la mano
La generosa stirpe: anzi coverte
Fien di stragi l'Europa e l'altra riva
Dell'atlantico mar, fresca nutrice
Di pura civiltà, sempre che spinga
Contrarie in campo le fraterne schiere
Di pepe o di cannella o d'altro aroma
Fatal cagione, o di melate canne,
O cagion qual si sia ch'ad auro torni.
Valor vero e virtù, modestia e fede
E di giustizia amor, sempre in qualunque
Pubblico stato, alieni in tutto e lungi
Da' comuni negozi, ovvero in tutto
Sfortunati saranno, afflitti e vinti:
Perchè diè lor natura, in ogni tempo
Starsene in fondo. Ardir protervo e frode,

drip milk and honey, or even dance
to the music of a waltz. The power
of the alembics and retorts and the machines
that compete with heaven has grown so great,
and will be even greater in the future,
for the seed of Shem and Ham and Japheth
is flying and will fly
higher and higher forever without end.

Surely, though, the world won't feed on acorns,
if hunger doesn't force it to; won't put away
cruel iron, though it will very often
disdain silver and gold, content with paper
currency. Nor will our noble sons
abstain from shedding the beloved blood
of their own. Indeed,
Europe and the Atlantic's other shore,
the new nurse of pure civilization,
will be bathed in slaughter every time
that it sends bands of brothers on the field
against each other, let the cause be pepper,
cinnamon, another spice, or sugarcane,
or whatever can be turned to gold.
True bravery and virtue, modesty and faith
and love of justice, under whatever form
of government, will be unpopular
and rare in public life, persecuted,
vanquished, and defeated every time;
for nature decided these would fail
in every instance. Violence and fraud,

Con mediocrità, regneran sempre,
A galleggiar sortiti. Imperio e forze,
Quanto più vogli o cumulate o sparse,
Abuserà chiunque avralle, e sotto
Qualunque nome. Questa legge in pria
Scrisser natura e il fato in adamante;
E co' fulmini suoi Volta nè Davy
Lei non cancellerà, non Anglia tutta
Con le macchine sue, nè con un Gange
Di politici scritti il secol novo.
Sempre il buono in tristezza, il vile in festa
Sempre e il ribaldo: incontro all'alme eccelse
In arme tutti congiurati i mondi
Fieno in perpetuo: al vero onor seguaci
Calunnia, odio e livor: cibo de' forti
Il debole, cultor de' ricchi e servo
Il digiuno mendico, in ogni forma
Di comun reggimento, o presso o lungi
Sien l'eclittica o i poli, eternamente
Sarà, se al gener nostro il proprio albergo
E la face del dì non vengon meno.

Queste lievi reliquie e questi segni
Delle passate età, forza è che impressi
Porti quella che sorge età dell'oro:
Perchè mille discordi e repugnanti
L'umana compagnia principii e parti
Ha per natura; e por quegli odii in pace
Non valser gl'intelletti e le possanze
Degli uomini giammai, dal dì che nacque

destined to stay afloat, will always reign
with mediocrity. However much you want
empire and power consolidated or diffused,
whoever has them will abuse them,
in whomever's name. Nature and fate
inscribed this law in adamant at the outset,
and neither Volta nor Davy will repeal it
with their lightning, nor will all of England
with her machines, nor the new century
with a Ganges of political screeds.
The good always unhappy and the bad
and scoundrels glad: the world will always be
united in arms against exalted souls.
Calumny and hate and rage will dog
the footsteps of true honor, and the weak will be
fodder for the strong, the starving beggar
the rich man's flatterer and slave, in every form
of social order; whether the ecliptic
or the poles be near or far, it will be so
forever, while our race's dwelling place
and the torch of day don't disappear.

It's vital that this rising golden age
preserve these frail remains, this evidence
of former times, because the human family
naturally contains a thousand warring
and opposing principles and parties,
and men's intellects and powers
have never managed to bring peace
to these antagonists,

L'inclita schiatta, e non varrà, quantunque
Saggio sia nè possente, al secol nostro
Patto alcuno o giornal. Ma nelle cose
Più gravi, intera, e non veduta innanzi,
Fia la mortal felicità. Più molli
Di giorno in giorno diverran le vesti
O di lana o di seta. I rozzi panni
Lasciando a prova agricoltori e fabbri,
Chiuderanno in coton la scabra pelle,
E di castoro copriran le schiene.
Meglio fatti al bisogno, o più leggiadri
Certamente a veder, tappeti e coltri,
Seggiole, canapè, sgabelli e mense,
Letti, ed ogni altro arnese, adorneranno
Di lor menstrua beltà gli appartamenti;
E nove forme di paiuoli, e nove
Pentole ammirerà l'arsa cucina.
Da Parigi a Calais, di quivi a Londra,
Da Londra a Liverpool, rapido tanto
Sarà, quant'altri immaginar non osa,
Il cammino, anzi il volo: e sotto l'ampie
Vie del Tamigi fia dischiuso il varco,
Opra ardita, immortal, ch'esser dischiuso
Dovea, già son molt'anni. Illuminate
Meglio ch'or son, benchè sicure al pari,
Nottetempo saran le vie men trite
Delle città sovrane, e talor forse
Di suddita città le vie maggiori.
Tali dolcezze e sì beata sorte
Alla prole vegnente il ciel destina.

since the day the glorious race was born;
and no treaty or newspaper in our time,
no matter how wise or powerful, will change it.
But in the most important things,
human happiness will be perfected,
as never seen before. Silk and wool clothing
will be softer daily. Farmers and workers,
shucking their rough duds in haste,
will dress their leathery hides in cotton
and cover their backs with beaver pelts.
Better-made, or lovelier to look at,
surely, rugs and blankets,
chairs and sofas, stools and tables,
beds and other furniture will grace
apartments with their beauties-of-the-month,
and new designs in pots and pans
will illuminate the smoky kitchen.
From Paris to Calais, Calais to London,
London to Liverpool, the train will be as fast
as flying, faster than anyone dare imagine,
and underneath the wide ways of the Thames
a tunnel will be opened:
inspired, immortal work
meant to be unveiled for many years.
The less traveled streets of major cities
will be better lit at night than now,
but just as safe, and perhaps someday,
the major streets of lesser towns as well.
So much sweetness, such a blessed fate,
does heaven promise to the rising generation.

Fortunati color che mentre io scrivo
Miagolanti in su le braccia accoglie
La levatrice! a cui veder s'aspetta
Quei sospirati dì, quando per lunghi
Studi fia noto, e imprenderà col latte
Dalla cara nutrice ogni fanciullo,
Quanto peso di sal, quanto di carni,
E quante moggia di farina inghiotta
Il patrio borgo in ciascun mese; e quanti
In ciascun anno partoriti e morti
Scriva il vecchio prior: quando, per opra
Di possente vapore, a milioni
Impresse in un secondo, il piano e il poggio,
E credo anco del mar gl'immensi tratti,
Come d'aeree gru stuol che repente
Alle late campagne il giorno involi,
Copriran le gazzette, anima e vita
Dell'universo, e di savere a questa
Ed alle età venture unica fonte!

Quale un fanciullo, con assidua cura,
Di fogliolini e di fuscelli, in forma
O di tempio o di torre o di palazzo,
Un edificio innalza; e come prima
Fornito il mira, ad atterrarlo è volto,
Perchè gli stessi a lui fuscelli e fogli
Per novo lavorio son di mestieri;
Così natura ogni opra sua, quantunque
D'alto artificio a contemplar, non prima
Vede perfetta, ch'a disfarla imprende,

Lucky are they whom, as I write,
the midwife welcomes mewling in her arms!
It's envisioned that they'll see
those sighed-for days when, thanks to long research,
we'll know, and every infant will imbibe
with the milk of its beloved nurse,
how much weight of salt and how much meat,
how many bushels of wheat his native city
devours each month, and as well how many
births and deaths the old prior marks down:
when, by the agency of mighty steam,
newspapers, printed by the thousands
in a second, the universe's soul and life
and the one font of wisdom
for this time and times to come!
will cover plain and hill
and even the vast tracts of the sea, I think,
as often an array of cranes in flight
will hide the light from the broad countryside.

The way a young child, with obsessive care,
builds a structure out of scraps of paper
and twigs, shaped like a temple, tower, or palace,
and once he sees it finished
turns and destroys it
because he needs these very scraps and twigs
in order to make something new,
so Nature, with each work of hers,
no matter how complex to contemplate,
no sooner sees it done than she undoes it,

Le parti sciolte dispensando altrove.
E indarno a preservar se stesso ed altro
Dal gioco reo, la cui ragion gli è chiusa
Eternamente, il mortal seme accorre
Mille virtudi oprando in mille guise
Con dotta man: che, d'ogni sforzo in onta,
La natura crudel, fanciullo invitto,
Il suo capriccio adempie, e senza posa
Distruggendo e formando si trastulla.
Indi varia, infinita una famiglia
Di mali immedicabili e di pene
Preme il fragil mortale, a perir fatto
Irreparabilmente: indi una forza
Ostil, distruggitrice, e dentro il fere
E di fuor da ogni lato, assidua, intenta
Dal dì che nasce; e l'affatica e stanca,
Essa indefatigata; insin ch'ei giace
Alfin dall'empia madre oppresso e spento.
Queste, o spirto gentil, miserie estreme
Dello stato mortal; vecchiezza e morte,
Ch'han principio d'allor che il labbro infante
Preme il tenero sen che vita instilla;
Emendar, mi cred'io, non può la lieta
Nonadecima età più che potesse
La decima o la nona, e non potranno
Più di questa giammai l'età future.
Però, se nominar lice talvolta
Con proprio nome il ver, non altro in somma
Fuor che infelice, in qualsivoglia tempo,
E non pur ne' civili ordini e modi,

scattering the broken parts around.
And in a futile effort to protect himself
and others from the evil game whose reason
is kept from him forever, the mortal creature
hastens to perform a thousand feats expertly
in a thousand ways; but, scorning all his work,
cruel Nature, that undaunted child,
indulges her capriciousness and endlessly
enjoys herself destroying and rebuilding.
And so a various, unending family
of incurable ills and pains oppresses
the frail mortal, ineluctably
born to die: a hostile, unrelenting,
fierce destructive power, within
and everywhere around him, drives him
from the day he's born. Inexhaustible itself,
it wears him down and out, until at last he lies
defeated and undone by his pitiless mother.
These, noble spirit, are the ultimate
miseries of mortal beings: old age and death,
which start back when the infant mouth
sucks at the tender breast that instills life.
The happy nineteenth century won't manage
to improve on it, I think,
any better than the tenth or ninth,
nor will future times improve on now.
Yet, if sometimes it's permissible
to call truth by its proper name,
then, all in all, each creature born will be
simply unhappy, in whatever era,

Ma della vita in tutte l'altre parti,
Per essenza insanabile, e per legge
Universal, che terra e cielo abbraccia,
Ogni nato sarà. Ma novo e quasi
Divin consiglio ritrovàr gli eccelsi
Spirti del secol mio: che, non potendo
Felice in terra far persona alcuna,
L'uomo obbliando, a ricercar si diero
Una comun felicitade; e quella
Trovata agevolmente, essi di molti
Tristi e miseri tutti, un popol fanno
Lieto e felice: e tal portento, ancora
Da *pamphlets*, da riviste e da gazzette
Non dichiarato, il civil gregge ammira.

Oh menti, oh senno, oh sovrumano acume
Dell'età ch'or si volge! E che sicuro
Filosofar, che sapienza, o Gino,
In più sublimi ancora e più riposti
Subbietti insegna ai secoli futuri
Il mio secolo e tuo! Con che costanza
Quel che ieri schernì, prosteso adora
Oggi, e domani abbatterà, per girne
Raccozzando i rottami, e per riporlo
Tra il fumo degl'incensi il dì vegnente!
Quanto estimar si dee, che fede inspira
Del secol che si volge, anzi dell'anno,
Il concorde sentir! con quanta cura
Convienci a quel dell'anno, al qual difforme
Fia quel dell'altro appresso, il sentir nostro

and not in civil laws and customs only,
but in every other part of life,
which is essentially incurable,
by universal law, which takes in earth and heaven.
But the exalted spirits of my century
discovered a new and practically divine
idea: having failed to make a single
person on earth happy, they abandoned man
and tried to find a universal bliss;
and having found it easily,
out of many wretched and unhappy persons
made a joyful, happy race:
and this miracle, not yet proclaimed by "pamphlets,"
papers, or reviews, the public herd admires.

Oh intellects, oh wisdom, superhuman
foresight of the age unfolding now!
And what sure philosophy, what wisdom, Gino,
my century and yours teaches to the future
on ever more sublime and abstruse topics.
How faithfully it falls down and adores today
what it scorned yesterday and will knock down tomorrow,
only to pick up the pieces and reinstate them
amidst the fumes of incense the next day!
How worthy, how inspiring of belief,
is this new century's sense of common purpose,
or rather, this year's. How painstakingly
we should avoid comparing what we feel
today with what will certainly
be otherwise next year,

Comparando, fuggir che mai d'un punto
Non sien diversi! E di che tratto innanzi,
Se al moderno si opponga il tempo antico,
Filosofando il saper nostro è scorso!

Un già de' tuoi, lodato Gino; un franco
Di poetar maestro, anzi di tutte
Scienze ed arti e facoltadi umane,
E menti che fur mai, sono e saranno,
Dottore, emendator, lascia, mi disse,
I propri affetti tuoi. Di lor non cura
Questa virile età, volta ai severi
Economici studi, e intenta il ciglio
Nelle pubbliche cose. Il proprio petto
Esplorar che ti val? Materia al canto
Non cercar dentro te. Canta i bisogni
Del secol nostro, e la matura speme.
Memorande sentenze! ond'io solenni
Le risa alzai quando sonava il nome
Della speranza al mio profano orecchio
Quasi comica voce, o come un suono
Di lingua che dal latte si scompagni.
Or torno addietro, ed al passato un corso
Contrario imprendo, per non dubbi esempi
Chiaro oggimai ch'al secol proprio vuolsi,
Non contraddir, non repugnar, se lode
Cerchi e fama appo lui, ma fedelmente
Adulando ubbidir: così per breve
Ed agiato cammin vassi alle stelle.
Ond'io, degli astri desioso, al canto

although they never differ in the slightest.
And if we contrast
modern times and ancient, look how much
we've gained in wisdom, from philosophy!

One of your former colleagues, worthy Gino,
a true master of poetry, indeed of every science
and art and human faculty and branch
of knowledge that was, is, and ever shall be,
doctor and reformer, told me:
Forget your own affections. This manly age,
concerned with the hard facts of economics,
immersed in politics, can have no interest
in them. What good does exploring
your heart do you? Don't go looking
for a source of song inside yourself.
Sing our century's needs and its ripe hope.
Memorable advice! To which I answered
with solemn laughter, the word "hope"
sounding like a joke to my profane ears,
or a baby's tongue
that's sucking air.
Now I turn back and take a different path
than in the past,
having learned from sure experience
that one must never contradict or criticize
one's own time if one longs for praise and fame,
but faithfully, obediently fawn:
and by this short and easy route attain the stars.
Which means that I, who do desire fame,

Del secolo i bisogni omai non penso
Materia far; che a quelli, ognor crescendo,
Provveggono i mercati e le officine
Già largamente; ma la speme io certo
Dirò, la speme, onde visibil pegno
Già concedon gli Dei; già, della nova
Felicità principio, ostenta il labbro
De' giovani, e la guancia, enorme il pelo.

O salve, o segno salutare, o prima
Luce della famosa età che sorge.
Mira dinanzi a te come s'allegra
La terra e il ciel, come sfavilla il guardo
Delle donzelle, e per conviti e feste
Qual de' barbati eroi fama già vola.
Cresci, cresci alla patria, o maschia certo
Moderna prole. All'ombra de' tuoi velli
Italia crescerà, crescerà tutta
Dalle foci del Tago all'Ellesponto
Europa, e il mondo poserà sicuro.
E tu comincia a salutar col riso
Gl'ispidi genitori, o prole infante,
Eletta agli aurei dì: nè ti spauri
L'innocuo nereggiar de' cari aspetti.
Ridi, o tenera prole: a te serbato
È di cotanto favellare il frutto;
Veder gioia regnar, cittadi e ville,
Vecchiezza e gioventù del par contente,
E le barbe ondeggiar lunghe due spanne.

don't think that I can make what this age needs
the subject of my song now, for the merchants
and the factories look to it already
far and wide, and more so every hour.
But hope I'll surely sing of, hope, to which the Gods
so clearly pledge allegiance: for young faces
already flaunt the coming happiness,
sporting sideburns and enormous beards.

All hail, O salutary symbol,
first light of the famous rising age.
See how earth and sky brighten before you,
how the looks of the young ladies sparkle,
how the bearded heroes' fame begins
to spread in meetings and at parties. Grow,
grow for your fatherland, O truly manly
modern race. In the shadow of your fleece
Italy will grow, and all of Europe
from the headwaters of the Tagus
to Hellespont, and the world will be secure.
And start smiling for your bearded fathers,
infant offspring, meant for golden days;
don't let the harmless darkening
of those beloved faces frighten you.
Smile, sweet offspring; the results
of all this chattering are meant for you:
to see joy reign in city and in country,
old age and youth both happy equally,
and beards flowing, two spans long.

XXXIII

IL TRAMONTO DELLA LUNA

Quale in notte solinga,
Sovra campagne inargentate ed acque,
Là 've zefiro aleggia,
E mille vaghi aspetti
E ingannevoli obbietti
Fingon l'ombre lontane
Infra l'onde tranquille
E rami e siepi e collinette e ville;
Giunta al confin del cielo,
Dietro Apennino od Alpe, o del Tirreno
Nell'infinito seno
Scende la luna; e si scolora il mondo;
Spariscon l'ombre, ed una
Oscurità la valle e il monte imbruna;
Orba la notte resta,
E cantando, con mesta melodia,
L'estremo albor della fuggente luce,
Che dianzi gli fu duce,
Saluta il carrettier dalla sua via;

Tal si dilegua, e tale
Lascia l'età mortale

XXXIII

THE SETTING OF THE MOON

As in the solitary night
over silvered countryside and water
where Zephyr gently breathes
and far-flung shadows
project a thousand lovely
insubstantial images and phantoms
onto still waves and branches,
hedges, hills, and farms;
reaching the horizon,
behind Apennine or Alp, or on the boundless
breast of the Tyrrhenian,
the moon descends, the world goes colorless,
shadows disappear, and one same darkness
falls on hill and valley.
Night is blind,
and singing with a mournful melody,
the carter on his way salutes
the last ray of the fleeting light
that led him on before.

So youth fades out,
so it leaves mortal life

La giovinezza. In fuga
Van l'ombre e le sembianze
Dei dilettosi inganni; e vengon meno
Le lontane speranze,
Ove s'appoggia la mortal natura.
Abbandonata, oscura
Resta la vita. In lei porgendo il guardo,
Cerca il confuso viatore invano
Del cammin lungo che avanzar si sente
Meta o ragione; e vede
Che a se l'umana sede,
Esso a lei veramente è fatto estrano.

Troppo felice e lieta
Nostra misera sorte
Parve lassù, se il giovanile stato,
Dove ogni ben di mille pene è frutto,
Durasse tutto della vita il corso.
Troppo mite decreto
Quel che sentenzia ogni animale a morte,
S'anco mezza la via
Lor non si desse in pria
Della terribil morte assai più dura.
D'intelletti immortali
Degno trovato, estremo
Di tutti i mali, ritrovàr gli eterni
La vecchiezza, ove fosse
Incolume il desio, la speme estinta,
Secche le fonti del piacer, le pene
Maggiori sempre, e non più dato il bene.

behind. The shadows
and the shapes of glad illusions
flee, and distant hopes,
that prop our mortal
nature up, give way.
Life is forlorn, lightless.
Staring ahead, the wayward traveler
searches unavailingly
for goal or reason on the long
road he senses lies ahead,
and sees that man's home truly has become
alien to him, and he to it.

Our miserable fate was judged
too glad and carefree up above
if youth, whose every happiness
is the product of a thousand pains,
should last for life;
the sentence that condemns
all living things to death too lenient
if first they were not given
a half-life far more cruel
than terrifying death itself.
The eternal gods invented—
great creation of immortal minds—
the worst of all afflictions:
old age, in which desire is unfulfilled
and hope extinguished,
the fonts of pleasure withered,
pain ever greater, and with no more joy.

Voi, collinette e piagge,
Caduto lo splendor che all'occidente
Inargentava della notte il velo,
Orfane ancor gran tempo
Non resterete; che dall'altra parte
Tosto vedrete il cielo
Imbiancar novamente, e sorger l'alba:
Alla qual poscia seguitando il sole,
E folgorando intorno
Con sue fiamme possenti,
Di lucidi torrenti
Inonderà con voi gli eterei campi.
Ma la vita mortal, poi che la bella
Giovinezza sparì, non si colora
D'altra luce giammai, nè d'altra aurora.
Vedova è insino al fine; ed alla notte
Che l'altre etadi oscura,
Segno poser gli Dei la sepoltura.

You, hills and shores,
the splendor past that turned
the veil of night to silver in the west,
will not stay orphaned long,
for in the opposite
direction soon you'll see
the sky turn white again and dawn arise,
after which the sun,
flaming with potent fire
everywhere,
will bathe you and the heavenly fields
in floods of brilliance.
But mortal life, once lovely youth
has gone, is never dyed
by other light or other dawns again.
She remains a widow all the way.
And the Gods determined that the night
which hides our other times ends in the grave.

XXXIV

LA GINESTRA

O,

IL FIORE

DEL DESERTO

Καὶ ἠγάπησαν οἱ ἄνθρωποι μᾶλλον τὸ σκότος ἢ τὸ φῶς.

E gli uomini vollero piuttosto le tenebre che la luce.

GIOVANNI, III, 19

Qui su l'arida schiena
Del formidabil monte
Sterminator Vesevo,
La qual null'altro allegra arbor nè fiore,
Tuoi cespi solitari intorno spargi,
Odorata ginestra,
Contenta dei deserti. Anco ti vidi
De' tuoi steli abbellir l'erme contrade
Che cingon la cittade
La qual fu donna de' mortali un tempo,
E del perduto impero
Par che col grave e taciturno aspetto

XXXIV

BROOM,

OR

THE FLOWER OF

THE DESERT

Καὶ ἠγάπησαν οἱ ἄνθρωποι μᾶλλον τὸ σκότος ἢ τὸ φῶς.

And men loved darkness rather than light.

JOHN 3:19

Here on the dry flank
of the terrifying mountain,
Vesuvius the destroyer,
which no other tree or flower brightens,
you spread your solitary thickets,
scented broom,
at home in the desert. And I've seen your shoots
embellishing the lonely plain
around the city
that once was mistress of men,
and whose grave and silent aspect
seems to bear witness, telling the traveler

Faccian fede e ricordo al passeggero.
Or ti riveggo in questo suol, di tristi
Lochi e dal mondo abbandonati amante,
E d'afflitte fortune ognor compagna.
Questi campi cosparsi
Di ceneri infeconde, e ricoperti
Dell'impietrata lava,
Che sotto i passi al peregrin risona;
Dove s'annida e si contorce al sole
La serpe, e dove al noto
Cavernoso covil torna il coniglio;
Fur liete ville e colti,
E biondeggiàr di spiche, e risonaro
Di muggito d'armenti;
Fur giardini e palagi,
Agli ozi de' potenti
Gradito ospizio; e fur città famose
Che coi torrenti suoi l'altero monte
Dall'ignea bocca fulminando oppresse
Con gli abitanti insieme. Or tutto intorno
Una ruina involve,
Dove tu siedi, o fior gentile, e quasi
I danni altrui commiserando, al cielo
Di dolcissimo odor mandi un profumo,
Che il deserto consola. A queste piagge
Venga colui che d'esaltar con lode
Il nostro stato ha in uso, e vegga quanto
È il gener nostro in cura
All'amante natura. E la possanza
Qui con giusta misura

of her lost empire.
Now I see you here again,
lover of sad places that the world has left
and constant friend of fallen greatness.
These fields
strewn with sterile ashes, blanketed
by hardened lava
that echoes to a wanderer's steps,
where the snake nests and coils under the sun
and the hare goes home
to his familiar cave-like den—
these were happy, prospering farms.
They were blond with wheat
and echoed with lowing cattle;
here were gardens, villas, welcome
respite for the powerful,
and famous cities, which, with rivers
pouring from its fiery mouth,
the implacable mountain crushed,
along with their inhabitants.
Now one ruin envelops everything
where you take root, noble flower,
and, as if sharing in the pain of others,
send a waft of sweetest scent
into the sky, consoling the desert.
Let him who loves to praise our state
come to these slopes and see how well our kind
is served by loving nature.
And he can also fairly judge
the power of the human race

Anco estimar potrà dell'uman seme,
Cui la dura nutrice, ov'ei men teme,
Con lieve moto in un momento annulla
In parte, e può con moti
Poco men lievi ancor subitamente
Annichilare in tutto.
Dipinte in queste rive
Son dell'umana gente
Le magnifiche sorti e progressive.

Qui mira e qui ti specchia,
Secol superbo e sciocco,
Che il calle insino allora
Dal risorto pensier segnato innanti
Abbandonasti, e volti addietro i passi,
Del ritornar ti vanti,
E procedere il chiami.
Al tuo pargoleggiar gl'ingegni tutti,
Di cui lor sorte rea padre ti fece,
Vanno adulando, ancora
Ch'a ludibrio talora
T'abbian fra se. Non io
Con tal vergogna scenderò sotterra;
Ma il disprezzo piuttosto che si serra
Di te nel petto mio,
Mostrato avrò quanto si possa aperto:
Ben ch'io sappia che obblio
Preme chi troppo all'età propria increbbe.
Di questo mal, che teco
Mi fia comune, assai finor mi rido.

whom their cruel nurse,
when they fear it least,
with the slightest movement in a moment
partly destroys,
and can with movements not much greater
suddenly and totally annihilate.
Represented on these slopes you see
the magnificent, progressive destiny
of humankind.

Look here and see yourself reflected,
proud and foolish century,
who gave up the way forward
indicated by resurgent thought,
and, having changed course,
boast of turning back
and call it progress.
While you babble, all the geniuses
unlucky enough to have had you as a parent
sing your praises,
although among themselves they often scorn you.
Not so shamefully
shall I go to my death;
rather, the disdain for you
that is locked inside my breast
I'll have displayed as openly as possible,
though well aware oblivion obscures
him who was too disliked in his own time.
I've always laughed at this misfortune,
which will be yours as well.

Libertà vai sognando, e servo a un tempo
Vuoi di novo il pensiero,
Sol per cui risorgemmo
Della barbarie in parte, e per cui solo
Si cresce in civiltà, che sola in meglio
Guida i pubblici fati.
Così ti spiacque il vero
Dell'aspra sorte e del depresso loco
Che natura ci diè. Per questo il tergo
Vigliaccamente rivolgesti al lume
Che il fe palese: e, fuggitivo, appelli
Vil chi lui segue, e solo
Magnanimo colui
Che se schernendo o gli altri, astuto o folle,
Fin sopra gli astri il mortal grado estolle.

Uom di povero stato e membra inferme
Che sia dell'alma generoso ed alto,
Non chiama se nè stima
Ricco d'or nè gagliardo,
E di splendida vita o di valente
Persona infra la gente
Non fa risibil mostra;
Ma se di forza e di tesor mendico
Lascia parer senza vergogna, e noma
Parlando, apertamente, e di sue cose
Fa stima al vero uguale.
Magnanimo animale
Non credo io già, ma stolto,
Quel che nato a perir, nutrito in pene,

You dream of freedom, but at the same time
want thought to be enslaved again—
the one thing because of which we partly
rose out of barbarism, the one thing
that civilizes us, the one thing
that brings improvement of the common good.
The truth about the bitter fate
and miserable condition nature handed us
made you so unhappy that
you turned your backs like cowards on the light
that made it patent. And while you run from it,
you call the man who follows it a coward,
and a great spirit only him
who, wise or foolish, fooling himself or others,
extols human nature above the stars.

A man who's poor and weak of limb by nature,
though he have a generous, noble soul,
doesn't believe or boast
of being rich or powerful
or laughably display
a life of luxury
or his own prowess publicly,
but without shame lets himself
appear to have no wealth or power,
and says so openly, and values
what he has according to the truth.
I consider a man foolish
and not noble who, though born to die
and raised on pain,

Dice, a goder son fatto,
E di fetido orgoglio
Empie le carte, eccelsi fati e nove
Felicità, quali il ciel tutto ignora,
Non pur quest'orbe, promettendo in terra
A popoli che un'onda
Di mar commosso, un fiato
D'aura maligna, un sotterraneo crollo
Distrugge sì, che avanza
A gran pena di lor la rimembranza.
Nobil natura è quella
Che a sollevar s'ardisce
Gli occhi mortali incontra
Al comun fato, e che con franca lingua,
Nulla al ver detraendo,
Confessa il mal che ci fu dato in sorte,
E il basso stato e frale;
Quella che grande e forte
Mostra se nel soffrir, nè gli odii e l'ire
Fraterne, ancor più gravi
D'ogni altro danno, accresce
Alle miserie sue, l'uomo incolpando
Del suo dolor, ma dà la colpa a quella
Che veramente è rea, che de' mortali
Madre è di parto e di voler matrigna.
Costei chiama inimica; e incontro a questa
Congiunta esser pensando,
Siccome è il vero, ed ordinata in pria
L'umana compagnia,
Tutti fra se confederati estima

says, I was made for pleasure,
and fills his pages up
with rank pride, high-flown destinies,
and new joys that the heavens,
and not this planet only, have never heard of,
making promises on earth to men
whom a typhoon from the stormy sea,
a blast of ill wind, or an earthquake
may so destroy that all that's left,
to their great sorrow, is the memory.
The noble nature is the one
who dares to lift his mortal eyes
to confront our common destiny
and, with honest words
that subtract nothing from the truth,
admits the pain that is our destiny,
and our poor and feeble state;
who shows he's great and strong in suffering
and doesn't add his brother's hate or anger,
worse than any evil, to his ills
by blaming man for his unhappiness,
but assigns responsibility
to the truly guilty: she who is
mother of mortals when she gives us birth,
stepmother when she rules us.
Her he calls his enemy, and believing
the whole human company
arrayed against her,
as they are in fact,
considers all men allies from the outset

Gli uomini, e tutti abbraccia
Con vero amor, porgendo
Valida e pronta ed aspettando aita
Negli alterni perigli e nelle angosce
Della guerra comune. Ed alle offese
Dell'uomo armar la destra, e laccio porre
Al vicino ed inciampo,
Stolto crede così qual fora in campo
Cinto d'oste contraria, in sul più vivo
Incalzar degli assalti,
Gl'inimici obbliando, acerbe gare
Imprender con gli amici,
E sparger fuga e fulminar col brando
Infra i propri guerrieri.
Così fatti pensieri
Quando fien, come fur, palesi al volgo,
E quell'orror che primo
Contra l'empia natura
Strinse i mortali in social catena,
Fia ricondotto in parte
Da verace saper, l'onesto e il retto
Conversar cittadino,
E giustizia e pietade, altra radice
Avranno allor che non superbe fole,
Ove fondata probità del volgo
Così star suole in piede
Quale star può quel ch'ha in error la sede.

Sovente in queste rive,
Che, desolate, a bruno

and embraces all of them
with true love, offering
and expecting real and ready aid
in the alternating dangers and concerns
of our common struggle. But to take up arms
against a man, or set a trap
or make trouble for his neighbor
seems to him as stupid as,
surrounded by hostile soldiers
during the heaviest fighting on the field,
to forget your enemies
and battle fiercely with your friends,
inciting your own men to run
by threatening them with your sword.
When such ideas become
known to the populace as they once were,
and the fear
that first joined mortals in a common pact
against unholy nature
shall be revived to some extent
out of real wisdom, then an honest,
just society of citizens
and right and piety will take root
from something more than vain mythologies;
and on this foundation
the people's probity may stand as firm
as something that depends on error.

Often I sit at night on these deserted
slopes which the hardened flood

Veste il flutto indurato, e par che ondeggi,
Seggo la notte; e su la mesta landa
In purissimo azzurro
Veggo dall'alto fiammeggiar le stelle,
Cui di lontan fa specchio
Il mare, e tutto di scintille in giro
Per lo vóto seren brillare il mondo.
E poi che gli occhi a quelle luci appunto,
Ch'a lor sembrano un punto,
E sono immense, in guisa
Che un punto a petto a lor son terra e mare
Veracemente; a cui
L'uomo non pur, ma questo
Globo ove l'uomo è nulla,
Sconosciuto è del tutto; e quando miro
Quegli ancor più senz'alcun fin remoti
Nodi quasi di stelle,
Ch'a noi paion qual nebbia, a cui non l'uomo
E non la terra sol, ma tutte in uno,
Del numero infinite e della mole,
Con l'aureo sole insiem, le nostre stelle
O sono ignote, o così paion come
Essi alla terra, un punto
Di luce nebulosa; al pensier mio
Che sembri allora, o prole
Dell'uomo? E rimembrando
Il tuo stato quaggiù, di cui fa segno
Il suol ch'io premo; e poi dall'altra parte,
Che te signora e fine
Credi tu data al Tutto, e quante volte

clothes in a black that seems to undulate,
and over the sad plain
I see the stars
burning up above in purest blue,
which the sea reflects in the far distance
and, twinkling everywhere, the world
glistens in the empty sky.
And once my eyes have focused on those lights,
which seem a tiny point to them,
though they're enormous, so that next to these
the earth and sea
are in truth no greater than a speck
to which not only man
but this globe where man is nothing
is totally unknown; and when I see
these still more infinitely distant
nuclei, it seems, of stars
that look like haze to us, to which
not only man and earth but all our stars
together, infinite in size and number,
the golden sun among them,
are unfamiliar or else they appear
the way these look to earth: a point
of nebulous light—
how do I think of you then, sons of men?
And, considering
the way you are down here,
to which the earth I walk upon bears witness,
and that even so you see yourself
as lord and end assigned to Everything,

Favoleggiar ti piacque, in questo oscuro
Granel di sabbia, il qual di terra ha nome,
Per tua cagion, dell'universe cose
Scender gli autori, e conversar sovente
Co' tuoi piacevolmente, e che i derisi
Sogni rinnovellando, ai saggi insulta
Fin la presente età, che in conoscenza
Ed in civil costume
Sembra tutte avanzar; qual moto allora,
Mortal prole infelice, o qual pensiero
Verso te finalmente il cor m'assale?
Non so se il riso o la pietà prevale.

Come d'arbor cadendo un picciol pomo,
Cui là nel tardo autunno
Maturità senz'altra forza atterra,
D'un popol di formiche i dolci alberghi,
Cavati in molle gleba
Con gran lavoro, e l'opre
E le ricchezze che adunate a prova
Con lungo affaticar l'assidua gente
Avea provvidamente al tempo estivo,
Schiaccia, diserta e copre
In un punto; così d'alto piombando,
Dall'utero tonante
Scagliata al ciel profondo,
Di ceneri e di pomici e di sassi
Notte e ruina, infusa
Di bollenti ruscelli,
O pel montano fianco

and how you were often flattered to relate
that the authors of the universe
came down to this mere grain of sand called earth
for love of you, and often condescended
to speak with you and yours,
and how you keep retailing absurd notions
insulting to the wise, down to our day,
which seemingly surpasses every other
in knowledge and civility; what emotion, then,
mortal unhappy race, what notion of you
finally assails my heart? It's hard to say
whether it's laughter or pity that prevails.

As a little apple, falling from a tree,
which there in the late autumn
no other force but ripeness brings to earth,
breaks, in an instant emptying and burying
the sweet nests of a multitude of ants
dug out of the soft soil at great cost,
and the works and wealth
that the hardworking nest
had stored up by long labor
providently in the summertime;
so, plummeting like lead from overhead,
hurled out of the thundering womb
deep into the sky,
night and ruin of ashes,
dirt, and stones,
infused with boiling rivers
or steaming in the grass

Furiosa tra l'erba
Di liquefatti massi
E di metalli e d'infocata arena
Scendendo immensa piena,
Le cittadi che il mar là su l'estremo
Lido aspergea, confuse
E infranse e ricoperse
In pochi istanti: onde su quelle or pasce
La capra, e città nove
Sorgon dall'altra banda, a cui sgabello
Son le sepolte, e le prostrate mura
L'arduo monte al suo piè quasi calpesta.
Non ha natura al seme
Dell'uom più stima o cura
Che alla formica: e se più rara in quello
Che nell'altra è la strage,
Non avvien ciò d'altronde
Fuor che l'uom sue prosapie ha men feconde.

Ben mille ed ottocento
Anni varcàr poi che spariro, oppressi
Dall'ignea forza, i popolati seggi,
E il villanello intento
Ai vigneti, che a stento in questi campi
Nutre la morta zolla e incenerita,
Ancor leva lo sguardo
Sospettoso alla vetta
Fatal, che nulla mai fatta più mite
Ancor siede tremenda, ancor minaccia
A lui strage ed ai figli ed agli averi

of the mountain flank,
an enormous downward flood
of liquid boulders,
metal, burning sand,
fused and broke apart
and buried within instants
the cities that the sea lapped
there on the far shore; so that now goats graze
on top of them and nearby new towns rise
for which the buried ones are stepping stones
and the tyrant mountain seems
to trample on the felled walls with its foot.
Nature has no more esteem
or care for the seed of man
than for the ant. And if annihilation
is rarer for the one than for the other
it's because of nothing more
than that man has less fertile progeny.

More than eighteen hundred years have passed
since these crowded places disappeared,
extinguished by the power of fire,
and yet the farmer bending to his vines
which the scorched and poisoned earth
nurtures poorly in these fields
still lifts his anxious eyes
to the fatal peak,
in no way gentler,
which sits there still tremendous,
still threatening ruin

Lor poverelli. E spesso
Il meschino in sul tetto
Dell'ostel villereccio, alla vagante
Aura giacendo tutta notte insonne,
E balzando più volte, esplora il corso
Del temuto bollor, che si riversa
Dall'inesausto grembo
Su l'arenoso dorso, a cui riluce
Di Capri la marina
E di Napoli il porto e Mergellina.
E se appressar lo vede, o se nel cupo
Del domestico pozzo ode mai l'acqua
Fervendo gorgogliar, desta i figliuoli,
Desta la moglie in fretta, e via, con quanto
Di lor cose rapir posson, fuggendo,
Vede lontan l'usato
Suo nido, e il picciol campo,
Che gli fu dalla fame unico schermo,
Preda al flutto rovente,
Che crepitando giunge, e inesorato
Durabilmente sovra quei si spiega.
Torna al celeste raggio
Dopo l'antica obblivion l'estinta
Pompei, come sepolto
Scheletro, cui di terra
Avarizia o pietà rende all'aperto;
E dal deserto foro
Diritto infra le file
Dei mozzi colonnati il peregrino
Lunge contempla il bipartito giogo

for him, his children,
and their mean possessions.
And often the poor man sleepless on the roof
of his country hovel,
lying in the open air all night,
jumps up time and time again to watch
the progress of the fearful boiling,
spilling out of the inexhaustible womb
onto the sandy mountainside,
on which the shore of Capri gleams reflected,
and the port of Naples, and Mergellina.
And if he sees it coming close, or hears
his well water gurgle agitated,
he frantically collects his wife and children,
and, fleeing with as many of their things
as they can carry, watches from afar
their longtime nest and the small field
that was their one defense from hunger
fall prey to the burning flood,
which advances hissing and unstoppable,
to pour over them unendingly.
Extinct Pompeii
returns to the celestial light
from her immemorial oblivion
like a buried skeleton
that greed or piety has raised out of the earth
into the air, and from the empty forum
the wanderer, gazing
down the rows of broken colonnades,
contemplates the distant double peak

E la cresta fumante,
Che alla sparsa ruina ancor minaccia.
E nell'orror della secreta notte
Per li vacui teatri,
Per li templi deformi e per le rotte
Case, ove i parti il pipistrello asconde,
Come sinistra face
Che per vóti palagi atra s'aggiri,
Corre il baglior della funerea lava,
Che di lontan per l'ombre
Rosseggia e i lochi intorno intorno tinge.
Così, dell'uomo ignara e dell'etadi
Ch'ei chiama antiche, e del seguir che fanno
Dopo gli avi i nepoti,
Sta natura ognor verde, anzi procede
Per sì lungo cammino
Che sembra star. Caggiono i regni intanto,
Passan genti e linguaggi: ella nol vede:
E l'uom d'eternità s'arroga il vanto.

E tu, lenta ginestra,
Che di selve odorate
Queste campagne dispogliate adorni,
Anche tu presto alla crudel possanza
Soccomberai del sotterraneo foco,
Che ritornando al loco
Già noto, stenderà l'avaro lembo
Su tue molli foreste. E piegherai
Sotto il fascio mortal non renitente
Il tuo capo innocente:

and its smoking crest,
still menacing the scattered ruin.
And in the horror of the hidden night,
in the empty theaters, the broken temples,
and ruined houses where the bat
conceals its offspring,
advancing cruelly through vacant buildings
like an evil torch the gleaming,
deadly lava flows,
and glows red among the distant shadows,
dyeing everything around.
So, ignorant of man and of the age
that he calls ancient, and of the descendants
following their ancestors,
nature stays evergreen; indeed she travels
such a long road she might as well
be standing still. Meanwhile kingdoms fall,
languages and peoples die; she doesn't see.
Yet man takes it upon himself to praise eternity.

And you, too, pliant broom,
adorning this abandoned countryside
with fragrant bushes,
you will soon succumb
to the cruel power of subterranean fire,
which, returning to the place it knew before,
will spread its greedy tongue
over your soft thickets. And unresisting,
you'll bow your blameless head
under the deadly scythe;

Ma non piegato insino allora indarno
Codardamente supplicando innanzi
Al futuro oppressor; ma non eretto
Con forsennato orgoglio inver le stelle,
Nè sul deserto, dove
E la sede e i natali
Non per voler ma per fortuna avesti;
Ma più saggia, ma tanto
Meno inferma dell'uom, quanto le frali
Tue stirpi non credesti
O dal fato o da te fatte immortali.

but you will not have bowed before,
hopeless abject supplicant
of your future oppressor; you were never raised
by senseless pride up to the stars
or above the desert, which for you
was home and birthplace
not by choice, but chance;
no, far wiser and less fallible
than man is, you did not presume
that either fate or you had made
your fragile kind immortal.

XXXV

IMITAZIONE

Lungi dal propio ramo,
Povera foglia frale,
Dove vai tu? Dal faggio
Là dov'io nacqui, mi divise il vento.
Esso, tornando, a volo
Dal bosco alla campagna,
Dalla valle mi porta alla montagna.
Seco perpetuamente
Vo pellegrina, e tutto l'altro ignoro.
Vo dove ogni altra cosa,
Dove naturalmente
Va la foglia di rosa,
E la foglia d'alloro.

XXXV

IMITATION

Where are you going,
tender little leaf,
so far from your bough?
The wind tore me away
from the beech where I was born.
Whirling as he flies, he spirits me
from wood to meadow
and from hill to valley.
I wander with him endlessly,
disregarding everything.
Where all else goes I go,
where by nature rose
and laurel leaf go, too.

XXXVI

SCHERZO

Quando fanciullo io venni
A pormi con le Muse in disciplina,
L'una di quelle mi pigliò per mano;
E poi tutto quel giorno
La mi condusse intorno
A veder l'officina.
Mostrommi a parte a parte
Gli strumenti dell'arte,
E i servigi diversi
A che ciascun di loro
S'adopra nel lavoro
Delle prose e de' versi.
Io mirava, e chiedea:
Musa, la lima ov'è? Disse la Dea:
La lima è consumata; or facciam senza.
Ed io, ma di rifarla
Non vi cal, soggiungea, quand'ella è stanca?
Rispose: hassi a rifar, ma il tempo manca.

XXXVI

SCHERZO

When as a child
I came to be schooled by the Muses,
one of them took me by the hand,
and all day long
she took me through
their workshop.
One by one she showed
the tools of their art
and the different uses
each of them is put to
as they do the work
of prose and rhyme.
I was amazed, and asked her:
Muse, where's your file? The Goddess
answered: Gone; we do without today.
And I: But when it's worn,
don't you replace it?
Said she: We ought to, but there isn't time.

FRAMMENTI

[FRAGMENTS]

XXXVII

ALCETA

Odi, Melisso: io vo' contarti un sogno
Di questa notte, che mi torna a mente
In riveder la luna. Io me ne stava
Alla finestra che risponde al prato,
Guardando in alto: ed ecco all'improvviso
Distaccasi la luna; e mi parea
Che quanto nel cader s'approssimava,
Tanto crescesse al guardo; infin che venne
A dar di colpo in mezzo al prato; ed era
Grande quanto una secchia, e di scintille
Vomitava una nebbia, che stridea
Sì forte come quando un carbon vivo
Nell'acqua immergi e spegni. Anzi a quel modo
La luna, come ho detto, in mezzo al prato
Si spegneva annerando a poco a poco,
E ne fumavan l'erbe intorno intorno.
Allor mirando in ciel, vidi rimaso
Come un barlume, o un'orma, anzi una nicchia,
Ond'ella fosse svelta; in cotal guisa,
Ch'io n'agghiacciava; e ancor non m'assicuro.

XXXVII

ALCETA

Listen, Melisso: I want to tell you a dream
I had last night, which comes to mind,
seeing the moon again. I was standing
at the window that looks out on the meadow
staring up, when suddenly the moon
unhooked herself. And it seemed to me
that as she fell,
the nearer she got the bigger she looked, until
she hit the ground in the middle of the meadow,
big as a bucket, and vomited
a cloud of sparks that shrieked as loud
as when you dunk a live coal in the water
and drown it. So, as I said,
the moon died in the middle of the meadow,
little by little slowly darkening,
and the grass was smoking all around.
Then, looking up into the sky, I saw
something still there, a glimmer or a shadow,
or the niche that she'd been torn away from,
which made me cold with fear. And I'm still anxious.

MELISSO

E ben hai che temer, che agevol cosa
Fora cader la luna in sul tuo campo.

ALCETA

Chi sa? non veggiam noi spesso di state
Cader le stelle?

MELISSO

Egli ci ha tante stelle,
Che picciol danno è cader l'una o l'altra
Di loro, e mille rimaner. Ma sola
Ha questa luna in ciel, che da nessuno
Cader fu vista mai se non in sogno.

MELISSO

You were right to be afraid, when the moon
fell so easily into your field.

ALCETA

Who knows? Don't we often see
stars fall in summer?

MELISSO

There are so many stars
that if one or another of them falls
it's no great loss, since there are thousands left.
But there's just this one moon up in the sky,
which no one saw fall ever—except in dreams.

XXXVIII

Io qui vagando al limitare intorno,
Invan la pioggia invoco e la tempesta,
Acciò che la ritenga al mio soggiorno.

Pure il vento muggia nella foresta,
E muggia tra le nubi il tuono errante,
Pria che l'aurora in ciel fosse ridesta.

O care nubi, o cielo, o terra, o piante,
Parte la donna mia: pietà, se trova
Pietà nel mondo un infelice amante.

O turbine, or ti sveglia, or fate prova
Di sommergermi, o nembi, insino a tanto
Che il sole ad altre terre il dì rinnova.

S'apre il ciel, cade il soffio, in ogni canto
Posan l'erbe e le frondi, e m'abbarbaglia
Le luci il crudo Sol pregne di pianto.

XXXVIII

Lurking here around the threshold, I
pray for rain and storm without success,
so that I can keep her here with me.

But the wind bellows in the forest
and the vagrant thunder bellows in the clouds
before dawn can be revived in the sky.

O dear clouds, O heaven, O earth, O trees,
my lady's leaving! Pity me, if an unhappy
lover can find pity in this world.

O whirlwind, rouse yourself now, try
to drown me now, O clouds, until the time
the sun brings daylight back in other lands.

The sky opens, the wind dies; everywhere,
the grass and leaves lie still; and the cruel sun
dazzles my eyes, which are heavy with tears.

XXXIX

Spento il diurno raggio in occidente,
E queto il fumo delle ville, e queta
De' cani era la voce e della gente;

Quand'ella, volta all'amorosa meta,
Si ritrovò nel mezzo ad una landa
Quanto foss'altra mai vezzosa e lieta.

Spandeva il suo chiaror per ogni banda
La sorella del sole, e fea d'argento
Gli arbori ch'a quel loco eran ghirlanda.

I ramuscelli ivan cantando al vento,
E in un con l'usignol che sempre piagne
Fra i tronchi un rivo fea dolce lamento.

Limpido il mar da lungi, e le campagne
E le foreste, e tutte ad una ad una
Le cime si scoprian delle montagne.

In questa ombra giacea la valle bruna,
E i collicelli intorno rivestia
Del suo candor la rugiadosa luna.

XXXIX

The light of day had died out in the west,
and the houses' smoke had disappeared,
as had the sounds of dogs and people, too,

when she, heading to love's rendezvous,
found herself in the middle of a heath
more gay and charming than she'd ever known.

The sun's sister spread her brightness
with every ray, and silvered
the trees that made a garland for that place.

The little boughs were singing in the wind
and together with the bird that always weeps
among the trees a river was lamenting.

The sea was bright in the distance,
the countryside and forests, and one by one
the tops of the mountains could be seen.

The dark valley lay in silent shadow
and the dewy moon was cloaking
the little hills around it with its brightness.

Sola tenea la taciturna via
La donna, e il vento che gli odori spande,
Molle passar sul volto si sentia.

Se lieta fosse, è van che tu dimande:
Piacer prendea di quella vista, e il bene
Che il cor le prometteva era più grande.

Come fuggiste, o belle ore serene!
Dilettevol quaggiù null'altro dura,
Nè si ferma giammai, se non la spene.

Ecco turbar la notte, e farsi oscura
La sembianza del ciel, ch'era sì bella,
E il piacere di colei farsi paura.

Un nugol torbo, padre di procella,
Sorgea di dietro ai monti, e crescea tanto,
Che più non si scopria luna nè stella.

Spiegarsi ella il vedea per ogni canto,
E salir su per l'aria a poco a poco,
E far sovra il suo capo a quella ammanto.

E veniva il poco lume ognor più fioco;
E intanto al bosco si destava il vento,
Al bosco là del dilettoso loco.

E si fea più gagliardo ogni momento,
Tal che a forza era desto e svolazzava
Tra le fronde ogni augel per lo spavento.

The lady went her silent way alone
and she felt the wind that wafts its odors
gently pass across her face.

There's no point in asking if she was happy:
the sight gave her pleasure, yet the good
her heart promised her was even greater.

How quickly you flew, lovely, serene hours!
Nothing else that is delightful lasts
down here, nothing ever lasts, but hope.

See the night cloud over, and the face
of the sky that was so beautiful turn dark,
and her pleasure turn to fright.

A turbid cloud, the father of a storm,
rose from behind the hills, and grew so huge
that moon and stars no longer could be seen.

She saw it spreading everywhere,
gradually rising through the air
and making a mantle above her head.

The faint light grew dimmer all the time;
meanwhile the wind rose in the grove,
where they were supposed to rendezvous.

And moment by moment it grew stronger,
so every bird was wakened by its force
and darted in the foliage from fear.

E la nube, crescendo, in giù calava
Ver la marina sì, che l'un suo lembo
Toccava i monti, e l'altro il mar toccava.

Già tutto a cieca oscuritade in grembo,
S'incominciava udir fremer la pioggia,
E il suon cresceva all'appressar del nembo.

Dentro le nubi in paurosa foggia
Guizzavan lampi, e la fean batter gli occhi;
E n'era il terren tristo, e l'aria roggia.

Discior sentia la misera i ginocchi;
E già muggiva il tuon simile al metro
Di torrente che d'alto in giù trabocchi.

Talvolta ella ristava, e l'aer tetro
Guardava sbigottita, e poi correa,
Sì che i panni e le chiome ivano addietro.

E il duro vento col petto rompea,
Che gocce fredde giù per l'aria nera
In sul volto soffiando le spingea.

E il tuon veniale incontro come fera,
Rugghiando orribilmente e senza posa;
E cresceva la pioggia e la bufera.

E d'ogn'intorno era terribil cosa
Il volar polve e frondi e rami e sassi,
E il suon che immaginar l'alma non osa.

And the cloud, as it increased, descended
to the shore, till one of its edges
touched the hills and the other met the sea.

Now, in the womb of blind obscurity,
the shudder of the rain began to be heard
and the sound grew as the cloud came nearer.

Lightning flared inside the clouds
in a fearful shape that made her blink,
and the land was sad, the air was red.

The poor girl felt her knees give way
and now the thunder bellowed like the roar
of a river pouring from the heights.

At times she stood stock-still and watched
the dark air in dismay and then she ran,
her clothes and hair streaking behind her.

And the wild wind struck her breast
and cold rain was spattering her face
in the darkness while she gasped for breath.

And the thunder struck like something wild,
howling horribly, unendingly,
and the rain and storm intensified.

And everything around was terrible
flying dust and leaves, branches and stones,
and a sound the soul dare not imagine.

Ella dal lampo affaticati e lassi
Coprendo gli occhi, e stretti i panni al seno,
Gia pur tra il nembo accelerando i passi.

Ma nella vista ancor l'era il baleno
Ardendo sì, ch'alfin dallo spavento
Fermò l'andare, e il cor le venne meno.

E si rivolse indietro. E in quel momento
Si spense il lampo, e tornò buio l'etra,
Ed acchetossi il tuono, e stette il vento.

Taceva il tutto; ed ella era di pietra.

She, covering her miserable, tired eyes
from the lightning, clutched her clothes to her breast
and hurried faster through the cloud.

But the burning lightning stayed in sight,
so that in the end she wasn't
moving in her terror, and lost courage.

And she turned back. And at that very moment
the lightning ceased, the air went dark,
the thunder subsided, and the wind.

Everything was still; and she was stone.

XL

DAL GRECO DI SIMONIDE

Ogni mondano evento
È di Giove in poter, di Giove, o figlio,
Che giusta suo talento
Ogni cosa dispone.
Ma di lunga stagione
Nostro cieco pensier s'affanna e cura,
Benchè l'umana etate,
Come destina il ciel nostra ventura,
Di giorno in giorno dura.
La bella speme tutti ci nutrica
Di sembianze beate,
Onde ciascuno indarno s'affatica:
Altri l'aurora amica,
Altri l'etade aspetta;
E nullo in terra vive
Cui nell'anno avvenir facili e pii
Con Pluto gli altri iddii
La mente non prometta.
Ecco pria che la speme in porto arrive,
Qual da vecchiezza è giunto
E qual da morbi al bruno Lete addutto;
Questo il rigido Marte, e quello il flutto

XL

FROM THE GREEK OF SIMONIDES

Every earthly happening
is in the power of Jove, of Jove, my son,
who according to his will
decides how everything is done.
But our blind brain is tortured
planning a long future,
although the human state,
as heaven decides our fate,
proceeds from day to day.
Lovely hope feeds all of us
on sweet appearances,
and we all suffer from them to no end:
some await the friendly dawn,
some the time to come,
and no one lives on earth
who hasn't told himself
that Pluto and the other gods
will be kind and lenient next year.
Yet before hope comes to port,
some of us have reached old age
and some are brought
by illness to dark Lethe.

Del pelago rapisce; altri consunto
Da negre cure, o tristo nodo al collo
Circondando, sotterra si rifugge.
Così di mille mali
I miseri mortali
Volgo fiero e diverso agita e strugge.
Ma per sentenza mia,
Uom saggio e sciolto dal comune errore
Patir non sosterria,
Nè porrebbe al dolore
Ed al mal proprio suo cotanto amore.

One gets taken by hard Mars,
another by the river of the ocean;
someone else, devoured by black cares,
or putting a sad noose around his neck,
flees underground. So a many-headed
wild swarm of a thousand ills
chases and ruins miserable mortals.
But I say the man who's sane
and free of common error won't put up
with suffering, or lavish so much love
on his own misery and pain.

XLI

DELLO STESSO

Umana cosa picciol tempo dura,
E certissimo detto
Disse il veglio di Chio,
Conforme ebber natura
Le foglie e l'uman seme.
Ma questa voce in petto
Raccolgon pochi. All'inquieta speme,
Figlia di giovin core,
Tutti prestiam ricetto.
Mentre è vermiglio il fiore
Di nostra etade acerba,
L'alma vota e superba
Cento dolci pensieri educa invano,
Nè morte aspetta nè vecchiezza; e nulla
Cura di morbi ha l'uom gagliardo e sano.
Ma stolto è chi non vede
La giovanezza come ha ratte l'ale,
E siccome alla culla
Poco il rogo è lontano.
Tu presso a porre il piede
In sul varco fatale
Della plutonia sede,
Ai presenti diletti
La breve età commetti.

XLI

BY THE SAME AUTHOR

Human things last only a short time,
and what the sage of Chios claimed
is very sure:
that leaves and human beings
are similar by nature.
Yet few are comfortable with this idea.
We all give room
to restless hope,
the young heart's creature.
While the flower
of our green age blooms,
our empty, prideful soul
feeds a hundred sweet ideas in vain,
expecting neither death nor age,
and strapping, healthy youth
won't hear of sickness.
But he's a fool who doesn't see
how swift the wings of youth are, and how near
the cradle lies to the grave.
You, about to take
the fatal step
that leads to Pluto's kingdom,
commit to present pleasure
your brief life.

Other Texts

LE RIMEMBRANZE

Idillio

Era in mezzo del ciel la curva luna,
E di Micon la povera capanna
Sol piccola da un lato ombra spandea.
Chino sul destro braccio, ed appoggiando
Alle ginocchia il cubito, dell'uscio
Sul facile gradin sedea Micone.
Egli era triste, e muto. Il tenerello
Dameta il figliuolin, che ad ogni istante
Temea la mamma udir chiamarlo al sonno,
Scherzavagli d'intorno, e saltellando
La mano gli prendeva, e or d'una cosa
Or d'altra il ricercava: un panierino
Mostravagli talor da lui tessuto,
Talor raccolto un fresco fior, talora
Nella socchiusa man lucido insetto
Sorpreso in aria da sagace colpo:
E il rimirava in faccia, e avidamente
Plauso chiedea col guardo, e col sorriso.

MEMORIES

Idyll

The crescent moon was high up in the sky
and Micon's poor hut offered
only a little shadow on one side.
Leaning on his right arm,
with his elbow on his knee,
Micon sat in the wide threshold of his door.
He was sad and silent. Tender young Dametas,
his little boy, who was afraid of hearing
his mother call him to bed at any moment,
was playing near him, and, jumping,
took his hand and begged for his attention
for one thing or another: now he showed him
a little basket that he'd woven,
now a fresh flower that he'd picked,
now a gleaming insect in his hand,
caught in midair with a shrewd maneuver.
He looked into his face and greedily
sought his approval with his eyes and smile.

Quel, serio, e taciturno a stento ai detti,
O a fuggitivo riso i labbri apriva.
Alfin proruppe:

MICONE

O amabile Dameta,
Dì, figlio mio, del tuo maggior fratello
Non ti ricordi tu? più non rammenti
Il tuo Filino? Ei t'ha lasciato, e un anno
È che nol vedi più. Le prime rose
Spuntavano, com'or, su quella fratta,
Quando, i suoi giuochi abbandonati, il vidi
Seder pallido, e muto. Io gli chiedea:
Figlio, perchè qui sei? perchè non giuochi?
Perchè non vai con tuo fratello al prato?
Su scendi a sollazzarti. Hai forse male?
No, padre, ei mi dicea, no, nulla io sento,
Ma stanco io sono, e qui riposo; or ora
Tornerò con Dameta a trastullarmi.
Così sempre ei dicea, ma sempre il male
Più gli apparia sul viso. Un dì di Festa
Alfine ei si levò l'estrema volta,
Poi più non sorse. Oh come, allor che a casa
La sera mi vedea tornar dal campo,
Lieto in chiamarmi mi tendea le mani,
E la mia mi baciava, e mi chiedea
Se stanco fossi, e sempre a se vicino
M'avria voluto. Un giorno alfin (dimani

The other, serious, and taciturn, was having trouble
speaking or even smiling a fleeting smile.
Finally he broke out:

MICON

O adorable Dametas,
tell me, son, don't you remember
your older brother? Don't you recall
your Filinos? He left you, and it's been a year
since you've seen him. The first roses
were budding, as they are now, on that cliffside
when I saw him leave his games
and sit down pale and mute. I asked him:
Son, why are you here? Why aren't you playing?
Why don't you go to the meadow with your brother?
Sit here and rest. Are you not feeling well?
No, Father, he told me, I don't feel a thing,
but I'm tired, I'm resting here.
Soon I'll go back to playing with Dametas.
Which was what he always said, but illness
was more and more apparent on his face.
At last one Sunday he got out of bed
one final time, and then no more. Oh, when he saw me
coming from the field back to the house
he'd hold his hands out, happily
calling me, and kiss my hand and ask me
if I was tired and always wanted me
beside him. At last one day (tomorrow

Quel dì funesto riconduce il sole)
Mi levai, corsi a lui, chino sul letto
Gli diedi un bacio, e come stasse il chiesi.
Ei più non rispondea: l'occhio mi volse
Cui luccicante lacrima copria:
Ma nulla dir potè, più non dischiuse
Il moribondo labbro. Un opportuno
Rimedio al male, il vecchio Alcon, quel Saggio,
Cui sì spesso vedesti, e cui sì spesso
Della villa consultano i pastori,
Indicato ci avea. Per procacciarlo
Impaziente alla città mi volsi.
Saliva il sole in cielo, e la marina
Di lontano splendea: ma la campagna
Era tacita ancor. Passai non lungi
A quell'alto palagio, che alla luna
Or vedi biancheggiar dietro alle piante,
Colà vicino alla maestra via.
Della villa i Signori eran sepolti
Nel dolce sonno del mattin. Pur vidi
Aperta una finestra, intorno a cui
Sporgea ferrea ringhiera, e dentro l'ampia
Camera Signoril, sul pavimento
E il lucido apparato, che l'opposta
Parete ricopria, dal sol dipinta
L'immagine mirai della finestra.
A cui dinanzi con negletta veste
Un dei servi passar vidi, che intento
Sulla scopa pendea. Quanto lugubri
Per me fur quei momenti! Alla cittade

will be the deadly anniversary)
I rose and ran to him, lay on his bed,
gave him a kiss, and asked him how he was.
He didn't answer any more: he turned to me,
eyes full of glistening tears,
but he couldn't speak; he never opened
his dying lips again. Old Alcon,
the wise man you saw often, whom the shepherds
of the farm always turned to,
suggested an effective remedy
for his illness, so to get it
I rushed impatiently to town.
The sun rose in the sky, the sea was shining
in the distance: but the countryside
was quiet still. I passed not far
from the high palace you now can see
turn white in the moonlight
behind the hedge, beside the main street there.
The Masters of the place were buried
in sweet morning sleep. And yet I saw
one window with an iron balcony
and inside the ample Master Chamber,
both on the floor
and on the room's rich furnishings,
covering the wall opposite, I saw
the windows' image painted by the sun.
In front of which I saw one of the servants
pass, out of uniform, leaning on his broom.
How unhappy
these moments were for me!

Giunsi, tolsi il rimedio, e qua tornai.
Fra speme, e fra timor, tremante, incerto
Entrai sospeso . . . Morto era Filino.
Pallido il rimirai: finito io vidi
Il respirar sulle gelate labbra:
Serrate le palpebre, e rilucenti
Pel ghiacciato sudor l'umide chiome.
Ahi mio Filino! Da quel tempo ancora
Quel mesto orror, quei funebri momenti,
Quel tristo dì dimenticar non posso.

DAMETA

Ben men sovvengo anch'io: che nel levarmi
Quella mattina, oltre l'usato io vidi
Trista la mamma. Al mio Filino io tosto
Correr voleva: ella il vietò, mi disse
Che ancor dormiva, e uscir mi fece al prato.
Ma nel tornar con festa, e saltellando
Pianger la vidi. Io m'acchetai, pian piano
Le venni appresso, e presale la gonna,
Mesto le dimandai perchè piangesse.
Ella china abbracciommi, ed appoggiando
Alla mia la sua fronte, ah figlio, disse,
Caro Dameta mio, Filino è morto.
Allor piansi ancor io. La mamma invano
Trattenermi volea: poi ch'ella il guardo
Rivolse altrove, al letticciuolo io corsi
Del mio caro Filin. Fiso dapprima

I reached town, got the medicine, and ran back here.
I came in trembling, hanging uncertain
between hope and fear . . . Filinos was dead.
I saw that he was pale, I saw the breath
was finished on his icy lips,
his lids were closed, his wet locks
shone with icy sweat.
Oh my Filinos! From that moment on
I can't forget that melancholy horror,
those mournful moments, that sad day.

DAMETAS

I myself remember less: but when I rose
that morning, I saw my mother was much sadder
than normal. I wanted to run to my Filinos
right away. She stopped me, saying
he was still asleep, and made me go out in the meadow.
But as I came back joyful, jumping,
I saw her weeping. I went silent, slowly
I came up to her and pulled her skirt,
sadly asking her why she was crying.
She bent down to hold me, and as she pressed
her forehead to mine, said, Oh son,
My dear Dametas, Filinos is dead.
Then I cried, too. Mamma wanted
to hold me back but couldn't. While she
was looking elsewhere, I ran to the little
bed of my dear Filin. At first I stared at him

Il rimirai, poi sullo smorto viso
Mille baci gli diedi, e colla mano
Toccai la fredda guancia, e gli occhi chiusi
Di riaprir gli cercai. Deh quanto io piansi
In veder come più non si movea!
Filin! fratello! io gli dicea, oh Dio!
Tu non mi vedi più . . . Che far giammai
Potrò senza di te? Quanto t'amava!
Quanto m'amavi! alla selvetta, al prato
Sempre eravamo insieme: oh quante volte
Corremmo a gara, e a gara tra le foglie
Cogliemmo i più bei fior! quante sull'erba
La sera assisi al raggio della luna,
Cantammo insiem! Tu m'insegnavi il suono
Sopra le canne a modular, che spesso
Di tua man m'apprestavi; o a far panieri
Per empirli di fiori; o a lanciar sassi
A un albero lontan. Spesso nel bosco
Tendemmo insidie agli augelletti, e insieme
Ci partimmo la preda. Entro un canneto
Spesso nascosto io l'amor tuo cercai
Deludere un momento: ansioso allora
Tu di me givi in traccia. Il riso mio,
O lo scrosciar delle vicine canne
Mi tradiva talor: tu mi scoprivi,
E lieto a me correvi, e in abbracciarmi
Del mio crudo piacer mi riprendevi.
Oh quanto ci amavamo! Ah tutto tutto
È finito per noi. Caro fratello
Tu mi lasciasti . . . Al giuoco, in casa io sempre

intently, then I kissed his pallid face
a thousand times, and touched his frigid cheek
with my hand, and tried to open
his shut eyes. Oh, how I cried,
seeing that he no longer moved!
Filin! My brother! I said to him, oh God!
You don't see me anymore . . . What will I ever
manage to do without you? How I loved you!
How you loved me! We were always together
in the woods and field: oh how many times
we raced, and competed in picking the prettiest flowers
in the leaves. How often we sat on the grass
in the evenings and sang
by the light of the moon! You taught me
how to make notes with the canes
you often lent me, or weave baskets
to fill with flowers, or throw rocks
at a tree in the distance. Often in the woods
we set traps for the birds, and shared our catch
together. Often hidden in a canebrake
I tried to fool your love for just a moment:
then how anxiously
you'd dog my footsteps. My laughter,
or the rustling of the canes nearby
would betray me and you'd find me out,
and gladly run to me, and hug me,
reprimanding me for my cruel pleasure.
How much we loved each other! Oh everything,
everything is over for us.
Dear brother, you left me . . . Must I always be alone,

Solo restar dovrò? No, che la vita
Menar più non potrei . . . Caro Filino,
Ah tu moristi, ah morir voglio anch'io.

Egli piangea; tra le ginocchia il prese
Il buon Micone, e gli asciugava il pianto,
E consolando il gia.

MICONE

Diman condurti
Alla cittade io vo', diman la tomba
Ti mostrerò di tuo fratello, e voglio
Che venga insiem con noi la mamma ancora.
Ah figlio! ah tu sei morto! il padre tuo
Che sì t'amò, dimenticar sapresti?

playing, and at home? No, I couldn't
go on living . . . Dear Filinos,
you died, and I want to die myself.

He wept. Good Micon took him
between his knees and wiped his tears,
and kept on consoling him.

MICON

Tomorrow
I want to take you into town, I'll show you
your brother's grave,
and I want your mother to come, too.
Ah son! Ah, you're dead! How could your father
who loved you so, forget you?

IL CANTO DELLA FANCIULLA

Canto di verginella, assiduo canto,
Che da chiuso ricetto errando vieni
Per le quiete vie; come sì tristo
Suoni agli orecchi miei? perchè mi stringi
Sì forte il cor, che a lagrimar m'induci?
E pur lieto sei tu; voce festiva
De la speranza: ogni tua nota il tempo
Aspettato risuona. Or, così lieto,
Al pensier mio sembri un lamento, e l'alma
Mi pungi di pietà. Cagion d'affanno
Torna il pensier de la speranza istessa
A chi per prova la conobbe.

THE GIRL'S SONG

Young girl's song, insistent song
wafting from a hidden room and wandering
in the quiet streets—why do you sound
so sad to me? Why do you tear at my heart
so fiercely it brings me to tears?
And yet you're happy; joyous voice of hope:
each note of yours rehearses
the expected moment. Yet though you're happy,
you seem like a lament to me,
and pierce my soul with pity. The idea
of hope itself comes back, a cause of pain
to him who's known it.

CORO DI MORTI NELLO STUDIO DI FEDERICO RUYSCH

Sola nel mondo eterna, a cui si volve
Ogni creata cosa,
In te, morte, si posa
Nostra ignuda natura;
Lieta no, ma sicura
Dall'antico dolor. Profonda notte
Nella confusa mente
Il pensier grave oscura;
Alla speme, al desio, l'arido spirto
Lena mancar si sente:
Così d'affanno e di temenza è sciolto,
E l'età vote e lente
Senza tedio consuma.
Vivemmo: e qual di paurosa larva,
E di sudato sogno,
A lattante fanciullo erra nell'alma
Confusa ricordanza:
Tal memoria n'avanza
Del viver nostro: ma da tema è lunge
Il rimembrar. Che fummo?

CHORUS OF THE DEAD IN THE STUDY OF FREDERICK RUYSCH

Alone eternal in the world,
toward which all creation tends,
Death, our naked being
rests in you:
not happy, but secure
from age-old suffering.
A deep night in our troubled minds
obscures the terrible idea;
the arid spirit lacks
the breath for hope and desire:
thus freed from strife and fear,
peaceably it spends
the empty, inexorable years.
We lived, and like
a terrifying ghost
a nursing infant's fitful dream,
the vague memory of living
flickers in our soul.
But memory's a far cry
from fear. What were we?

Che fu quel punto acerbo
Che di vita ebbe nome?
Cosa arcana e stupenda
Oggi è la vita al pensier nostro, e tale
Qual de' vivi al pensiero
L'ignota morte appar. Come da morte
Vivendo rifuggia, così rifugge
Dalla fiamma vitale
Nostra ignuda natura;
Lieta no ma sicura;
Però ch'esser beato
Nega ai mortali e nega a' morti il fato.

What was that bitter
moment they called life?
Today we see it as
a secret, fearful thing,
the way that death seems alien
to those who are alive.
As living it fled death,
so our naked being
shrinks from the vital flame,
not happy, no, but safe;
since fate prohibits happiness
for mortals and the dead.

AD ARIMANE

Re delle cose, autor del mondo, arcana
Malvagità, sommo potere e somma
Intelligenza, eterno
Dator de' mali e reggitor del moto,

io non so se questo ti faccia felice, ma mira e godi ec. contemplando eternam. ec.

produzione e distruzione ec. per uccider partorisce ec. sistema del mondo, tutto patimen. Natura è come un bambino che disfa subito il fatto. Vecchiezza. Noia o passioni piene di dolore e disperazioni: amore.

I selvaggi e le tribù primitive, sotto diverse forme, non riconoscono che te. Ma i popoli civili ec. te con diversi nomi il volgo appella Fato, natura e Dio. Ma tu sei Arimane, tu quello che ec.

E il mondo civile t'invoca.

Taccio le tempeste, le pesti ec. tuoi doni, che altro non sai donare. Tu dai gli ardori e i ghiacci.

E il mondo delira cercando nuovi ordini e leggi e spera perfezione. Ma l'opra tua rimane immutabile, perchè p. natura dell'uomo sempre regneranno L'ardimento e l'inganno, e la sincerità e la modestia resteranno indietro, e la fortuna sarà nemica al valore, e il

TO AHRIMAN

King of the real, creator of the world,
hidden malevolence, supreme power and supreme
intelligence, eternal
giver of pain and arbiter of movement,

I don't know if this will make you happy but look and enjoy, etc., *contemplando aeternam* [contemplating eternity], etc.

production and destruction etc. gives birth to kill etc., system of the world, all *patimen* [suffering]. Nature is like a baby who suddenly destroys what has been created. Old age. Boredom or passions full of pain and despair: love.

The savages and primitive tribes, in different forms, recognize only you. But civilized peoples etc. the crowd call you Fate, nature, and God by different names. But you are Ahriman, you who etc.

And the civilized world calls to you.

I leave out the storms, plagues, etc. your gifts, for you don't know how to give anything else. You give ardors and ice.

And the world raves seeking new orders and laws and hopes for perfection. But your work remains immutable, because given man's nature Courage and illusion will always reign, and sincerity and modesty will lag behind, and luck will be the enemy of valor, and

merito non sarà buono a farsi largo, e il giusto e il debole sarà oppresso ec. ec.

Vivi, Arimane e trionfi, e sempre trionferai.

Invidia dagli antichi attribuita agli dèi verso gli uomini.

Animali destinati in cibo. Serpente Boa. Nume pietoso ecc.

Perchè, dio del male, hai tu posto nella vita qualche apparenza di piacere? l'amore? . . . per travagliarci col desiderio, col confronto degli altri, e del tempo nostro passato ec.?

Io non so se tu ami le lodi o le bestemmie ec. Tua lode sarà il pianto, testimonio del nostro patire. Pianto da me per certo Tu non avrai: ben mille volte dal mio labbro il tuo nome maledetto sarà ec.

Mai io non mi rassegnerò ec.

Se mai grazia fu chiesta ad Arimane ec. concedimi ch'io non passi il 7° lustro. Io sono stato, vivendo, il tuo maggior predicatore ec. l'apostolo della tua religione. Ricompensami. Non ti chiedo nessuno di quelli che il mondo chiama beni: ti chiedo quello che è creduto il massimo de' mali, la morte. (non ti chiedo ricchezze ec. non amore, sola causa degna di vivere ec.). Non posso, non posso più della vita.

merit will not manage to make its way, and the just and the weak will be oppressed, etc. etc.

You live, Ahriman, and triumph, and you will always triumph.

Envy of men attributed to the gods by the ancients.

Animals destined to be food. Boa Constrictor. Pitying god etc.

Why, god of evil, have you set some semblance of pleasure in life? love? . . . to torment us with desire, with comparing our fate with others, and our past etc.?

I don't know if you love praise or blasphemy etc. Your praise will be weeping, testimony of our suffering. Weeping from me certainly. You will not have: more than a thousand times will your name be cursed by my lips, etc.

But I will not be resigned etc.

If ever mercy was asked of Ahriman etc. grant that I will not pass the 7th lustrum. I have been, while I lived, your greatest preacher etc. the apostle of your religion. Give me recompense. I ask you for none of what the world calls goods: I ask you for what is considered the worst of evils, death. (I don't ask you for wealth etc. not love, the only thing worth living for etc.) I cannot, cannot bear to go on living.

CHRONOLOGY

THE STRUCTURE
OF THE CANTI

NOTES

SELECT BIBLIOGRAPHY

ACKNOWLEDGMENTS

INDEX OF TITLES
AND FIRST LINES

CHRONOLOGY

1798

Giacomo Taldegardo Francesco di Sales Saverio Pietro Leopardi is born on June 29 in Recanati, a small town not far from Ancona in the Marche, a region then belonging to the backward Papal States. He is the first of five surviving children—the others are Carlo (1799–1878) and Paolina (1800–1869), to whom Giacomo will be particularly close; Luigi (1804–28); and Pierfrancesco (1813–51)—of Count Monaldo Leopardi (1776–1847) and Marchesa Adelaide Antici (1778–1857). The reactionary Monaldo is cultivated, affectionate, a man of letters, and an avid book collector; his wife, by contrast, is cold, severe, dedicated to restoring the family's finances, which had been compromised by her spendthrift husband. Leopardi, in a portrait sketch thought to be of her in his *Zibaldone* (353–55, 25 November 1820), writes of a woman "reduced by religion" to hating life, beauty, and pleasure to the point where "not only does she not share in the grief of parents who lost their infant children, but she envied them intimately and sincerely, because they had flown to heaven without danger."

1807–12

Giacomo, Carlo, and Paolina are taught by priests until 1812, when, as Giacomo's father would write, "Giacomo's scholarly studies came to an end because the teacher had nothing more to teach him." Indeed, from 1808, it can be said that he educates himself. Beyond Italian and Latin, he eventually teaches himself Greek, Hebrew, French, Spanish, and English, and writes poems, translations, and philological works that will be admired by the litterateurs of the time.

1809

Writes various poetic texts, the first of which is the sonnet "La morte di Ettore" (The Death of Hector). Also writes his first prose works and, between the ages of ten and eleven, translates the *Odes* of Horace: twenty-nine from the first book and fifteen from the second.

1810

Writes other poems, in Italian and Latin, notably "Il diluvio universale" (The Universal Flood).

1811

Writes the tragedy *La virtù Indiana* (Indian Courage) and his first *Dissertazioni filosofiche* (Philosophical Dissertations). Translates Horace's *Ars poetica* into ottava rima.

1812

Begins the "seven years of insane and desperate study," in his father's library of sixteen thousand volumes, that will ruin his health; develops a serious hunchback. *Epigrammi. Pompeo in Egitto* (Pompey in Egypt), tragedy.

1813

Storia dell'astronomia dalla sua origine fino all'anno MDCCCXI (History of Astronomy from Its Beginnings to 1811).

1814

Philological studies of the Greek Esichios [of Milo], Plotinus, and early Christian rhetoricians. Translates *Scherzi epigrammatici* (Epigrammatic Scherzi) and *Fragmenta Patrum Graecorum* (Fragments from the Greek Fathers) (unfinished) from the Greek.

1815

In two months writes the *Saggio sopra gli errori poplari degli antichi* (Essay on the Popular Errors of the Ancients). After the Austrians defeat Murat he writes the *Orazione agli Italiani in occasione della liberazione del Piceno* (Oration to the Italians on the occasion of the liberation of Piceno), which reflects his father's anti-French and antirevolutionary biases. Translates the *Idilli* (Idylls) of Moschus and the pseudo-Homeric *Batracomiomachia*, titled "La guerra dei topi e delle rane" (The War Between the Mice and the Frogs), which he will later revise twice, in 1821–22 and 1826.

1816

Writes a discourse on the life and works of the Roman rhetorician M. Cornelius Fronto and translates his works, which had been discovered and published by the librarian and philologist Angelo Mai. Writes the *Notizie storiche e geografiche sulla città e chiesa arcivescovile di Damiata* (Historical and Geographical Notes on the City and Archiepiscopal Church of Damiata), printed in Loreto in June, his first published work; "Parere sul salterio ebraico" (A View of the Hebrew Psalter); "Della fama di Orazio presso gli antichi" (On Horace's Fame among the Ancients). Writes "Le rimembranze" (Memories), and the "Inno a Nettuno" (Hymn to Neptune), which purports to translate a Greek original; when it is published in *Lo spettatore* in Milan the following year it will fool even the most erudite critics. Writes (in Greek, with translations into Latin) two *Odae adespotae* (Anonymous Odes). Convinced that his death is imminent, writes the canticle "Appressamento della morte" (Approach of Death), of which a fragment will appear in the *Canti* (no. XXXIX). Translates the first book of the *Odyssey* and the second of Virgil's *Aeneid*, the *Iscrizioni greche triopee* (Greek Inscriptions from Triopio),and the pseudo-Virgilian poem *Moretum* or *La torta* (The Cake). Outlines a tragedy about Marie-Antoinette. Sends *La biblioteca italiana* a letter, which goes unpublished, in response to Mme de Staël's article "L'esprit des traductions."

1817

Translates the fragments of the *Roman Antiquities* of Dionysus of Halicarnassus discovered by Mai. Begins an epistolary friendship with the man of letters Pietro Giordani, who becomes his first great friend and admirer.

Writes the first notes of the *Zibaldone*, the collection of his literary and philosophical reflections and observations that will eventually be published between 1898 and 1900 by a commission led by Giosué Carducci under the title *Pensieri di varia filosofia e di bella lettera* (Thoughts on Various Philosophies and Belles Lettres). Translates Hesiod's *Titanomachia*. Writes the "Sonetti in persona di Ser Pecora fiorentino" (Sonnets in the Voice of the Florentine Ser Pecora) and the sonnet "Letta la vita dell'Alfieri scritta da esso" (On Reading Alfieri's Autobiography).

In December, Monaldo's twenty-six-year-old cousin Geltrude Cassi-Lazzari visits Recanati. Leopardi's overwhelming infatuation with her inspires his "Elegia I" (which becomes "Il primo amore") and the prose *Diario del primo amore* (Journal of First Love).

1818

Writes "Elegia II" and the *Discorso di un italiano intorno alla poesia romantica* (An Italian's Discourse Concerning Romantic Poetry). In September, Giordani visits Recanati for five days and the two travel to Macerata together, Leopardi's first foray away from his family. Toward the end of the year writes the canzoni "All'Italia" and "Sopra il monumento di Dante," which are published in Rome by Bourlié.

1819

Begins to suffer from a fatigue of the eyes, which prevents him "not only from any reading or study whatsoever, but from the slightest attempt at thinking" (letter to Leonardo Trissino, 27 September 1819).

Writes the canzoni "Per una donna inferma di malattia lunga e mortale" (For a Woman Suffering from a Long and Fatal Illness) and "Nella morte di una donna fatta trucidare col suo portato dal corruttore per mano di un chirurgo" (On the Death of a Woman Murdered with Her Fetus by Her Corruptor at the Hand of a Surgeon), which he will later disavow.

In July applies in secret for a passport for Milan, hoping to escape from Recanati, but his plan is discovered and foiled. Writes the *Ricordi d'infanzia e di adolescenza* (Memories of Childhood and Adolescence) and, it seems, begins to plan a tragedy, *Telesilla.*

In September, writes "L'infinito"; writes "Alla luna" and the fragment "Odi, Melisso . . ."

1820

Writes the canzone "Ad Angelo Mai" in ecstatic response to Mai's discovery in the Vatican of the manuscript of Cicero's *De re publica.* The poem is published by Marsigli in Bologna.

First glimmerings of the *Operette morali.* On September 4, he writes to Giordani: "Almost to take revenge on the world, and on courage, I've imagined and sketched out certain satirical prose pieces."

In the fall, writes "La sera del dì di festa" and, most likely, "Il sogno."

1821

Applies for but fails to obtain a post as writer in Latin under Mai at the Vatican Library.

Convinced of the absolute "uselessness of human things," he envisions writing several *Inni cristiani* (Christian Hymns), of which only the "Inno ai patriarchi" (1822) is completed. In all likelihood writes "La vita solitaria," "Nelle nozze della sorella Paolina," "A un vincitore nel pallone," and "Bruto minore."

1822

"Alla primavera," "Ultimo canto di Saffo," "Comparazione delle sentenze di Bruto minore e di Teofrasto vicini a morte" (Comparison of the Sayings of Brutus Minor and Theophrastus Before Dying).

Translates from the Latin the French patrologist François Combefis' *Martirio de' santi padri nel Monte Sinai* (Martyrdom of the Holy Fathers on Mount Sinai).

Is invited to travel to Rome with one of his maternal uncles, but is gravely disappointed by the culture of the capital. Orcel (331): "He walks a bit in the city, weeps at the grave of Tasso, becomes aware of his unsuitability for any kind of worldly life, and fails in his attempts to find a post in Italy or abroad."

1823

Returns to Recanati on May 3. In September, writes the Platonic canzone "Alla sua donna," translates the "Satira di Simonide sopra le donne" (Simonides' Satire on Women), and returns to his philological studies, writing over thirteen hundred pages in the *Zibaldone*.

1824

Writes the first twenty of the *Operette morali* (moral sketches; satirical and philosophical dialogues in the style of Lucian) as well as the "Discorso sopra lo stato presente dei costumi degl'italiani" (Discourse on the Present State of the Morals of the Italians), which remains unpublished until 1906.

Is invited by G. B. Vieusseux to contribute to his distinguished Florentine review, *L'Antologia*, but declines, saying it's impossible for him to keep au courant of contemporary literary fashion in Recanati.

At the end of August, the *Canzoni*, of which there are ten, along with their "Annotazioni" are published by Nobili in Bologna. Between December 1824 and early 1825 translates the *Operette morali* of Isocrates.

1825

In July, is invited by A. F. Stella to edit the complete writings of Cicero. Leaves for Milan, stopping at Bologna, where he is met by Giordani. After declining a minor appointment at the University of Rome, returns to Bologna at the end of

September, where he will remain for more than a year, working on a translation of the *Manual* of Epictetus and, in particular, a critical edition of Petrarch's *Rime* for Stella.

1826

Refuses an ecclesiastical benefice left vacant on the death of one of his uncles. Several of the *Operette morali* are published in *L'Antologia*.

Interrupting a long poetic silence, which otherwise runs from September 1823 to April 1828, composes the epistle "Al Conte Carlo Pepoli," which he is invited to deliver at the Bolognese Accademia dei Felsinei. But it is poorly received: "His voice is low and timid, and his philosophy decidedly too despairing" for popular consumption (Orcel, 331).

In the springtime, meets and is briefly infatuated with Countess Teresa Carniani Malvezzi, a friend of the poet Vincenzo Monti.

Stella publishes his Petrarch edition in Milan; the *Versi* are issued by the Stamperie delle Muse in Bologna.

Returns to Recanati on November 11. Translates the "Orazione di G. Gemisto Pletone in morte della imperatrice Elena Paleologina" (Oration of G. Gemisto Pleto on the death of the Empress Elena Paleologina) with an introductory "Discorso."

1827

Leopardi's *Crestomazia italiana: La Prosa* (Italian Anthology: Prose), compiled for Stella, is published in Milan, while Leopardi is correcting the proofs for the *Operette morali* (also published by Stella).

In Bologna from April 26 to June 20, when he travels to Florence. Meets Vieusseux, Gino Capponi, and other leading intellectuals, including Niccolò Tommaseo, for whom he forms an intense dislike, Manzoni, and Stendhal. Also encounters a young Neapolitan admirer, Antonio Ranieri, who will become his companion in his last years. Writes further *operette morali*.

On November 1 transfers to Pisa.

1828

Stella publishes Leopardi's *Crestomazia italiana poetica* (Anthology of Italian Poetry), or "Selection of passages in Italian verse outstanding for feeling or expression, chosen and arranged according to the age of the authors, by Count Giacomo Leopardi." Reads with great enjoyment Manzoni's *I promessi sposi* (The Betrothed).

Beginning in Pisa of a major return to poetry. Writes "Scherzo," "Il risorgimento," and "A Silvia."

Declines a chair in Dante studies at the University of Bonn.

Meets the Jesuit Vincenzo Gioberti in Florence and with him returns to Recanati at the end of November. Death of his brother Luigi.

1829

Writes "Le ricordanze," "La quiete dopo la tempesta," "Il sabato del villaggio"; begins the "Canto notturno di un pastore errante dell'Asia."

Plans a "Parallelo della civiltà degli antichi (cioè Greci e Romani) e di quella dei moderni" (Comparison of the Civilization of the ancients [i.e, Greeks and Romans] with that of the Moderns), as well as an "Enciclopedia delle cognizioni inutili" (Encyclopedia of Useless Knowledge).

1830

The *Operette morali* fail to win the quinquennial prize of 1000 *scudi* awarded by the Accademia della Crusca; it goes instead to Carlo Botta's *Storia d'Italia* (History of Italy).

Finishes the "Canto notturno" On April 30, leaves for Florence, where Pietro Colletta has arranged for a consortium of friends to offer him a yearlong stipend. Meets and falls in love with the beautiful but unmoved Fanny Targioni Tozzetti, inspiration for the five poems in the so-called Aspasia cycle: "Consalvo," "Il pensiero dominante," "Amore e Morte," "A se stesso," and "Aspasia."

Meets the Swiss philologist Louis de Sinner, to whom he gives all his own philological works, hoping that de Sinner will publish them abroad. In November, joins forces with Antonio Ranieri, who will remain with Leopardi until his death.

1831

Begins the *Paralipomeni della Batracomiomachia* (Omissions from the [pseudo-Homeric] War Between the Mice and the Frogs, twice translated by Leopardi in his youth); the poem, in eight eventual cantos of 375 octaves, is a relentless satire on political and religious idealism, an allegory of the Neapolitan revolution of 1820—"the shrimp are the Germans [i.e., the Austrians], the rats are the Italians of 1820; and the frogs are the priests" (wrote Marc Monnier in 1860)—which he will work on until his death and which will be published by Ranieri in Paris in 1842.

After the revolution of 1831, the provisional government of Recanati names him a deputy to the National Assembly in Bologna, but this is aborted with the return of the Austrians.

In April the first edition of the *Canti* is published in Florence by Piatti, dedicated to "his Tuscan friends," to whom he writes: "I am nothing more than a torso that feels and suffers."

Writes (possibly) "Il pensiero dominante," then leaves with Ranieri for Rome, where he may draft "Sopra un basso rilievo antico sepolcrale."

1832

Returns with Ranieri to Florence. Writes the preamble to the Florentine journal *Lo spettatore fiorentino*, planned by some friends. Writes, perhaps, "Amore e Morte" and "Consalvo."

Writes the last two *operette* and, on December 4, the last entry in the *Zibaldone*. Begins compiling the *Pensieri* (Thoughts), 111 short pieces largely drawn from the *Zibaldone*, on "the characters of men and their conduct in Society." The book will be published posthumously in Ranieri's 1845 edition of Leopardi's works.

1833

Writes "A se stesso" and sketches the hymn to Ahriman.

On September 2, leaves Florence for Naples with Ranieri, stopping in Rome; arrives October 2.

1834

Writes "Aspasia." Friendship with the German poet August von Platen. Publication in Florence of the second edition of the *Operette morali*.

1835

Signs a contract with the Neapolitan publisher Saverio Starita for a collected edition of his writings, planned in no fewer than six volumes, of which the first would contain the *Poesie*, the second and third the *Operette morali*, and the rest his uncollected works.

The second edition of the *Canti* is published in September, including the Aspasia poems and "Il passero solitario" (written between 1831 and 1835), as well as "Sopra un basso rilievo antico sepolcrale," "Sopra il ritratto di una bella donna," and the "Palinodia," most of these likely written in this year.

Probably also writes "I nuovi credenti" (The New Believers), verse satire on the Neapolitan Catholic spiritualists, analogous to his critique of Florentine liberals in the "Palinodia."

1836

The first and second volumes of Starita's edition are sequestered by the Bourbon government. Due to an outbreak of cholera in Naples, Leopardi, Ranieri, and Ranieri's sister Paolina retire to the Villa Ferrigni at the foot of Vesuvius, between Torre del Greco and Torre Annunziata.

Writes "Il tramonto della luna" and "La ginestra," which will be published in Ranieri's posthumous edition (Florence: Le Monnier, 1845).

1837

In the spring, returns to Naples. Dies on June 14 and is buried in the church of San Vitale at Fuorigrotta. Giordani's inscription on his tomb reads:

> TO COUNT GIACOMO LEOPARDI OF RECANATI / PHILOLOGIST ADMIRED OUTSIDE ITALY / GREATEST WRITER OF PHILOSOPHY AND POETRY / COMPARABLE ONLY WITH THE GREEKS / WHO FINISHED HIS LIFE AT AGE 39 / IN CONTINUAL MOST MISERABLE ILLNESS / ANTONIO RANIERI / WITH HIM FOR SEVEN YEARS TO THE LAST HOUR / MADE THIS FOR HIS ADORED FRIEND. MDCCCXXXVII

1845

Postumous edition of Leopardi's *Opere*, edited by Ranieri, published by Le Monnier in Florence.

1898–1900

Publication of the *Zibaldone* under the title *Pensieri di varia filosofia e di bella letteratura* (Thoughts on Various Philosophies and on Belles Lettres), edited by a national commission headed by Giosué Carducci, in seven volumes by Le Monnier, Florence.

1939

The poet's remains are interred in a monument next to the so-called tomb of Virgil near Piedigrotta (Mergellina).

THE STRUCTURE OF THE CANTI

The forty-one canti are generally seen as organized in the following groupings:

1 the ten canzoni (I–IX and XVIII), written between 1818 and 1823, on public and historical themes;

2 the intimately personal elegies and idylls (X–XVI), written at much the same time (1818–21), with the exception of XI, "Il passero solitario," begun in this period but completed in the early 1830s and inserted at the beginning of the idylls; this alternation between public and private, historical and pastoral, is in fact the essential organizing characteristic of all of Leopardi's work;

3 the epistle to Carlo Pepoli (XIX, 1826), written during the period when Leopardi had turned from poetry to the social criticism of the *Operette morali*;

4 the return to lyric with the canti of memory of the great Pisa-Recanati period, XX–XXV (1828–30);

5 the so-called Aspasia cycle, inspired by Leopardi's unhappy love for Fanny Targioni Tozzetti (XXVI–XXIX) (1830–35), which also includes "Consalvo" (XVII), though the poem was eventually placed earlier in the book;

6 the paired meditative, neoclassical sepulchral songs (XXX and XXXI) of the early 1830s;

7 the bitterly ironic verse epistle, the "Palinodia" (XXXII) (1835);

8 the last great testamentary poems, "Il tramonto della luna" and "La ginestra" (XXXIII and XXXIV), written at Naples in 1836, not long before the poet's death;

9 a group of seven short texts (XXXV–XLI): translations, epigrams, and fragments drawn from the poet's early unpublished work.

The variety of style, theme, and tone among the book's components makes its formal organization difficult to discern. As Nicola Gardini writes in "History and

Pastoral in the Structure of Leopardi's *Canti*" (79), the book is "the work of one man, but includes the most diverse poetic forms, styles and voices: Petrarchan canzoni, free canzoni, epistles, elegies, Horatian satire, love poems, dramatic monologues, imitations and translations. The book grew over the years from a slender collection of relatively traditional canzoni to its final form, progressively incorporating and adapating to an ever-changing design the poet's ongoing meditations and stylistic experiments." Though the poems appear in a basically chronological order, "temporal discontinuities as well as breaks and shifts of various kinds govern the whole. The publishing history of the book shows that the *Canti* have a highly dynamic structure and that contradiction and self-emendation or even recantation are distinctive features of Leopardi's mind."

Gardini (91) sees the book as divided into four sections: "(1) Historical decline ('All'Italia'–'Ultimo canto di Saffo'). (2) The pastoral/*infinito* ('Il primo amore–'Al conte Carlo Pepoli'). (3) Critique of the pastoral/*infinito* ('Il risorgimento'–'A se stesso'). (4) Historical catastrophe ('Aspasia'–'La ginestra') . . . While seeming solely to represent a fatal progression towards total historical ruin, this subdivision expresses an essential characteristic of Leopardi's mind: a passionate preoccupation with beginnings." He adds (92): "In the *Canti* . . . the positive follows, and tends to replace, the negative. Alternation within progression appears to be the leading principle of construction of the book."

Much perplexity has been expressed about why Leopardi himself, in the 1835 Naples edition, chose to end his greatest book "in a minor key." Dotti (146) quotes Mario Fubini's proposal that the poet wanted to give the reader "a little taste of his less serious work"; others have suggested that the poet wanted to make the book a little longer; but neither option seems plausible for such a premeditated artist.

The last two compositions, being, as Leopardi believed, translations of Simonides, the dominant figure of "All'Italia," the first of the canti, in a sense bring "full circle the stylistic and philosophical variety of the book as a whole under the unifying sign of antiquity," Gardini asserts (82), making Simonides and Leopardi "inextricably one" as the young Leopardi had hoped, "in spite of all historical decadence and difference" (92).

Franco d'Intino, in an illuminating analysis of fragment XXXIX ("Spento il diurno raggio in occidente," (700), contends that "the secret heart of the epilogue to the *Canti*" is "the rediscovery of the self in artistic labor—and in the book. A rediscovery which compensates for the loss—the vertiginous mutation—of the modern subject, hostage to a time which swallows up everything" (see notes, p. 478). Expanding on a suggestion of María de las Nieves Muñiz Muñiz, he asserts that "the frame of the epilogue exhibits and represents the theme of human time, opposed (in the 'Scherzo') to the time of artistic labor and the book," adding that "its central nucleus puts this opposition center stage, presenting old texts that go back to a now very distant past, reinterpreted (and, in part changed) in the new context of the book of the *Canti*." For d'Intino (716), it's not impossible that, "more ironic than his commentators," Leopardi, in a coda that is notable for its variety, irony, and, finally its spirited embrace of the classical acceptance of the limits of human time, "intended to laugh at himself, and his own obstinate dedication to an eternity in which he no longer believed."

NOTES

This is not a scholarly edition. Leopardi's work has been so thoroughly and authoritatively interpreted that to attempt something original in the way of commentary would have been a fool's errand for an amateur. I have confined myself in my notes to trying to offer a fuller context for the poetry than has hitherto been available for English-language readers, selectively pointing out sources and echoes along the way—though the poet draws incessantly on his inspirations, ancient and modern. It goes without saying that the commentary to these texts could have been endless.

NOTE: "M1" and "M2" refer, respectively, to Mondadori's Meridiani editions of Leopardi's poetry (edited by Mario Andrea Rigoni) and prose (edited by Rolando Damiani). See Bibliography, p. 487.

Introduction: Poet of Problems

1. The first complete English translation, edited by Michael Caesar and Franco d'Intino of the Leopardi Center at Birmingham University, will be published by Farrar, Straus and Giroux in 2012.

2. Ugo Dotti, in his exemplary critical edition of the *Canti* (6th ed.; Feltrinelli, 2008), 160.

3. "[T]he present, however it is, cannot be poetic; and the poetic, in one way or another, always turns out to consist in the distant, the undefined, the vague." *Zibaldone* 4426 (1 January 1829).

4. Gary Brown, in a note to his translation of "History in the Service and Disservice of Life," the second of Nietzsche's *Unzeitgemässe Betrachtungen* (*Un-*

modern Observations, otherwise translated as *Untimely Meditations*) (1873–76) (New Haven: Yale University Press, 1990), writes (93*n*–94*n*): "Nietzsche, like Schopenhauer, felt intense admiration [for Leopardi's poetry and prose]. Schopenhauer had seen in Leopardi the supreme contemporary poet of human unhappiness; and it was to Nietzsche . . . that Hans von Bulow . . . dedicated his translation of Leopardi into German . . . Of Leopardi Nietzsche remarked [in "We Classicists," the last of the *Unmodern Observations*] that he was "the modern ideal of a classicist" and one of "the last great followers of the Italian poet-scholars" ["Richard Wagner in Bayreuth," the fourth of the *Unmodern Observations*] . . . who, along with Merimée, Emerson, and Landor, could rightly be called 'a master of prose' [*The Gay Science*, 92]."

In his introduction (xiv) to the Yale edition of the *Unmodern Observations*, William Arrowsmith writes of Nietzsche's conviction that to "fulfill themselves art and philosophy must be fused in a powerfully unified vision. Thus, Nietzsche could speak of the poetry of Heraclitus and Empedocles as philosophy *en acte* and . . . praise Pindar and Leopardi as 'poets who think.'"

5. By Domenico De Robertis, Nicola Gardini, Franco d'Intino, and others. See Gardini's "History and Pastoral in the Structure of Leopardi's *Canti*" and d'Intino's "'Spento il diurno raggio.'" See also "The Structure of the *Canti*," pp. 375–77.

6. For an illuminating discussion of the significance of Leopardi's title and the formal development of his poetry, see Michel Orcel's essay "Leopardi et le procès des formes" in Orcel (9–20), in which he asserts (10) that the poet's primary inspirations for his title were Mme de Stäel's "Dernier chant de Corinne," in chapter XX of her celebrated eponymous novel, and Cesarotti's versions of Ossian, the *Canti di Selma*. Orcel also associates the new title for the book with the "return to life" that was also a "return to song" in the new lyricism of the Pisa-Recanati period, as recorded in "Il risorgimento," adding that Bellinian "bel canto" offered the poet a model of "semantic plasticity" in his new "melodic expansion."

7. *Zibaldone* 4302 (15 February 1828): "One of the major results that I propose for myself and hope for my verses, is that they should warm my old age with the heat of my youth; it is to enjoy them in that time, and feel some residue of my past feelings, set within them there, to preserve them and give them dura-

tion, as if on deposit; it is to be moved myself in rereading them as often happens to me, and more so than in reading the poems of others: beyond remembering, reflecting on what I was, and comparing myself with myself; and finally the pleasure that is felt in enjoying and appreciating one's own work, and contemplating it oneself, taking pleasure in it, the beauties and the virtues of one's own child, with no other satisfaction than having made something beautiful in the world; whether or not it is recognized as such by others."

8. See Franco d'Intino's illuminating introduction to his edition of Leopardi's translations of *Poeti greci e latini*, xvi.

9. The ten canzoni are canti I–IX and XVIII, "Alla sua donna" (1823). See notes to "All'Italia" for a discussion of the form and its meaning for Leopardi.

10. Iris Origo, *Leopardi: A Study in Solitude*, 76.

11. "Lyric can be called the height the culmination the summit of poetry, which is the summit of human discourse." *Zibaldone* 245 (18 September 1820).

12. In his "Translator's Introduction: 'Attempts and Preludes'" (xviii), to his *Leopardi: Selected Poems*.

13. Nicholas J. Perella, "Translating Leopardi?" 358.

14. Quoted in Perella, 364.

15. John Heath-Stubbs, in the introduction (13) to his *Poems from Giacomo Leopardi*.

16. D. S. Carne-Ross, *Instaurations*, 262–63. As d'Intino (*Poeti greci e latini*, xvi) puts it, Leopardi in the *Zibaldone* "always described and greatly appreciated Greek as free and flexible, in opposition . . . with Latin, a logical and rational language par excellence."

17. See Orcel, p. 14.

18. I.e., from heart to chorus. Orcel (16) quotes *Zibaldone* 2804–2809 (21–23 June 1823): "I consider [the use of the chorus in ancient drama] as part of that vague, that indefinite that is the principal cause of the *charme* of ancient poetry and belles lettres . . . Maxims of justice, virtue, heroism, and compassion, of love of country, were spoken in ancient dramas in the mouth of the chorus, that is of an indefinite, and often unnamed, multitude . . . They were expressed in lyric verses, which were sung, and accompanied by musical instruments. What other impression could all these circumstances . . . produce if not an impression of the

vague and indeterminate, and therefore entirely great, entirely beautiful, entirely poetic? These maxims weren't put into the mouth of an individual, to be recited in an ordinary and natural tone . . . The entire nation, posterity, appeared on stage. She did not speak like each of the mortals who represented the action: she expressed herself in lyric verses, full of poetry. The sound of her voice was not that of human individuals: it was a music, a harmony . . . This was almost the same as uniting the real world and the ideal and moral world . . . on stage."

19. Leopardi wrote to Charles Lebreton in June 1836 about Starita's edition of his collected writings: "In spite of the magnificent title of *opere* which my bookseller has felt he must give to his collection, I have never made works, I have only made some attempts thinking always of making a start, but my career has gone no further"—an echo, perhaps, of his much-quoted mot by Mme De Staël that "dans la vie il n'y a que commencements." Quoted in Damiani, *All'apparir del vero*, 467.

20. *Zibaldone* 152 (4 July 1820). See also his "Discorso di un italiano intorno alla poesia romantica" (M2, 347–426).

21. Francesco De Sanctis, in his *History of Italian Literature*, trans. Joan Redfern, vol. 2 (New York: Barnes & Noble, Inc., 1968), 943–44.

22. Massimo Bontempelli, quoted in Rigoni (M1, 976).

23. See *Zibaldone* 2219–21 (3 December 1821).

24. Cyril Connolly, *The Unquiet Grave: A Word Cycle by Palinurus*, rev. ed. with an introduction by Cyril Connolly (New York: Persea Books, 1981), 22.

25. Nicola Gardini, "History and Pastoral in the Structure of Leopardi's *Canti*," pp. 84 and 92.

Canti

I. ALL'ITALIA / TO ITALY

This first canzone was written at Recanati in September 1818; it was published that year in Rome, along with "Sopra il monumento di Dante" and a dedicatory letter to the poet Vincenzo Monti (1754–1828), by Bourlié. Republished in the Bologna edition of the *Canzoni* (1824) and in the 1831 and 1835 editions of the *Canti*. Leopardi's "Argomento di una canzone sullo stato presente dell'Italia" (Rigoni [M1, 620]) outlines the themes developed in his first two canzoni.

Leopardi, in his notes on the *Canti* (1831) (M1, 147–48), derived from his letter to Monti: "The success of Thermopylae was truly celebrated by the one who is introduced to poetize in this canzone, i.e, Simonides; held by antiquity to be one of the best Greek lyric poets, who lived, what's more, at the time of the fall of Xerxes, and was a Greek citizen. Apart from the epitaph repeated by Cicero and others, his achievement is demonstrated by what Diodorus writes in book eleven, where he also quotes some words of this Poet on this theme, two or three of which are repeated in the fifth line of the last strophe . . . I don't believe another subject as worthy of a lyric poem has ever been found, nor one more fortunate, nor more truly achieved, than this one chosen by Simonides. Since if the enterprise of Thermopylae has such power for us who are distant from those who carried it out, and, in spite of all this, we cannot contain our tears reading about it simply as it transpired, and twenty-three centuries after it occurred; we have to conjecture as to the power of the memory of it in a Greek, and a poet, and among the principal ones, who, it can be said, had witnessed the event with his own eyes, traveling in the same cities victorious over an army much larger than any others recorded in the history of Europe, partaking in the celebrations, the marvels, the fervor of a whole very excellent nation, made even more magnanimous in nature through its awareness of the glory it had gained, and by the emulation of so many virtues demonstrated previously by its own. For these reasons, considering it due to much misadventure that the writings of Simonides on that occurrence had been lost, not that I presumed to repair that damage, but in order to belie the wish to, I tried to represent to myself in my mind the dispositions of the poet's spirit at that time, and in this way, apart from the disparity in our gifts, tried to go back and create his song; of which I offer this opinion, that either it was marvelous, or else the fame of Simonides was pointless and his writings were lost with little harm."

The term "canzone" signifies a poetic composition "of high rank and theme, lyric, principally, and later doctrinal and political, but always Dantesquely 'tragic' (lyric also in the sense of being linked, at least in origin, to music)" (Bertone, 38ff). It had Sicilian and Tuscan roots modeled on the Provençal *cansò*, and its primacy was established by Dante, who in his *De vulgari eloquentia* named it the highest of the poetic forms. Later, it was practiced with greater variation and freedom by Petrarch, and in modern times has been adopted by Carducci and d'Annunzio, and by Pasolini in his Friulian dialect poems.

The first of Leopardi's published poems already formally subverts its Petrarchan model, for the even stanzas follow one rhyme scheme and the odd stanzas another. In his hands, the canzone would gradually become *libera*, free, shedding its strict rhyming and rhythmic structures until, in "A Silvia" (1828), what remains of the ancient form's strictures is "mere alternation of *settenari* [seven-syllable lines] and hendecasyllables" and the rhyming of the last line of each stanza with an internal line of variable position.

The history of Leopardi's experimentation with the canzone reveals much about the development of the modern poetic voice. Bertone (43): "At the beginning, in 'All'Italia' and 'Sopra il monumento di Dante,' different rhyme schemes alternate, one for the odd stanzas and one for the even (but with an equal number of lines . . . and the succession of rhymes also corresponds in large part, though hendecasyllables replace *settenari* and vice versa). In 'Bruto minore' the number of unrhymed lines (nine out of fifteen) increases up to the 'Ultimo canto di Saffo,' in which the stanzas (eighteen lines) present fully sixteen unrelated hendecasyllables and a *combinatio* or conclusion to the stanza (*settenario* and hendecasyllable) with *rima baciata* [aa]." As Orcel (14) puts it: "The Leopardian *canto*—that is, the canzone freed from every pre-established model—is born of the conjunction between the canzone form and the suppleness of the loose hendecasyllable."

In a typically ironic preamble to the republication of his "Annotazioni" to the canzoni in the Milanese review *Il nuovo ricoglitore* in September 1825 (M1, 163–64), a signal text that largely summarizes Leopardi's thinking in poetry, he describes "ten Canzoni, and more than ten 'stravaganze' (eccentricities)" (for "'eccentricity' we are meant to read 'originality'" [Dotti, 44]). Of them, "not even one [is] amorous"; they are not particularly Petrarchan, nor do they follow the traditional forms of the Italian canzone from Chiabrera to Monti; in fact, "they are like no Italian lyric poem . . . [N]o one could guess the subjects of the Canzoni by their titles," but—and here, typically, as Dotti (45) puts it, "the ironic-polemical motif slowly gives way to an open declaration of the tragic truth" of man's condition—"they are all full of laments and melancholy, as if the world and men were a sad thing, and as if human life were unhappy." After declaring that his work needs to be read carefully to be understood ("as if the Italians read carefully") and emphasizing that "poetry is in fact thought" (Dotti, 45), Leopardi "enumerates what he considers the most notable 'discoveries' of his 'philosophy': that science and knowledge, in destroying our illusions and their 'errors,' have diminished the world; that at one time nature, without revealing herself, knew how to speak to hearts and inspire them; that the more we make progress in reason and consciousness, the more the imagination becomes sterile and the more the emptiness of things is revealed; that all is vain in the world except pain; that even this pain is better than boredom; and that in sum 'all is mystery in the Universe, except for our unhappiness.'" Thus Leopardi defines his "eccentricity": in Dotti's words "the mark of a vibrant ideological as well as stylistic originality."

Rigoni (M1, 916): "The reflection on the radical diversity of ancient and modern man and world was, from Winckelmann to Friedrich Schlegel, one of the fundamental elements of the revolution in Western consciousness that determined . . . the landscape of experience and thought in which we continue to live today. But no one in Europe in the 18th and 19th centuries, or after, has dedicated an attention and an analysis to this theme as profound as Leopardi's: the pages of the *Zibaldone*, from beginning to end, are a supreme document of this, so much more surprising if one considers Leopardi's distance from the great moment of German culture . . .

"Criticism of the first of the *Canti* initially underlined its public and patriotic and recently also its 'existential' aspects [Dotti (11) calls it "a singular admixture of libertarian and legitimist themes"], but it is important to recognize a much more vast and essential subject, i.e., the comparison and contrast between the decadence and obscurity of contemporary Italy, where its former greatness survives only in the fantasies of ruins, and the immortal glory of the 'adventurous and dear and blessed . . . ancient times' embodied by classical Greece . . . Though it is called '*All'Italia*,' the lyric is also and above all a hymn to Greece, the testimony—at the beginning of Leopardi's poetic work—of the idealization of antiquity repeated and varied upon as well in the other canzoni." Indeed, Gardini (82) calls it "a manifesto of literary anachronism and, as such, a distillation of all that poetry represents and entails for Leopardi."

Simonides' apologia, which makes up more or less the second half of the poem, and to a modern reader is striking in its vividness in contrast to the formulaic rhetoric of what precedes it—"the language of traditional civil and patriotic poetry" derived from Dante, Petrarch, and Virgil that is the vehicle of Leopardi's first canzoni (Dotti, 151)—is his first representation of the poet's self-consciousness, his definition of the poet's calling and his anxiety for fame. As such, it stands as a precursor of Leopardi's own autobiographical testimonies, and hence of our modern "confessional" lyric.

Dotti (12) quotes Luigi Blasucci on the young poet's sense "of his own unhappy condition, vague mania for greatness, awareness of an aristocratic sensibility though not without a painful awareness of exclusion"; indeed, for Blasucci the protagonist of these first two canzoni is Leopardi's own "heroic, eloquent ego." Here, then, Dotti adds, "we see not only a 'patriotic' young man . . . who, in the romantic-Risorgimento atmosphere at the dawn of the first national liberation movements, pays (and cannot not pay) his tribute to the great civil tradition of Parini, Alfieri, and Foscolo; we see a poet . . . beginning to raise his protest—individually and personally felt—against the indolence with which he is surrounded"; the first two canzoni also expound on the themes that bring "us to the heart of Leopardi's thought": "the inevitable unhappiness of modern man thrown into a world turned upside down yet aware of an irremediably lost 'happiness.' "

7 *Nuda la fronte* . . .: Orcel (288): "The personification of Italy is an originally Petrarchan topos (see the canzoni 'Italia mia' and 'Spirto gentil' [*Rime* CXXVIII and LIII]), which Monti had recently adopted in his 'Musogonia' and 'Il beneficio.' "

14 *senza velo*: The veil was the prerogative of Roman freewomen.

24 *Che fosti donna . . .*: Cf. Dante, *Purgatorio* VI, 78; Foscolo, "Bonaparte liberatore," 50–52; Ariosto, *Orlando furioso* XVII, lxxvi.

37 *L'armi, qua l'armi*: Cf. Virgil, *Aeneid* II, 668: "Arma, viri, ferte arma."

38 *procomberò*: I'll fall forward, facing the enemy.

41 *Dove sono i tuoi figli?*: Taken from the letter of 19–20 February 1799 in Foscolo's novel, *Ultime lettere di Jacopo Ortis* (1798–1801): "Ove dunque sono i tuoi figli?"

43 *In estranie contrade*: A division of Italian soldiers fought in Napoleon's disastrous Russian campaign of 1812. See Leopardi's treatment of the theme in "Sopra il monumento di Dante."

65 *O tessaliche strette*: The pass of Thermopylae, where in 480 B.C. a band of three hundred Spartans under Leonidas resisted Xerxes' Persian army to the death.

69 *al passeggere*: Refers to the epigraph at Thermopylae, arributed to Simonides (*Palatine Anthology* VII, 241): "Stranger, when you come to / Lakedaimon, tell them we lie / Here, obedient to their will." In *Poems from the Greek Anthology*, trans. Kenneth Rexroth, expanded ed. (Ann Arbor: University of Michigan Press, 1973), 106.

75 *Serse per l'Ellesponto si fuggia*: After the great sea battle of Salamis, which followed the engagement at Thermopylae.

77 *Antela*: Town near the pass of Thermopylae.

78 *Si sottrasse da morte . . .*: Rigoni (M1, 918) notes that F. Sesler first remarked that this formulation derives from Simonides of Keos's epigram on the Spartans' defense of Plataea in 479 B.C. in the *Palatine Anthology* (VII, 251): "These men clothed their land with incorruptible Glory when they assumed death's misty cloak. / They are not dead in death; the memory / Lives with us and their courage brings them back." In *The Greek Anthology and Other Ancient Greek Epigrams: A Selection in Modern Verse Translations*, ed. and trans. Peter Jay (New York: Oxford University Press, 1973), 40.

79 *Simonide*: Simonides of Keos (556–468/9 B.C.), Greek lyric poet, rival of Aeschylus and Pindar, often considered the first national poet of Greece, a fragment of whose poem about Thermopylae (480 B.C.), as quoted by Diodorus of Sicily, had been translated by Leopardi's mentor Pietro Giordani. In the C. H. Oldfather translation (*Diodorus of Sicily*, vol. IV, Books IX–XII. 40, Loeb Classical Library. [Cambridge: Harvard University Press, 1946], 153), the fragment reads: "Of those who perished at Thermopylae / All glorious is the fortune, fair the doom; / Their grave's an altar, ceaseless memory's theirs / Instead of lamentation, and their fate / Is chant of praise. Such winding sheet as this / Nor mould nor all-consuming time shall waste. / This sepulcher of valiant men has taken / The fair renown of Hellas for its inmate. / And witness is Leonidas, once king / Of Sparta, who hath left behind a crown / Of valour mighty and undying fame."

88 *Nell'armi e ne' perigli*: Hendiadys.

93 *passo*: The (Petrarchan) step of death. Originally, "passo" was "fato."

95 *splendido convito*: Dotti (212) calls this a "probable allusion to the famous remark . . . made by Leonidas before the battle in front of his soldiers: 'Forward with courage, O Spartans; tonight perhaps we shall dine in the Underworld.'"

97 *Tartaro*: Tartarus is Hades, but as G. De Robertis says (8), Leopardi should have said Elysium, where heroes are supposed to reside after death.

102 *immortale*: I.e., endless.

108 *L'ira de' greci petti e la virtute*: Cf. Foscolo, *Dei sepolcri*, 201: "La virtù greca e l'ira."

125 *La vostra tomba è un'ara*: The formulation again derives from Simonides.

137 *Così la vereconda . . .*: Leopardi's formulaic expression here of the poet's desire for immortality is a classic trope that he will later reject. (See in particular the critique of the "vana" and "cieca" Goddess Gloria at the end of "Al Conte Carlo Pepoli," and the "Palinodia.")

138 *appo*: from the Latin *apud.*

II. SOPRA IL MONUMENTO DI DANTE / ON THE MONUMENT TO DANTE BEING ERECTED IN FLORENCE

This second canzone was written at Recanati in September and October 1818, soon after "All'Italia" (the "Argomento di una canzone sopra lo stato presente dell'Italia" outlines ideas employed in both poems) and a little more than a month after the announcement of a plan to erect a monument to Dante, to be sculpted by Stefano Ricci, in the Florentine church of Santa Croce, the Italian Westminster Abbey or Panthéon. The poem was published in Rome with "All'Italia" in 1819.

Rigoni (M1, 919): The composition's "denunciation of past French rule and, in contrast, its silence on the current Austrian hegemony in Italy, must have been displeasing to liberal circles, but Leopardi, who could certainly not openly proclaim himself as against the Restoration, was aiming in fact to attack every form of foreign oppression, using the example of Napoleon."

"At once both fatiguing and emphatic" (Rigoni [M1, 920]), and rife with Petrarchan allusions to the reduced condition of modern Italy, the canzone is most effective poetically in its evocation of the miserable death of Italian soldiers on the Russian steppe during Napoleon's retreat from Moscow in 1812, in strict antithesis with the heroic death of the Spartans at Thermopylae described in "All'Italia." Rigoni notes that Leopardi's deploring of the shame of Italians fighting for a foreign power echoes his remarks in the *Zibaldone* (896–99 [30 March–4 April 1821]) on the unnatural nature of modern wars, no longer conducted by nations and states, but by governments.

It is worth observing, too, that each poem's conclusion is dominated by the figure of a poet: here Dante, there Simonides of Keos. Leopardi's impersonation or inhabiting of the Greek poet in "All'Italia" makes for vivid and convincing writing in the first canzone; here, the poem gains in power when he abandons apostrophe for a powerful imagining of the deaths of Italian soldiers.

2 *Pace*: The Congress of Vienna (September 1814–June 1815), at which the structure of post-Napoleonic Europe was determined, and hopes for Italian unification were disappointed.

9 *contrade* (plural): Petrarchan.

14 *Che senza sdegno omai*: The harsh alliteration here is characteristic of Alfieri's tragic style.

21 *colui per lo cui verso*: Dante died in exile in Ravenna in 1321 and was buried there.

22 *Il meonio cantor*: Homer, thought by some to be a native of Maeonia, or Lydia, in Asia Minor.

60 *Lunge sia*: Cf. Virgil, *Aeneid* VI, 258: "Procul, o procul este, profani."

74 *etrusco*: Etruscan, for Tuscan.

76 *costei che tanto alto locasti*: Beatrice.

81 *bronzi e marmi*: Cf. Horace, *Odes* III, 30: "Exegi monumentum aere perennius."

82 *unqua*: from Latin *umquam*, to avoid repetition of *mai*.

94 *di novo salisti al paradiso*: Dante had already been to heaven once, in his vision.

100 *la più recente . . .*: Napoleon. This line originally read: "Ma non la Francia scellerata e nera" (But not France, criminal and black).

111–12 *de' folti / Carri . . .*: Napoleon ordered numerous Italian artworks transported to Paris, many of which entered the collections of the Louvre.

131–32 *morto / Io non son per la tua cruda fortuna*: Cf. "All'Italia," 135–36, where Simonides expresses regret that he has not fallen in battle for Greece, and that his contribution must be different.

137 *Padre*: Leopardi now addresses Dante directly.

151 *Quando più bella a noi l'età sorride*: When we are young.

156 *Così vennero al passo*: The moment of death. See "All'Italia," 93.

163 *infinita . . . sciagura*: Dotti (224) notes that the bitterness of the heroes' fate is aggravated by the fact that it is the same as the cowards' and quotes G. L. Bickersteth: "Being confused with cowards, simply because their suffering was unknown, was the tragedy of these men, as it was Leopardi's."

164 *e questo vi conforti*: Orcel (290–91): "This tragic epigram is the fruit of a psychological observation on the 'pleasure brought on by despair,' the masochistic and megalomaniacal components of which Leopardi will later describe acutely" (see *Zibaldone* 2217–21 [3 December 1821]).

172–73 *chi vi spinse / A pugnar contra lei*: Napoleon.

178 *affaticata e lenta*: Cf. Petrarch's description of Italy in the canzone "Spirto gentil" (*Canzoniere* LII): "vecchia, oziosa e lenta, / Dormirà sempre . . ."

190 *andrò sclamando*: Cf. Dante, *Purgatorio* XXIV, 52–54: "I' mi son un che, quando / Amor mi spira, noto, e a quel modo / Ch'e ditta dentro vo significando." Also Petrarch, "Italia mia": "I'vo gridando."

200 *Meglio l'è rimaner*: Cf. *Purgatorio* VI, 112–13: "Vieni a veder la tua Roma che piagne, / Vedova e sola . . ." [Come see your Rome, which weeps, / a widow and alone . . .]

III. AD ANGELO MAI / TO ANGELO MAI

Written at Recanati "in ten or twelve days" in January 1820; published in Bologna in July of the same year, with a dedicatory letter to Count Leonardo Trissino.

Abate Angelo Mai (1782–1854) of Bergamo, Jesuit philologist and writer on Oriental languages, was librarian of the Biblioteca Ambrosiana in Milan, and, from late 1819, of the Vatican. Leopardi first wrote to him in 1816 when, as a young scholar, he learned that Mai, one of the leading literary men of his time, had discovered a new manuscript by Marcus Cornelius Fronto, "an author almost wholly, and perhaps deservedly, unknown," as Origo (40) puts it, on whom Leopardi had written a Latin commentary in 1814, at a startlingly young age. Leopardi translated the new work with great alacrity and sent it to Mai, hoping to publish it, but Mai responded coolly—as he did to this poem, the occasion of which was the abbot's discovery of the manuscript of Cicero's *De re publica* in the Vatican Library. Gallo and Garboli assert nevertheless (21) that from 1816 on virtually all of Leopardi's properly philological work was based on Mai's discoveries or publications.

Rigoni (M1, 923): "The canzone to Mai . . . bears witness for the first time, at least in poetry, to that incompatibility between wisdom and life, between knowledge and existence, between history and happiness, that can be considered the original and definitive nucleus of all the thought and work of Leopardi"—what Francesco De Sanctis (as quoted by Dotti, 16) called "the horrible fanaticism" of Leopardi's "philosophy of history."

The poem is the first of what might be called the catalog canzoni (along with "Alla primavera" and the "Inno ai patriarchi"), in which a series of figures out of the past is evoked and celebrated, in the manner of the Homeric Hymns, as admonishment of and encouragement to the present age. For Ungaretti, who reportedly taught a course at the University of Rome that consisted of a close reading of the poem, it "is Leopardi's greatest undertaking. It even surpasses, in spite of some naïve passages, 'La ginestra.' In its emotional power, it recalls Beethoven, in its tragedy, Aeschylus . . . It treats two themes: the theme of the *Secol morto*, the dead century, or Leopardi's own time; and the theme of the *Clamor dei defunti*, the clamor of the dead. The dead—from every age from Dante on, but with the distant shadow of those risen from the times of *De Republica* [*sic*] . . . rise up again, and we are witness—contrasting our days, which are desert, with those of the ancients, which are furious—to the ebbing of the vital energy of a civilization, rousing itself here and there, with every new age; but ever more faintly [cf. the "Coro di morti," p. 352] . . . It is a chilling spectacle. The effect is obtained by the interweaving of words or images which respond to and evoke each other from stanza to stanza, via echoes and a thousand other means of verbal orchestration, which ends up, while complex in the extreme, clear in its slightest tones." "Secondo discorso su Leopardi" (1950), in *Vita d'un uomo: saggi e interventi*, ed. Mario Diacono and Luciano Rebay (Mondadori, 1974), 478ff.

1 *ardito*: "Indefatigable," but also "audacious, courageous" (Leone Piccioni, quoted in Orelli, 84), eager to measure himself against the past.

9 *Risorgimenti*: Of lost classical texts.

14–15 *O con l'umano / Valor forse contrasta il fato invano*: Dotti (228) notes that the typical Leopardian opposition of the hero and fate redounds to Petrarch (*Rime* LIII, 85–87: "Rade volte adiven ch'a l'alte imprese / fortuna ingiuriosa non contrasti, / ch'agli animosi fatti mal s'accorda" [It rarely happens that harmful fortune, which accords poorly with spirited deeds, doesn't interfere with great undertakings].)

50 *que' giorni allor*: "You bring us back to the times of the Petrarchs and the Poggi [allusion to the humanist Gian Francesco Poggio Bracciolini (1380–1459), who recovered many classical texts], when every day was illuminated by a new classical discovery, and the marveling and joy of the litterati knew no rest." Leopardi to Mai, 10 January 1820.

53–54 *a cui natura/ Parlò senza svelarsi . . .*: I.e., without revealing the sad truth of man's destiny, though suggesting it in myth and fable. De Sanctis (quoted in Gallo and Garboli, 27: "It means that nature wasn't revealed in her truth and nakedness, and appeared dressed in all her illusions, which were her deceiving veil. The phrase is too rapid in its profundity; it is a thought that flashes and that will later be the basis for another canzone ['Alla primavera']."

54–55 *i riposi / Magnanimi . . .*: Cf. "La ginestra," 28: "Agli ozi de' potenti."

62–63 *Non domito nemico / Della fortuna*: Allusion to Dante, *Inferno* II, 61: "amico . . . non della ventura . . ."

64 *Fu più l'averno che la terra amico*: Because there he could finally see the sins of his contemporaries punished.

68–69 *sfortunato / Amante*: Francesco Petrarca (1304–74), founder of the tradition of the Italian love lyric.

72 *Del tedio . . .*: "The unhappiness or desperation that comes from great passions or illusions or whatever misfortune in life, is not comparable to the suffocation that results from the certainty and the vivid sense of the nullity of all things, and the impossibility of being happy in this world, and the immensity of the void that is felt in the soul. Misfortunes, whether imaginary or real, can also bring on the desire for death, or even death itself, but that unhappiness has more of life, indeed, if above all it results from imagination and passion, it is full of life; but this other unhappiness I'm describing is all death; and that same death produced *immediately* by misfortunes is a more alive thing, whereas this other is more sepulchral, without action without movement without heat, and almost without pain, but rather with an unmeasured heaviness and a sadness similar to the one that derives from the fear of ghosts in childhood, or the idea of hell. This condition of the spirit is the effect of very great real misfortunes, and of a great soul once full of imagination and then totally stripped of it, and also of a life so evidently null and montonous, that it makes palpable the nullity and vanity of things, because without this the great variety of illusions that merciful nature sets before us every day, impedes this fatal and sensible evidence. And therefore, although this condition of the spirit is extremely reasonable, indeed the only reasonable one, being with all this extremely contrary, indeed the most directly contrary to nature, it is unknown except by a few who have felt it, like Tasso." *Zibaldone* 140–41 (27 June 1820).

74 *il fastidio*: Cf. the "negra cura" in "Al Conte Carlo Pepoli," 85, and the related notion of "ozio" throughout. Dotti (153): "No traditional poet could have written lines like these. [What is original here] . . . is poetry that translates thought, that tends to the allusive and brings together in a particular image, as powerful as it is naked, the repeated research of reflection. Classical argumentation is transformed into assertion, and assertion becomes figure."

77 *Ligure ardita prole*: Columbus, who was born in Genoa in 1447. Leopardi's "uniquely and typically" (Dotti, 18) radical view of the explorer's achievements centers on "its devasating consequences—the vastness of the world destroyed, the capacity for fantasy annihilated, the liquidation of the imagination, the triumph of science and reason at the expense of primitive natural sensibility"—and is "based on the opposition of nature and science, dream and reality, fantasizing ancient humanity and lucidly (and squalidly) prosaic modern world." See also the "Dialogo di Cristoforo Colombo e Pietro Gutierrez" (1824) in the *Operette morali*, quoted by William Carlos Williams in *In the American Grain* (1925).

78 *alle colonne*: The Straits of Gibraltar, known to the ancients as the Columns of Hercules.

87–88 *conosciuto il mondo / Non cresce . . .*: Leopardi's essential notion of the beauty of the *vago*, or indefinite, is relevant here. "Science destroys the principal pleasures of our spirit, because it determines things and shows us their boundaries, though in many things it has materially enlarged our ideas a very great deal. I say materially and not spiritually, since, for example, the distance from the sun to the earth was much greater to the human mind when we thought it was a few miles without knowing how many, rather than now, when it is known to be very precisely thousands. Thus science is the enemy of the greatness of ideas, though it has immeasurably enlarged our natural opinions. It has enlarged them as clear ideas, but a very small *confused idea* is always greater than a very big, entirely *clear* one. The uncertainty as to whether a thing entirely is or is not is also the source of a largeness which becomes destroyed by the certainty that the thing really is. How much greater the idea of the Antipodes was, when Petrarch said that *perhaps* they exist, than as soon as it was known that they did. What I'm saying about science, I'm saying about experience, etc., etc. The biggest, indeed the only greatness with which man can confusedly satisfy himself, is the indeterminate, as also results from my theory of pleasure . . . Therefore ignorance, which alone can hide the limits of things, is the principal source of indefinite ideas, etc. Therefore it's the greatest source of happiness, and thus childhood is the happiest time in a man's life, the most content with itself, least subject to boredom. Experience necessarily shows the limits of many things even to the natural, unsociable man." *Zibaldone* 1464–65 (7 August 1821).

96 *del maggior pianeta*: The sun, considered a planet by the ancients.

106 *Nascevi ai dolci sogni*: Ludovico Ariosto (1474–1533), author of the great romance *Orlando furioso*. Leopardi in his "Elogio degli uccelli" in the *Operette* *morali* (M2, 159) writes of Ariosto's imagination "not . . . profound, fervid and tempestuous, such as Dante and Tasso had: which is a very baleful gift, and the source of very deep and enduring cares and worries; but that rich, various, light, unstable and childlike one; which is the very broad source of pleasing and happy thoughts, sweet illusions, various delights and comforts; and the greatest and most fruitful gift with which nature is courteous to living spirits."

111 *O torri, o celle*: Allusion to the first line of the *Orlando furioso*: "Le donne, i cavalier, l'arme, gli amori."

121 *O Torquato*: Torquato Tasso (1544–95), author of the epic *Gerusalemme liberata* (1574), in the last twenty years of his life endured mental instability, exile, and imprisonment. Dotti (19): "In Tasso . . . Leopardi sees another self and . . . more than a man of the past, a contemporary."

129 *ultimo inganno . . .*: According to tradition, Tasso's unhappy love for Eleonora d'Este.

130 *Ombra reale e salda*: Leopardi, letter to Giordani of 6 March 1820: "Because this is the miserable condition of man, and the barbaric teaching of reason, that human pleasures and pains being mere illusions, the travail which derives from the certainty of the nullity of things is always and only just and true." And in the letter to Jacopsen of 13 June 1823: "The nullity of things was the only thing that existed for me. It was always present for me as a frightful phantom; I saw only a desert around me."

132 *Al tardo onore*: Tasso was to be crowned with the laurel wreath on the Capitoline Hill in Rome, as Petrarch had been, but died before this honor could be bestowed.

143 *Se, fuor che di se stesso . . .*: G. De Robertis (40), Leopardi's letter of 28 August 1820: "All the classes are tainted with the destructive egotism of all that is beautiful and all that is great."

155 *Allobrogo feroce*: The passionate and severe dramatist Vittorio Alfieri (1749–1803), a harsh critic of Italian colonization, whom Parini in fact called "fero [fierce] allobrogo" ("Il dono," 1) and who served as an essential model for the young Leopardi. In ancient times, the Allobrogians lived in the territory stretching from the Alps to the Rhone, which was later called Delfinato and Savoy. By extension, the Piedmontese, living near Savoy and ruled by the House of Savoy, were also called Allobrogians.

159 *in su la scena*: Alfieri's tragedies, among them *Filippo*, *Antigone*, *Oreste*, *Mirra*, and *Saul*, which are primarily concerned with the overthrowing of tyranny, made him one of the heroes of the Risorgimento.

175 *scopritor*: Refers again to Mai.

177 *arma*: Cf. lines 24–25: "ripor mano alla virtude / Rugginosa."

IV. NELLE NOZZE DELLA SORELLA PAOLINA / ON THE MARRIAGE OF HIS SISTER PAOLINA

Written at Recanati between October and November 1821, in anticipation of the marriage, which in fact failed to take place, of his beloved sister, Paolina (1800–1869), a cultivated enthusiast of music and translator of a biography of Mozart, and an admirer of Stendhal. Published in Bologna, along with the first three canzoni, already published and corrected, in 1824.

Leopardi, in *Disegni letterari* [Literary Outlines], 1821 (M2, 1205): "Canzone to the Roman Virginia where one imagines seeing her shadow in a dream, and speaking to her tenderly both about her situation and about the present ills of Italy." Cf. also "Dell'educare la gioventù italiana" (On the Education of Italian Youth) of 1818 or 1820 (M1, 623–24), where Leopardi indicates that the poem is based "on the taste [style] of Ode 2, Book III of Horace."

Orcel (293): "In spite of its metrical regularity, the canzone—of which De Sanctis wrote that it was more a 'funeral dirge' than an epithalamium—distances itself further from the Petrarchan model in assimilating in particular certain typically Horatian stylistic elements (inversions, ellipses)."

Rigoni (M1, 926): "The patriotic-educative themes, while present, serve nevertheless the expression of a much more general and intrinsic idea, particularly vivid in all the canzoni: the contrast between the happy, vital and heroic fullness of the dawn of the world and the sadness of being born "too late, / and in the evening of human life." Here Leopardi "leads the causes of general modern mediocrity back to the fatal historical exhaustion which marks the Earth in its final age."

16–17 *O miseri o codardi / Figliuoli avrai*: "Leopardi had already read of the association of greatness and unhappiness that will echo in the opening of the 'Dialogo della Natura e di un'anima' [in the *Operette morali*], 'be great and unhappy,' as in fact an imposition of nature rather than 'corrupted custom,' in D'Alembert's

Éloges, relating it in the *Zibaldone* to the theory of pleasure and to the tormented 'desire for happiness.' " D. De Robertis, quoted in Gavazzeni, 151.

17–18 *Immenso / Tra fortuna e valor*: Dotti (242): "The corrupt custom of the present times has imposed an enormous deviation (*dissidio*) between merit (*valor*) and *fortuna*, where the term means "fortunate social circumstances," which are favored by cowardice, submissiveness and conformism. Underlying this statement are at least two basic Leopardian convictions: the opposition of ancients and moderns, and the senescent condition of the contemporary world, represented historically by the Restoration." Cf. the opposition between the hero and fate in "Ad Angelo Mai" (14).

34 *il ferro e il foco*: Cf. Anacreontic 24: "She who is beautiful vanquishes iron and fire."

37 *a voi s'inchina*: In a marginal note, Leopardi cites Guarini's *Il pastor fido* III, 1399–1400: "a cui pur s'inchina / ogni cosa mortale."

38 *Ragion di nostra etate*: Dotti (243) quotes Mario Fubini: "The thought is closely linked to what precedes it: if the power of women is so great, they are responsible, if not for the present corruption, at least for the lack of attempts to combat it."

46 *atti egregi*: Cf. Foscolo, *I sepolcri*, 151: "egregie cose."

47 *chi ben l'estima*: Cf. Petrarch's canzone "Quell'antico mio dolce empio signore," 139: "Che son scala al Fattor, chi ben l'estima." G. De Robertis (48): Leopardi "wants to attenuate the crudeness of the preceding stanza. The vileness of the times is not so much and not only the fault of women, but of the ignorance of men, who don't know how to hear the claims of love, to read and see themselves in beauty."

52 *e fiede le montagne il rombo*: Cf. Virgil, *Georgics* I, 318 and 323–24. Cf. also the evocation of the storm in the "Ultimo canto di Saffo" and in fragment XXXIX ("Spento il diurno raggio in occidente").

60 *fanciulle*: Effeminate men.

75 *nel conservato scudo*: In *Zibaldone* (45), Leopardi tells the story of the Spartan mother who gives her son his shield, telling him to return "with it or on it" and at 2425 (6 May 1822) mentions that it was a point of honor among the Spartans to return from battle with their shields, whose size would prevent them from fleeing.

76 *Virginia*: The Roman Virginia, killed by her centurion father to save her from the advances of the decemvir Appius Claudius. Leopardi, inspired no doubt by one of Alfieri's most celebrated tragedies, *Virginia*, makes her a heroine who sacrifices herself voluntarily for the good of her country. Again, as in the first two canzoni, the poem gains in power once Leopardi characteristically moves from generalizing to a specific character and case.

80–81 *Eri pur vaga . . . / dolci sogni*: Dotti (156–57) cites this as a primary instance of Leopardi's "tendency," derived from Petrarch, "to fasten on the unknown in order to immerse his heart in the vague [*vago*] and indeterminate." Gardini (81) points out the "striking stylistic affinities" between the description of Virginia and the later masterpiece "A Silvia," the words "molcea," beltade," "vaga," and "dolci" occuring in both texts. For Dotti (246), Virginia at this moment "becomes the ideal sister of Silvia. The language's tone suddenly changes and takes on the accents of the major Leopardi, the poet who depicts his feminine creations from within . . . revealing their most human and painful emotions."

82–83 *ti ruppe / Il bianchissimo petto*: Orcel (293): "Beyond the probable Virgilian reminiscence (*candida pectora rumpit, Aeneid* IX, 432), one ought to question the recurrence in Leopardi's imagination of the symbolic association between whiteness and blood, which is itself linked to the theme of the moon. Cf. 'Bruto minore' (76–77): 'E tu dal mar cui nostro sangue irriga, / Candida luna . . .' and 'Alla primavera' (35–38): 'La faretrata Diva / Scendea ne' caldi flutti, e dall'immonda / Polve tergea della sanguigna caccia / Il niveo lato . . .' "

84 *Erebo*: Hades.

96 *la romulea prole*: According to myth, the Romans were the descendants of Romulus.

97–98 *di polve / Lorda il tiranno i crini*: Appius Claudius was dragged by the Romans through the streets after being murdered. As Dotti (247) notes, Leopardi is drawing on the tragic spirit of Alfieri.

105 *Femmineo fato*: As Orcel (294) points out, the suppression of the article gives the phrase an untranslatable force. Rome had first been aroused by the death of Lucretia, which had led to the fall of the Tarquins and the old Roman monarchy. This is the first evocation in the *Canti* of a woman's suffering and death, but the theme was already well established in Leopardi's work. Two early unpublished canzoni, "Per una donna inferma di malattia lunga e mortale" (For a Woman Suffering from a Long and Mortal Illness) (March–April 1819) and the contemporary "Nella morte di una donna fatta trucidare col suo portato dal corruttore per mano ed arte di un chirurgo," which Leopardi's father prohibited him from publishing along with the canzone to Angelo Mai, bear witness to Leopardi's intense interest in feminine suffering, which he posits as perhaps the most representative instance of human pain.

V. A UN VINCITORE NEL PALLONE / TO A CHAMPION AT FOOTBALL

Written at Recanati in November 1821, in honor of Carlo Didimi, an athlete from nearby Treia, who later became a hero of the Risorgimento. (The game was not soccer but *palla al muro*, an antecedent of the Basque *pelote* played in Italy since the sixteenth century.) Published in the Bologna 1824 edition of the *Canzoni*.

Orcel (294) compares this to the odes of Horace and Pindar—in spite of Leopardi's note asserting that this is not "an imitation of Pindar"—pointing out the difference in style from Chiabrera (1552–1638), whose Pindaric odes/canzoni included three on this very game: "In this piece, often quite obscure due to elision, one will note the praise of 'desire,' of physical energy, of heroism, as 'powerful,' vital 'illusions' as well as the provocative, but no less profound, equivalence that Leopardi establishes between life and game, illusion and reality." Bon (78): "Only in danger, or at least in risk, does life become fully valued."

Beyond its invidious comparison of heroic times and the decadent present, the poem evokes one of Leopardi's primary paradoxes: that since life in actuality is suffering and nullity, illusion, pleasure, and the game—which he could not bring himself to trust—are in fact the things that ultimately make it worth living. Cf. *Zibaldone*, 272 (11 October 1820): "All the pleasures are illusions or are made of illusion, and our life is formed and constructed from these illusions. Now if I can't have them, what pleasure remains to me? and why do I live? I speak likewise of the ancient institutions, etc., tending to foment enthusiasm, illusions, courage, activity, movement, life. They were illusions, but take them away, as they were taken. What pleasure remains? And what does life become? Similarly, I say: virtue, generosity, sensibility, true mutuality in love, faithfulness, constancy, justice, magnanimity, etc. humanly speaking are imaginary entities. And yet the sensible man, if he found them frequently in the world, would be less unhappy." And 339 (18 November 1820): "This was the idea that the ancients constructed of happiness and unhappiness. That is, they considered the man who was lacking such advantages in life, albeit illusory, to be really unhappy, and vice versa. And they never consoled themselves with the idea that these were illusions, recognizing that life consisted of them, or considering them as such or as reality. And they didn't hold happiness and unhappiness to be imaginary and chimerical things, but solid and solidly opposed to each other."

14 *in Maratona*: At the battle of Marathon, September 12, 490 B.C., the Athenians and Plataeans defeated the Persian army.

16 *il campo eleo*: Elis, the plain in the northwest Peloponnesus, where on the banks of the River Alpheus, especially at Olympia, the Olympic Games were celebrated every four years.

31 *Le meste rote*: Melancholy, because the wheels bring to light so much unhappiness.

33 *ed è men vano*: G. De Robertis (56) quotes a letter of Leopardi of 9 April 1821: "All the good things of this world are illusions. But do you therefore take away these illusions? What is wisdom? What else teaches us beside our unhappiness? In substance the happy man isn't happy, but the unhappy man is truly unhappy, for all that even unhappier wisdom tries to console him. There was a time when I trusted in virtue, and despised fortune: now after a very long battle I'm defeated, and down on the ground, because I've found in the end that if many wise men have known the sadness and vanity of things, I, like many others, have also known the sadness and vanity of wisdom." Dotti (250) notes that the movement of the line recalls the opening of Foscolo's *Sepolcri*.

40 *Tempo forse verrà*: Cf. Virgil, *Georgics*, 493ff, and Petrarch, *Rime* CXXVI: "Tempo verrà ancor forse." The fantasy, according to Rigoni (M1, 929), derives from the letter of 19–20 February 1799 in Foscolo's *Ortis*. Cf. the description of the ruins around Vesuvius in "La ginestra."

43 *i sette colli*: The seven hills of Rome.

45 *la cauta volpe*: Leopardi's habitual epithet for the fox, or vixen.

65 *più grata riede*: Having neared the infernal river, i.e., having risked death, it returns "più cara e più pregiata che innanzi" [dearer and more valued than before] ("Dialogo di Cristoforo Colombo e di Pietro Gutierrez" in the *Operette morali*). Dotti (253) notes Mario Fubini's observation that Leopardi transforms his athlete into a mythic hero like Hercules or Theseus, who triumphs over hell and death. But cf. also the suicidal fantasy and its aftermath, recounted in *Zibaldone* 82 (1819) (translated in the note to "Le ricordanze" 106–109), p. 446.

VI. BRUTO MINORE / BRUTUS

Written at Recanati in December 1821; published in Bologna in 1824, preceded by the "Comparazione delle sentenze di Bruto Minore e di Teofrasto vicini a morte" ("Comparison of the sayings of Brutus Minor and Theophrastus on the verge of death") (M2, 266–77) (1822), in which Leopardi writes: "We can say that the times of Brutus constituted the last age of the imagination, prevailed over, finally, by science and the knowledge of truth, which was disseminated among the people sufficiently to lead to the old age of the world. For if this had not been, neither would he have had occasion to flee from life, as he did, nor would the Roman Republic have died along with him. But not only this, but all of antiquity, I mean the ancient character and customs of nations, were close to disappearing, along with the opinions that had generated and fed them."

Marcus Junius Brutus (79?–42 B.C.) is known as Brutus Minor because of his older relative Decimus Junius Brutus (84–43 B.C.), likewise a trusted associate of and later conspirator against Julius Caesar, who also resisted Antony's attempt to gain absolute power. Marcus Brutus, the hero of Shakespeare's *Julius Caesar*, fought with Cassius against Antony in Macedonia before being defeated at Philippi.

Orcel (295): "The poem starts from the legendary blasphemy against virtue that Marcus Junius Brutus was supposed to have shouted at the moment of his suicide, after the defeat of the republican troops against the army of Octavian and Antony at the battle of Philippi in 42 B.C." [Florus, *Epitome* IV, 7: "But how much more efficacious is fortune than virtue and how true is what (Brutus) expressed as he died, *that virtue consists not so much in the thing but in the word . . .*]

"From this subject Leopardi draws a somber and vehement poem [a prime example of the violent "titanism" or disdain of the gods, found in the canzoni, with a vehement protagonist who owes much to the "titanic" heroes of Alfieri] in which, against the well-established background of the fracture between ancient and modern worlds, he develops . . . a blasphemous Prometheanism and an apologia for suicide (which, in spite of the future reservations of the 'Dialogo di Plotino e di Porfirio' [of 1827, in the *Operette morali*], will remain representative of the poet's attitude in the face of destiny)" and which Dotti (28) sets among the greatest of his achievements, the "tragic," "lucid and despairing monologue of a Shakespearean hero" (see Dotti, 25–33, for a brilliant discussion of the centrality of "Bruto minore" in defining Leopard's "philosophy").

As Leopardi wrote to de Sinner on 24 May 1832, in response to a German reviewer who saw "a religious tendency" in his work and related his pessimism to his physical ailments: "My feelings about destiny have been and still are those I expressed in 'Bruto minore.' It was due to the same courage that, having been led by my research to a despairing philosophy, I didn't hesitate to embrace it wholly; while on the other hand it was only because of the cowardice of men, who need to be convinced of the value of existence, that they wanted to consider my philosophical opinions the result of my personal suffering, and continue to attribute to my material circumstances what is only owed to my understanding. Before I die, I'm going to protest against this invention of weakness and vulgarity, and beg my readers to commit to destroy my observations and reasonings rather than blame my maladies."

1 *nella tracia polve*: G. De Robertis (60) quotes Leopardi (M2, 149): "We use here the license taken by diverse ancient authors to attribute to Thrace the city and the battle of Philippi, which were actually in Macedonia." Dotti (254) notes Leopardi's mention in his *Annotazioni* (M2, 182) that the beginning of the canzone is modeled on that of Book III of the *Aeneid.*

2 *ruina immensa*: Dotti (254): For Leopardi the defeat of Brutus brings the heroic age of the ancient world to a close.

4 *Esperia*: The Greek name for Italy, given its western location.

4 *al tiberino lido*: I.e., at Rome.

7 *l'Orsa algida*: The cold northern constellation of Ursus Major, known to us as the Big Dipper.

10 *fraterno sangue*: At Philippi, brothers fought against brothers, Octavian and Anthony against Brutus and Cassius, in civil war.

16 *Stolta virtù . . .*: Leopardi, in the manner of his expatiation on Simonides in "All'Italia," draws freely on Brutus's words as reported by Dio Cassius (*Roman History*, XLVII, 49) and Florus.

20 *Flegetonte*: River in Hades.

38 *Guerra mortale, eterna...*: Rigoni (M1, 931): "In the preamble to his translation of the *Manual of Epictetus* Leopardi writes [M2, 1046] that 'it is characteristic of great and strong spirits . . . to struggle, at least within themselves, against necessity, and wage fierce and mortal war against destiny, like the seven at Thebes of Aeschylus, and like the other great spirits of ancient times.' "

45 *E maligno alle nere ombre sorride*: Cf. *Zibaldone* 503–504 (15 January 1821): "But the ancients, always greater, more magnanimous, and stronger than we, in the excess of their bad fortune, and in their consideration of its necessity, and of the invincible power that made them unhappy and held them close and bound them to their misery without their being able to improve on it or liberate themselves, conceived hate and fury against fate, and cursed the Gods, declaring themslves enemies of heaven in a certain sense, though impotent and incapable of victory or vendetta, but not therefore dominated nor tamed, no less, but rather all the more desirous of revenge, the greater their misery and need."

60 *il non suo dardo*: I.e., the suicidal blow delivered not by nature but by man himself.

63 *al non previsto passo*: Cf. "All'Italia," 93; also the description of the lives of sheep in the "Canto notturno."

68–69 *nulla contesa / Legge...*: G. De Robertis (66): "Allusion to the Platonic idea of the afterlife. See the 'Dialogo di Plotino e di Porfirio': 'Why must primitive nature,which no longer prescribes laws for our life, prescribe laws for our death? Why must not reason govern death, since it governs life?' "

Dotti (29) underlines how the polemic on suicide—"central to Leopardi's meditation"—becomes "a polemic on theology and religion (Christianity above all)."

72 *Figli di Prometeo*: Rigoni (M1, 932): The Titan "Prometheus is the father of consciousness and civilization, and hence of human unhappiness."

75 *a voi Giove contende*: Cf. the "Coro di morti" from the "Dialogo di Federico Ruysch e delle sue mummie" in the *Operette morali* (translated on p. 352).

78–79 *la funesta / ... campagna*: The battlefield of Philippi.

79 *All'ausonio valor*: Ausonia was an ancient name for Italy.

84 *Lavinia prole*: The descendants of Lavinia, wife of Aeneas, the legendary Trojan founder of Rome.

85 *memorandi allori*: Laurel wreaths representing the victories for which they were awarded.

105 *Nè scolorò le stelle*: According to ancient fable, when great misfortunes afflicted humanity, the stars went dark (G. De Robertis, 69).

106 *Cocito*: Hell.

109 *dell'atra morte ultimo raggio*: Dotti (262): "Leopardi wants to say that Brutus doesn't turn, even in the extreme moment of his life, to his descendants who, aware of what the defeat at Philippi meant, and moved perhaps to indignation, could represent the last ray of hope for life in the black death that the hero is now about to embrace."

112–13 *In peggio / Precipitano i tempi*: Cf. Virgil, *Georgics* I, 199: "Sic omnia fatis in peius ruere."

VII. ALLA PRIMAVERA / TO SPRING

Written at Recanati in eleven days in January 1822; published in Bologna in 1824.

Leopardi, *Zibaldone* 63–64: "What a lovely time it was when everything was alive according to the human imagination and humanly alive, i.e., inhabited and shaped by beings equal to ourselves! When in the emptiest of woods it was judged certain that the lovely Hamadryads lived, and fauns and wood nymphs and Pan, etc. And arriving and seeing that all was solitude there you still believed all was inhabited and likewise of the springs lived in by Naiads, etc. And hugging a tree to your breast you almost felt it quiver in your hands, believing it to be a man or woman like Ciparissus, etc.! And likewise with flowers, etc., as indeed with children."

In the *Discorso di un Italiano intorno alla poesia romantica* (M2, 359–60), Leopardi offers his version of Schiller's "naïve," which the modern "sentimental" can only aspire to mourn: "What the ancients were we all were, and what the world was for some centuries, we were for some years, I mean children, and sharers in that ignorance and those fears and those joys and those beliefs and that endless activity of the imagination; when the thunder and wind and sun and stars and animals and plants and the walls of our houses—everything seemed to us to be either our friend or our enemy, none indifferent, none insensate, when every object we saw seemed somehow to be nodding to us, as if to show it wanted to address us; when we were never alone anywhere and asked things of images and walls and trees and flowers and clouds, and embraced stones and wood, and practically mistreated as if we'd been offended and almost embraced as helpful things that were incapable of offense or aid; when the marvel that is so welcome to us that very often we want to be able to believe in it in order to be able to marvel, possessed us constantly, when the colors of things when the light when the stars when fire when the flight of insects when the song of birds when the clearness of the springs was all new or unfamiliar to us, nor did we pass over any accident as ordinary, or know the reason for anything, and we imagined things according to our ability and embellished them according to our ability; when tears were a daily thing, and the passions were unconquered and intensely alive, not forcibly repressed, and broke out ardently. But what was our imagination then, how often and easily inflamed, how free and unrestrained, how it wandered impetuous and inexhaustible, how it magnified small things and loved simple things, and illuminated dark things, what living simulacra and breathing creatures, what lovely dreams what ineffable daydreams what magic what portents what lovely lands what chivalric finds, such material for poetry, such riches such vigor so much power so much commotion so much delight."

Orcel (296): "In spite of the highly classical density of its verbal material—its philological incandescence—and its formal relationship with 'Bruto minore,' this canzone . . . distances itself yet a little more from the model of the Horatian ode to prefigure the future freedom of the Leopardian canto (here, the stanza already has no more than eight rhymed lines out of 19) . . . the poem grafts onto the theme of the overwhelming return of spring the lament for the disappearance of the ancient myths [frequent since the end of the eighteenth century; cf. above all Schiller's *The Gods of Greece*], myths that Leopardi treats, not as metaphysical 'wisdom,' but, on the contrary, as a material and vital product of the primitive world (infantile or historic)." For Leopardi, myth is "a human creation to be understood as the reflection and personification of our own internal emotions, now happy, now unhappy; where the mythological landscape . . . is seen as an expression of the infancy of the world and corresponding, in the world of today, to the imagination of the child who still has the privilege . . . of giving life and feeling not only to animal existence but to the inanimate world as well" (Dotti, 34). Dotti (36) quotes Karl Vossler's suggestion that the linguistic archaisms of the canto were part of a literary game with the aim of seeing "Nature once again not as she is, but as she appeared to the Greeks."

Rigoni (M1, 933): "If Schiller and the philosophy of history of German romanticism, from Schlegel to Hölderlin, while perceiving the break between ancient and modern, believe in the possibility of reconstituting the blessed primitive harmony on another plane . . . Leopardi on the contrary nourishes no hope, sees no future. And in the canzone 'Alla primavera,' written in the firmest and most enchanted classicism, he has set loose the shadows and shivers of modern dereliction, creating a masterpiece of Grace and Melancholy at the same time."

1 *Perchè i celesti danni*: Cf. Horace, *Odes* IV, 7, 13: "Damen tamen celeres reparant coelestia lunae." See also, for contrasting tone, the opening lines of "La vita solitaria."

12–13 *l'atra / Face del ver*: Literally, the dark, i.e., sad, torch of truth, or scientific knowledge.

14 *Innanzi tempo*: Antognoni (quoted by Gallo and Garboli, 66): "Before its time, because nature, in taking illusions away from man, also had to deprive him of feeling; she did this partially, but not proportionally: she took the illusions all at once, feeling by degrees. One senses that a time will come when the heart of man will be totally cold; now, to the degree that it is not so, he suffers."

19 *Nel fior degli anni*: Leopardi frequently harps on the theme of his unspent youth; in "Il passero solitario," 23–25, e.g.: "Quasi romito, e strano / Al mio loco natio, / Passo del viver mio la primavera.") He wrote to Giulio Perticari (30 March 1821): "Fate has condemned my life to miss youth: because from childhood I made a leap to old age, indeed to decrepitude of the body as well as of the spirit. I've never ever experienced a single joy since I was born; hope for some years; for a long time since, not even that. And my external and internal life is such that, only imagining it, men would go chill with fear."

35 *La faretrata Diva*: Diana, goddess of the hunt, with her attributes of bow and arrows.

41 *la titania lampa*: The sun, offspring of the Titan Hyperion. Cf. Virgil, *Aeneid* VI, 725: "titaniaque astra."

44 *Ciprigna luce*: The moon, Venus, goddess of Cyprus.

55 *Dafne o la mesta Filli*: Daphne, pursued by Apollo, was transformed into a laurel tree by her father, Peneus. Phyllis, daughter of Lycurgus, king of Thrace, believing herself abandoned by Demophoön, killed herself and was turned into an almond tree.

55–56 *di Climene / . . . la sconsolata prole*: The Heliades, daughters of Helios and Clymene, sisters of Phaeton. After mourning at length the death of their brother, who was unable to control the chariot of the sun and fell from the sky, they were transformed into willows.

57 *Eridano:* River in Greek mythology associated with the Po.

61 *Eco*: Echo, hopelessly in love with Narcissus, wasted away until only her voice remained.

71 *Musico augel*: The nightingale.

76 *E d'ira e di pietà . . .*: Orcel (297–98): Because of the "criminal disgrace" committed against Philomela, "who was violated by her brother-in-law Tereus, king of Thrace. He cut out her tongue to prevent her from speaking, but Philomela embroidered her story on a piece of cloth and so told her sister Procne, who killed her own son Itys and gave him to Tereus to eat. Pursued by Tereus, she was transformed into a nightingale, Philomela into a swallow, Tereus into a hoopoe, and Itys into a robin. The composition of this line supposedly cost Leopardi much labor."

79 *e te di colpa ignudo . . . men caro*: Less adored because modern reason has destroyed the myth of the nightingale, and with it the possibility of our participating in her piteous fate.

85 *In freddo orror dissolve*: Conflation of two phrases from Virgil's *Aeneid*: "mihi frigidus horror / membra quatit" (III, 29–30) and "solvuntur frigore membra" (I, 29).

85 *e poi ch'estrano . . .*: Dotti (270): "and from the moment that even the earth on which we are born . . . is alienated from us and, indifferent to the fate of its children . . . nourishes, raises . . . their unhappy souls. Leopardi wrote in a marginal note [about lines that were later changed]: 'Thus these verses would say poetically, that today given the absence of illusions, the earth itself, and the very home of the living, has become the dwelling place of death and totally dead.'"

90 *Vaga*: See notes to lines 87–88 of "Ad Angelo Mai" (394) and passim on this essential Leopardian concept.

90 *la favilla antica*: Gallo and Garboli (70): the spark "of youth, as of the youth of the world."

91 *se tu pur vivi . . .*: Gallo and Garboli (70): "if you still live, and if there is something in heaven, on earth or on the sea that can in some way represent the metaphor of our life."

VIII. INNO AI PATRIARCHI / HYMN TO THE PATRIARCHS

Written at Recanati in seventeen days in July 1822; published in Bologna in 1824, the only one completed of ten planned hymns (the others were to be to God, the Redeemer, Maria, the Angels, Moses, the Prophets, the Apostles, the Martyrs, and the Hermits), along with a *Discorso intorno agl'Inni e alla Poes. Crist.* (Discourse on the Hymns and on Christian Poetry). Leopardi, in the "Annotazioni" to the canzoni (M2, 197): "I call this Hymn a Canzone, because it is a lyric poem, though it has neither stanza nor rhyme, and has achieved the true significance of the term canzone, which means the same as the Greek term *ode*, i.e., *canticle* [cantico]."

Leopardi, *Zibaldone* 2939 (11 July 1823): "From the long considerations made by me around the meaning of the tree of knowledge in Genesis, etc., from the fable of Psyche [. . .] and from other very ancient fables or beliefs, etc. [. . .] one can gather not only what is generally said, that the corruption and decadence of humankind from a better state was confirmed by a very distant, universal, constant and continuous tradition, but [. . .] that this corruption and decadence of humanity from a happy state, was born out of knowing, out of experiencing too much, and that the origin of its unhappiness was knowledge both of itself and of the world, and the overuse of reason."

Orcel (298): "Inspired by the Homeric and Alexandrian hymns, particularly rich in Latinisms, the poem forms with the canzone 'Alla primavera' a sort of diptych on the golden age." Dotti (35): "The hymn to the Biblical primitive after the one raised to the classical primitive [was] based on the conviction that Christian tradition, like that of all religions, had 'a great deal of that which, in resembling illusion, is optimal for poetry.'" Gallo and Garboli (71): Leopardi "admired the great book of the Jewish people, the Bible, the same way he admired the two poems of Homer: 'for nothing else than because being the most ancient books, they are the closest to nature, the sole source of beauty, greatness, life, variety' " (*Zibaldone* 1028 [11 May 1821]).

Bon (82–83) cites the influence of Chateaubriand and emphasizes the hymn's distance from Manzoni's devotional *Inni sacri* (1812–15 and 1822). "The notes that survive bear witness . . . to an unease ('O uomo Dio, Pietà di questa miseranda vita Che tu provasti'; *Inno al Redentore* [O man God, Have mercy on this miserable life Which you experienced; *Hymn to the Redeemer* [M1, 639]) which over time will move toward the vision of evil as prime mover of existence [cf. the hymn "To Ahriman"]." Orcel: "[The hymn is] globally less convincing than the preceding one ([and] its manuscripts attest in fact to its difficult elaboration)" and in fact the project of the hymns was abandoned.

The hymn joins the other odes-canzoni (Fubini, quoted in Dotti [37]) in "its taste for difficult and fugitive expression, arrived at via an elaboration that is especially laborious here, and an even more prominent and agitated syntax than in 'Alla primavera' . . . characterized especially by many forceful Latinate inversions."

For Dotti (38), "The theme . . . of the insane and insatiable human desire to know and its deleterious effects on society . . . having become the true bearing structure of the poem . . . ended by suffocating the more poetic, Miltonic part of its inspiration [i.e., on man's fall], which dedicated the hymn to the vast infinities of the primal world . . . one certainly reads the prose of the sketch [M1, 676–80] with more admiration than its translation into poetry . . . Its bitter and agonistic burden, its ideological obsession with the contrast between nature and reason, not only dominate but overwhelm the images making explicit what . . . was possibly better left inexplicit, in the background."

Rigoni (M1, 936): "The blessedness of the original state, imagined in the preceding poem in the form of Greek myth, is here sung in the Biblical version of the origins of humankind, through the evocation of the 'Patriarchs,' from Adam to Jacob, inhabitants of a world still immersed in a stupefied and solitary peace, ignorant of the mad and insatiable will to knowledge and of the unpropitious effects of society (whose foundation is laid at the feet of Cain, the first murderer). But the metaphor of the golden age is enriched in the last stanza, by another figure, no less dear to Leopardi's thought than ancient man, the child, and the animal: the savage, evoked in the species then believed to be most 'primitive,' and 'natural,' that is the savage of the 'California forests,' the same one which Leopardi's 'ultraphilosophy' posits as an ideal of happiness and, in a note in the *Zibaldone* of 21 May 1823, even of wisdom, precisely in that he 'doesn't know *thought*' . . . Here is the secret meaning of the canzoni: heroes of Thermopylae, great Italians of the past, Spartan and Roman virgins, winners in the game of *pallone*, Greek fables, patriarchs are not, in a poet like Leopardi, relics of a simple classicism or primitivism; they are projections and disguises of a flight from the condemnation of History, acts of exorcism of the nightmare of Time and the curse of Becoming."

5–6 *alma / Luce*: The sun; cf. *Aeneid* VIII, 455.

11–12 *vostro antico / Error*: Original sin.

21 *Erebo*: The kingdom of Death.

22 *Tu primo il giorno*: Adam. Leopardi imitates the mode of the Greek Homeric hymns and of Callimachus to "enumerate in a segment of brief portraits the most memorable facts about celebrated heroes" (G. A. Levi, cited by Dotti, 37).

34 *l'aurea luna*: Leopardi (in a marginal note quoted by Dotti, 273): "The color of the moon is between gold and silver. And *aureo* means *splendid*."

40 *fraterno scempio*: Adam and Eve's first son, Cain, a farmer, committed the first murder, killing his shepherd brother Abel, when God rejected Cain's sacrifice but accepted Abel's.

49 *aduna e stringe / Ne' consorti recetti*: Dotti (275) calls these lines "strongly elliptical."

57 *E tu dall'etra . . .*: Noah.

68 *illude*: Cf. Virgil, *Georgics* I, 181, and II, 375.

71 *padre de' pii*: Abraham.

77 *celesti peregrini*: Cf. *Genesis* 18:1–2, where Yahweh appeared to Abraham as three men.

78–79 *figlio / Della saggia Rebecca*: Jacob, son of Isaac and Rebecca.

83 *Della vezzosa Labanide*: Rachel.

85 *servaggio all'odiata soma*: Jacob had to serve Laban for fourteen years to obtain Rachel's hand in marriage. Cf. *Genesis* 29:1–30.

88 *L'aonio canto*: I.e., poetry. Mount Helicon, home of the Muses, is located in Aonia (Boeotia).

91 *Questa misera piaggia*: The earth.

91–92 *aurea corse / Nostra caduca età*: According to Orcel (299), Leopardi draws for this passage on Virgil's fourth eclogue, the final chorus of the first act of Tasso's *Aminta*, and the fourth act of Guarini's *Il pastor fido*.

105 *beata prole*: Leopardi believed that California was the last place on earth where "the golden age is not a fable" (M1, 164), and that its existence was threatened by colonialism. In his 1831 "Note ai Canti" to the canzoni (M1, 150) he wrote: "It's thought that the Californians, among the known nations, are the most distant from civilization, and the most hostile to it." Orcel (299) calls these last lines an "astounding denunciation of colonialism" but for Rigoni (M1, 938) "it would be incongruous to see" in this last stanza "a simple denunciation of white colonialism, rather than a despairing cry on the tragedy of civilization."

117 *ignuda / Felicità per l'imo sole incalza*: Dotti (280) quotes M. Fubini: "One can observe that the word *felicità* always occurs in the same position in Leopardi's verses: it's placed at the beginning of the line, separated by a strong enjambment from the adjective that accompanies it, as if the poet wants us to sense the unreachable distance of the good desired by everyone (cf. 'La vita solitaria,' 20; 'Al Conte Carlo Pepoli,' 24, 59, 87; 'Le ricordanze,' 24; 'Palinodia,' 31 and 258; 'La ginestra,' 104)."

IX. ULTIMO CANTO DI SAFFO / SAPPHO'S LAST SONG

Written at Recanati between May 13 and 19, 1822; published in the Bologna edition of the *Canzoni* in 1824. As Leopardi wrote (M1, 163), the poem "intends to represent the unhappiness of a delicate, tender, sensitive, noble, and warm soul contained in an ugly and young body."

Orcel (299): "This canzone, still representative of a verbal hyperclassicism . . . is presented as a metrical 'extravagance': the [eighteen-line] stanza includes only one *settenario* and only the last two lines are rhymed." Dotti (281) quotes Antognoni: "The first sixteen lines have the now placid, now solemn, now tragic movement of the free hendecasyllabic line . . . Sappho's disturbed mind finds the wave of harmony at the end of the stanza, and almost indulging in this, a relative calm in her despairing pain." Orcel: "This movement toward the Leopardian 'canto,' which will soon free itself of all formal constraint, corresponds to the poem's subject matter: through the voice of Sappho (Leopardi exploits both the Ovidian image of the 'small and dark' Sappho of the *Heroides* and the poetess's legendary unhappy love for Phaon) it is the poet's own subjectivity—the alienation of a 'noble' and 'tender' soul in a 'young and ugly' body—that for the first time finds pure expression here. A commentary on sources (see C. Muscetta, *Per la poesia italiana*, Rome, 1988) would mention among others . . . Mme. De Staël's 'Dernier chant de Corinne,' A. Verri's *Avventure di Saffo*, Cesarotti's Ossian, and Italian translations of Gray."

Rigoni (M1, 939–40): "The composition renounces all concrete classical orientation, instead letting erupt on the scene—for the first time in the series of the *Canti*—the pure voice of the Leopardian lyric 'I' . . . The inspiration for the canzone, which takes the theme of suicide—with its bitter and blasphemous notes—from 'Bruto minore,' is thus endowed with a transposed but nevertheless very evident personal theme and raises again the question, long debated by the critics, of the relationship between thought and biography in Leopardi. Even during the poet's life it was insinuated that his pessimism was determined by his deformity and illness, with the intent of limiting or invalidating it as an entirely private and particular case . . . Leopardi himself had responded to such an attitude with lucid and resentful certainty [in the letter to Louis de Sinner quoted on p. 402 (see also his bitter lines on the subject in the "Palinodia," 7–13)]. Anticipating on this point as well a notion that will be typical of Nietzsche . . . [the poet] exalted the exceptional decisive role of the various passions and the different states of organic and psychological alteration in the discoveries of thought (cf. *Zibaldone* 1975 [23 October 1822]) . . . The [irritated], incandescent autobiographical material is not only legitimized on the poetic plane by virtue of its high imaginative and stylistic development but manages, on the intellectual plane, to attain universal and objective truths about the human condition: the cruel blindness of destiny; the impossibility that inner worth can be affirmed on its own on earth; the brevity of youthful 'joyful illusions'; the indecipherable enigma of the universe where 'All is mystery except our pain.'"

G. De Robertis (97), however, asserts that "when he felt human unhappiness as something less causal, he made his deformity the subject of humor, and used it once to describe the origin of Socratic irony, which was also his irony (cf. the "Detti memorabili di Filippo Ottonieri" [in the *Operette morali*], chapter 1)."

Bon (83) notes that starting with the Florentine edition of 1825, the "Ultimo canto di Saffo," though it comes chronologically before the "Inno," is placed after it so that "the two classical canti open and close the mythical parenthesis, be it classical or biblical."

3 *la rupe*: The rock of Leucade above the Ionian Sea, from which, according to legend, Sappho is supposed to have thrown herself into the sea because of her unrequited love for Phaon.

4 *Nunzio del giorno*: The "star" of Venus, which is called Lucifer when it announces the day.

5 *l'erinni*: The Furies; by extension, the torments of passionate love.

7 *Spettacol molle*: The personal tone of this introductory evocation anticipates the similar opening of the autobiographical "Le ricordanze."

Leopardi wrote in the margin of his manuscript: (quoted in Dotti [282]): "Don't we say *spettacol dolce, dolce vista, dolce sguardo*? Why then can you apply a word from spoken language to the eyes, and not from touch? I admit that the metaphor is a stretch, but how many more stretches does Horace have. But if the poet, especially the lyric poet, isn't ardent in his metaphors, and is afraid of the unusual, he will also lack what's new."

10–11 *il flutto / Polveroso de' Noti*: Notus, or Auster: the south wind, here used generically.

12 *carro di Giove*: "It was a commonplace for poets to think of thunder as Jove's chariot." Leopardi, "Saggio sopra gli errori poplari degli antichi," XIII (M2, 807).

24 *grave ospite addetta*: The phrase is borrowed from Lucan, *Pharsalia* VIII, 157: "submissa . . . gravis hospita."

30 *colorati augelli*: Cf. "pictae volucres," Virgil, *Aeneid* IV, 525, and *Georgics* III, 243, as Leopardi himself notes (Rigoni [M1, 941]) in marginal notes on the poem manuscript.

41 *scemo*: Leopardi, "Here it does not mean *diminished*, but absolutely *lacking*."

43 *indomita*: Leopardi, in a marginal note quoted by Dotti (284): "Lachesis can very well be called indomitable, given that the ancients assigned the governance of the world to the Fates."

44 *ferrigno*: Leopardi: "i.e., iron-colored, dark," in a marginal note quoted by Gallo and Garboli (86).

46 *Arcano è tutto*: Dotti (154) gives this as an example of Leopardi's unique ability to "reshape the entire traditional linguistic patrimony . . . innovating it by inserting entirely personal terms . . . Leopardi's epigraphic Dantism has here assumed an entirely new form . . . through the insertion of a word [arcano] which certainly belongs to the tradition but which, as used, pertains, one could say almost exclusively, to the [poet's] ideal vocabulary."

49 *De' celesti si posa*: Leopardi, in a marginal note (Rigoni [M1, 941]), writes: "Homer and other poets in numerous places."

50 *il Padre*: Zeus.

54 *disadorno ammanto*: Leopardi to Giordani (2 March 1818): "Whoever it may be is forced to desire that virtue not be without some external embellishment, and finding it entirely naked, turns sad and, by force of nature that no wisdom can defeat, practically lacks the courage to love the virtuous one in whom only the soul is beautiful."

55 *Morremo*: Cf. the exclamation of Dido in *Aeneid* IV, 659–60: "Moriemur inulta, sed moriamur," which Leopardi cites in a marginal note. He glosses this Virgilian quotation in *Zibaldone* 2217 (3 December 1821): "Virgil wanted here to express (a refined and profound sentiment, and worthy of a man who knew hearts, and was expert in passions and misfortunes, as he was) the pleasure that the soul feels in considering and representing not only vividly, but minutely, intimately, and fully its misfortune, its pains; in exaggerating them, even to itself, if it can (and if it can, it certainly will), in recognizing, or representing, but certainly persuading itself and taking care with every effort to persuade itself firmly, that they are excessive, endless, limitless, without possible real remedy or impediment or compensation or consolation, without any circumstance that would alleviate them; in seeing, in sum, and feeling vividly that its misfortune is appropriately immense and perfect."

Dotti (43), commenting on the movement here from "io" to "noi," points out that the first person plural was used for the singular "as Leopardi well knew, having noted it in *Zibaldone* 2891 [5 July 1823] . . . according to the habit of the best Greek and Latin poets," adding that it nevertheless "has a choral force."

55 *Il velo indegno*: Continues the metaphor of the body as mantle in the previous line. The (Petrarchan) veil is the body in which Sappho's soul is dressed.

59 *fede*: Gallo and Garboli (87): "obsessive."

62 *nato mortal*: Leopardi (in a marginal note quoted by Gallo and Garboli

[87]): "The Gods according to the ancients were born but not mortal, and many of these had lived for some time on earth; and many were terrestrial, and always lived there, like the nymphs of the woods, rivers, seas, Pans, the sylvan gods, etc."

63 *del doglio avaro*: Leopardi is alluding, as he notes (Rigoni [M1, 941]), to "the jar full of happiness which Homer places in the house of Jove." Cf. *Iliad* XXIV, 527–30.

67 *Sottentra il morbo* . . .: Leopardi is translating Virgil, *Georgics* III, 66–69: "Optima quaeque dies miseris mortalibus aevi / prima fugit, subeunt morbida tristisque senectus / et labor, et durae rapit inclementia mortis." The ambiguous nature of "primo" (l. 66 here) is pointed out by Leopardi in a marginal note (Rigoni [M1, 942]): "Does *primo* depend on *età* or relate to *s'invola*? Ask Virgil."

68–69 *Ecco di tante / Sperate palme* . . .: Leopardi, in an unpublished note (19 May 1822) [M1, 681–82], wrote: "Latin poetry, Virgil and Horace, who are the most perfect . . . abound in such uncertain expressions . . . And the uncertain, and distant, and ardent, and unusual, and indefinite, and fugitive in this phrase gives it that *vago* [vagueness] which will always be greatly valued by whoever understands the true nature of poetry."

71 *tenaria*: Hecate or Proserpina, goddess of the underworld, is so named after Cape Tenaro, now Capo Matapàn, endpoint of the southern Peloponnese, which was near the entrance to Hades according to the Greeks.

X. IL PRIMO AMORE / FIRST LOVE

Written between December 14 and 16, 1817, at Recanati; published under the title "Elegia I," in the Bologna *Versi*, 1826; and then with its final title in the Florentine *Canti* of 1831. ("Elegia II," "Io qui vagando al limitare attorno," appears in revised form in the *Canti* without a title, as fragment XXXVIII). The poem was occasioned by a visit made to the Leopardi household by a cousin of Monaldo's, the twenty-seven-year-old contessa Geltrude Cassi-Lazzari of Pesaro, who had a powerful effect on the young Leopardi, arousing an emotion of "uncontaminated and pure fire."

Orcel (301): "Written before the first canzoni, and heavy with literary citations, this elegy is all the more disappointing when compared with the *Diario del primo amore* (written slightly later . . . [14–23 December 1817]) [M2, 1171–86], which relates the same psychological experience in prose with an entirely Stendhalian introspective clarity" (cf. the discrepancy in vividness between the sketch for the "Inno ai patriarchi" and the canzone itself). D'Intino, in the introduction to his edition of Leopardi's *Scritti e frammenti autobiografici* (xxi–xxv), finely analyzes his affinity with Stendhal, while Dotti (48) quotes Walter Binni on the "disruptive and liberating importance" of Leopardi's reading of Alfieri's *Vita* earlier in the year.

Orcel (301): "In spite of its having been written first, Leopardi placed this poem after the nine canzoni as an introduction to the intimism of the second section of the collection," i.e., the idylls. Dotti (47): After the "ideological-poetical group of canzoni" with its "heroically accented poetry of 'ideas,'" Leopardi here introduces "the more mournful and intimately descriptive voice of his own interior journey, of human suffering, of the singular 'adventure' of the poet's spirit that has likewise been preoccupying him at the same time."

Rigoni (M1, 942) sees the "cantabilità" of the poem as deriving from the decline of Petrarchism [like much of his work, the poem is riddled with Petrarchan echoes and citations, among others] into the terza rima of the typical eighteenth-century amorous elegy. "It is interesting to note three themes: the poet's turning back on his own heart ('Only my heart pleased me . . .'), destined to be noteworthy as his direct interlocutor in 'Il risorgimento' and above all in 'A se stesso'; the regret at not having enjoyed things . . . which will return in 'Il passero solitario'; and the presence of the 'idea' of love which looks ahead in its form and effects to 'Il pensiero dominante,' and in the three final lines connects closely to the canzone 'Alla sua donna.'"

1 *Tornami a mente*: Cf. Petrarch, sonnet CCCXXXVI, "Tornami a mente, anzi v'é dentro, quella."

1–2 *la battaglia / D'amor*: Cf. Petrarch, sonnets CCCXXXVI and CIV.

15 *t'era noia ogni contento*: Cf. *Zibaldone*, 59: "When a man conceives of love the whole world fades before his eyes, it is no longer seen except for the beloved object, he stands in the midst of the crowd in conversations, etc., as if he were all alone, abstracted and making those gestures which your ever immobile and all-powerful thought inspires in you with no care for the wonderment or disdain of others, everything is forgotten and becomes boring, except for that one idea and that sight."

31–32 *qual tra le chiome / D'antica selva*: Cf. "Alla primavera," 71: "chiomato bosco." The source is Horace, *Odes* IV, III, 11: "nemorum comae."

34 *taccio . . . contendo*: Narrative present tense.

41 *i destrier che dovean farmi deserto*: Because they would soon carry his love away.

65 *Olimpo*: I.e., the heavens.

68 *a pianger nato*: Cf. Petrarch, *Rime* CXXX, 6: "e di lacrime vivo, a pianger nato."

79 *da me sì vario fui*: Echoes *Aeneid* II, 274: "Ei mihi, qualis erat, quantum mutatus ab illo," which in Leopardi's youthful (1816) translation reads: "quanto da quel diverso."

81 *nui*: Literary form of Sicilian origin (Dotti, 293).

88–89 *la candida imago / . . . pinta nel seno*: Cf. Petrarch, *Rime* XCVI, 5–6: "Ma'l bel viso leggiadro che depinto / Porto nel petto . . ." Orcel (301): "One sees here the first signs of the very personal 'Platonism' which Leopardi will develop especially in 'Alla sua donna' and 'Il pensiero dominante.'" Cf. also "il mio possente errore" in "Le ricordanze," 66.

103 *sol di lei*: Or, "it in itself fulfills me." Cf. Petrarch, *Rime* CXXIX, 37: "che del suo proprio error l'alma s'appaga."

XI. IL PASSERO SOLITARIO / THE SOLITARY THRUSH

Begun in 1819, when the first idylls, which it introduces, were being written, it was probably worked on again at Recanati in 1829–30, and finished in Florence in the autumn of 1830 or later. First published in the Neapolitan edition of 1835.

Rigoni (M1, 943–44): "This is the first example, in the arrangement of the *Canti*, of the so-called free, or Leopardian, canzone, typical of the Pisa-Recanati period . . . Unlike the 'regular' canzoni, this one is made up of strophes [or *lasse*, varying stanzas, derived from medieval French and Spanish poetry] that differ among themselves as to number of lines and rhyme scheme." The poem is positioned "as prelude to the idylls, whose atmosphere it recalls, even if its formal and metrical structure presumes the experience of the great Pisa-Recanati canti of 1828–1830 . . . The goal of this operation seems to be that of vitalizing the perspective on the first idylls and reinforcing their unity with his later poetic production [Bandini] . . .

"Attention to the animal world—characteristic of Leopardi's sensibility and thought and already touched on . . . both in 'Bruto minore' and 'Alla primavera' —turns here to a species, birds, which the magnificent 'Elogio degli uccelli' in the *Operette morali* (1824) had celebrated for their existence consisting purely in song and flight, almost as emblems of their lightness, mobility, and freedom, which are associated with the air, their proper and natural element. But, while in the operetta they are described as 'the happiest creatures in the world' (birds are in fact compared to children . . . they are the children of the animal kingdom, they overflow with 'extrinsic life,' are unfamiliar with boredom, and share in the sovereign pleasure of 'laughter' [like ancient man in "Alla primavera"]), in this canto, infused with springtime exultation as well as the melancholy of imminent sunset, Leopardi concentrates on the particular and sorrowful image of one, distinguished instead by its self-exclusion from the lively and joyful life of its fellows. Counter-figure of the poet in not belonging to the mobile, distracted and active life, the solitary thrush yet remains much more fortunate than he because, obedient in its way to its own nature, it is free of the curse of awareness which, in addition to paralysis of feeling and separation from the whole, will bring bitterness and regret for the youth renounced [by the poet]."

Dotti (910): The canto "belongs (at least ideally) to a particular period at Recanati, the period . . . of memory [which would include the composition of "A Silvia" and "Le ricordanze"] which in reconstruing the inner life interprets and dramatizes it in contrast with the truth . . . After memory . . . has evoked a given moment of existence . . . in its fleeting beauty . . . as always, in its second part, the poem turns to reflection, makes the 'negative' emerge and proposes the sorrowful lesson of the truth. All the pain of the real is expressed here in the closing questions (the questions that will lend its poetic tone to the 'Canto notturno'), and it's as if the poet, with these, has tried to distance for some time—in a future avoidable only in death—imminent and fatal misfortune."

1 *della torre antica*: Dotti (296): The campanile of the church of Sant'Agostino in Recanati.

3 *Cantando vai . . .*: Cf. Petrarch, *Rime* CCCLIII, 1, "Vago augelletto che cantando vai." But see also the celebrated opening of *Purgatorio* VIII, to which Leopardi's lines are rich in references: "Era già l'ora che volge il disio / ai navicanti e 'ntenerisce il core / lo dì ch'han detto ai dolci amici addio; / e che lo novo peregrin d'amore / piange, se ode squilla di lontano / che paia il giorno pianger che si more."

53 *Quando muti questi occhi . . .*: On "what man loses losing youth," Dotti (443) points to *Pensieri* LXI and *Zibaldone* 4284 (1 July 1827): "The age in which man senses he no longer inspires anything is very sad. Man's great desire, the great mover of his actions, his words, his looks, his attitudes all the way to old age, is the desire to inspire, to communicate something of himself to his spectators or hearers."

57 *che di me stesso?*: Cf. Leopardi's letter to G. P. Vieusseux (4 March 1826): "My life, at first through necessity of circumstance and against my will, later by inclination born of a habit converted into nature and become indelible, has always been, and is, and will perpetually be solitary, even in the midst of conversation, in which, to put it in English, I am more 'absent' than a blind and deaf man would be."

XII. L'INFINITO / INFINITY

This first and most famous of the idylls was supposedly written at Recanati in the spring-autumn of 1819. It was published as "L'infinito. Idillio I," along with "La sera del dì di festa," "Alla luna," "Il sogno," "La vita solitaria," and "Fragment XXXVII" (where it is called "Lo spavento notturno") under the overall title *Idilli*, in two successive numbers (December 1825 and January 1826) of *Il nuovo ricoglitore* in Milan; all were subsequently included in the Bologna edition of 1826, in which "L'infinito" stands as the first poem.

An idyll is an extended lyric of ancient origin with a bucolic, pastoral setting, originally accompanied by a flute. Traces can be found in Homer, but the first complete idylls are those of Theocritus, which appealed strongly to the young Leopardi. The form has a long history of literary recuperation and imitation in Latin literature (cf. Virgil's *Eclogues*) and in the Renaissance, starting with the eclogues attributed to Dante and including Sannazaro's *Arcadia*, Tasso's *Aminta*, etc. (Bertone, 106). For Leopardi, however, the idyll represents an attempt to cut through to the directness and simplicity of the Greek lyric, as Pound and H. D. strove to do several generations later; in this sense, his idylls may be considered the first modern lyric poems in Italian.

In a note on the manuscript of his version of Theocritus's "Il predatore di favi" (M1, 897), Leopardi preferred the "grace" and "simple" qualities of the Greek poet to the "sublime" Horace; as d'Intino notes (*Poeti greci e latini*, xvii), "The 'simple' means, in this its first appearance, the spontaneous, i.e., the *natural*, but also the *real*, in opposition to the sublime life of concepts and ideas, or worse, of ideals." (Leopardi had also translated the idylls of the Greek poet Moschus, whom he erroneously considered a contemporary of Theocritus and whom he called "the Virgil of the Greeks, but a Virgil who invents and doesn't transcribe, and who in addition writes in a more delicate language, and in a time which preserves something more of the ancient simplicity." Moschus's poems were, no doubt, an inspiration in naming his own pastoral poems; Dotti (53), however, cites Fubini in suggesting that Leopardi's own writing was probably more influenced by pre-romantic works such as Monti's *Pensieri d'amore* and *Sciolti a Sigismondo Chigi*, Goethe's *Werther*, and Foscolo's *Ortis*.

Rigoni (M1,946): "The structure of this idyll . . . is clear, and easy to define: a visual sensation (the hedge that hides from sight 'so much of the last horizon') arouses the imagination of spatial infinity and its 'depthless calm'; a subsequent auditory sensation (the wind stirring in the leaves), compared with that superhuman silence, calls up the imagination of temporal infinity and the comparison between 'the dead seasons and the present, / living one and how it sounds.' And in this double, oceanic immensity it is sweet, to the poet's way of thinking, to founder. It is not a matter, however, of abandonment to a theological infinity, nor in fact to an experience of the 'sacred,' as many have claimed or suggested: numerous notes in the *Zibaldone*, along an arc that stretches at least from 1820 to 1827, attest in fact to Leopardi's polemic against any metaphysical interpretation . . . The most important of these—even if it comes after the date of composition of the idyll—denies infinity is real insomuch as it is contradictory of that *principium individuationis* which rules every form of being. Everything that exists is necessarily an *individual* entity, marked and distinguished by a contour and a boundary, i.e., *finite*. An infinite individual or an individual infinity is a philosophical absurdity, a contradiction in terms: without a limit, everything vanishes into the absolute Indistinct, into *nothingness*, which alone seems infinite. 'It seems that only what does not exist, the negation of being, nothingness, can be without limits, and that the infinite comes to be essentially the same as nothing. It seems above all that the individuality of existence naturally involves a limitation of some sort, in such a way that the infinite does not admit individuality and these two terms are contradictory; therefore one cannot suppose an individual entity that does not have limits' (*Zibaldone* 1478, 2 May 1826). But in a later clarification, Leopardi will reject this 'hypostatisization' of infinity itself as nothingness, granting it a purely mental and linguistic existence (cfr. *Zibaldone* 4181–82, 4 June 1826). The infinite is reduced to being the imagination of what is not seen or the nevertheless very real boundaries of which are not known, i.e., the *indefinite*, a key concept in his theory of pleasure as well as in Leopardi's poetics: 'Not only the cognitive faculty, or that of loving, but the imaginative, too, is incapable of infinity, or of knowing infinitely, but only of the indefinite, and of conceiving indefinitely. Something delights us because the soul, not seeing its limits, receives the impression of a kind of infinity, and confuses the indefinite with the infinite . . .' (*Zibaldone* 472, 4 January 1821)." Compare the lover's "amorosa idea" of the beloved in "Aspasia," 39ff. As we have seen, the adjective "vago" incorporates this sense of indefinite pleasure and beauty. (See *Zibaldone* 100 [8 January 1820].)

D'Intino ("Coleridge-Leopardi," 100): "Leopardi's poetics of the indefinite, in effect, derives precisely from the rejection of the seen (which is limited to the recognition of the actual) and from that broadening of the horizon beyond the limits of the visible of which Coleridge speaks . . . The romantic locus par excellence [of Leopardi's poetics] is the one in which 'in the place of vision the imagination goes to work and the fantastic takes its place. The soul imagines what it doesn't see, what that tree, that hedge, that tower, hides from it, and goes wandering in an imaginary space, and conceives for itself things that it could not if its sight extended everywhere, because the real would exclude the imaginary.' " (*Zibaldone* 171 [12 –23 July 1820]).

For Ungaretti (1950), " 'L'infinito' is an idyll that is ironic in tone starting with its title. The idyll of infinity will in fact be a representation of the finite." But according to Rigoni (M1, 947): "In the immediacy of the psychological experience and its poetic expression, it's natural that the illusion of the loss of limits be lived as reality and therefore present the characteristics proper to ecstasy, with the inevitable admixture of fear and pleasure: this alone, in the end, determines the meaning of the poem, as it does the deep emotion it provokes in the soul of the reader."

1 *ermo colle*: Monte Tabor, not far beyond the Porta di Monte Morello of Recanati, near Palazzo Leopardi. The expression is derived from classic Italian writers such as Galeazzo di Tarsia. Gardini (86) also sees the first line of the poem as derived from Leopardi's translation of the idylls of Moschus and from Theocritus and relates the "colle" to the hill of Antela in "All'Italia." He calls "L'infinito" "a modern version of pastoral . . . which, through temporal suspension and utopian evasion, saves the individual from despair, providing some kind of reprieve from historical decay."

11 *mi sovvien l'eterno*: Dotti (301) quotes Fubini, according to whom "the immediate antecedent of 'L'infinito' and in particular of these lines" is a passage from Leopardi's *Ricordi d'infanzia e di adolescenza* (also written in 1819): "My considerations on the plurality of worlds and the nothingness of us and of this earth and on the greatness and power of the nature that we measure with its torrents, etc. which are a nothing on this globe which is a nothing in the world and, aroused by a voice calling me to dinner, our life and time and celebrated names and history, etc. then seemed a nothing." Cf. also the great apostrophe on the insignificance of man on earth in "La ginestra," 167–200.

14 *Immensità*: Originally "infinità." Cf. the description of a similar situation in Alfieri's *Vita* (Parte I, Epoca III, cap. IV) (1790): "Sitting on the shore with my shoulders leaning on a tallish rock which deprived me of all sight of the earth from behind, in front of me and around me I saw nothing but sky and sea; and so between these two immensities . . . I spent an hour of delights daydreaming."

15 *E il naufragar m'è dolce . . .*: Orcel (304) asserts that this phrase likely has mystical origins.

XIII. LA SERA DEL DÌ DI FESTA / THE EVENING OF THE HOLIDAY

Written at Recanati between 1819 and 1821, and usually assigned to 1820; first published in the Milanese journal *Il nuovo ricoglitore* in December 1825, under the title "La sera del giorno festivo. Idillio II." The situation from which the poem derives is described in *Zibaldone* 50–51: "My unhappiness at hearing late at night after some feast day the nocturnal song of peasants passing. Infinity of the past that came to mind, thinking of the Romans [fallen] thus after so much noise and of so many events now past which I compared mournfully with the profound stillness and silence of the night, making me realize what was pleasing in the prominence of that peasant's voice or song."

Orcel (304): "Written in a single stanza of blank hendecasyllables (which . . . testifies to internal unity of the text in the eyes of the poet) . . . From the transparent initial nocturne—of an entirely Homeric freshness—to the song lost in the night of the last lines . . . the poem braids by subtle movements of leaps and reprises the typical Leopardian themes of alienation, of repetitive and destructive time, of destiny and loss. The subject of History, introduced by the classic *Ubi sunt?*, radically differentiates the experience incorporated in the second idyll from 'L'infinito.'" Cf. also the letter to Giordani of 6 March 1820. Dotti (58): "A canto like 'La sera . . .' . . . in which the poetry of memory is overwhelmingly present, evoking the historical as well as the personal . . . presents itself with all the summary characteristics of a 'conception of the world' and . . . as such is bound to impose itself on European culture." It was translated by Sainte-Beuve, Amiel, and Aulard, and imitated (and in part plagiarized) by Laforgue in his "Soir de carnival."

3–4 *rivela / Serena ogni montagna*: Cf. *Iliad* VIII, 555ff, a passage cited and translated by Leopardi himself in his *Discorso di un italiano intorno alla poesia romantica* as an example of the ancients' ability to imitate nature "in such a way that it does not seem imitated but transported into their lines." The attribution of the adjective "serena" is ambiguous: it can refer either to "luna" or to "ogni montagna."

5 *Già tace ogni sentiero*: Cf. Virgil, *Aeneid* IV, 525.

13 *l'antica natura*: Dotti (303) quotes *Zibaldone* 2263 (20 December 1821): "*Antichi, antico, antichità; posteri, posterità* are very poetic, etc., words because they contain one idea: 1. vast, 2. undefined and uncertain, maximal *posterities* of which we know nothing, and *antiquity* similarly is a very obscure thing for us." Dotti adds: "Here, however, the adjective *antica* by which nature is defined, followed immediately by *onnipossente*, seems to assume a tone that is polemical, setting the 'I' in opposition to destiny."

14 *mi fece all'affanno*: Cf. "Il primo amore": "a pianger nato" (68).

In his letter to Giordani of 6 March 1820, Leopardi writes: "A few nights ago, before going to bed, having opened the window of my room and seeing a clear sky, a lovely ray of moonlight, and feeling warm air and hearing certain dogs baying in the distance, certain old images were awakened in me and I thought I felt a commotion in my heart, thanks to which I started screaming like a madman, begging for mercy from nature, whose voice I thought I was hearing after so long."

Dotti (58) notes how the calm, "majestically Goethean" opening of the canto is characteristically soon revealed as illusion, yielding to a "lyrically agitated climate reminiscent of some of Monti's ["pre-romantic"] *Pensieri d'amore*."

33–34 *dov'è il suono / Di que' popoli antichi*: Dotti (304) reminds us that this is an instance of the time-honored classic—and medieval—trope of *Ubi sunt?* Cf. also the evocation of the "perduto impero" of Rome at the beginning of "La ginestra." Garboli and Gallo (111): "More than almost any other poet Leopardi loves the effect of pathetic precision which derives from the demonstrative pronoun."

It is notable how important the *sound* of the past is to Leopardi (see "Sopra il monumento di Dante," 114ff and elsewhere), as is the sound of the season in "L'infinito," and of Silvia's—and others'—singing throughout the *Canti*; indeed, the very title of the book implies how vital the aural aspect of poetry, and of experience as a whole, is for this poet.

43 *Premea le piume*: Cf. *Purgatorio* VI, 150 and elsewhere for this commonplace idiom (cf. also "Il primo amore," 20).

44–45 *Un canto . . . / Lontanando*: Cf. *Zibaldone* 1928 (16 October 1821), where Leopardi describes the effect of "a song . . . heard from afar . . . which little by litte grows distant," becoming insensible, lost in the vastness of space.

XIV. ALLA LUNA / TO THE MOON

The fourth idyll, written at Recanati, perhaps in July 1819 or 1820, and possibly before "L'infinito" (Orcel, 305); first published in *Il nuovo ricoglitore* (as "La ricordanza. Idillio III"), then in the Bologna edition of 1826. Until the Florentine edition of 1831, the poem was called "La luna o la ricordanza," or simply "La ricordanza"; the title was changed to avoid confusion with "Le ricordanze" (1829). Dotti (53) suggests that here and in "L'infinito" (and later, perhaps, in "A se stesso" as well), "Leopardi in his own way wanted to compete with the sonnet."

Rigoni (M1, 950–51): "Leopardi's emotional world and philosophical mythmaking are animated . . . in the twilight or nighttime light of the stars, and, par excellence, of the moon, certainly no longer a divinity but not yet the desolate land of astronautical exploration. If modern man, who has only been brushed by the wing of metaphysical disenchantment, can no longer devote himself in any way to the cult and the celebration of the image of the sun, in the moon . . . he still continues to recognize a pregnant, though altered, symbolic entity. The attributes and imagery that Leopardi gives her are a sublime example of loving, extreme mythological reintegration, culminating in the 'Canto notturno . . .' (*q.v.*). Young virgin, pensive, immortal, aware of The All, silent but consoling presence (her setting means grief on Earth, her fall from the sky—imagined in the wonderful fragment, 'Odi, Melisso'—pure cosmic alarm), she is also the patroness of memory . . . In this idyll, 'wholly plaintive confession of a lonely and bitter life . . . curiously it's less suffering or the past that dominates but the milky image of the feminine star: the irony of myth that it surprises cold reason.' (Orcel 1982)."

2 *or volge l'anno*: Cf. Petrarch, *Rime* LXII, 9: "Or volge, signor mio, l'undecimo anno." Dotti (59)—noting the importance of anniversaries for Leopardi, and citing a sketch for an elegy written on June 29, 1818, in which he writes: "Today ends my 20th year. Miserable me what have I done? Still no great accomplishment" (M1, 617)—suggests that the canto was composed on the poet's birthday, June 29, 1819.

2 *questo colle*: Again, Monte Tabor, the "ermo colle" of "L'infinito," outside Recanati.

13–14 *Nel tempo giovanil . . . il corso*: These two lines were a late addition of Leopardi's, first appearing in the Neapolitan edition of 1835.

15 *Il rimembrar delle passate cose*: Cf. *Zibaldone* 1987–88 (25 October 1821): "As with impressions, memories of childhood in whatever era are more vivid than those of any other period. Even the remembering of images or things that were unhappy, or frightening, etc., in childhood are pleasing due to their vividness. And for the same reason unhappy memories are also pleasing in life, even when the cause of the sadness isn't past, or when memory occasions them or intensifies them, as in the death of our dear ones, the remembering of the past, etc." See also *Zibaldone* 60 (May–June 1819).

XV. IL SOGNO / THE DREAM

Written in December 1820 or at the beginning of 1821, at Recanati; published on August 13, 1825, in Brighenti's Bolognese review, *Notizie teatrali bibliografiche e urbane, ossia il Caffè di Petronio*, then in *Il nuovo ricoglitore* (December 1825) as "Il sogno. Idillio IV," and in the Bologna edition of 1826.

Despite its formal echoes of Petrarch, of Cesarotti's Ossian, and of Monti, the poem, for Orcel (305), marks a lowering of quality in Leopardi's inspiration. "The figure of the young dead girl is perhaps inspired by Teresa Fattorini, daughter of the coachman of Palazzo Leopardi, who died in September 1818, and who [will later be] idealized in the canzone 'A Silvia' " and (Gallo and Garboli, 117) "whose image is fixed in the *Ricordi d'infanzia e d'adolescenza* and suggested in the canzone 'Per una donna inferma di malattia lunga e mortale' written in March and April 1819 and never published by Leopardi."

For Rigoni (M1, 951–52), " 'Il sogno' is not so much an amorous canto as a nod in the direction of a multiplicity of themes and tones which Leopardi will develop later and which show how far the poem diverges from its Petrarchan models (*Rime* CCCLIX; *Il Trionfo della Morte* II [in both of which "the old poet intones an emotional dialogue with Laura in heaven" {Dotti, 63}]) . . . but the interest of the idyll, beyond its function as a prelude, is also in the authentically Romantic frisson with which life and death are suspended and almost assimilated by the mournful magic of the dream, however much the rhetorical-literary model does not always end up perfectly adequate and resolved."

Dotti notes that in Leopardi's dream-dialogue "there is no motive of Christian transcendence whatsoever" and in fact he imagines the dead beloved not more beautiful in heaven, but exactly as she was on earth, writing (in the relevant "disegno letterario" mentioned below) that " 'even the increase of beauty is prejudicial to feeling and memory,' " something "he adds with the boldness of youth 'that was not understood by our poets, not even by Petrarch.' "

4 *Quando in sul tempo . . .*: Gallo and Garboli (119) compare these lines to Leopardi's translation of the second idyll of Moschus, 4–8: "Quando il sopor su le palpèbre / più soave del mèl siede e le membra / lieve rilassa, ritenendo intanto / in molle laccio avvilupati i lumi." [When sleep sits on the eyelids / more softly than honey / and lightly relaxes the limbs, while keeping / the eyes enclosed in a soft noose.]

24 *or son più lune*: Dotti (63) thinks the "Disegno letterario, VII" (M2, 1213), which mentions an "incontro di Petrarca morto, con Laura per la prima volta" (meeting of the dead Petrarch with Laura for the first time) could have been the nucleus of this elegy; as the plan also includes notes for "Nelle nozze della sorella Paolina" and "Bruto minore," written in November and December of 1821, he conjectures that "Il sogno" may also date from this period.

30 *ha poco andare*: The image of life as a journey is Petrarchan. Cf. *Rime* LXXV, 14: "Questi avea poco andare ad esser morto."

32 *e duro è il fato . . .*: I.e., hope extinguished by premature death, and not by experience. The theme recurs in "Sopra un basso rilievo antico sepolcrale," 33–43.

49 *Intenderlo potessi*: On Leopardi's desire to die see his letter to Brighenti of 12 April 1820: "It's time to die. It's time to yield to fate."

52 *come vecchiezza*: Leopardi to Giulio Perticari (30 March 1821): "Fortune condemned my life to go without youth; for from childhood I passed to old age." Cf. also Leopardi's treatment of the theme in "Il passero solitario."

55 *Nascemmo al pianto . . .*: See the same phrase in "Ultimo canto di Saffo," 48.

63 *il cor t'assalse*: Cf. Petrarch's similar question to Laura in the second chapter of *Il Trionfo della Morte*, 76–84. Dotti (311) notes Petrarchan borrowings throughout this passage and the poem as a whole.

95 *La fe*: In editions before 1835, this read as "L'amor."

99 *incerto raggio*: Dotti (312) quotes Fubini: " 'To this adjective, above all—which Leopardi found used thus in Virgil (cf. *Aeneid* III, 203 and VI, 270) and more frequently in Cesarotti's Ossian, to indicate the light of the sun or the stars veiled by clouds or something else—is entrusted the task of recreating, at the end of the composition, that precious suggestion of the indefinite with which it was begun.' "

XVI. LA VITA SOLITARIA / THE SOLITARY LIFE

Possibly written at Recanati in the summer of 1821; first published in *Il nuovo ricoglitore*, Milan, in January 1826 as "La vita solitaria. Idillio VI," and then in the Bologna edition of 1826.

Orcel (306): "The last of the idylls . . . preserving the traces of the 18th-century taste for poems on the four parts of the day (Parini, Pindemonte), alternating somewhat conventional passages with the ecstatic song of Leopardi at his greatest, needs to be re-established in its subtle internal unity, the end of each stanza calling up the following one by a game of thematic analogies (stanza I: death as refuge → stanza II: annihilation at midday → stanza III: coldness of heart and solitude → stanza IV: the moon as sole companion)."

Rigoni (M1, 953): "The 'solitary life' tends in fact to configure itself—beyond certain conventional situations or images—as a refuge in which a man tired and disillusioned by the world rediscovers in some degree his confidence in things and in the beings of nature and attempts the renewal of feeling and imagination through forgetting the truth, understood and suggested here in both its 'social' and 'metaphysical' senses. Except that the effects of this forgetfulness, already precarious in itself, are different, and even, at least apparently, contradictory: on the one side, in fact, it is represented as an experience that renews and comforts, refreshes and enlivens; on the other, in the description of the sunstruck, silent, immobile midday ["a regressive ecstasy, nirvana-light that devours sensibility and consciousness along with things, dispensing the peace of extinction and oblivion" (950)], rendered by means of an enchanting series of negative tropes, as the diving into a state of insensibility and unconsciousness similar to the 'ancient stillness' of death. From this comes the impression of uncertainty and emotional hesitation that the reading of the idyll leaves up to its last lines, which express a mixed wish of resignation and hope."

6 *alla capanna mia*: The rustic country house of the Leopardi family at San Leonardo, outside Recanati. The poem's opening echoes that of "Alla primavera," although in a different, intimate key, "Arcadian, not to say Tassian" (Dotti, 313).

12 *là dove segue*: Before the Neapolitan edition of 1835, this passage read: "dove si piglia [*or* prende] / lo sventurato a scherno" [where the unfortunate man / is held in contempt].

22 *il ferro*: Ferretti (104) notes that the Bologna edition lacked this strong Alfierian endorsement of suicide; "ferro" there was "pianto" [complaint], perhaps imposed, according to Moroncini (Dotti, 314), by the Bolognese censors.

23 *Talor m'assido in solitaria parte . . .*: The scene recurs in "Le ricordanze," 104–109, where Leopardi recalls suicidal fantasies in a similar setting. The contemplation of "altissima quiete" also evokes the "profondissima quiete" of "L'infinito." Fubini (Dotti, 314) draws attention to a similar passage in "Appressamento della morte," IV, 70–72, adding that they may derive from Cesarotti's translation of Gray's "Elegy" (1772), or from Foscolo's version of the same in letter XXXV of the *Ortis* (1798).

37 *lor quiete antica*: See the discussion of the term "antico" in the notes to "La sera del dì di festa."

44–45 *Era quel dolce / E irrevocabil tempo . . .*: This theme is expanded on in "Le ricordanze," 119–35, for which this poem almost seems a kind of preliminary sketch. Leopardi, *Zibaldone* 1534 (20 August 1821): "The words *irrevocabile, irremeabile* [irremediable], and others like them will always produce a pleasing sensation . . . because they arouse an idea that is without limits and impossible to be entirely conceived. And therefore they will always be extremely poetic and the true poet knows how to make use of and enjoy such words to very great effect."

65 *Odo sonar nelle romite stanze*: Cf. *Zibaldone* 4421 (1 December 1828): "On my solitary walks through the city, it's usual for the view inside the rooms I see from below in the street through open windows to excite very pleasing sensations and lovely pictures in me. Which rooms would interest me not at all if I saw them from inside. Is this not an image of human life, of its states, its goods and joys?" Cf. the similar setting of "A Silvia."

91 *Infesto alle malvage menti . . .*: Note the triple repetition of "infesto" in the last stanza. For Dotti (318), Leopardi here "is competing with a kind of Ossianic poetry, and in particular with the opening lines of Parini's "La notte." "Ossianic" poetry was inspired by Macpherson's *Fragments of Ancient Poetry* published in 1760 and translated by Melchiore Cesarotti as *Canti di Ossian* in 1763, which enjoyed an enormous vogue in the late eighteenth century and was highly influential for the romantic writers in the nineteenth. The largely invented "primitive" odes of the so-called Homer of the North spoke to a pre-romantic taste for a melancholic, pessimistic, death-haunted, "authentic" view of nature and man's place in it in contrast to the resolutely sunny rationality of the Enlightenment. Among the leading Italians of this school were Ippolito Pindemonte (1753–1828), author of *I cimiteri*, and Ugo Foscolo (*I sepolcri*) (1778–1827).

107 *Se core e lena a sospirar m'avanza*: Cf. Petrarch, *Rime* CCXCIV, 11: "altro che sospirar nulla m'avanza."

XVII. CONSALVO

Probably written in the spring of 1833 during the period of Leopardi's love for the Florentine socialite Fanny Ronchivecchi (1801–89), wife of the naturalist Antonio Targioni Tozzetti, whom Leopardi had met in Florence in 1830 (and who was in turn infatuated with Leopardi's friend Antonio Ranieri); published in the Neapolitan edition of 1835, where for tonal and thematic reasons it was placed between the idylls and the canzone "Alla sua donna."

The poetic "novella" 's dramatic situation, and its Spanish names, are derived from the poem in the style of Tasso, *Il conquisto di Granata* (The Conquest of Granada) by Girolamo Graziani (1604–75), of which Leopardi had anthologized a part in his *Crestomazia italiana poetica* (1828).

In the *Disegno letterario* (XII) of 1818 (M2, 1218–19) he wrote: "Farewell to Telesilla (dying) . . . Comic or tragic scenes. Historical or ideal characters. For example a man in my situation who speaks of love to a woman for the first time." This in fact does happen for the first time for Leopardi "(if only in poetic fiction) in the course of his long, silent and despairing love" (Dotti, 67) for Fanny.

Orelli (76) notes the "nearness" of the name Elvira to "Silvia," and demonstrates numerous linguistic affinities in the two texts. Orcel cites the "sadomasochistic aperçus" in the piece and writes (307): "One fails to understand how Leopardi, whose poetry is always of a great formal restraint, could have been attached to this melodramatic, weepy 'novella,' contrary to his own aesthetic." The poem nevertheless was among Leopardi's most popular works in his own day.

Rigoni (M1, 955), remarking on de Sanctis, who, "betrayed by his taste for passion and the popular," called it "a masterpiece," as well as on Carducci's highly critical denunciation, notes how the poem is related to other, even great canti—"Il pensiero dominante," "Amore e Morte"—especially in its "deep anxiety in the face of a supreme state of happiness. But will not the failure of the attempt also depend on the fact that Leopardi has tried for once to imagine and represent the *achievement* of such a moment?"

3–4 *a mezzo / Il quinto lustro*: Originally, "al mezzo di sua vita." Dotti (320): "The correction was intended to conceal the poet's allusion to himself, as he was thirty-five at the time of his love for Fanny Targioni Tozzetti."

24 *Ma ruppe alfin* . . .: Dotti (166–68) notes how Leopardi here, as in "Il primo amore" fifteen years earlier, has recourse to echoes of Petrarch and Dante (the latter drawn from the episode of Paolo and Francesca in *Inferno* V) as he tries "to sublimate his own amorous experience by reliving it and fusing it with exemplary models." In the "atmosphere of extreme agitation and turbulent transgression" that animated Leopardi's "most secret inspiration," he relied on his great predecessors to present it "in more reassuring forms."

39 *Addio per sempre*: For Leopardi's meditation on the emotion caused by final farewells, see *Zibaldone* 644–46 (11 February 1821) and 2242–43 (10 December 1821), where he writes that the reason for such emotion is linked "to that *infinity* which contains in itself the idea of a *finished* thing, beyond which there is *nothing* more; of a thing that is finished *forever*, and that will *never* come *again*."

99 *Due cose belle* . . .: Cf. the canzone "Amore e Morte" (XXVII), written at about the same time as "Consalvo."

111–112 *ma cotanto / Esser beato no consente il cielo* . . .: Cf. the last lines of the "Coro di morti," translated in the section "Other Texts," p. 352. Fubini (quoted in Dotti, 325) cites a passage from the first of the *Operette morali*, "La storia del genere umano": "[Love] very rarely brings two hearts together, embracing one and the other at the same time, and bringing about reciprocal ardor and desire in both; though he is asked for this with the the greatest insistence by all of those whom he occupies; but Jove doesn't allow him to satisfy them, except for a few; for the happiness that results from such a benefit, is surpassed by that of the divine by too small a degree." See also "Alla sua donna," 30–33.

148 *Dimani all'annottar*: I.e., at the end of the first day following his death.

XVIII. ALLA SUA DONNA / TO HIS LADY

Written at Recanati in six days in September 1823, at "the moment in which the poet, before throwing himself with the *Operette* [*morali*] into speculation on the arid truth of existence, before assuming the look and attitude of the Lucian of his age, stops to reflect on the consoling value of the illusions" (Dotti, 68); published in the Bolognese edition of 1824, as the tenth of the canzoni, it was moved to sixteenth position in the Florentine edition, and finally to the eighteenth in the Naples edition of 1835.

Moroncini, quoted in Rigoni (M1, 956), suggests that Leopardi first wrote the second, third, and fifth stanzas, later adding the first and fourth. Like "Il primo amore" and fragment XXXVIII, "Alla sua donna" was in some degree inspired by Leopardi's feeling for his father's cousin Contessa Geltrude Cassi-Lazzari, who visited the Leopardi household in December 1817 and again in 1818.

Orcel (308) credits Rigoni with finding Leopardi's source in a brief prose piece of the seventeenth-century moralist Saint-Evremond, "Idée de la femme, qui ne se trouve point, et qui ne se trouvera jamais," adding that "in this love inspired from afar, it's not forbidden to hear an echo of the '*amor de lonh*'" of the Provençal troubador Jaufré Rudel. (But the absent beloved is a central, indispensable feature of the Italian lyric tradition, from Dante's Beatrice to Petrarch's Laura all the way to Montale's Clizia.)

Leopardi wrote in his preamble to the reprinting of the first ten canzoni—"ten canzoni and not even one amorous"—in *Il nuovo ricoglitore* (I, 9, 1825 [Rigoni (M1, 163–65)]): "The lady, who is the beloved of the author, is one of those images, one of those celestial and ineffable phantoms of beauty and virtue, which often occur to our imagination during sleep or sleeplessness, when we are little more than children, and then on rare occasions in sleep, or in a sort of alienation of the mind, when we are young. Finally, she is *the woman who can't be found*. The author doesn't know whether his lady (and calling her this, he shows he loves only her) has ever been born till now, or will ever be born: he knows that now she does not live on earth, and that we are not her contemporaries; he looks for her among the ideas of Plato, he looks for her in the moon, in the planets of the solar system, in the constellations. If this canzone wants to be called amorous, it will nevertheless be true that love such as this can neither arouse nor suffer jealousy, because apart from the author no tender lover wants to make love with a telescope."

Orcel (308): "The 'hymn' . . . which borrows the form of a canzone almost totally liberated from classic schemes"—anticipating "the so-called 'free canzone' characteristic of the years 1826–30" (Rigoni [M1, 956])—"concludes Leopardi's first great poetic season . . . The canzone is in effect the purest example of Leopardi's peculiar [Petrarchan] 'Platonism' which, far from contradicting his radical materialism, is its despairing countersong. Among the numerous pieces in this group, beyond 'Il pensiero dominante' and 'Aspasia,' one should mention the letter to Jacopsen (23 June 1823): ["In love, all the joys that vulgar souls experience aren't worth the pleasure that one sole instant of ravishment and deep emotion give. But how to make this emotion last, or be renewed often in life? or find a heart that responds to it? Several times I've avoided for several days meeting the object who had charmed me in a delicious dream. I knew that this charm would have been destroyed by approaching reality. Yet I always thought of this object, but I didn't consider her according to how she was; I contemplated her in my imagination, the way she had appeared in my dream."]; and *Zibaldone* 4418 (30 November 1828): 'For the sensitive and imaginative man . . . the world and things are in a certain sense double.'" (See notes to "Le ricordanze.")

Rigoni (M1, 957): "The precise *meaning* of this canzone, born of an incurable nostalgia for Elsewhere," has not always been agreed upon. "A mind of the subtlety and penetration of Manzoni, though abyssally far from the intellectual and poetic universe of Leopardi, declared . . . that he understood nothing of it . . . The canzone constitutes a hymn to Woman, to Beauty, to an archetypal universe or one at least superior to the real because it would be the *only one* capable of redeeming and beatifying 'this arid earth,' this 'deathly life'—*if it ever existed.* From such paradoxical but anything but extrinsic Platonism, from the point of view of an absolute materialism which nevertheless doesn't seem to be *from down here* ('the world doesn't seem to me to have been made for me,' he once wrote to his brother Carlo), from a sort of extraordinary 'atheistic idealism' (Orcel, 1982), emerges the miracle of this, with its suspension in dream, with its piercing images of two antithetical conditions, with the fluctuations and reversals and continual returns from one to the other, embodied in the recurrence of the conditional, interrogative, adversative forms of its poetical music."

Fubini (quoted in Dotti, 69) sees the canzone as the "synthesis of all his preceding work, both canzoni and idylls, of which modes, themes, voices of one and the other are discreetly re-evoked," and as the linchpin between the first canti and those that follow the epistle to Pepoli.

13 *Nulla spene*: "Spene" is an alternative of "speme," preferable here, according to Straccali (Dotti, 329), to avoid "cacophony with the word that follows ["m'avanza"]."

14 *ignudo e solo*: I.e., devoid of his body. Cf. Petrarch, *Rime* CXXVIII, 101–102: "Ché l'alma ignuda e sola / conven ch'arriva a quel dubbioso calle."

15 *peregrina stanza*: An unknown dwelling place. In a marginal annotation Leopardi cites Petrarch, *Rime* LXIX, 9–11: "et per camino, / . . . / m'andava sconosciuto e pellegrino."

30 *Or non aggiunse*: Adversative, but less so than the original "Ahi, ma" (Dotti, 330).

33 *Simile a quella che nel cielo india*: Cf. Petrarch, *Rime* LXXIII, 68: "simile a quella ch'è nel ciel eterna," though "the Petrarchan 'eterna' is replaced with the Dantesque 's'india' (Dotti, 330); see *Paradiso* IV, 28.

37 *Del giovanile error*: Cf. the "antico error" of the canzone to his sister, Paolina, and Petrarch, *Rime* I, 3: "In sul mio primo giovenil errore."

Leopardi wrote to Jacopsen (13 June 1823): "Pour moi, je regrette le temps où m'était permis de l'y chercher, et je le vois avec une sorte d'effroi que mon imagination devient sterile."

43–44 *dell'imago, / . . . m'appago*: Cf. the end of "Il primo amore": "Spira nel pensier mio la bella imago / . . . / . . . e sol di lei m'appago."

45 *eterne idee*: The Ideas of Plato, "immaterial and primitive forms of things" as Leopardi describes them in a note to Petrarch's sonnet (*Rime* CLIX): "In qual parte del ciel, in qual idea" (Rigoni [M1, 958]).

46 *L'una sei tu*: Orcel (309) cites C. Galimberti's suggestion that "l'una" in some sense stands for "luna," the moon: "the 'traveler' of the hymn effectively evokes the 'companion' of 'Alla primavera' and the 'eternal pilgrim' of the 'Canto notturno' and of so many other canti."

50 *ne' superni giri*: Cf. Dante, *Purgatorio* XXX, 93.

55 *Questo . . . ricevi*: Dotti (332): "The line constitutes the principal proposition that subordinates the two propositions of uncertainty in a complex and insuperably harmonious syntactical ensemble, an ensemble that suggests, rhythmically as well, the indefinite miracle of archetypal Beauty."

XIX. AL CONTE CARLO PEPOLI / TO COUNT CARLO PEPOLI

Written at Bologna in March 1826 and published as the final text in the Bologna edition of the *Versi* that year.

Conte Carlo Pepoli (1796–1881), a Bolognese nobleman and scholar, was a friend of Leopardi from 1825 to 1830; in 1826, he was vice president of the Bolognese Accademia dei Felsinei. A political liberal imprisoned and then exiled after the riots of 1831, he eventually taught Italian literature at London University, where Carlyle judged him "a very pretty man." He wrote the libretto for Bellini's *I Puritani* (1835), which for Rigoni (M1, 960) shows some traces of Leopardi's influence.

Orcel (309) notes that the poem falls exactly between the publication of the first twenty *operette morali* (1824) and the poetic "risorgimento" of 1828, "a moment of transition and perhaps of artistic uncertainty" (Rigoni [M1, 959]) i.e., of Leopardi's "so-called conversion from the beautiful to the true" (Dotti, 72). The "epistle"—as it was originally called, in recognition of its Horatian inspiration—was commissioned by the Accademia dei Felsinei and read there publicly on the evening of Easter Monday, where it was coolly received (see Damiani, *All'apparir del vero*, 282–83). The poem, "which is modeled on Horatian *sermo* and on Parinian 'verso sciolto' [unrhymed hendecasyllables imitative of classical hexameters]" (Dotti, 70), can fairly be characterized as "versified prose" (Orcel, 309), argued in "a protracted and gray argumentative style" (Rigoni [M1, 959]), though it does rise to lyricism at certain points, particularly its last forty lines. Rigoni (959): "We are naturally . . . in the atmosphere of so-called 'cosmic pessimism' . . . the causes of evil and unhappiness have been extended, from the arena of civilization and history, to the order of nature itself, to the original and intrinsic condition of things."

Leopardi wrote to Giordani (6 May 1825): "As to the type of work I am engaged in, as I have changed from what I was, so has my work changed. Everything that adheres to the affectionate and eloquent bores me, has the flavor of a joke and ridiculous childishness. I am looking for nothing more than the truth, which I so hated and detested before. It pleases me ever more to discover and touch with my hand the misery of man and things, and to shiver coldly, examining this unhappy and terrible mystery of the life of the universe. I see well now that, since my passions are spent, there is no other source and base for pleasure in my work than an empty curiosity, the satisfaction of which still has much power to delight; a thing that before, while the last spark remained in my heart, I could not understand."

6 *ozio*: from Latin *otium*, or ease, where it has far less pejorative sense than it takes on soon after the poem's opening, coming as it does to represent emptiness, boredom, lack of energy; elsewhere Leopardi uses the term (cf. "Ad Angelo Mai," 164) to characterize the lack of ambition and aspiration of pre-Risorgimento Italians.

13 *franger glebe* . . .: Cf. Tasso, *Gerusalemme liberata* I, 63: "Il ferro uso a far solchi, a franger glebe."

23–24 *la bella / Felicità*: Rigoni (M1, 959): "the real and single goal of life" for Leopardi.

30 *Di medicina in loco* . . .: Cf. Leopardi's bitter denunciation of the gods' "gift" to man of illness, old age, and death in "Il tramonto della luna," 34–50.

36–37 *men loco avesse / Al travagliarne il cor*: On this theme, Orcel (309) refers the reader to the "Storia del genere umano," the great introductory allegory to the *Operette morali*.

43 *Nè la lentezza accagionar dell'ore*: Cf. "A un vincitore nel pallone," 62–63: "nè delle putri e lente / Ore il danno misura."

61–62 *quell'una / Cui natura apprestò* . . .: See the apologia for suicide in "Bruto minore," 55–70.

63 *Lui delle vesti* . . .: The following two stanzas constitute a variation on Virgil, *Georgics* II, 503ff.

71 *adamantina* . . .: Dotti (337): "The whole image quite closely evokes Horace *Odes* II, 24, 5–7: '*si figit adamantinos / summis verticibus dira Necessitas / clavos*' . . . except that instead of the figure of *Necessitas* in Leopardi there is that of *Noia*."

84-85 *s'asside / Su l'alte prue . . .*: Cf. Horace, *Odes* II, XVI, 18–22; "la negra cura" is the "atra cura" of *Odes* III, I, 40.

96-97 *di remoti / Lidi turbando . . .*: Cf. Leopardi's critique of colonialism in the last lines of the "Inno ai patriarchi."

127 *Or quando al tutto irrigidito e freddo . . .*: Cf. "Il passero solitario," 53ff.: "Quando muti questi occhi all'altrui core."

135-36 *ogni alto senso, / Ogni tenero affetto . . .*: Cf. the apostrophe to Nerina at the end of "Le ricordanze," 171ff: "D'ogni mio vago immaginar, di tutti / I miei teneri sensi . . ."

138 *Altri studi*: Dotti (340): "philosophical, political and moral reflections, the outlines of which can be read in a series of *Disegni letterari* (IX, X, XI, XII) [M2, 1214–19] datable starting in 1825 (up to 1829) . . . Yet Fubini notes: 'In reality [Leopardi] also signals, even as he writes this epistle, that his spirit is returning to sensibility and to poetry, a sensibility and a poetry that are different but no less genuine than those of another time."

149 *d'ammirar son pago*: Cf. *Zibaldone* 4257–58 (21 March 1827): "The great mastery of nature, the incomparable order of the universe, is endlessly praised . . . Let us admire . . . this order, this universe: I admire it more than others: I admire it for its depravity and deformity, which to me seem extreme. But let's wait to praise it until we know at least, with certainty, that it is not the worst of all possibilities."

150 *gli ozi*: Originally Leopardi wrote "anni" (years). Gallo and Garboli suggest that Leopardi is referring to the *Operette morali*, which Leopardi was then writing and which would be published the following year.

151 *ancor che tristo*: Cf. "Alla luna," 15–16: "Il rimembrar delle passate cose, / Ancor che triste . . ."; "Le ricordanze," 60: "ancor tristo."

154 *O mal grati . . .*: Cf. "La ginestra," 68: "Ben ch'io sappia che obblio / Preme chi troppo all'età propria increbbe."

155 *vago*: Dotti (342): " 'inagnnoso e dolce' [deceiving and sweet] in one of Leopardi's many variants."

158 *Diva più cieca*: Dotti (342): "Glory is not only a vain thing, but a divinity who grants her favors even more arbitrarily and capriciously even than fortune and love."

XX. IL RISORGIMENTO / THE REAWAKENING

Written at Pisa from April 7 to 13, 1828; published in the Florentine edition of 1831. The poem, Leopardi's first since "Alla sua donna" of 1823 with the exception of the epistle to Carlo Pepoli (Bologna, 1826), inaugurates the great Pisa-Recanati period of 1828–30.

Leopardi here adopts a songlike, Metastasian meter used by Parini in a poem, "Brindisi," anthologized in the 1828 *Crestomazia italiana poetica*, and which, as Orcel (310) puts it, "often evokes the language of 18th-century Italian opera." Rigoni (M1, 962): "The singularity of this ['sort of summary interior autobiography'] comes from the fact that this inner history [of the devastating loss of early illusions; followed by a period of deep indifference; and, finally, a new rebirth of feeling, to which the poem's title alludes], including as it does the negative assertions of Leopardi's philosophy, is countermanded by the tremendously light and singable meter of the Metastasian, Arcadian canzonetta, thereby creating—at least in [the first and second parts]—a certain dissension between tone and content . . . [This is] the only time that Leopardi has made use in the *Canti* of a meter so inappropriate for him." Yet this very paradox betrays the poet's grateful reattachment to the "salutary illusions" that make life worth living. As he wrote to his sister, Paolina, from Pisa (2 May 1828): "I have now finished the *Crestomazia poetica*: and after two years I wrote some verses this April; but verses really in the old style, and with my heart of previously." Still, this is a "reawakening that does not deny the painful discoveries made about illusions and truth, about what should be and is instead, on what the heart conceives of and what is really real" (Dotti, 75).

Dotti (77–78) also discusses Emilio Bigi's views of the development of Leopardi's thought between the end of 1824, the year of the *Operette*, and the beginning of 1828, during which he adopted an extreme material nihilism, while also focusing on the human suffering that the nothingness of existence involves, the paradoxical disjunct between nature's tendency to preserve life and man's desire for happiness. For Dotti "it is probable that his continual immersion in 'negative' thought ended in awakening—by reaction—the desire for song in the poet."

3–4 *i dolci affanni / Della mia prima età*: Cf. "Il passero solitario"; "Il risorgimento" is almost an abstract of the ideas embodied there.

6 *del cor profondo*: Cf. Petrarch, *Rime* XCIV, 1.

10–12 *nel novo stato, / Quando . . . / Prima il dolor mancò*: Leopardi described his state of depression thus to Giordani (19 November 1819): "If in this moment I were to go mad, I believe that my madness would be to sit with my eyes always lowered, with my mouth open, with my hands between my knees, without laughing or crying, or moving from the place in which I found myself except from necessity. I have no more breath to understand any desire, not even for death, not because I fear it in any way, but I see no disparity between death and this life of mine, where not even pain comes to console me. This is the first time that boredom not only oppresses and tires me, but exhausts me and lacerates me like a heavy pain; and I am so appalled by the vanity of all things, and by the condition of men, with all the passions dead as they are spent in my soul, that I go beyond myself, considering that my desperation, too, is also a nothing." The return of feeling after this paralyzing anomie is the "novo stato" of "Il risorgimento."

43 *beato errore*: And "error beato" (86): "salutary illusions."

57 *E voi, pupille tenere*: Orcel (310) notes that this line is borrowed from a famous aria in Cimarosa's *Gli Orazi ed i Curiazi* (libretto by Antonio Sografi) (1797).

62 *Candida ignuda mano*: Cf. Petrarch, *Rime* CC, i: "Non pur quell'una bella ignuda mano."

81–82 *dalla grave, immemore / Quiete*: Leopardi's trance recalls the evocation of death by the souls in the "Coro di morti" (1824).

92 *Nella novella età*: Cf. *Inferno* XXXIII, 88: "Innocenti facea l'età novella."

95 *Tutto un dolor mi spira*: Cf. Metastasio, *Demetrio* II, XII: "Tutto non è dolor."

105–106 *o povero / Mio cor*: Dotti (348) notes Fubini's observation that "the 'heart' . . . is the true protagonist or object of this Leopardian canto." Cf. also *Zibaldone* 513–14 (16 January 1821): "It takes very little for illusions to retake possession of and reconquer our soul, even in spite of us; and man (as long as he is alive) returns infallibly to hope for that happiness he had despaired of; he knows the consolation he had believed and judged impossible; he forgets and discredits the bitter truth which had sent down deep, deep roots into his mind; and the most secure, total, and repeated, even daily, disenchantment, doesn't resist the forces of the nature that evokes errors and hopes again."

115 *con la vista impura*: Dotti (349): "Fubini justly observes that *impura* here has an active value, and that therefore the expression is understood: with the aspect that takes away from things the natural purity, the natural capacity to have illusions and to feel"; and that "the image 'makes us think of the malevolent look of a hostile divinity,' the *infausta verità* of line 116. One can read, in any case, of the inauspicious effects that Truth, in the 'Storia del genere umano,' the first of the *Operette morali*, has on men."

119 *So che natura è sorda*: The characterization of nature as indifferent to man is a Leopardian commonplace; cf. the closing lines of "Sopra un basso rilievo antico sepolcrale."

156 *Il mondo*: Dotti (351): "capacity to communicate, to know how to live."

158 *concedi al fato*: Latinism meaning "to die." Cf. Tasso, *Gerusalemme liberata* IV, 44: "Quando il mio genitor, cedendo al fato/ forse con lei si ricongiunse in cielo."

XXI. A SILVIA / TO SILVIA

Written at Pisa soon after "Il risorgimento," on August 19 and 20, 1828; published in the Florentine edition of 1831.

Orcel (311): "'A Silvia' is the first true '*canzone libera*' (or 'leopardiana'), in which the amplitude of the stanza, the alternating of hendecasyllables and *settenari*, the number and placement of the rhymes, are freed from every preestablished rule. The transparent and melancholy speed of the verse, whose rhythmic syntax acts contrapuntally with the apparent measure, and the miraculous weight of a language capable of amplifying in two words its historic measure ('paterno ostello') or of making literary profundity and the flavor of dialect resonate in the same word ('tenerella,' 'innamorati') are at the heart of this masterpiece of the Italian lyric".

The figure of Silvia—the name, like that of Nerina in "Le ricordanze," derives from Tasso's *Aminta*—was inspired by Teresa Fattorini, the daughter of the coachman of the Leopardi household, who died of consumption on September 30, 1818. Rigoni (M1, 963) draws our attention to two passages in the *Zibaldone* that can be helpful to our understanding the genesis of the poem. At 2242–43 (10

December 1821) Leopardi discusses the emotion that a sensitive individual feels realizing that something "is over forever, especially if it was once his and familiar to him." And at 4310–11 (30 June 1828) he discusses the ineffable impression that the pure and innocent freshness of young girls who have not yet become women can arouse without reference to desire or passion, especially if one thinks of the fragility of their situation and the painful destiny that awaits them.

In any case, the inspiration for "Silvia" becomes irrelevant when the reader realizes that she is a universal emblem of the mortality of "youthful hope" (Orcel), a Persephone figure, like her "cousin" Nerina (see d'Intino, "I misteri di Silvia"). Rigoni (M1, 964): "To reintegrate and reanimate in song the experience of destruction, to restore feeling and the enchantment of being in the very description of its vanity and ruin, this is the secret and miracle of Leopardi's poetry and this is also the mysterious effect that a note of the *Zibaldone* [259–60 (4 October 1820)] attributes to art itself: "Works of genius have this property, that even when they bring to life the nullity of things, even when they show clearly and make felt the inevitable unhappiness of life, even when they express the most terrible desperation, nevertheless to a great soul who finds himself in a state of extreme despondency, disenchantment, nothingness, anomie and discouragement with life or in the most bitter and *deadly* misfortune . . . they always offer consolation, reignite enthusiasm, and, though discussing and representing only death, restore, at least momentarily, the life he had lost."

Dotti (87–88) notes that De Sanctis and Carducci both referred to the poems of the Pisa-Recanati period as a new group of "idylls" but makes the convincing argument that only the poems so-called by Leopardi are deserving of the term. "Is it truly a matter only of the poet's abandonment to memory, of foundering in it, his consolation and refuge? . . . ["A Silvia" and "Le ricordanze"] don't hesitate to turn to the denunciation of nature, and even let us say of life . . . to read these lyrics without prejudice it doesn't take long to see that the lesson of the *Operette*, far from being surpassed, has not been forgotten at all."

4 *fuggitivi*: Darting, from modesty and shyness; cf. "erranti" in "Il risorgimento." But Rigoni (M1, 965) quotes R. Bacchelli: "More distantly, in a veiled way, the adjective insinuates the idea of transitoriness implicit in the previous expression: 'of your mortal life.' " The line originally read, "ne la fronte e nel sen tuo verginale" [in your forehead and virgin breast]; it was changed to "e ne gli sguardi incerti e fuggitivi" [and in your hesitant, startled eyes]. Dotti (352) alludes to the passage in *Zibaldone* 4310 (30 June 1828) written soon after this poem, in which Leopardi writes that a woman in her twenties is more likely to inspire passion, while a young girl from sixteen to eighteen still has something of the angelic and divine, which, though it may not cause us to fall in love, elevates our soul and leads us to imagine the unhappiness that awaits her, the fleetingness of her beauty, and the compassion she arouses in us—for her, for us, for human fate, and life itself.

6 *salivi*: Stefano Agosti, in *Il testo poetico* (Milano: Rizzoli, 1972, 40), notes that the word is a virtual anagram for Silvia's name. Cf. also "solevi" in the next stanza (Orelli [76], who notes numerous assonantal echoes throughout).

9 *al tuo perpetuo canto*: For Rigoni (M1, 965) the phrase recalls Virgil's description of Circe's song, "adsiduo resonat cantu . . . / arguto tenues percurrens pectine telas" in *Aeneid* VII, 12 (cf. also the "assiduo canto" of "Il canto della fanciulla," translated in the section of "Other Texts" in the "Argomenti di idilli").

12 *vago*: Leopardi wrote "dolce" (sweet) in the manuscript margin. But "vago," as we have seen, is an altogether broader, more comprehensive, characteristically open Leopardian term, suggesting indefinite, untested possibility, "that divine wavering in the imagination of confused and brilliant ideas, essential to true poetry and similar to the joys experienced in childhood, of which Leopardi speaks in *Zibaldone* 100" (8 January 1820) (Dotti, 353). See also the introductory notes to "L'infinito."

16 *sudate carte*: Literally, "sweated-over." Cf. "A un vincitore di pallone," 4: "sudata virtude." Orelli (74) sees an echo from a Latin letter of Petrarch's, *Impia mors*, which Leopardi translated in March 1827 ("Epistola di Francesco Petrarca al Cardinale Giovanni Colonna") (M1, 608–10, ll. 65ff.): "indarno / ti fien gli studi e le trattate carte?"

22 *Che percorrea la faticosa tela*: Cf. Virgil, *Aeneid* VII, 14: "arguto tenuis percurrens pectine telas."

41 *chiuso morbo*: In his brilliant essay "I misteri di Silvia: Motivo persefoneo e mistica eleusina in Leopardi," Franco d'Intino (229–30) argues that Silvia's murderous illness was "contracted . . . in a mortal struggle with an *icy* principle of authority" and quotes Claudio Colaiacomo's suggestion that "chiuso" should be taken in an active sense, incorporating the notion of military siege "that belongs to the Latin 'claudere.'" D'Intino's psychologically motivated interpretation sees the canto as enacting a conflict between "the creative desire of the imagination and an authoritarian principle simultaneously both loved and hated" (237) and finds numerous affinities with the early "Appressamento della morte" (see notes to XXXIX, p. 480).

46 *innamorati*: According to Rigoni (M1, 965), citing Leopardi's commentary on Petrarch's *Rime* XLII, 13, and LXXIII, 69 (*Zibaldone* 4140 [6 October 1825]), the term means "to inspire love, to fascinate."

51–52 *negaro i fati / La giovinezza*: Cf. "La sera del dì di festa," 14–15: "A te la speme / Nego, mi disse, anche la speme."

61 *Tu*: Dotti (356): "Refers to hope which nevertheless ... is incarnated in Silvia."

62 *una tomba ignuda*: The closing foreshadows the Gods' imposition of the grave as the endpoint of human life in Leopardi's last poem, "Il tramonto della luna."

63 *Mostravi di lontano*: D'Intino ("I misteri di Silvia," 255–56) notes that "the idea of this gesture is not new" and refers us to Leopardi's letter on Tasso "which contains the Eleusinian theme of the *contemplation* of the death-life paradox": "You understand the great crowd of emotions that is born of considering the contrast between the greatness of Tasso and the humbleness of his tomb" (L, 390). He also cites "All'Italia," 125–27: "La vostra tomba è un'ara; e qua mostrando / Verran le madri ai parvoli le belle / Orme del vostro sangue" and "Le rimembranze," 136–37: "diman la tomba / Ti mostrerò di tuo fratello."

D'Intino (257) also points to the "sudden movement from the perfect tense of 'cadesti' to the imperfect of 'mostravi,' which, linking with the canto's initial imperfects ('splendea,' 'salivi') in a certain sense points it . . . toward a new beginning and a rebirth"—in an eternal cycle of memento mori.

XXII. LE RICORDANZE / THE RECOLLECTIONS

Written at Recanati from August 26 to September 12, 1829. First published in the Florentine edition of 1831. The title recalls the 1816 idyll, "Le rimembranze" (translated in "Other Texts," pp. 339ff.), which was excluded from the *Canti*, and

"La ricordanza," the original title of the poem that was eventually titled "Alla luna."

In contrast with the summary abstraction of "Il risorgimento," here, in his most relaxed, descriptive, and evocative poem, Leopardi indulges in description, detail, local color, in reifying the emotions evoked by vivid memories, and with great success. Written at a time when he had returned to Recanati forever, as he thought, from his sojourn in Bologna, feeling that the trajectory of his life was over, the poem, "the true lyric realization, long dreamed of, of the poet's plan to write a proper autobiography (interior), his *Storia di un'anima* [History of a Soul]" (Fubini, quoted in Dotti [83]), "entrusts itself to the free movement of memory, the themes and tones of his interior and 'idyllic' autobiography aroused by the return to places objects images emotions dreams of one time and the comparison between what he was and felt then and what he is and feels now" (Rigoni [M1, 964]), celebrating "memory as partial compensation for the *souffrance* of life" (Dotti, 83). The figure of Nerina, a kind reprise of Silvia—much as the meditation on Silvia's fate was a kind of spur to the personal evocation of regret here—appears at the end of the poem as its ex post facto interlocutor and justification, the embodiment of Leopardi's idea "of a thing that is finished *forever*, and that will *never* come *again*." (See notes to "Consalvo," p. 431.) Rigoni: "In the whole last and longest *lassa* of the canto, an insistent elegiac variation on this painful theme, Leopardi projects in reality the very figure of farewell, of the curtain that, unrealized and fatal, falls on his and on all experience."

1 *Vaghe*: Once again, evocative of unknown, untested potential, undefined mystery and beauty. (See notes to "L'infinito" and "A Silvia.")

10 *seduto in verde zolla*: The setting is reminiscent of "L'infinito" and "Alla luna" and of the ending of "Aspasia." Typically, Leopardi conceives of himself as a solitary figure, surrounded by and alien from inanimate nature.

28 *Nè mi diceva* . . .: Among the numerous letters in which Leopardi expresses his disdain for his hometown is this one to Karl Bunsen (5 September 1829), written at the time he was working on "Le ricordanze": "Condemned by lack of means to this horrible and detested residence, and already dead to all enjoyment and all hope, I live only to suffer, and pray only for the rest of the tomb."

34 *Per invidia non già* . . .: Dotti (359) recalls *Zibaldone* 83–84 (1819), in which Leopardi, responding to some observations of Mme de Staël's, sees the envy of common people for those superior to them as a combined "disdain, compassion, and ill-will for those who don't think the way they do." Superior people thus are not envied for something common people don't understand, but are simply felt sorry for; and when it involves the young, it is believed that when they are grown, they'll see things differently and think like everyone else. "And this precisely," Leopardi concludes, "is the experience I've had and am having."

56–57 *un'immagin dentro / Non torni*: Cf. *Zibaldone* 4418 (30 November 1828): "To the sensitive and imaginative man, who lives, as I have long lived, continually feeling and imagining, the world and objects are in a certain sense double. He will see a tower and countryside with his eyes; he will hear with his ears the sound of a bell; and at the same time in his imagination he will see another tower, hear another sound. In this second sort of object consists all that is beautiful and pleasing in things. Sad is that life (and yet life is commonly like this) that doesn't see, hear, sense if not simple objects, only those from which the eyes, ears and other senses receive the sensation." Cf. also "the amorous idea" of the beloved, often starkly contrasting with the person herself, in "Aspasia," 39ff.

60 *ancor tristo*: Cf. "ancor che triste" at the end of "Alla luna."

60 *e il dire: io fui.* Dotti (361): "The acknowledgment that all is ineluctably past." Cf. *Inferno* XVI, 84: "quando ti gioverà dicere I' fui."

62 *queste dipinte mura*: Leopardi is describing frescoes in the rooms of Palazzo Leopardi.

74 *Il garzoncel, come inesperto amante*: Cf. the "dolce / E irrevocabil tempo" of "La vita solitaria," 44–52. Dotti (362) notes that "celeste beltà" is grammatically the object of both "fingendo" and "ammira." The line "fuses the image of the life dreamed of by the young boy and also the 'celestial beauty' he dreams of."

92 *Che di cotanta speme oggi m'avanza*: Cf. Petrarch, *Rime* CCLXVII, 32: "Questo m'avanza di cotanta spene," earlier evoked by Foscolo in his sonnet "In morte del fratello Giovanni," 11: "Questo di tanta speme oggi mi resta." And see the description of similar emotions in "La sera del dì di festa," 21–22: "Intanto io chieggo / Quanto a viver mi resti . . ."

102–103 *la dolcezza / del dì fatal tempererà d'affanno*: This is almost the inverse of the last image of "Consalvo," because here the poet is mourning "a life not lived" (Dotti, 364).

108 *Pensoso di cessar . . .*: Cf. *Zibaldone* 82 (1819), in which Leopardi recalls suicidal fantasies: "I was extremely bored by life, on the edge of the pool in my garden, and looking at the water and bending over it with a certain shudder, thought: if I threw myself in here, and immediately having floated on the surface, I would clamber over this rim, and having forced myself to come out after having been terrified of losing my life, coming back unharmed I would feel a few moments of happiness at having saved myself, and of fondness for this life that I now so despise, and which would then seem more valuable to me. The tradition around the leap from Leucade [the rock from which Sappho jumped to her death (see notes to "Ultimo canto di Saffo")] could be based on an observation like this one." Cf. the similar emotions evoked at the end of "A un vincitore nel pallone."

118 *funereo canto*: A reference to Leopardi's youthful canticle, "Appressamento della morte" (The Coming of Death), written in 1816. (Fragment XXXIX is a revision of the beginning of the poem.) The line itself recalls Ovid, *Metamorphoses* XIV, 430: "carmina iam moriens canit exequalia Cygnus."

136 *O Nerina!*: Like her "twin sister" Silvia (Dotti [85], though he finds Nerina "much less autobiographical . . . much more allusive and intentionally symbolic"), her name, like Silvia's, as we have seen, is borrowed from Tasso's *Aminta*. To some, she is a refiguring of Silvia, or evokes another young girl from Recanati, Maria Belardinelli, who died at twenty-six; in any case, she exists as a fiction, the poet's symbolic interlocutor and memento mori.

141 *Terra natal*: Recanati, her birthplace. G. De Robertis (222): "Whence the capital letter."

162 *Se torna maggio . . .*: The ancient festival of Calendimaggio, on the first of May, "when young men, accompanied by music and singing, carry a flowering branch to the girls's houses to hang on their doors" (Fubini, quoted by Dotti [367], who adds that these lines echo the ballads of Poliziano).

164–165 *non torna / Primavera . . .*: Orcel (313) cites Francesco Flora's identification of the end of the stanza as an echo of Guarini's *Il pastor fido* III, i, 1–10: "O primavera . . . / tu torni ben, ma teco / non tornano i sereni / e fortunati dì . . . ; ma teco altro non torna, / che del perduto mio caro tesoro / la rimembranza misera e dolente."

XXIII. CANTO NOTTURNO DI UN PASTORE ERRANTE DELL'ASIA / NIGHT SONG OF A WANDERING SHEPHERD IN ASIA

The last canto of the Pisa-Recanati period, written at Recanati between 22 October 1829 and 9 April 1830; published in the Florentine edition of 1831 under the title "Canto notturno di un pastore vagante in Asia."

The idea for the poem was suggested by an article by the Baron de Meyendorff, "Voyage d'Orenbourg à Boukhara, fait en 1820," which appeared in the *Journal des savants* of September 1826. In *Zibaldone* 4399–400 (3 October 1828) Leopardi noted: "Many [of the Kirghiz] spend the night sitting on a rock looking at the moon and improvising very sad words on melodies which are no less so." Rigoni (M1, 967) quotes Mario Fubini and Emilio Bigi: this citation "was found among other testimony relative to the existence of oral lyric song even among the most primitive and ignorant people, prior to the more complex epics, not to mention dramatic works: and all these observations confirmed in him the conviction that the lyric is the 'first-born of all' genres, indeed the one genuinely poetic genre, 'belonging to every man even uneducated who tries to amuse or console himself with song.' Indeed, in this last phase of his meditation about poetry, and a few months before the composition of the 'Canto notturno,' he came to the point of recognizing the similarity between the condition of primitive and modern men, who cannot recognize any other poetry than the lyric, the pure and simple voice of the heart."

Dotti (92 –93), quoting Bigi, asserts that the "Canto notturno" represents a different way of confronting the same material as in the two preceding canti, i.e., "the unhappiness and desolation of existence, but no longer from the viewpoint of autobiographical memory, but of compassion for a general condition, human and non-human . . . After the lyric song of memory we see Leopardi confront the lyric song of thought" (94). Cf. *Zibaldone* 4175 (22 April 1826): "Not only men, but the human race was and will always be necessarily unhappy. Not only the human race but all animals. Not only animals but all other beings in their way. Not individuals but species, races, globes, systems, worlds"—which passage is followed (4176–77) by the famous description of a garden "as a vast hospital (a place much more deplorable than a cemetery), and if these beings feel, or we mean, felt, it's certain that not being would be much better for them than being."

Once again, as in "Alla luna," the moon—"detached from her traditional sacredness and from her interior and supersensible reality" (Guido Ceronetti)—serves as the poet's interlocutor, inspiration, and supreme alter ego. Rigoni (M1, 968): "Only in the forms of *existence* devoid of or poor in *life* (according to a distinction noted in the *Zibaldone* between *existence* as pure exteriority and *life* as sentient interiority), only in the inorganic or animal world does that happiness denied to man who has discovered, with consciousness and history, the uselessness and boredom of everything seem imaginable (and it is to be remembered that the lines on the flock directly inspired the beginning of the second of Nietzsche's *Unzeitgemässe Betrachtungen* [*Untimely Meditations* or *Unmodern Observations*], 'History in the Service and Disservice of Life', focused in fact on the theme of happiness as 'oblivion,' as the ability to feel, while it lasts, in a *non-historical* way)."

Rigoni, who calls this the Leopardi poem most worthy of the term "canto," notes its vivid, reduced, and essential syntax, and the musical, rhythmic effect of "the disconsolate repercussion, like an echo in the desert," of the rhyme in *-ale* at the end of each stanza.

Orcel (313) cites De Sanctis: "a biblical poem, a page out of Job," though he hears echoes of Ecclesiastes in its repetitive, desolate rhythms.

Gardini (89) sees the poem as "anti-bucolic, a reversal of 'L'infinito,' in which references to the pastoral . . . are ironically antiphrastic . . . Nothing is left but despair."

For Dotti (96) "the mythical Asian shepherd represents the mourning voice of humanity both ancient and modern, as if the centuries had been erased and the poetry of mythic antiquity, even oral, is one with that of modern times . . . It's from this perspective, into which ideological attitudes, established convictions, esthetic considerations, and, naturally, determined states of mind flow and blend, that Leopardi seems to have finally found the key to representing in powerful synthesis his complex conception of the world, and for embodying it 'lyrically.'"

14 *Poi stanco si riposa in su la sera*: Cf. Petrarch's description of the shepherd's life in *Rime* L, 29–38.

21 *Vecchierel bianco* . . .: Cf. Petrarch, *Rime* XVI, 1: "Movesi il vecchierel canuto e bianco." Leopardi's allegorical vision of human life here derives from *Zibaldone* 4162–63 (17 January 1826).

40 *Ed è rischio di morte il nascimento*: Cf. the description of parents' duties and behavior toward their children and Leopardi's bemusement about it in *Zibaldone* 68 (1819) and 2607 (13 August 1822): "By God! what is man born for? and why does he have children? so that he can then console the children he's had for the mistake of having been born?"

60 *poco ti cale*: Cf. the end of "Sopra un basso rilievo antico sepolcrale," where Leopardi asserts that nature has no care for human good or ill.

101 *degli eterni giri*: Cf. *Purgatorio* XXX, 93. Cf. the "superni giri" of "Alla sua donna," 50.

105 *O greggia mia . . .*: Rigoni (M1, 969) notes that G. Negri, in the late nineteenth century, cited Edward Young's *Night Thoughts* (1741) as a source for this passage. The poem was translated into Italian prose by Ludovico Antonio Loschi, under the title *Notti* (Nights) (Venice, 1726). Dotti (374) quotes from part II, p. 22: "Guida la tua gregge in un pascolo pingue. Tu non la udirai belare mestamente [. . .] Ma la pace di cui godono esse [le pecore] è negata ai loro padroni. Un tedium, una scontentezza che non dà mai tregua rode l'uomo e lo tormenta da mane a sera." (Guide your flock into a rich pasture. You won't hear them bellow mournfully [. . .] But the peace they [the sheep] enjoy is denied to their masters. A tedium, a discontent that never lets up gnaws at man from morning to evening.)

107 *Quanta invidia ti porto!*: Cf. Petrarch, *Rime* CCC, i: "Quanta invidia io ti porto . . . avara terra!"

112 *tedio non provi*: For Leopardi's views on the innocence and contentedness of animals see *Zibaldone* 69 (1819) and 2221 (3 December 1821). Cf. also the related discussion in "Bruto minore," 61–70.

122 *E pur nulla non bramo*: Fubini (quoted in Dotti [375]) cites as a source lines 89–91 of the third act of Alfieri's *Mirra*: "io non trovo mai pace / Né riposo né loco. Eppure sollievo / Nessuno io bramo." [I never find peace / Or rest or room. And yet / I desire no relief.] What the shepherd says is different, however. It is not that he does not desire relief; he wants for, desires, nothing.

132 *il tedio*: Boredom, anomie, which Leopardi calls the most noble of the emotions (*Pensieri* LXVIII) is "the absence of any special sensation of good or evil" in which one experiences "the natural unhappiness of man" (*Zibaldone* 4498 [4 May 1829]). Cf. *Zibaldone* 4043 (8 March 1824): "Boredom is manifestly an evil, and being bored is an unhappiness. Now what is boredom? It's neither evil nor particular pain (in fact the idea and nature of boredom exclude the presence of any particular ill or pain whatsoever), but simple life fully felt, experienced, known, wholly present to the individual, and occupying him. Therefore life is simply an evil: and living, or living without, whether by extension or intension, is simply a good, or a lesser evil, or else preferable in itself and absolutely to life." See also the introductory notes to "La quiete dopo la tempesta" below.

133 *Forse* . . .: Dotti (375) cites Angelo Monteverdi, who believes that the canto was written in several stages: the first, second, and fourth stanzas at first, to which the third was later added, followed by the fifth, which, "given its inconclusive character" (94), was originally set between the second and third. Finally, Leopardi moved this stanza to fifth position and added the sixth and final stanza. For Monteverdi, the first "forse" of this last stanza is soon "rejected" by another "forse" in line 139, which begins "the second part of the stanza and which, repeated again [in 141], seems almost to transform into a 'certainly.' "

133 *Forse s'avess'io l'ale*: Cf. the refrain "Deh, l'ali avessi anch'io / Qual tu da girne a volo" from Celio Magno's "Vago augellin," which Leopardi anthologized in his *Crestomazia italiana poetica*, as well as the lines "Credevi d'aver l'ale / Da volar su le nubi" from the canzone "Ressurga su la tumba avara e lorda" attributed to Andrea da Basso (fifteenth century).

135 *E noverar le stelle* . . .: Cf. Petrarch, *Rime* CXXVII, 85: "Ad una ad una annoverar le stelle."

143 *funesto*: Originally "misero." In *Zibaldone* 2671 (8 February 1823) Leopardi copied from Barthélemy's enormously popular novel *Voyage du jeune Anacharsis en Grèce*: "Among many of the nations which the Greeks call barbarian, a child's day of birth is a day of mourning in his family."

XXIV. LA QUIETE DOPO LA TEMPESTA / THE CALM AFTER THE STORM

Written at Recanati between September 17 and 20, 1829; published in the Florentine edition of 1831.

This great *canzone libera* and the following one, both written before the

"Canto notturno," make a kind of diptych, "a true *unicum*, conceived and realized as such" (Dotti, 99). Each is a "parable" (Dotti again) richly dressed in exquisitely observed local detail, "a country scene illustrated and sung so as to point to a precise and unequivocal meaning" concerning Leopardi's theory of pleasure and, more precisely, the negativity of pleasure and the tension between opposites: "everything is animated by contrast, and languishes without it" (*Zibaldone* 2156 [24 November 1821]); and the following year, after discussing uniformity as the cause of boredom, Leopardi writes (*Zibaldone* 2600–2602 [7 August 1822]): "Here is how ills come to be necessary for happiness itself, and take on the true and real essence of goods in the general order of nature: mainly that indifferent things, i.e., not good and not bad, are the cause of boredom per se, as I have shown elsewhere, and also do not interrupt pleasure, and therefore don't destroy its uniformity, so vividly and fully as ills do, and can only do. From which the convulsions of the elements and other such things that cause anguish and the evil of fear in natural or civilized man, and equally in animals, etc. Illnesses and a hundred other inevitable evils for the *living* are recognized as conducive, and in a certain way necessary to the happiness of the living, and therefore with reason contained and collocated and received into the natural order, which looks in all ways toward predicted happiness. And this is not only because these evils give prominence to the good, and because health is enjoyed more after illness, and calm after the storm: but because without these evils, goods would not even be good in the short run, coming to be boring, and not being enjoyed nor felt as goods and pleasures, and the sensation of pleasure not being able, inasmuch as it is truly pleasing, to last long."

Orcel (314): "The first stanza, marked formally by an echo of Tasso's madrigals and a dancing rhythm of phrase, launched by an internal rhyme in the first two lines, links with the more gnomic form of the two that follow, in which Promethean sarcasm (culminating in the madrigalesque rhyme 'assai felice / se respirar ti lice') is appeased in view of the final peace of death."

Rigoni (M1, 970–71): "It is nevertheless clear that compared to the tone of detached philosophical observation of these notes, which predate the radicalization of Leopardi's 'pessimism,' the canto is distinguished by an attitude of precise and bitter reaction, which ironizes on the benevolence and generosity of nature and laments how even the rare and miraculous pleasures allowed to man, far from having their own consistency and reality, are only the effect of the suspension of pain. The dynamic of contraries, form and law of multiplicity, now appears as an intrinsic and permanent evil, a perverse and irremediable system: that convulsive disequilibrium, that 'violent state' which life is cannot be reordered and cured except in the 'quiet,' which is indeed truly blessed, of death."

4 *ripete il suo verso*: Cf. Petrarch, *Rime* CCXXXIX, 3: "E li augeletti incominciar lor versi."

13 *a prova*: Dotti (378): "Competing with others. An archaic locution of which Leopardi was fond." Cf. "Il risorgimento," 127, and "La quiete dopo la tempesta," 13.

29 *studi*: Occupations or concerns. Leopardi uses the word in its Latin sense, as he does "famiglia" and "mostro" elsewhere in the poem.

35 *El paventò la morte*: Leopardi notes in several places that the man who has been in danger of death comes to love life again. Cf. the end of "A un vincitore nel pallone" and *Zibaldone* 82 (Dotti, 379).

51 *cara agli eterni*: Originally, "degna di pianto." Dotti (379): "In his definitive version the poet chose to accentuate the polemical and sarcastic."

XXV. IL SABATO DEL VILLAGGIO / SATURDAY IN THE VILLAGE

Begun after September 20, 1829, and finished on the twenty-ninth, at Recanati; published in the Florentine edition of 1831.

This perfect companion piece to the canto that precedes it, likewise a *canzone libera*, Rigoni writes (M1, 971–72), "manifests the idea that pleasure is never actual (in both the philosophical and temporal senses of the term) but always and only future or, secondarily, past, because pleasure consists in the undefined"—it is "an intellectual, not real, subject" ("Dialogo di Torquato Tasso e del suo genio familiare" in the *Operette morali*)—"and the undefined, irreconcilable with reality and the present, lives only in the imagination or eventually in memory." The poem "faithfully mirrors ... the theoretical reflections of Leopardi, who strictly locates pleasure only in the future as various notes attest, from *Zibaldone* 532–35 (20 January 1821) to *Zibaldone* 4492 (April 1829), which cites Rousseau ...: 'L'on n'est heureux qu'avant d'être heureux.' " (Cf., however, "Alla luna," which evokes the masochistic pleasure painful memories can arouse in youth.)

"In analogy with the last stanza of the preceding canto, which turned the 'storm' and 'calm' into metaphors not only for 'suffering' and 'pleasure,' but also for 'life' and 'death,' the last stanza of this canto transforms the Sabbath into a metaphor for a first stage of life, with the exhortation to the unthinking 'boy' . . . to enjoy it as long as possible and not be unhappy if his 'Sunday,' his so painfully antiphrastic 'feast day,' is slow in coming."

29 *il zappatore*: Cf. "l'avaro zappador" of Petrarch, *Rime* L, 15–24.

37 *fornir l'opra*: Cf. Petrarch, *Rime* XL, 9: "Ma però che mi manca a fornir l'opra."

44 *Cotesta età fiorita*: Gallo and Garboli (204) cite Iacopo (or Giacomo) Marmitta's "Sopra la primavera," which Leopardi included in his *Crestomazia*: "Quanto diletta e piace / questa stagion novella! / Però tu, che la face / spregi d'amore, o bella / e più che orsa crudel, mia pastorella; / mentre che primavera / nel tuo bel viso appare, / non gir superba e fera:/ ch'a queste dolci e chiare / verran poi dietro l'ore fosche, amare: / e di tua vita in breve / porteran seco il verno, / e la pioggia e la neve: / onde, oh dolor interno! / te stessa avrai, com'or me lasso, a scherno."

50 *ma la tua festa*: Many, including Rigoni and Orcel, interpret the last two lines as follows: "But don't be sorry / that your holiday is slow in coming." As Nicola Gardini has pointed out, however, this is not grammatically defensible. But G. De Robertis (250) writes: "Everyone sees however how much the poet's particular arrangement of his words contributes to their total effect, especially in the anticipating of *la tua festa*, in immediate contrast with the grieving and piteous *ma*, which suddenly casts a sad shadow and denies, almost before it's said, the promised and awaited joy."

The lines resonate with the close of fragment XLI, the last lines in the *Canti*: "Ai presenti diletti / La breve età commetti."

XXVI. IL PENSIERO DOMINANTE / THE DOMINANT IDEA

Written at Florence in 1831, or between the spring of 1833 and the spring of 1835; published in the Naples edition of 1835. Inspired, like the three following canti and "Consalvo," by Leopardi's unhappy love for Fanny Targioni Tozzetti.

This *canzone libera*, "of a singular and nearly abstract beauty and a very interior musicality—comparable in some respects to another 'canto-manifesto' [Dotti, 110], 'Il risorgimento'—in which the loving emotion that is its object is never named"—"because [Karl Vossler, quoted in Dotti (110)] in the face of the newness of the experience it would have seemed too insignificant, because every reference to past things . . . might have given the impression of a diminution: 'I have no word for this.' "—"blends a polemic against the vulgarity of the century with its Platonic" exaltation of the idea of love. The singularity of the poem is enriched by a language in which, in the light of a strange atheist idealism, echoes of Petrarch . . . [and of Dantean stilnovism] blend with a [Latinate] vocabulary that is often neutral or willfully dry" (Orcel, 316).

For Rigoni (M1, 973), "the beauty of 'Il pensiero dominante' consists in its dreamlike enchantment no less than in its sure knowledge of the truth. In fact, Leopardi here renews, albeit in a different register, the miracle of the canzone "Alla sua donna," which was to bring together—in a sublime paradox—the experience of metaphysical disillusionment with the capacity to lose oneself in the joy of Platonic illusion. The entire canto is an exaltation of the idea of love, which not only dominates the mind, distancing it from every other idea, dissolves death itself into a 'game,' and raises the poet up above the utilitarian baseness of the century, but is enough to make one forget the truth by inspiring visions equal to 'the dreams of the immortals.' [Dotti (113) cites Walter Binni's observation that the fourteen stanzas of the poem are like rays, "miraculous effects" projecting from a central nucleus in which love reigns over the poet's entire spirit.] This idea is certainly an illusion and 'patent error' but an illusion and an error of a divine nature, which holds out against the truth and often even 'approximates' it, being confused with life itself: as Leopardi had written stupendously at the end of the 'Storia del genere umano' [in the *Operette morali*]: 'it will not be given to Truth, though all-powerful and battling with it continually, either ever to exterminate it from the earth, or to defeat it, except rarely,' for 'it is not given to the nature of genius to oppose the Gods.' " This blending of "two apparently contradictory attitudes also explains, beyond the return of the antitheses which had woven together 'Alla sua donna,' its singularly suggestive tone and rhythm."

Cf. *Pensieri* LXXXII: "No one becomes a man before he has had a great experience of himself, which in revealing him to himself, and determining his opinion of himself, in some way determines his fortune and condition in life. For this great experience, before which no one in the world is much more than a child, ancient life provided infinite and ready material; but today private life is so poor in occasions, and universally of such a nature, that, for lack of opportunities, many men die before the experience I am speaking of, and therefore live as children little differently than if they hadn't been born.

"But once it happens, either early in life, as for some, or later on, and after other loves of minor importance, as seems to happen more often, certainly at the end of a great and passionate love, man knows the mediocrity of his familiars, among whom he was used to walking with intense desires, and grave needs, perhaps not felt before; he knows *ab esperto* the nature of the passions, because when one of them burns it inflames all the others; he knows his own nature and temperament, knows the measure of his own faculties and powers; and from now on he can judge if and how much it behooves him to hope or despair for himself, and, for as much as he can understand of the future, what place in the world is destined for him. Finally, life in his eyes has a new look, already transformed in him from something heard about to something seen, from imagined to real; and he feels himself in the midst of it, perhaps no longer happy, but, so to speak, more powerful than before, that is, more able to make use of himself and of others."

12 *Par novo ad ascoltar ciò ch'ei ragiona*: Cf. Petrarch, *Rime* LXXI, 7–13, and Dante's canzone "Amor che ne la mente mi ragiona."

15 *a far dimora*: Cf. Dante's canzone "Tre donne intorno al cor mi son venute," 3–4: "ché dentro siede Amore / Lo quale è in segnoria de la mia vita."

17 *Gli altri pensieri miei . . .*: Cf. Petrarch LXXII, 40–45. Cf. Leopardi's description of the single-mindedness of love in *Zibaldone* 59 (1819).

50 *Necessitade estrema*: Tacitus's "ultima necessitas," death.

65–66 *A scherno / Ho gli umani giudizi*: Cf. the "Palinodia" and "La ginestra," with its denunciations of credulous modern notions of progress. Dotti (112): "Rarely has Leopardi declared his own superiority with such energy and passion . . . in what amounts to a declaration of principle, a challenge to the world."

67 *A' bei pensieri*: "The study of beauty, the emotions, the imagination, the illusions" (Leopardi to Giordani, 24 July 1828): the very things necessary "to make existence useful and bearable" (Dotti, 389).

69 *A quello onde tu movi . . .*: Leopardi here is referring by extension to the Aristotelian notion of God as the prime, or unmoved, mover of the universe. "The insistence on the moment of reasoning and the celebration of Love's effects on man typical of this stanza bring the canto ever nearer to the great ideological canzoni of our stilnovistic poetry and its heirs" (Dotti, 389–90).

106 *il ver pongo in obblio*: Cf. Petrarch CCCXXV, 45: " 'l mio mal posi in oblio."

116 *in grembo a morte*: Cf. Alfieri, *Alceste* II, iii: "di morte in grembo."

123 *Altri gentili inganni* . . .: Orcel (316): "Actually seeing had the tendency to weaken the beauty of the poet's fantasies . . . The idea is already expressed in the letter to Jacopsen of [23 June] 1823" (quoted in the notes to "Alla sua donna").

126 *colei*: Most likely Fanny Targioni Tozzetti.

143 *Nella terrena stanza*: Cf. "Alla sua donna," 15: "peregrina stanza."

XXVII. AMORE E MORTE / LOVE AND DEATH

Written at Florence in 1832 or 1833 and, like both its predecessor and "Consalvo," inspired by the poet's attachment to Fanny Targioni Tozzetti, to whom Leopardi wrote on 26 August 1832: "Love and death are the only beauties the world possesses, and the only things, absolutely the only ones, worthy of being desired"; published in the Neapolitan edition of 1835. Cf. the inscription for a bust of Raphael that Leopardi composed in 1832 (Damiani [M2, 1016]): "RAFFAELE D'URBINO / PRINCE OF PAINTERS / AND MIRACLE OF GENIUS / INVENTOR OF INDESCRIBABLE BEAUTY / HAPPY FOR THE GLORY IN WHICH HE LIVED / HAPPIER FOR THE LOVE IN WHICH HE BURNED / HAPPIEST FOR HIS DEATH OBTAINED IN THE FLOWER OF HIS YEARS / NICCOLÒ PUCCINI THESE LAURELS THESE FLOWERS / SIGHING FOR THE MEMORY OF SO MUCH HAPPINESS. / MDCCCXXXII"

Rigoni (M1, 975–76): "It is the ancient *topos* of the twinship of Love and Death, widely taken up again in European poetry of the early 19th century" and in fact evoked by Leopardi's friend August von Platen in his poem "Tristan": "Wer die Schönheit angeschaut mit Augen / Ist dem Tode schon anheimgegeben" [He who sees Beauty with his eyes / is already in the lap of Death]. "Exactly the opposite of Leopardi, in whom paradoxically the song of Death becomes the song of Life and Youth, the only form of life not destroyed but dissolved in eternal Nothingness" (Dotti, 116).

Leopardi develops the theme in the context of his own philosophical considerations discussed passim in the *Zibaldone*, e.g., "on 'the physical pleasure of death,' experienced not as active but 'highly languid' pleasure (2567 [16 July 1822]). In respect to the stormy raging of desire, death is shown wearing the features of beauty, and of liberating pity: from this derives both the personification of Love's companion as a sweet child, and the more or less 'languid' or at least distended and melodic development of the canto [in which rhyme, uncharacteristically in the later Leopardi, abounds]. But the last stanza, in which the craving to fall asleep on death's 'virgin breast' is associated with the repudiation of all other puerile consolation and the refusal to kiss and bless the despised hand of fate, testifies precisely to [Leopardi's fundamental] nature as an 'implacable innocent' (to use an expression of Bontempelli [1937])."

3 *Cose quaggiù sì belle*: Cf. "Consalvo" (also written in 1832), 99–100: "Due cose belle ha il mondo: / Amore e morte."

7 *per lo mar dell'essere*: Cf. *Paradiso* I, 112.

10 *Bellissima fanciulla*: Death. Angiola Ferraris (Dotti, 114) notes the "neoclassical spirit" (one imagines a staue by Canova) of this description.

16 *saggio core*: Stilnovistic. Cf. Cavalcanti: "Beltà di donna, e di saccente core."

17 *Nè cor fu mai più saggio*: Dotti (396): "The syntax of these lines recalls the first stanza of Guinizelli's canzone 'Al cor gentil rempaira sempre amore.' "

27 *Quando novellamente*: Cf. Petrarch, *Rime* CCLXIV, 110: "Quando novellamente io venni in terra." "Nel cor profondo" is Petrarchan, too (XCIV, 1), as in "Il risorgimento," 6.

30–31 *Languido e stanco . . . / desiderio di morir*: Cf. the "Dialogo di Federico Ruysch e delle sue mummie" in the *Operette morali*, the introductory chorus to which is translated in "Other Texts."

35 *Allor questo deserto*: Life, without love.

52 *Abbandonando all'alba il corpo stanco*: I.e., to sleep.

63 *L'uom della villa*: Cf. *Purgatorio* IV, 23.

81 *sprona*: Used by both Dante and Petrarch. Literally, spurs.

85 *Pongon le membra giovanili in terra*: Cf. Petrarch, *Rime* XXXVI, 11: "colle mie mani avrei gìa posto in terra / queste membra noiose."

104–105 *t'inchina / A disusati preghi*: Cf. Petrarch's canzone to the Virgin, *Rime* CCCLXVI, 11: "al mio prego t'inchina." Orcel (317) notes "the slippage of the 'Vergine bella' toward the 'beautiful child' whose features Leopardi gives to Death."

107 *dell'età reina*: Literally, queen of the age. The phrase likewise derives from Petrarch's canzone to the Virgin, 13.

108 *Me certo troverai . . .*: A typical Leopardian close in which he portrays himself alone and apart, observing life without illusions; cf. the end of "Aspasia" and "La vita solitaria."

116 *antica viltà*: Dotti (401): "Indicates the age-old secular intellectual misery of the common people, enslaved to prejudices. Cf. this passage from the 'Dialogo di Tristano e di un amico' [in the *Operette morali*]: 'And men are cowards, weak, with ignoble and narrow spirits; docilely always hoping for good . . . ever ready and ever resolved to console themselves for whatever ill fortune, to accept whatever recompense in exchange for what has been denied them or what they've lost, to accommodate themselves in whatever condition to a however more iniquitous and barbarous fate, and when they are deprived of every desirable thing, to live according to false beliefs, as healthily and vigorously as if they were the truest or most well-founded in the world. I for myself laugh at the human race in love with life; and I judge very unmanly their wanting to be fooled and deluded like idiots, and beyond the evils they suffer, to be almost the laughingstock of nature and destiny.' In these and the following lines, ever more decisively, Leopardi excoriates beliefs in the beyond and, above all, Christian resignation before the suffering of life."

XXVIII. A SE STESSO / TO HIMSELF

Written at Florence before the spring of 1835, quite possibly in 1833, following the end of his attachment to Fanny Targioni Tozzetti; published in the Neapolitan edition of 1835.

The poem (Orcel, 318) "is closely related to the sketch for the hymn 'Ad Arimane' (the god of darkness of pre-Islamic Iran) [likely written in 1833] . . . Flowing in the dimensions of the most peaceful of the idylls ('L'infinito' and 'Alla luna'), allying concision with internal pulverization (broken phrases, brutal coups, enjambments, etc.), this darkly beautiful piece illustrates marvelously the pre-Nietzschean paradox that Leopardi developed at the beginning of the *Zibaldone* (260) [quoted in the notes to "A Silvia," p. 441] to the effect that works of genius, while speaking only of death give back to the soul the life that it had lost." Croce and Cesare Luporini, among others, however, have found it poetically wanting, reading it as "a kind of note left on the table" (Dotti [116], who in contrast cites Monteverdi's analysis of the artful tripartite construction of the canto [119], each five-line section beginning with an exhortation to the poet's heart to be still).

As Beckett wrote in his *Proust* (1931) (New York: Grove Press, 1970, 7): "The wisdom of all the sages, from Brahma to Leopardi . . . consists not in the satisfaction but in the ablation of desire." Rigoni (M1, 977): "Such extinction is realized in this canto, however, not in the form of a serene—philosophical or mystical—renunciation, but rather in the desperate tension between the vindication of the solitary and sovereign, albeit futile, dignity of his heart . . . and disdain for everything that exists, the denunciation of universal filth, the two poles of a tragic wisdom that sees Ahrimanic malevolence superseded in the *vanitas vanitatum* of Ecclesiastes."

2 *l'inganno estremo*: The illusion of love. "Ad Angelo Mai," 129: "Amor, di nostra vita ultimo inganno."

3 *Perì*: Cf. Foscolo, "Di se stesso": "Non son che fui. Perì di noi gran parte . . ."

4 *In noi*: Dotti (403): "In me and in my heart."

6 *Assai*: Enough, or too much.

10 *fango*: Cf. "Ad Angelo Mai," 179: "Questo secol di fango."

14–15 *il brutto / Poter . . .*: Cf. the beginning of "Ad Arimane" and *Zibaldone* 4175–77 (22 April 1826): "Everything is evil. That is to say that everything that exists is evil."

16 *l'infinita vanità del tutto*: Cf. the "vanity of vanities" of Ecclesiastes 12:8.

XXIX. ASPASIA

Written, or finished, at Naples in the spring of 1834 or 1835; published in the Neapolitan edition of 1835.

Aspasia of Miletus was the celebrated *hetera* allied with Pericles. The name was used by Parini (cf. "Il mattino," 681) for Ninon de Lenclos (1620–1705), the French author and courtesan.

Like its predecessor—though now from a removed distance, and "on the safe shore of the intellect" (Croce, quoted in Dotti [123])—the canto, "a letter-confession directed to himself" (Dotti, 126), bears acerb witness to the end of

Leopardi's infatuation with Fanny Targioni Tozzetti (as Leo Spitzer [Dotti, 120] puts it, "singing about disenchantment is a harder thing than singing the intoxication of feeling"). "Aspasia"—"a poem of the intellect . . . returning to itself after the shipwreck of amorous passion" (Dotti, 127)—"describes the oxymoron of a Platonic passion, in which the loved one is revealed to be unworthy of the archetype imprinted on her, having failed to incarnate 'the woman who can't be found' [see notes to "Alla sua donna"]" (Damiani, *All'apparir del vero*, 446).

"Aspasia" is an autobiographical expatiation, in a neoclassical mode, on the ideas in "Alla sua donna" and "Il pensiero dominante" (and in its own way a disabused rewriting of "Consalvo"), "where love is likewise conceived as error and illusion but sung in all its radiant vital potential"; here, however—in "bitter confirmation that reality has defeated the ideal forever" (Dotti, 123)—"Leopardi changes tone, mixes the lexicon of mourning with that of ecstasy, carries out . . . a final and definitive act of destruction of both love and woman, who returns now only as a 'beloved ghost' " (Rigoni [M1, 979]).

10 *erinni*: Literally, the Furies.

20 *arcana*: Literally, hidden, secret.

27 *Novo ciel, nova terra . . .*: Cf. Revelation 21:1: "And I saw a new heaven and a new earth."

31–32 *finch'a quel giorno / Si fu due volte ricondotto il sole*: I.e., until two years had passed.

34 *Simile effetto*: See *Zibaldone* 1785–86 (24 September 1821) for a discussion of the similar effects on man of music and feminine beauty. See also the conclusion of "Sopra il ritratto di una bella donna."

39 *l'amorosa idea*: Cf. "Il pensiero dominante."

57–58 *in chi dell'uomo al tutto / . . . è minor*: Cf. Ovid, *Heroides* XIX, 6–7: "fortius ingenium suspicor esse viris; / Ut corpus teneris ita mens infirma puellis."

Dotti (408–409) quotes Fubini: "Note . . . the crudely and polemically misogynist tone, in correspondingly impacted and heavy language."

61 *Nè tu finor giammai . . .*: Cf. "La sera del dì di festa," 9–10: "e già non sai nè pensi / Quanta piaga m'apristi in mezzo al petto."

87–88 *un lungo / Servaggio*: Cf. the "lunghi affanni / E di servaggio" under Laban that Jacob had to submit to in order to win the hand of Rebecca in the "Inno ai patriarchi" (84–85).

90–91 *a cui piegar sostenni / L'altero capo*: Cf. the broom, bending in response to necessity at the end of "La ginestra," 303–305: "E piegherai / Sotto il fascio mortal non renitente / Il tuo capo innocente."

98–99 *a' tuoi superbi / Fastidi*: Cf. Virgil, *Eclogues* II, 15: "superba . . . fastidia."

112 *Il mar*: The mention of the sea argues for the poem's being written after Leopardi had arrived in Naples in 1833.

XXX. SOPRA UN BASSO RILIEVO ANTICO SEPOLCRALE / ON AN ANCIENT FUNERAL RELIEF

Marti (Dotti, 124) argues that the canto was drafted in Rome in 1831–32, where, in the studio of the neoclassical Carrarese sculptor Pietro Tenerani (1789–1869), principal disciple of the great Danish sculptor Bertel Thorvaldsen (1770–1844), Leopardi saw "the bas-relief for the burial of a young woman, full of sadness and sublime constancy" (letter to Carlotta Lenzoni, 29 October 1831) now in the Roman church of San Lorenzo in Lucina (significantly, he makes the sculpture ancient in his poem); published in the Neapolitan edition of 1835.

Rigoni notes "conceptual and rhythmic analogies" with the last part of the "Dialogo di Plotino e di Porfirio" (1827) in the *Operette morali* and with *Zibaldone* 4277–78 (9 April 1827). These concern whether the subject should be considered fortunate or unhappy "in correlation with the problem of the immortality of the soul" (Dotti, 414). The poem represents a clear break with the Aspasia poems occasioned by Leopardi's relationship with Fanny Targioni Tozzetti. Orcel (320): "A song of an entirely ancient *pietas*." To G. A. Levi (1931), "one of the most delicate and even sublime things" written by Leopardi.

"Here too as in 'A Silvia,' 'Le rimembranze,' and elsewhere, the death of a young woman—a subject Leopardi had long contemplated (see "Disegni letterari," XII [M2, 1218])—is the occasion for a sober reflection on the 'marvel that cannot be praised' of nature and her contradictions, the blind hurtling of human consciousness against the insoluble and inextricable . . . a lucid and sensible argument on the paradoxical relationship between life and death, between him who goes and him who stays, which is reflected . . . in the contrast/conflict between the logic of the intellect and the natural, unsuppressible reaction of . . . the spirit" (Rigoni [M1, 980–81]).

The opening of the poem also suggests that of "Nelle nozze della sorella Paolina."

27 *Mai non veder la luce . . .*: Best not to be born (cf. Sophocles, *Oedipus at Colonus*, 1289). Leopardi repeats this classical commonplace, first expressed by Theognis, 425–28, several times; he quotes it from Barthélemy's *Voyage* in *Zibaldone* 2672 (10 February 1823), and in both the autobiographical "Detti memorabili di Filippo Ottonieri" and the "Dialogo di Tristano e di un amico" in the *Operette morali.*

36 *Come vapore in nuvoletta accolto . . .*: Cf. Wisdom of Solomon 2:4: "Our life shall pass away as the trace of a cloud, and shall be dispersed as a mist," and Job 7:9: "As the cloud is consumed and vanisheth away."

47 *Che per uccider partorisci e nutri*: Cf. "Ad Arimane" (356): "per uccider partorisce ec . . ." (See also *Zibaldone* 4257–58 [21 March 1827], quoted in the notes to "Al Conte Carlo Pepoli.") Dotti (416): "In this epigrammatic phrase Leopardi summarizes one of the central themes of his thought." Cf. also *Zibaldone* 4485–86 (11 April 1829): "Nature necessarily, according to the law of destruction and reproduction, and to maintain the current state of the universe, is essentially, regularly, and perpetually the persecutor and mortal enemy of all individuals of all kinds and species to whom it gives life; and it begins to persecute them from the very moment it produced them."

The passage foreshadows the complaint against divine cruelty toward the human race in "Il tramonto della luna" (1836), 34–50. Indeed, the two poems are closely interrelated throughout.

55 *Misera ovunque miri*: Cf. *Imitatio Christi* I 22: "Miser es ubicumque fueris et quocumque te verteris." Also the "Canto notturno," 21–38.

58 *Piacqueti che delusa*: Cf. the similar argument in "Il tramonto della luna," 35. Fubini (quoted in Dotti [417]) notes that "Piacqueti" "corresponds to the Latin expression *placuit*: it was your decree."

87–88 *scemo / Rimaner di se stesso*: Cf. *Purgatorio* XXX, 49–50: "scemi / di sé."

XXXI. SOPRA IL RITRATTO DI UNA BELLA DONNA / ON THE PORTRAIT OF A BEAUTIFUL LADY

As with the previous poem, with which this makes a pair known as the *canzoni sepolcrali*, or sepulchral odes, this was written at Naples between 1831 and 1835, and may likewise have been inspired in part by plaster models made in 1831 by

Pietro Tenerani for a memorial for Margaret Compton, Marchioness of Northampton, who died in Rome in 1830. The sculpture is now in the Ashby Castle Church, Northamptonshire. (See Novella Bellucci, "Lo scultore della Psiche," in Novella Bellucci and Luigi Trenti, eds., *Leopardi a Roma*, catalogue of an exhibition at the Museo Napoleonico, Rome, 10 September–10 December, 1998. Milano: Electa, 1998, 227).

Rigoni (M1, 982) notes that the poem "is distinguished . . . by its insistence on the specific baroque theme of *desengaño*, the miserable and vile transformation into 'mud' and 'bones' performed by death on . . . feminine beauty." If "Sopra un basso rilievo" is classical in its detachment, its companion's violent conceptual and formal antitheses, expressive of two opposing realities, recall the structure—and the disenchantment—of "Aspasia," suggesting, as Marti has argued (Dotti, 124), that this second sepulchral ode was written later, in the wake of the final detachment from the illusion of love that is the burden of the "Aspasia" cycle, and as such is part of it, "or at least documents it" (Dotti, 126).

Ezra Pound's translation, "Her Monument, the Image Cut Thereon," was published in his *Canzoni*, 1911.

6–7 *il simulacro / Della scorsa beltà*: Orcel (321): "D. De Robertis notes with finesse that these lines constitute a kind of 'anti-*Sepolcri*,' evoking the image in Foscolo of the Muses (with their immortal song) as 'guardians of tombs.' "

9 *quel labbro, ond'alto*: Cf. Parini's sonnet "Quando costei": "Volo al bel labbro onde il piacer trabocca." The imagery here recalls the protagonist's enraptured reactions to his beloved in "Consalvo" and "Aspasia."

16 *di pallor si tinse*: The line is drawn from a loose translation of Archilochos made by Leopardi in 1823–24 (M1, 605).

22 *Misterio eterno*: Dotti (421) calls this asseveration "a bit emphatic."

26 *Quale splendor* . . .: Cf. the "Raggio divino" of the beloved's beauty in "Aspasia," 33.

38 *Ammirabil concetto*: The "amorosa idea" of "Aspasia," 39, which the poet has evoked once more in the preceding lines.

42 *natural virtù*: Music, by the very nature of its sounds, expresses emotion immediately and purely. Cf. *Zibaldone* 79 (1819): "The other arts imitate and express nature, from which feeling is derived, but music imitates and expresses only the same feeling in person, which is derived from itself and not from nature"; Leopardi also approvingly quotes Mme de Staël's claim about music that "c'est celui qui agit le plus immédiatement sur l'âme." Dotti (422) also recalls the relations between music and feminine beauty in "Aspasia," 34–37 and 67–70.

52 *polve ed ombra*: Cf. Petrarch, *Rime* CCXIV, 12: "Veramente siam noi polvere et ombra," which in turn derives from Horace, *Odes* IV, 7, 16: "pulvis et umbra sumus."

56 *Da sì basse cagioni*: Dotti (423): "Entirely material causes, motives (like the flowering and disappearance of beauty)." G. De Robertis (301): "These last lines have a flavor of the distant gnomic, and a quick rhythm that is not at all in keeping with the weight and meaning of their miserable questioning"—questioning "destined to have no answers" (Dotti, 423): "eternal mystery / of our being."

XXXII. PALINODIA AL MARCHESE GINO CAPPONI / RECANTATION FOR MARCHESE GINO CAPPONI

Written in 1834 or 1835 at Naples; published in 1835 as the culminating poem of the Neapolitan edition of the *Canti*.

A palinode is a Greek recantation; this is Leopardi's satire, inspired by Parini's "Il giorno," and based on Virgil's fourth eclogue, on the optimistic fantasies and the fads and foibles of his time—"Science, Culture, Technology, Industry, Politics, Newspapers, Progress, Happiness, expressions of the absurd faith in the advent of a new golden age" (Rigoni [M1, 984])—which gives brilliant, biting expression to "the polemical (and very often visionary) side of Leopardi's historical and metaphysical nihilism" (Orcel, 321). The Greek term "is used with an ironic and polemically bitter intention" (Dotti, 424); the poem's tone is closely allied with that of the "Dialogo di Tristano e di un amico" (1832), which brings the *Operette morali* to a close. Gino Capponi (Florence, 1792–1876), was an economist and politician, author of a history of the Florentine republic, and founder with G. P. Vieusseux of the influential liberal review *L'Antologia*. He met Leopardi in 1827 and was apparently the one judge who voted to give the *Operette morali* the prize of the Accademia della Crusca in 1829. Capponi accepted Leopardi's dedication of the "Palinodia" to him, though he was in fact one of the "ingenuous" optimists excoriated in the poem. As he wrote to Niccolò Tommaseo in November 1835: "Leopardi has offloaded some of his attacks onto my back, kindly deriding me as a believer in newspapers, whiskers, cigars, and the wisdom and the blessedness of the century" (quoted in Rigoni [M1, 985]).

EPIGRAPH *Il sempre sospirar nulla rileva*: Petrarch, *Rime* CV: "Mai non vo' più cantar com'io soleva, / Ch'altrui non m'intendeva, ond'ebbi scorno; / et pu-ossi in bel soggiorno esser molesto. / Il sempre sospirar nulla rileva." [I'm never going to sing again the way I did, / For no one understood me, and I was scorned; / and it can be harmful in a lovely place. / Always sighing redeems nothing.] Marti (quoted in Dotti [132]) sees the epigraph as marking "a shift" on Leopardi's part away from personal suffering in favor of an active, dynamic opposition to the progressive ideology of his time.

1 *candido Gino*: Orcel (321): "The epithet is to be understood in the Latin sense of 'sincere,' 'well-meaning' (Italian publishers used to address [their offerings to] the 'candid reader'); but the adjective's ironic resonance is very probable." Cf. Horace's salutation, "candide iudex," to his friend Tibullus in *Epistles* I, 4, 1.

12–13 *del mio mal consorte / L'umana specie*: Leopardi always rejected the insinuation of his contemporaries that his own ideas were the result of his personal predicament. Cf. the letter to de Sinner of 24 May 1832 quoted in the notes on "Bruto minore," p. 402.

13–14 *fumo / . . . onorato*: Glorious, like the smoke of battle. The trope continues in the following lines. Leopardi's satirical view of newspapers is also mooted, among other places, in the "Dialogo di Tristano e di un amico": "I believe in and embrace the profound philosophy of the newspapers which, killing every other literature and every other occupation, massively grave and displeasing, are the lords and light of the present age."

25 *Come nulla quaggiù dispiace e dura*: Parody of a line of Petrarch, *Rime* CCXI, 14: "Come nulla quaggiù diletta e dura" [How nothing down here pleases and survives].

38 *Aureo secolo . . .*: Literal translation of a passage in Simmacus quoted in *Zibaldone* 1181 (18 June 1821), and which itself recalls Virgil, *Eclogues* IV, 46–47. The ostentatious, highly familiar classical reference underlines the satirical thrust of the passage (Dotti, 427)—and the distance of this golden age from the emotional and spiritual one imagined in "Sopra il ritratto di una bella donna."

42 *Universale amore*: Rigoni (M1, 986): For Leopardi, a pernicious myth that has "produced universal egotism" (*Zibaldone* 890 [30 March–4 April 1821]).

44 choléra: Leopardi uses the French spelling, as if to underline the snobbish exoticism of the disease; there was a widespread cholera epidemic in France in 1832.

46–47 *pino o quercia / Suderà latte e mele*: Parody of Virgil's fourth eclogue and of the last chorus of the first act of Tasso's *Aminta.*

50 *E le macchine al cielo emulatrici*: Cf. Virgil, *Aeneid* IV, 89: "aequataque machine caelo"; for Virgil "machine" refers to high buildings or constructions but the hubristic intention is the same. Dotti (427) notes that Leopardi had already satirized the nineteenth-century faith in machinery in the "Proposta dei premi fatta dall'Accademia dei Sillografi" (*Operette morali*).

54 *Di Sem, di Cam e di Giapeto il seme*: Shem, Ham, and Japeth were the sons of Noah, from whom the human race descended.

55 *Ghiande*: In the first Golden Age, men ate acorns.

65 *Contrarie in campo le fraterne schiere*: Cf. the denunciation of internecine strife in "La ginestra," 135–44.

77 *A galleggiar sortiti*: Cf. the like political predictions of "Ad Arimane."

82 *Volta nè Davy*: Alessandro Volta (1745–1827), Italian inventor of the voltaic pile, an early electric battery, from which he obtained the first electric current; the English chemist and physicist Humphry Davy (1778–1829) invented the miner's safety lamp and isolated several elements, including chlorine and iodine.

84 *un Gange*: I.e., a river of ink.

94 *l'eclittica*: The sun's orbit, i.e., anywhere on earth.

94–95 *eternamente / Sarà . . .*: Cf. the "Proposta di premi fatta all'Accademia di Sillografi" in the *Operette morali*, in which the academy hopes one day or another to find "some thread of healthy or other genius" that will save men "from egotism, from the predominance of mediocrity, from the prosperous fortune of the insensate, the ribald, and the low, from the universal not-caring and the misery of the wise, the costumati and the magnanimous." See also "To Ahriman" (357): "And the world raves seeking new orders and laws and hopes for perfection."

97 *Queste lievi reliquie*: Cf. the also parodic line in Virgil's fourth eclogue, 31: "*Pauca tamen suberunt priscae vestigia fraudis.*"

102 *e por quegli odii in pace*: Dotti (431) makes reference to the long pages of the *Zibaldone* 3773–810 (25–30 October 1823) on human unsociability.

113 *coton*: Cotton clothes were more expensive; Dotti (431) notes that the cotton industry was then being broadly developed in Britain and in the United States.

121 *l'arsa cucina*: The irony here derives from the association of an elevated, literary epithet like *arsa* (blackened by smoke) and a common term like *cucina* (kitchen) (Dotti, 431–32).

123 *Liverpool*: Hub of the English cotton and slave trades.

125–26 *sotto l'ampie / Vie del Tamigi*: The tunnel from Wapping to Rotherhithe, begun in 1804 and finally completed in 1842.

143 *quanti*: For Leopardi's sardonic view of statistics, see the "Dialogo di Tristano e di un amico": "But long live statistics! long live economic, moral, and political science, portable encyclopedias, manuals, and the very beautiful creations of our century." And in a letter to Giordani (24 July 1828): "Most of all it doesn't enter my mind that the high point of human wisdom lies in political knowledge and statistics."

145–46 *per opra / Di possente vapore*: Steam-powered typographical machines.

149 *Come d'aeree gru . . .*: This exquisitely modulated classical simile is "probably the most finely ironic" (Dotti, 433) moment of the poem.

154 *Quale un fanciullo . . .*: With this next simile, Leopardi abandons irony for his customary grave, disabused consideration of human nature. The same comparison of nature to a child who continually destroys what he creates can be found in *Zibaldone* 4421 (2 December 1828); cf. also the sketch for the hymn "Ad Arimane." The simile also foreshadows that of the apple and the ants in "La ginestra," 202ff.

172 *Distruggendo e formando*: Leopardi, in the "Frammento apocrifo di Stratone da Lampsaco" in the *Operette morali*: "But given that the said power [of nature] never stops operating on and modifying matter, therefore those creatures that it continually forms, it also destroys, making new creatures from their matter." Cf. also the discussion of the related notion of hostile mother nature, who creates only to destroy, in the notes to "Sopra un basso rilievo sepolcrale," p. 462.

182 *Queste . . . miserie estreme*: Cf. "La quiete dopo la tempesta," 42–45: "O natura cortese, / Son questi i doni tuoi, / Questi i diletti sono / Che tu porgi ai mortali." Cf. also the "necessità diverse" which nature provided to keep humans busy in "Al Conte Carlo Pepoli," 32–36.

193–94 *E non pur . . . / . . . altre parti*: These two lines were not printed in the Neapolitan edition of 1835.

204–205 *un popol fanno / Lieto e felice*: Leopardi wrote to Fanny Targioni

Tozzetti (5 December 1831): "I laugh at the happiness of the *masses* because my little brain cannot conceive of a happy *mass* made up of unhappy individuals." And in the "Dialogo di Tristano e di un amico" (1832) he caricatures the newly popular notion of the "masses": "*Individuals have disappeared before the masses*, the modern thinkers elegantly say. Which means that it's unnecessary for the individual to put up with any inconvenience . . . Let the masses do it; what they are going to do without individuals, being made up of individuals, I wish and hope the intendants of individuals and masses, who today illumine the world, will explain to me."

211–12 *In più sublimi ancora e più riposti / Subbietti*: Orcel (322) calls this "raillery against the religious and spiritualist renewal then particularly present at Naples (Leopardi also wrote a satirical in terza rima, 'I nuvoi credenti,' 'The New Believers' [likely also 1835], not included in the *Canti*)." These "exponents of Neapolitan Catholic spiritualism constitute a target analogous and parallel to that represented by the Florentine liberals in the "Palinodia" (Rigoni [M1, 1065]).

214–15 *prosteso adora / Oggi*: Recalls the last lines of Parini's "Notte": "La gloria e lo splendor di tanti eroi / Che poi prosteso il cieco vulgo adora."

217 *Tra il fumo degl'incensi*: I.e., on the altars of religion.

227 *Un già de' tuoi . . .*: The liberal Catholic thinker Niccolò Tommaseo (1802–74), one of Capponi's principal collaborators on the *Antologia* and a bitter enemy of Leopardi's, who by 1833 had moved to Paris. See Leopardi's brilliant and bitter satire on Tommaseo's intellectual arrogance and self-certainty, "Potenze intellettuali: Niccolò Tommaseo" (1836) (M2, 1017–20). Capponi (Rigoni [M1, 988]), however, believed Leopardi was referring here to Manzoni, whom Leopardi also met in Florence.

238 *la matura speme*: The Italian hope for liberty.

242–43 *un suono / Di lingua che dal latte si scompagni*: Cf. Petrarch's canzone "Tacer non posso" (*Rime* CCCXXV), 87–88: "con voci, anchor non preste, / di lingua che dal latte si scompagne."

247–48 *se lode / Cerchi e fama*: Cf. "La ginestra," 68–69: "Ben ch'io sappia che obblio / Preme chi troppo all'età propria increbbe." And in the "Dialogo di Tristano e di un amico," the friend says: "Or more probably you'll be disdained, as understanding modern philosophy badly, and caring little for the progress of society and its lights."

250 *vassi alle stelle*: Parodic version of Virgil, *Aeneid* IX, 641: "sic itur ad astra."

252 *Del secolo i bisogni*: Fubini (Dotti, 439) notes that Leopardi, repeating this phrase, first used in ll. 237–38, is satirizing the journalistic parlance of the day.

259 *enorme il pelo*: Young Italian liberals sported sideburns and big beards to symbolize their opposition to the Austrians and their "collaborators." The aulic vocabulary—"conceda,""ostenta," etc.—is patently satirical.

265 *Qual de' barbati eroi . . .*: "Verse of Parinian coinage, both for the image of the 'barbati eroi' and for the ironically aulic hypermetric line" (Fubini, quoted in Dotti [440]).

271 *comincia a salutar col riso*: Cf. Virgil's fourth eclogue, 60: "Incipe, parve puer, risu cognoscere matrem." The entire passage is rife with parodic echoes of Virgil's poem.

XXXIII. IL TRAMONTO DELLA LUNA / THE SETTING OF THE MOON

Written in the Villa Ferrigni at Torre del Greco in the spring of 1836; published in the Florentine edition of 1845. According to legend—since disproved—Leopardi was supposed to have dictated the last six lines to Ranieri (or to the German historian Heinrich Wilhelm Schulz, who was visiting him at the time) six hours before his death.

The analogical development of the poem, in which the setting of the moon is likened to the disappearance of youth, recalls that of "Il passero solitario," though this new *canzone libera* is infinitely more impersonal and detached. This is not a return to the idyllic evocation of the world by moonlight, but a highly structured translating of "radical conceptual convictions into images ["not allegorical but symbolic" (Dotti, 197)]—having hidden the proposition so as to have it blossom like a flower born in the heart of the man who suffers" (Dotti, 139). Dotti (193): Strongly characteristic of Leopardi's late poetry is "the disappearance of the 'I' into a collective voice: the overwhelming and seemingly conclusive imposition of thinking; the translation of this thinking into imagery; the development, in fact, and often in highly dramatic forms, of the poetry which, in a lower and almost psalm-like tone, began with the restless questioning of the

'Canto notturno' . . . It's certain that all the canti of the late Leopardi are *operette morali* in verse, so to speak, canti that open on a complex, and highly articulate, ideological landscape."

3 *zefiro*: The spring wind.

20 *Tal si dilegua* . . .: The second stanza functions as the corresponding part of a an extended simile, comparing the moon ("Quale . . .") with youth ("Tal . . ."). Dotti (442): "The poet takes up the suggestive images created by the lunar night . . . to fix and render them precisely in their allusiveness . . . The simile is taken up point for point and laden with allegorical values, though with a very delicate touch."

30 *Del cammin lungo*: Cf. "Alla luna," 13–14: "Nel tempo giovanil, quando ancor lungo / La speme e breve ha la memoria il corso." After youth, "man realizes [Dotti, 443] that the years that remain to him will be particularly long, oppressive . . . devoid of the pleasure of youth . . .

"The image of the traveler in life is very frequent in the ancients and in Petrarch, but in Leopardi it takes on a very different meaning. While in the first the traveler seeks above all to reach his goal well, which for the Christian world is also eternal salvation, in [Leopardi] the *viatore* asks to no effect what the endpoint of the road he must still travel is. In the first, the traveler knows and rushes; in Leopardi he knows nothing and wanders in confusion. Or if he knows something, he knows that the world in which he finds himself is alien to him, as is he in the world's eyes."

32 *l'umana sede*: Man's home, the earth.

45–46 *estremo / Di tutti i mali* . . .: Cf. *Pensieri* VI: "Old age is the worst of all evils: because it deprives man of all his pleasures, leaving him with his appetites; and carries along it all his pains." Cf. Petrarch, *Rime* CCXXVII, 4: "Che il desir vive e la speranza è morta." "The definition that the ancients gave to death Leopardi reserves for old age" (Dotti, 444, who also notes that the collocation of "trovato" and "ritrovar" "has a hard polemical significance").

63 *Ma la vita mortal* . . .: Cf. Catullus V, 4–6: "Soles occidere et redire possunt; / nobis cum semel occidit brevis lux, / nox est perpetua una dormienda."

66–67 *alla notte / Che l'altre etadi oscura*: Old age, which erases the memory of the other times of life.

XXXIV. LA GINESTRA / BROOM

Written, like the preceding poem, at the Villa Ferrigni, Torre del Greco, in 1836 and published in the Florentine edition of 1845.

"La ginestra" is widely considered a kind of "spiritual testament" of the poet (Rigoni [M1, 989]). Its critique of nineteenth-century notions of progress, addressed more baldly and prosaically in the "Palinodia," is here "personified" in the anthropomorphized figure of the broom, often referred to as the national flower of Italy, with its wise way of bending before the cruel vicissitudes of nature.

The poem has been criticized by Croce and others for the mixture of "poetry and non-poetry," i.e., for the alternation between lyric description and philosophical argument—which in essence is the primary alternation in the *Canti*, what Heidegger called "pensiero poetante," or "thinking in poetry," "the transfiguration of reflection into imagery" (Dotti, 143) that marks the ultimate stage of Leopardi's poetic achievement.

Orcel (323): "From the aesthetic viewpoint, one could not deny that the most discursive strophes are close to a versified prose, but beyond the hammering or sarcastic power that the versification justly imprints them with, it is worth remembering that . . . Croce's distinction is the fruit of a post-romantic confusion between poetry and lyricism"—a feeling, I would submit, that Leopardi's own greatest lyrics are in part responsible for.

Dotti (200) notes "the progressive moving of Leopardi's thought and poetry in the direction of approaches always less attuned to lyrical subjectivity and always closer to the conquest—wished for by the poet himself, though he considered it debatable—of a 'truth' which could stand as the basis for a renewal of humanity. If, in other words, in the shepherd's song, the night sky was the symbol of the irrational and fatal alienation of the universe from man, that same sky in 'La ginestra' teaches us how such alienation may, at least in certain respects, be healed through understanding."

Leopardi's poem (which involves and subsumes numerous themes and gestures of his earlier work) is a national poem in much the same way that the song of Simonides in "All'Italia" is—it seeks to define a national spirit, a civic life, that has always been one of Leopardi's major themes. In this sense, the poems balance each other and create the arena for the consideration of these themes that is the *Canti*.

EPIGRAPH *le tenebre che la luce*: With his epigraph, Leopardi underlines his belief, underscored in the lines that follow, in rational enlightenment, in opposition to the spiritualism of his era.

10 *donna de' mortali*: Ancient Rome.

16 *d'afflitte fortune*: Cf. Petrarch, *Rime* CXXVIII, 59: "le fortune afflicte e sparte."

29 *fur città famose*: Herculaneum, Pompeii, and Stabia, destroyed by the eruption of Vesuvius in A.D. 79.

32 *Con gli abitanti insieme*: According to Orcel (324), Leopardi's meditations on the desolate ruins around Vesuvius throughout the poem derive from the reminiscences of Jacopo Sannazaro (1457/8–1530), court poet to Ferdinand I of Naples (in his elegy *Ad ruinas Cumarum* and prose *Arcadia*, chapter XII).

32–33 *Or tutto intorno / Una ruina involve*: Cf. Petrarch's canzone "Spirto gentil," *Rime* LIII, 35: "e tutto quell ch'una ruina involve."

39 *Il nostro stato*: The "umano stato" and "stato mortale" of the "Canto notturno"; the "mortale stato" of "Sopra un ritratto di una bella donna." Dotti (449) notes the "harsh ironic accent" of these lines. The aulic term "possanza" (for "potenza") in 41, e.g., "is used in an ironic sense in regard to the 'progressive' intellectuals and their optimistic faith in the century" (Dotti, 448).

51 Le magnifiche sorti e progressive: The phrase, which has become proverbial, was coined by Leopardi's cousin Terenzio Mamiani (1799–1885), a Catholic-optimist writer from Pesaro, in the preface to his *Inni sacri* (Paris, 1832). "Words of a modern, which explains all their elegance," wrote Leopardi, in his notes on the *Canti* (M1, 151).

Rigoni (M1, 991) asserts that "there is not, definitively, a political nor, *a fortiori*, a progressive Leopardi," though he notes the poet's approval of the demythifying rational or "destructive" tendencies of Renaissance and Enlightenment thought, which for Leopardi involved a return to the healthy scepticism of classical culture. Cf. *Zibaldone* 4192–93 (1 September 1826): "Bayle's observation that reason is rather an instrument of destruction than of construction, applies very well, in fact returns to what I seem to have observed elsewhere, that the progress of the human spirit, from the Renaissance on, and especially in these times, has consisted and consists more and more primarily not in the discovery of positive truths, but of substantially negative ones; or rather, in other words, in knowing the falsity of what in the past, more or less long ago, was considered sure, or rather the ignorance of what was thought to be known: though in fact, *faute de bien observer ou raisonner*, many similar negative discoveries are considered positive. And that the ancients, in metaphysics and morals principally, and also in politics . . . were equal to or more advanced than us, solely because and to the degree that they preceded the supposedly positive discoveries and realizations of the truth, to which we slowly and laboriously arrived and continually arrive at by renouncing, and discovering and knowing their falseness, and persuading ourselves of this, and promulgating such new discoveries and popularizing them."

55 *Dal risorto pensier*: The resurgence of classically inspired rational thought in what we today know as the Renaissance but was called the Risorgimento in the eighteenth century.

60 *Di cui lor sorte rea padre ti fece*: G. De Robertis (335): "Who through their ill fortune were born from you, like you, insanely proud like you."

63–64 *Non io / Con tal vergogna . . .*: I.e., by encouraging your infantile fantasies. Cf. the proud self-assertion of "All'Italia," 37–38: "io solo / Combatterò, procomberò sol io." Dotti (449) also mentions "Bruto minore," 106, in this vein.

The Le Monnier edition of 1845 includes the following three lines, which were dropped in the Mestica edition (1886) because they had been crossed out in the manuscript:

> E ben facil mi fora
> imitar gli altri, e vaneggiando in prosa
> farmi agli orecchi tuoi cantando accetto.

[And it would be very easy for me / to imitate others, and, raving in prose, / make my singing acceptable to your ears.]

69 *Preme . . .*: Obscures in its own night, buries (diction from Foscolo). Cf. also the "Palinodia," 246–50, on this theme. Fubini (quoted in Dotti [449]): "The future perfect relates to an understood 'before I go underground': Leopardi is conscious of speaking his last words." The line evokes a canzone of Dante (*Rime* XLIX, 59: "Per che parlar con voi si vole aperto," "and the Dantesque atmosphere is also emphasized by the inversions that call attention to the vibrant moral tension."

72 *Libertà vai sognando*: Cf. Dante, *Purgatorio* I, 71: "Libertà va cercando . . ."

72–73 *e servo . . . / Vuoi di novo il pensiero*: Leopardi is referring to the "utopian humanitarianism" (Dotti, 450) and religious idealism of the French thinkers of the restoration like Lammenais and the Baron d'Eckstein, who were also widely influential in Italy.

75 *in parte*: Rigoni (M1, 992): "The limiting expression '*in parte*' becomes clear only if we interpret correctly Leopardi's historical notion, according to which the best orientation of modern civilization is a continuous and incomplete return to the antique." See *Zibaldone* 4289 (18 September 1827): "The present progress of civilization is another Renaissance; it still consists, in large part, in retrieving what has been lost." Cf. also Leopardi's plan (1829) for a "Parallelo della civiltà degli antichi e quella dei moderni" (M2, 1217).

100 *nato a perir, nutrito in pene*: Fubini (quoted by Dotti [451]): "repeats epigrammatically the ideas expressed in the 'Palinodia,' 173–81."

103 *Empie le carte*: Dotti (452): "The expression, also found in the *Paralipomeni della Batracomiomachia*, IV, 14, 5, indicates the stupid and prideful volume of writings by the 'new believers.' "

112 *Che a sollevar s'ardisce*: Cf. Lucretius, *De rerum natura* I, 66–67, referring to Epicurus: "mortales tollere contra / Est oculos ausus, primusque obsistere contra."

125 *e di voler matrigna*: Cf. the expostulation against nature, "illaudabil maraviglia," marvel that cannot be praised, in "Sopra un basso rilievo antico sepocrale," 45ff. "My philosophy makes nature evil in all things, and totally exculpates men, directs its hatred, or if not its complaint, to a higher principle, to the true origin of the suffering of the living" (*Zibaldone* 4428 [January 1829]).

126–27 *e incontro a questa / Congiunta . . .*: The idea of the alliance of men in a constant war—"which Leopardi imagines being against nature and fate" (Dotti, 453)—is found in Hierocles of Alexandria, cited in *Zibaldone* 4226–27 (16 November 1826). Cf. also the passage in *Zibaldone* 4279–80 (13 April 1827) that ends: "This could serve as the 'Letter to a young man of the 20th century.' "

146 *come fur*: As they were in ancient times.

147 *quell'orror che primo*: Cf. Leopardi's description of the formation of society in "Inno ai patriarchi," 43–50.

152 *Conversar*: Society, from Latin *conversor*, to abide, frequent.

155 *probità del volgo*: Dotti (454): "Ironic and polemical (hence the use of the Latin term *volgo*): man's intellectual honesty, his way of thinking and conceiving."

158 *Sovente in queste rive*: Gardini (90–91) sees this as a reappearance of "the restless ghost of the pastoral" and notes that "sovente" and "queste" "are patently reminiscent of the first line of 'L'infinito.' . . . Whatever is left of the juvenile pastoral . . . here becomes one with the historical embodiment of Nature's destruction."

163 *Veggo dall'alto fiammeggiar le stelle*: Cf. Petrarch, *Rime* XXII, 11 ("poi quand'io veggio fiammeggiar le stelle"). See also the "Canto notturno," 84.

184–85 *o prole / Dell'uomo*: For Dotti (456) the vocative is "inspired more by compassion than by polemical scorn . . . [In contrast, see *Zibaldone* 3171–72 (12 August 1823),] where, Pascal-like, he had interpreted man's awareness of his smallness as a sign 'of his nobility, of the power and immense capacity of his mind, which, enclosed in such a small and minimal being' had yet been able to succeed in 'knowing and understanding things so superior to his nature' and embracing with his thought the immensity 'itself of existence and of things.'"

194–95 *i derisi / Sogni*: Religious beliefs, the object of scorn on the part of eighteenth-century Enlightenment philosophers.

203 *là*: G. De Robertis (345) notes that this is "one of the many indeterminate expressions dear to Leopardi. It imparts a sense of vagueness and fable."

220 *liquefatti massi*: Leopardi is quoting Sannazaro (*Arcadia* XII), who in turn quotes Virgil, "*liquefacta saxa*" (*Georgics* I, 473).

230 *quasi calpesta*: Cf. Isaiah 66:1: "Thus saith the Lord, The heaven is my throne and the earth is my footstool" (see also Acts 7:49).

240 *il villanello*: Cf. "lo villanello," *Inferno* XXIV, 7.

246–47 *ancor minaccia / A lui strage . . .*: Cf. Statius, *Silvae* IV, iv, 84–85: "necdum letate minari / cessat apex."

255 *riluce*: Cf. Virgil, *Aeneid* II, 312: "Sigea igni freta lata relucent," translated in 1816 by the young Leopardi: "Riluce la sigea vasta marina."

257 *Mergellina*: In Leopardi's day, a northern suburb of Naples.

269–71 *Torna al celeste raggio / . . . l'estinta / Pompei*: Systematic excavations of Pompeii began in 1768, but only became regularized at the beginning of the nineteenth century. Under Napoleonic rule (1806–14) they were particularly vigorous and methodical, but continued after the Bourbon restoration.

272–73 *cui di terra / Avarizia o pietà rende all'aperto*: Cf. the different attitude of "Ad Angelo Mai," in which Mai is praised for this very activity.

275 *Diritto*: Can modify either "il peregrino" (standing) or "lunge contempla" (looking directly).

280 *E nell'orror della secreta notte*: Dotti (460) observes that these lines (280–88) "seem to want to vie with Ossianic poetry." Cf. Foscolo, *Sepolcri*, 207–208: "e all'orror de'notturni / silenzi."

295 *Passan genti e linguaggi*: Cf. Petrarch, "*The Triumph of Time*," 112–14: "Passan vostre grandezze e vostre pompe / passan le signorie, passan i regni: / Ogni cosa mortal Tempo interrompe."

295 *ella nol vede*: Cf. Dante's description of Fortuna, *Inferno* VII, 94: "ma ella s'è beata e ciò non ode."

296 *E l'uom d'eternità s'arroga il vanto*: Cf. Tasso, *Gerusalemme liberata* XV, 20, 3–6: "Muoiono le città, muoiono i regni / Copre i fasti e le pompe arena ed erba, / e l'uom d'esser mortal par che si sdegni: / o nostra mente cupida e superba!"

304 *tue molli foreste*: Cf. *Lentae genistae*, Virgil, *Georgics* II, 12.

313 *Non per voler ma per fortuna*: For Dotti (462), this anticipates Heidegger's notion of man "thrown" into the universe.

315 *inferma*: Weak, but also foolish.

XXXV. IMITAZIONE / IMITATION

Imitation of a poem, "La feuille," written in 1815–16 by the French poet Antoine-Vincent Arnault (1766–1834), on his having to leave France after the defeat of Napoleon. It was published anonymously with no title in the *Spettatore italiano* XI, 12 (1818). Leopardi's version was written in 1828 and published in the Neapolitan edition of 1835. The original text follows:

De ta tige détachée,
Pauvre feuille desséchée,
Où vas-tu?—Je n'en sais rien.
L'orage a brisé la chêne

Qui seul était mon soutien;
De son inconstante haleine
Le zéphir ou l'aquilon
Depuis ce jour me promène
De la forêt à la plaine,
De la montagne au vallon;
Je vais où le vent me mène,
Sans me plaindre ou m'effrayer;
Je vais où va toute chose,
Où va la feuille de rose
Et la feuille de laurier.

Rigoni (M1, 995) writes that Leopardi's imitation stands between the two extremes of the tradition of the fallen leaf as emblem of human mortality—these being represented by *Iliad* VI, 146–50: "Very like leaves / upon this earth are the generations of men— / old leaves, cast on the ground by the wind, young leaves / the greening forest bears when spring comes in. / So mortals pass; one generation flowers / even as another dies away" (tr. Robert Fitzgerald), and Verlaine's "Chanson d'automne," 13–18: "Et je m'en vais / Au vent mauvais / Qui m'emporte / Deçà, delà / Pareil à la / Feuille morte." "Leopardi occupies an equidistant point, offering a version of the theme which partakes of the world of each but does not coincide with either: he keeps intact the purity of vision of the Ancient, though without being able to have its ingenuity; he already feels all the melancholy of the *Décadence* without yet knowing its aromas and poisons, its *vent mauvais*. And in this consists the faultless singularity of his work, as of his spirit." The theme is also touched on in fragment XLI.

9 *Vo pellegrina*: Dotti (464) quotes Bacchelli: "Wanderer, outsider, exile. It has all three meanings."

9 *e tutto l'altro ignoro*: Fubini (quoted by Dotti [464]): "not only the goal but everything else that is not its sad experience."

XXXVI. SCHERZO

Written at Pisa, 15 February 1828, after the completion of the *Operette morali*; published in the Naples edition of 1835.

Rigoni (M1, 996) notes that the ironic tone of this sketch "connects to Leopardi's assiduous and revolutionary meditation on the absolute value of style; on the knowledge and inimitable practice of the ancients in exact opposition to the moderns, who are concerned only with ideas and content; on the consequent immortality of the works of the former and on the ephemeral fate of the books of the latter." The theme is common in the *Zibaldone*; on "the universal negligence as to style" (Dotti, 465) see 4268–71 (2 April 1827). Dotti (466) also mentions Leopardi's following observations (4271–72) on "the hurry with which books were being written in Leopardi's day, having now become real and proper merchandise." See also "Parini" and the "Dialogo di Tristano e di un amico" in the *Operette morali.*

María de las Nieves Muñiz Muñiz (497) suggests that canti XXXV and XXXVI—united by theme, metrics, and "a certain madrigalesque lightness"—constitute a related pair, "a kind of prologue to the epilogue of the *Canti*," and that both turn on the idea of repetition. "The secret heart of the epilogue to the *Canti*, then," adds d'Intino ("Spento il diurno raggio," 702) "is . . . the rediscovery of the self in artistic labor—and in the book . . . The frame of the epilogue exhibits and represents the theme of human time, opposed (in the 'Scherzo') to the time of artistic labor and of the book of the *Canti*."

5 *La*: A "vividly Tuscan pleonasm" (Dotti, 465) used with an ironic nod to the Tuscan Accademia della Crusca (Gallo and Garboli, 293), which considered itself the arbiter of Italian style. Other aulic expressions—"Mostrommi," the Petrarchan "a parte a parte," "hassi a far"—are employed with strong ironic intent.

14 *La lima*: The "lima," or file, was used for correction and polishing. Cf. Horace, *Ars poetica*, 291: "limae labor."

Frammenti / Fragments

XXXVII

This "Arcadian" fragment, written at Recanati in 1819, was originally titled "Lo spavento notturno" (Nocturnal Fear), though the manuscript bears the title "Il sogno" (The Dream). It appears in Leopardi's "Argomenti e abbozzi di poesia" as "Argomenti di Idilli, I" (M1, 636), where its source is given as an actual dream of the poet's. Rigoni (M1, 997) cites Leopardi's mention of ancient beliefs that the moon could fall from the sky in chapter IV of his *Saggio sopra gli errori poplari degli antichi*, and notes the "Greek manner" of the fragment, adding that a characteristic of the piece is that the poet has dreamed and is amazed by his dream, just like the ancients.

It was first published as "Lo spavento notturno. Idillio V" in *Il nuovo ricoglitore* no. 12 (December 1825), but it was too different in tone and language from the other idylls, which express "situations, affections, historical adventures" of the poet's soul ("Disegni letterari, XX" [M2, 1218]), and was not republished after the Bologna edition of 1826 until the Naples edition of 1835, where it appeared among the "Frammenti" as no. XXXV.

The piece makes frequent use of both archaic and popular forms of speech—"contarti," "dar di colpo," "vomitava," "Anzi," "intorno intorno," "svelta," "Egli ci ha"—in its attempt to create an atmosphere of timeless Arcadian comedy.

10 *Grande quanto una secchia*: The image is drawn from Dante, *Purgatorio* XVIII, 76–78: "La luna [. . .] / fatta come'un secchion che tutt'or arda."

23 *Chi sa?*: Dotti (468): "Alceta doesn't pick up on his companion's irony and continues with his ingenuous reflections. Even in this brief passage you sense that he incarnates the figure of the child, the ancient primitive, lost in his dreams and illusions (compared with the more expert and detached Melisso)."

XXXVIII

Fragment in terza rima of an elegy, an echo of "Il primo amore" and like it inspired by Leopardi's cousin Geltrude Cassi-Lazzari. Written at Recanati at the end of 1818, after Cassi's second visit to Recanati; published in the Bologna *Versi* of 1826 under the title "Elegia II" ("Elegia I" was later retitled "Il primo amore" and inserted in the *Canti*), it appeared among the "Frammenti" as no. XXXVI in the Naples edition of 1835. For the inspiring theme, see the fifth "argomento di elegia" (1818) (M1, 617), which is also related to the taste for tempestuous nature evoked in the "Ultimo canto di Saffo" and elsewhere (including fragment XXXIX, below).

XXXIX

This is the first canto, slightly revised, of Leopardi's youthful Dantesque canticle in terza rima, "Appressamento della morte" (Approach of Death), written in November–December 1816; the selection was published in the Naples edition of 1835, among the "Frammenti," as no. XXXVII.

A storm was supposed to be the subject of one of the idylls (cf. "Le fanciulle nella tempesta" [M1, 636]) and also appears in a passage of chapter XIII, "Del tuono" (On Thunder), of the *Saggio sopra gli errori popolari degli antichi* [M2, 804–20]. The lines are rich in borrowings from and allusions to Virgil, Ovid, Theocritus, Dante, and Petrarch.

Straccali (1), opens his edition of the *Canti* with this text: "It's not improbable that the poet chose to select . . . this fragment, and modify its subject [from "the Poet himself, *intent on reaching an exalted goal*" to "a woman seeking *an amorous goal*"] and its ending as well as its form, having the thought of the premature death of this girl which always remained in his mind as the image of youth, and of all the deceptions and illusions that make this time of life joyful . . . And in fact as Silvia, in the poem that bears her name, while still in the time of sweet dreams, dies overcome and defeated by crude sickness, so the girl of this fragment, totally smiled on by hope (see vv. 25–27), falls overcome and defeated by the forces of nature which suddenly turn inimical . . . With a poet's intellect, Carducci [writes]: 'Let us call her the pilgrim of love and truth and put this *symbolic* poem at the beginning of the volume of loving and despairing poems.' "

For d'Intino ("Spento il diurno raggio"), this early, never published fragment is an "archeological find" (702), a critical reading of the "Appressamento" (714), which he interprets as the record of an unresolved struggle between a classically inspired, secular Leopardi and a Leopardi under the Dantesquely inflected influence of the religious ideology of the poet's mother. The passage, rewritten as described by Straccali, is included in the *Canti* to memorialize Leopardi's movement from the "ingenuous poetry of the ancients" that he had previously translated, "to the sentimental and philosophical"(702) poetry of the moderns—and his determination to be a poet over and against the expectations of his parents. It "represents, in 1835, a kind of coming to terms with his own education" (712).

16 *In questa ombra giacea la valle bruna*: Cf. "Il tramonto della luna," 13–14: "ed una / Oscurità la valle e il monte imbruna."

76 *di pietra*: Dead.

XL. DAL GRECO DI SIMONIDE / FROM THE GREEK OF SIMONIDES

Written at Recanati between 1823 and 1824; published in the Naples edition of 1835 among the "Frammenti" as no. XXXVIII.

Leopardi's poem is a free translation of an iambic fragment by Semonides of Samos, called Semonides of Amorgos, a Greek poet of the seventh century B.C. whom Leopardi confused with the more renowned Simonides of Keos (556–468 B.C.), celebrated in "All'Italia." The translation can be related to Leopardi's discovery, as he was beginning to write the *Operette morali*, of ancient pessimism through reading Jean-Jacques Barthélemy's celebrated novel, *Voyage du jeune Anacharsis en Grèce* (1787), in which a young Scythian is supposed to visit Greece and report on the customs and conditions of her various republics after Alexander's defeat of the Persians.

The 1826 Florence edition of the *Versi* included another text of 1823, the so-called "Volgarizzamento della satira di Simonide sopra le donne" (Translation of Simonides' satire on women) (M1, 601–604), though it is in fact by Semonides of Samos.

10 *La bella speme . . .*: Lines 10–18, with some variations, are quoted in chapter X of "Il Parini, ovvero della gloria" (1824) in the *Operette morali*. The fragment was also published separately, under the title "La speranza," in the *Corriere delle dame* of Milan, no. 45, 10 November 1827.

15 *E nullo in terra vive*: Our unrealistic expectations for the future receive a witty ironic treatment in the "Dialogo di un venditore d'almanacchi e di un passeggere" (1832) in the *Operette morali*. Pluto here is the dispenser of wealth (Orcel, 327).

19 *pria che la speme in porto arrive*: Cf. the use of the same image in "Sopra un basso rilievo antico sepolcrale," 74.

XLI. DELLO STESSO / BY THE SAME AUTHOR

Written at Recanati between 1823 and 1824; published in the Neapolitan edition of 1835 as no. XXXIX. The authorship of the fragment—whether it is by Semonides of Samos or Simonides of Keos—is uncertain, though for Leopardi (see notes to fragment XL) this was not an issue.

1 *Umana cosa . . .*: The first line does not correspond to the Greek text. Dotti (479) observes that it seems to have been inspired by a line of Petrarch's, "come nulla qua giù diletta e dura" (*Rime* CCCXI, 14), which is also parodied in the "Palinodia," 25.

3 *il veglio di Chio*: Homer was supposed to have hailed from Chios.

5 *Le foglie e l'uman seme*: See *Iliad* VI, 146: "Very like leaves / upon this earth are the generations of men" (tr. Robert Fitzgerald). Cf. the use of the same trope in fragment XXXV, "Imitazione."

23 *Ai presenti diletti*: Dotti (480): "The finale of the whole, more than the Greek text, is inspired by an Horatian atmosphere." G. De Robertis (377): "This is the ancient wisdom that Leopardi was not willing to accept, and that here, at the end of the *Canti*, seems to mark the difference, and the distance, between two civilizations." Cf. also the end of "Il sabato del villaggio."

Other Texts

LE RIMEMBRANZE / MEMORIES

Idyll written at Recanati in 1816 and repudiated by Leopardi in the index of his works. The characters' names come from Theocritus. The evocations of memory prefigure especially the apostrophe to Nerina at the end of the similarly named "Le ricordanze."

63 *Pur vidi / Aperta una finestra . . .*: Foreshadows the evocation of the "romite" and "quete" "stanze" of "La vita solitaria" and "A Silvia." See p. 429 for Leopardi's description in the *Zibaldone* of how his imagination was excited by looking into the rooms of a house.

IL CANTO DELLA FANCIULLA / THE GIRL'S SONG

Probably written in April 1818 and subsumed into "A Silvia."

7 *il tempo / Aspettato*: Cf. the "festa / Ch'anco tardi a venir" of "Il sabato del villaggio."

10 *Cagion d'affano*: Cf. the contrasting argument of "Alla luna" (1819), where the memory of even sad things is welcome.

CORO DI MORTI NELLO STUDIO DI FEDERICO RUYSCH / CHORUS OF THE DEAD IN THE STUDY OF FREDERICK RUYSCH

The eerily eloquent "Coro di morti," which James Thomson (204) called "one of the marvels of literature," appears at the beginning of the dark and brilliant "Dialogo di Federico Ruysch e delle sue mummie" (Dialogue of Frederick Ruysch and His Mummies) (August 1824) in the *Operette morali*. The embalmer Ruysch is awakened by the singing of his mummies at the moment that a cosmic cycle is coming to an end, during which the dead are allotted fifteen minutes in which to speak. Ruysch questions them about their dying and how they knew they were dead, but the time is up before they can answer.

Damiani (M2, 1324): "The dead intone their chorus in a spirit of resignation as to the incomprehensibility of life, similar to that which the living have in respect to death. In the negation of happiness, which fate imposes on mortals, returns the impossibility of knowing the mystery which oversees the cycles of life and death. If in fact the living don't know about death, though it is 'alone eternal in the world,' neither do the dead answer the last question of the embalmer—'How do you know you're dead?'—which remains hanging in the void . . . Prevented from knowing their fundamental nature, the beings are naturally inclined toward pleasure, which yet has no place or time except in the interstices between life and death, in the instant in which the pain of existence ceases, to which the living are bound to the point of always hoping that 'an hour or two of life' remains."

Ruysch (d. 1731) was a renowned Dutch anatomist, doctor, and naturalist. Leopardi's note on the manuscript: "Fontenelle Éloge de M. Ruysch. Thomas Éloge de Descartes, not. 32." Thomas writes (M2, 1325): "M. Ruysch's mummies prolonged their life in some respect, said M. Fontenelle, whereas those of ancient Egypt only prolonged their death. One could have said that they were men asleep, ready to speak at their awakening."

1 *si volve*: Damiani (M2, 1325): "Latininism. The eternal totality of death embraces creation as a negative and all-comprehensive horizon of being, of that 'causa sui' [cause of itself] which Spinoza defined, in the first line of his *Ethics*, as 'id, cuius essentia involvit existentiam' [that, the essence of which involves being]."

3 *si posa*: Rests, but also has an end.

8 *Il pensier grave*: Damiani (M2, 1325): "The painful thought" (of the life that is past). In the "deep night" in which oblivion involves everything, one seems to hear, up close, the echo of Foscolo's *Sepolcri* (lines 17–19) and, more distantly, the fragment of Pindar reported by Plutarch: "from there vomit endless darkness / the slow rivers of the dismal night."

21–22 *quel punto acerbo / Che di vita ebbe nome*: "The terrifying sacred hymn sung by the dead . . . acts as a prelude to the dialogue, imbued with black humor, between scientist and mummies. The universal question, the one out of which every poem is born in being posed as a way of considering life . . . is asked in tragic terms under a comic halo. Neither of the two elements elides or excludes the other. Rather, they touch each other in a certain zone. And in three lines surfaces . . . the 'interrogating doctrine of Leopardi': 'What were we? / What was that bitter instant / known as life?'" Andrea Zanzotto, "Tentativi di esperienza poetica (Poetiche-lampo)," in *Il Verri*, 1–2, 1987.

31 *Però ch'esser beato*: The rhythm of the last line recalls that of the closing sentence of "Sopra un basso rilievo antico sepolcrale": "Ma da natura / Altro negli atti suoi / Che nostro male o nostro ben si cura."

AD ARIMANE / TO AHRIMAN

Damiani (M2, 1099): "Ahriman or Angra Mainyu is the divine spirit of Evil in Mazdeism or Zoroastrianism, the religion of pre-Islamic Iran. The sketch for the hymn is of interest above all as testimony to or confirmation of Leopardi's idea of the absolute sovereignty of evil in the universe: not foreseeing the opposition to Ahriman by any Omuzd (Ohrmazd, Ahura Mazdah), the notion professed by Leopardi assumes in fact . . . the character of a black monism. Thus are explained also the noted pages of *Zibaldone* 4174–4178 of 22 April 1826, which affirm with repetitive obsession that 'All is evil' without distinction or possible exception (and are consonant, surprisingly, with the 'system' exposed by Saint-Fond at the end of the second part of Sade's *Juliette*). But the sketch is also important in relation to some passages in the *Canti*, which lead back to it: 'A se stesso,' 14–5; 'Sopra un basso rilievo antico sepolcrale,' 47; 'Palinodia,' 154–64; 'La ginestra,' 124–5," as well as the closing of "Amore e morte."

A probable source is Byron's *Manfred*, in which Ahriman is a character.

e il giusto e il debole sarà oppresso: Cf. the very similar argument in the "Palinodia," 69–81.

7° *lustro*: The Latin *lustrum* was a period of five years. Leopardi is asking not to live beyond his thirty-fifth birthday, 29 June 1833; it is therefore presumed that the sketch was written shortly before this date.

SELECT BIBLIOGRAPHY

Editions of Leopardi

Geoffrey L. Bickersteth, trans., *The Poems of Leopardi.* Cambridge: Cambridge University Press, 1923.

Rolando Damiani, ed. *Giacomo Leopardi: Lettere.* Milano: I Meridiani, Arnoldo Mondadori Editore, 2006.

Rolando Damiani e Mario Andrea Rigoni, eds. *Giacomo Leopardi: Poesie e Prose.* 5 vols. Milano: Edizioni della Meridiana, Arnoldo Mondadori Editore, 1987. *Poesie*, ed. Mario Andrea Rigoni con un saggio di Cesare Galimberti [M1]. *Prose*, ed. Rolando Damiani [M2]. *Zibaldone*, ed. Rolando Damiani.

Domenico De Robertis, ed. *Canti di Giacomo Leopardi.* 2 vols. Edizione critica e autografi. Milano: Edizioni Il Polifilo, 1984.

Giuseppe De Robertis, ed. *Giacomo Leopardi: Canti.* Firenze: Felice Le Monnier Editore, 1925.

Franco d'Intino, ed. *Giacomo Leopardi: Poeti Greci e Latini.* Roma: Salerno Editrice, 1999.

———, *Giacomo Leopardi: Scritti e frammenti autobiografici. Testi e Documenti di Letteratura e di Lingua, XVI.* Roma: Salerno Editrice, 1995.

Ugo Dotti, ed. *Giacomo Leopardi: Canti.* Milano: Universale Economica Feltrinelli, sixth edition, 2008.

Niccolò Gallo e Cesare Garboli, *Giacomo Leopardi: Canti, con un' appendice di scritti del poeta.* Torino: Giulio Einaudi Editore, 1993.

Franco Gavazzeni e Maria Maddalena Lombardi, eds. *Giacomo Leopardi: Canti.* Milano: BUR Poesia, fourth edition, 2004.

Francesco Moroncini, *Canti di Giacomo Leopardi: Edizione critica.* Bologna: Licino Cappelli, 1961.

Carlo Muscetta e Giuseppe Savoca, eds. *Giacomo Leopardi: Canti, Paralipomeni, Poesie Varie, Traduzioni Poetiche e Versi Puerili con le concordanze dell'opera poetica leopardiana.* Parnasso Italiano IX. Torino: Giulio Einaudi Editore, 1968.

Alfredo Straccali, ed. *I Canti di Giacomo Leopardi commentati da.* Firenze: G. C. Sansoni, Editore, 1892.

English Translations

Jean-Pierre Barricelli, *Giacomo Leopardi: Poems.* Translated and with an introduction. New York: Las Americas Publishing Company, 1963.

Giovanni Cecchetti, *Giacomo Leopardi: Operette Morali: Essays and Dialogues.* Translated with an introduction and notes. Berkeley: University of California Press, 1982.

Patrick Creagh, "Giacomo Leopardi: Ten Odes," *PN Review* 9, no. 3 (1982): 11–21.

W. S. Di Piero, *Pensieri.* Translated with an introduction. Baton Rouge: Louisiana State University Press, 1981.

Angel Flores, ed. *Leopardi: Poems and Prose.* Introduction by Sergio Pacifici. Bloomington: Indiana University Press, 1966.

Eamon Grennan. *Leopardi: Selected Poems.* Princeton: Princeton University Press, 1997.

John Heath-Stubbs, *Poems from Giacomo Leopardi.* Translated and with an introduction. London: John Lehmann, 1946.

Paul Lawton, *Giacomo Leopardi: Canti.* Selected and introduced by Franco Fortini. Dublin: UCD Foundation for Italian Studies, 1996.

J. G. Nichols, *Giacomo Leopardi: The Canti, with a selection of his prose.* Manchester: Carcanet Press Limited, 1994.

Iris Origo and John Heath-Stubbs, ed., trans., and introd., *Giacomo Leopardi: Selected Poetry and Prose.* London: Oxford University Press, 1966.

G. Singh, ed. *I Canti di Giacomo Leopardi nelle traduzioni inglesi.* Bibliographic essay and anthology of versions from the Anglo-Saxon world. Preface by Mario Luzi. Introduction by Mario Foschi. Recanati: Centro Nazionale di Studi Leopardiani TranseuropA, 1990.

James Thomson ("B.V."), *Essays, Dialogues and Thoughts (Operette Morali and Pensieri) of Giacomo Leopardi.* Edited by Bertram Dobell. London: George Routledge and Sons Ltd., 1905.

Joseph Tusiani, *Leopardi's Canti.* Introduction and notes by Piero Magno. Preface by Franco Fortini. Fasano: Schena, 1998.

Arturo Vivante, *Giacomo Leopardi: Poems.* Translated and with an introduction. Wellfleet, Mass.: Delphinium Press, 1988.

Other Translations

María de las Nieves Muñiz Muñiz, *Giacomo Leopardi: Cantos.* Madrid: Ediciones Cátedra, 1998.

Michel Orcel, ed. *Leopardi, Chants/Canti.* Translation, introduction, and bibliography by Michel Orcel. Preface by Mario Fusco. Paris: Flammarion, 2005.

Biographical Works

Rolando Damiani, *All'apparir del vero: Vita di Giacomo Leopardi.* Milano: Arnoldo Mondadori Editore, 1998. Revision of *Vita di Leopardi,* 1992.

Iris Origo, *Leopardi: A Study in Solitude.* Introduction by Shirley Hazzard. New York: Books & Co. / Helen Marx Books, 1999.

Critical Works

Adriano Bon, *Invito alla lettura di Giacomo Leopardi.* Milano: Mursia, 1985.

Yves Bonnefoy, *L'enseignement et l'exemple de Leopardi.* Bordeaux: William Blake & Co. Edit., 2001.

D. S. Carne-Ross, "Leopardi: The Poet in a Time of Need." In *Instaurations: Essays in and out of Literature, Pindar to Pound.* Berkeley: University of California Press, 1979, pp. 167–192.

Francesco De Sanctis, *History of Italian Literature.* 2 vols. Translated by Joan Redfern. New York: Barnes & Noble, Inc., 1968.

———, *Leopardi.* Edited by Carlo Muscetta and Antonio Ernati. Turin: Einaudi, 1983.

Franco d'Intino, "Coleridge-Leopardi: per una poesia potenziale?" *La questione Romantica: Organicism/Meccanismo* I, no. 1 (Autunno 1995): 93–107.

———, "I misteri di Siliva. Motivo persefoneo e mistica eleusina in Leopardi." *Filologia e critica* XIX, no. ii (maggio–agosto 1994): 211–71.

———, "Spento il diurno raggio." In A. Maglione, ed. *Lectura leopardiana: I quarantuno canti e 'I nuovi credenti.'* Venezia: Marsilio, 2003, 697–717.

Nicola Gardini, "History and Pastoral in the Structure of Leopardi's *Canti.*" *Modern Language Review* 103, no. 1 (January 2008): 76–92.

Giorgio Orelli, "Connessioni leopardiane." *Strumenti critici* n.s. a. ii, no. 1 (gennaio 1987): 73–96.

Nicolas J. Perella, "Translating Leopardi?" *Italica* 77, no. 3 (Autumn 2000): 357–85.

Antonio Prete, *Il pensiero poetante: Saggio su Leopardi.* Expanded edition. Milan: Feltrinelli, 2006.

Natalino Sapegno, "Giacomo Leopardi." In Emilio Cecchi and Natalino Sapegno, eds. *Storia della letteratura italiana.* Vol. 7, *L'Ottocento.* Milano: Garzanti, 1965, 733–865.

Giuseppe Ungaretti, *Vita d'un uomo: Saggi e interventi.* Ed. Mario Diacono and Luciano Rebay. Milan: Arnoldo Mondadori Editore, 1974.

J. H. Whitfield, *Giacomo Leopardi.* Oxford: Basil Blackwell, 1954.

Other Works

Giorgio Bertone, *Breve dizionario di metrica italiana.* Torino: Piccola Biblioteca Einaudi, Saggistica letteraria e linguistica, 1999.

Marco Sonzogni, ed. *Or volge l'anno/At the Year's Turning: An Anthology of Irish Poets Responding to Leopardi.* Dublin: Dedalus, 1998.

ACKNOWLEDGMENTS

In preparing this book, I have drawn largely on the work of a few editors, first of all Mario Andrea Rigoni, whose 1987 Meridiani edition incisively synthesizes and interprets the vast library of Leopardi criticism. Leopardi's leading modern biographer, Rolando Damiani, has also created exemplary editions of the poet's prose and letters. I am also indebted to Ugo Dotti's rigorous and suggestive scholarship, in which he often quotes incisively from his own predecessors, in particular Mario Fubini. And I have been encouraged and inspired by the excellent French translation and commentary of Michel Orcel (2005), who, while largely relying on Rigoni, contributes much that is fresh in the way of psychoanalytic and other perspectives. My gratitude to these scholars is boundless.

For other help of various kinds, I would also like to express my great thanks to the following: Frank Bidart; Patrizio Ceccagnoli; Eric Chinski; Jeff Clark; Bill Clegg; Jesse Coleman; Nicola Crocetti; Franco d'Intino, whose criticism of my commentary was essential; Stuart Dybek; Jane Elias; James Fenton; Enrico Ferorelli, who gave me his mother's schoolgirl copy of Giuseppe De Robertis's edition of the *Canti*; Susan Galassi; Louise Glück; Susan Goldfarb; Eliza Griswold; Walter Kaiser; Andrew Mandel; Maureen McLane; Susan Mitchell; Paul Muldoon; Michael Palma; Tim Parks, who first set me on the course of trying to translate Leopardi; Francesco Rognoni; Jeff Seroy; Robert Silvers; Alyson Sinclair; my gifted editor Lorin Stein; Leon Wieseltier; C. K. Williams; Christian Wiman; and, most of all, Frederick Seidel, who worked tirelessly to try to free me from the bonds of translationese.

My daughters, Beatrice and Isabel Galassi, have been constant sources of tenderness and encouragement.

And with Tom Le I have known a happiness that daily disproves the great Giacomo's contention that love is illusory.

I have dedicated these versions to two friends whose interest in and support of my engagement with Leopardi over the years has been deeply sustaining: Nicola Gardini, brilliant, fecund writer and critic, who has helped me to cut my own path through the forest of Leopardi studies; and Shirley Hazzard, great novelist and *cultrice* of Italy and her artists, who knows Leopardi and so much else by heart.

INDEX OF TITLES AND FIRST LINES